T0211158

Foundations
of
Object-Oriented
Languages

Foundations
of
Object-Oriented
Languages
Types
and
Semantics

Kim B. Bruce

The MIT Press
Cambridge, Massachusetts
London, England

© 2002 Massachusetts Institute of Technology

All rights reserved. No part of this book may be reproduced in any form by any electronic or mechanical means (including photocopying, recording, or information storage and retrieval) without permission in writing from the publisher.

Library of Congress Cataloging-in-Publication Information

Bruce, Kim B.
    Foundations of object-oriented languages: types and semantics /
    Kim B. Bruce.
      p.   cm.
    Includes bibliographical references and index.
    ISBN 978-0-262-02523-2 (hc. : alk. paper)–978-0-262-52573-2 (pb.)
    1. Object-oriented programming (computer science). 2. Programming languages (Electronic computers). I. Title.

QA76.64 .B776   2002
005.1'17–dc21   2001054613

The MIT Press is pleased to keep this title available in print by manufacturing single copies, on demand, via digital printing technology.

To my mother and the memory of my late father

Contents

I Type Problems in Object-Oriented Languages   1

IV Extending Simple Object-Oriented Languages 289

List of Figures

Preface

I wrote this book to provide a description of the foundations of statically typed class-based object-oriented programming languages for those interested in learning about this area. An important goal is to explain how the different components of these languages interact, and how this results in the kind of type systems that are used in popular object-oriented languages. We will see that an understanding of the theoretical foundations of object-oriented languages can lead to the design of more expressive and flexible type systems that assist programmers in writing correct programs.

Programmers used to untyped or dynamically typed languages often complain about being straitjacketed by the restrictive type systems of object-oriented languages. In fact many existing statically typed object-oriented languages have very restrictive type systems that almost literally force programmers to use casts or other mechanisms to escape from the static type system. In this work we aim to meet the needs of a programmer who wants a more expressive type system. Thus another goal of this text is to promote richer type systems that reduce the need for bypassing the type checker.

Because of the semantic complexity of the features of object-oriented languages, particularly subtyping and inheritance, it is difficult to design a static type system that is simultaneously safe and flexible. To be sure that there are no holes in the type system we need to prove that the type system is safe (essentially that no type errors can occur at run time), but we cannot do that without a description of the meaning of programs. Thus this book contains careful formal descriptions of the syntax, type system, and semantics of several progressively more complex object-oriented programming languages. With these definitions, it is possible to prove type safety.

Object-oriented programming languages have been of great practical and theoretical interest, but most of the interesting developments in foundations have been accessible only to researchers in the area. Moreover, papers in the area have taken quite different approaches, as well as using different notation and even different terminology from each other. As a result, it has been difficult for outsiders to learn the basic material in this area.

This book differs from other recent books in the foundations of object-oriented languages in several ways. First, the focus of attention is class-based object-oriented languages, rather than object-based or multi-method languages. Thus our study is very relevant to the most popular kind of object-oriented languages in use today.

Second, this book approaches the foundations from the point of view of a programmer or language designer wishing to understand the type systems of object-oriented languages and to see how to extend the type systems to increase the expressiveness of these languages. The semantics presented suggest extensions to the language and provide the foundations for verifying the safety of the type system.

Third, we base the foundation of object-oriented programming languages on the classical typed lambda calculus and its extensions rather than introducing new calculi to explain the fundamental constructs. Thus we can rely on classical results, only including a brief review of the lambda calculus to introduce readers to the notation.

This book is intended for several different audiences. My intention has been to make it accessible to students, especially advanced undergraduates and graduate students, to practitioners wishing to have a deeper understanding of the foundations of object-oriented programming languages, and to researchers who wish to understand developments in the foundations of object-oriented languages. It can be used as the main text for a course in the foundations of object-oriented programming languages or as a supplementary text for a course with a broader focus that includes object-oriented programming languages.

We have designed the first part of the book, comprising the first seven chapters, to be especially accessible to a wide variety of readers. These chapters provide a relatively non-technical introduction to key issues in the type systems of object-oriented programming languages. As such, this part may be especially appropriate for use in a general undergraduate or graduate course covering concepts of object-oriented programming languages or as the basis for self-study.

The next part, comprising Chapters 8 and 9, provides a relatively quick introduction to the simply typed lambda calculus and many of its extensions. The goal of this part is to have the reader understand how the lambda calculus can provide a formal description of programming language constructs. This part also introduces the formalism for writing the syntax and type-checking rules for programming languages. For readers with a solid understanding of programming languages as provided for by Pierce's text, *Type Systems for Programming Languages* [Pie02], or Mitchell's *Foundations for Programming Languages* [Mit96], for example, these chapters will simply provide a quick review. Others will need to spend more time to understand how such a primitive language can be used as a model of important programming language concepts and to learn how to read and understand the type-checking rules. It is not necessary to understand the deep results about the lambda calculus found in more specialized texts in order to understand the use of lambda calculus in this book.

The third part of the book, comprising Chapters 10 through 14, presents the core foundational material on class-based object-oriented languages. We begin by providing a formal definition of a simple object-oriented language, $\mathcal{SOOL}$, and its type system. Chapters 11 and 12 explore understanding the semantics of $\mathcal{SOOL}$ by translating terms into a very rich extension of the typed lambda calculus. With this understanding of the language, Chapter 13 presents a proof of soundness and safety of $\mathcal{SOOL}$. This chapter is the technically most difficult of the book. The details of the proof in the first section of that chapter may be skipped on the first reading, but the statement of the soundness and safety theorems and the other material in the chapter are important as they illustrate how a careful formal definition of a language can lead to provable safety.

The language $\mathcal{SOOL}$ was kept very simple so that the proof of soundness could avoid as many complications as possible. The last chapter of this part discusses many of the more specialized concepts commonly found in object-oriented languages that were left out of $\mathcal{SOOL}$. These include references to methods from the superclass, more refined access control in classes, nil objects, and even a discussion of multiple inheritance.

The final part of this book explores extensions of the type systems of object-oriented languages suggested by our understanding of the semantics of $\mathcal{SOOL}$. The extensions include F-bounded polymorphism, a new type keyword, MyType, standing for the type of self, and a relation, matching, that is more general than subtyping. We will find that the addition of these features adds considerably to the expressiveness of object-oriented languages, yet we will prove that they do not compromise the type safety of the language. We end with the presentation of a language that incorporates MyType, matching, and a new form of bounded polymorphism using matching, but that no longer contains the notion of subtyping. We will see that this simpler language is still very expressive, even without subtyping.

The topics covered in this book represent an active area of research, with new papers appearing every year. There are many topics that I would have liked to have included, but could not because of a desire to keep the size of this book manageable. The best way to keep up with current research in the area is to attend or examine the proceedings of major conferences and workshops in this area. The major conferences presenting new research in the broad area of programming languages are the Principles of Programming Languages (POPL) and Programming Language Design and Implementation (PLDI) conferences. The most important conferences presenting research on object-oriented languages are the annual Object-Oriented Programming, Systems, Languages, and Applications (OOPSLA) conference and the European Conference on Object-Oriented Programming (ECOOP). The annual Foundations of Object-Oriented Languages (FOOL) workshop provides an important, though less formal, forum for new results in the area covered by this book. Information on the FOOL workshops is available at

```
http://www.cs.williams.edu/~kim/FOOL/.
```

One of my favorite quotes, first encountered as a signature tag on e-mail, is the following:

> "The difference between theory and practice is greater in practice than in theory" *Author unknown*

In pursuing my own research on topics central to the issues covered in this book, I have tried to keep this quote in mind. As a result, rather than just theorizing about issues in programming language design, my students and I have implemented interpreters and compilers for languages similar to those discussed here. (For pedagogical reasons the languages described in the text are different in inessential ways from the languages we have implemented.)

The experience of implementing and using these languages has provided better insight to the strengths and limitations of the type systems discussed here. It is my hope, and indeed one of the reasons for writing this book, that the knowledge obtained by the research community in the foundations of object-oriented programming languages will eventually work its way into practical and widely used programming languages. The growing interest in the extension, GJ, of Java described in Section 4.1 provides evidence that this kind of technology transfer has already begun.

The material presented in this book is the result of the dedicated and creative work of many researchers. The *Historical Notes and References* sections at the end of each of the four parts of the book credit the contributions of many of those doing research in this area. I have also benefitted greatly from personal and professional interactions from many researchers in this area.

Primary credit for helping me get started doing research in the semantics of programming languages goes to Albert Meyer, from whom I learned an enormous amount, both about semantics and about the process of doing research, while on my first leave from Williams College. A ten-year-long professional collaboration with Guiseppe Longo was extremely productive and enjoyable, while incidentally introducing me to the beauty of Italy and France. Peter Wegner deserves credit for introducing me to object-oriented programming languages and asking annoying questions that led to many interesting results. John Mitchell and Luca Cardelli provided key influences (and funding) during a visit to Palo Alto in the spring of 1991 that led to my work on the design and proofs of type safety of object-oriented programming languages.

A three-month visit to the Newton Institute of Mathematical Sciences in the fall of 1995 during the special program on Semantics of Computation provided a great opportunity to work with other researchers in the semantics of programming languages. The interaction with Benjamin Pierce and Luca Cardelli there led to our joint paper comparing different styles of semantics for object-oriented languages.

Similarly, early meetings of the workshops on the Foundations of Object-Oriented Languages (the FOOL workshops) resulted in many interesting discussions (and arguments), some of which led to the paper "On binary methods" [BCC+95], a paper with 8 co-authors who at times seemed to have at least 10 different opinions on how best to approach the issues involved. I have learned more through writing these papers (in spite of the difficulty of writing conclusions!) than through almost any other activity as a researcher. Teaching a graduate programming languages course while on a visiting professorship at Princeton University allowed me to begin writing this book while trying out the material on students.

Opportunities for collaboration with my computer science honors students at Williams College and my co-authors have taught me a great deal over the years. My honors students in computer science include Robert Allen, Jon Burstein, David Chelmow, John N. (Nate) Foster, Benjamin Goldberg, Gerald Kanapathy, Leaf Petersen, Dean Pomerleau, Jon Riecke, Wendy Roy, Angela Schuett, Adam Seligman, Charles Stewart, Robert van Gent, and Joseph Vanderwaart. Aside from the researchers and students mentioned above, my co-authors in programming language research papers include Roberto Amadio, Giuseppe Castagna, Jon Crabtree, Roberto DiCosmo, Allyn Dimock, Adrian

Fiech, Gary Leavens, Robert Muller, Martin Odersky, Scott Smith, and Philip Wadler.

I owe a great debt of gratitude to the National Science Foundation, most recently through the offices of Frank Anger, for their long-standing support for my research. NSF research grants supporting the research reported here include NSF CCR-9121778, CCR-9424123, CCR-9870253, and CCR-9988210. Any opinions, findings, and conclusions or recommendations expressed in this material are those of the author and do not necessarily reflect the views of the National Science Foundation.

Special thanks go to those who provided comments and corrections on drafts of this manuscript. Narciso Martí-Oliet, John N. Foster, and an anonymous reviewer provided very detailed and helpful comments on a complete draft of this book. Andrew Black provided very useful and detailed comments on an early survey paper that evolved into this book. Others who provided useful comments on different portions of the book, suggested approaches, or were helpful in clearing up historical details included Martín Abadi, Luca Cardelli, Craig Chambers, Kathleen Fisher, Cheng Hu, Assaf Kfoury, John Mitchell, Benjamin Pierce, and Jack Wiledon. Thanks to my editor Bob Prior for his friendship, for his faith in this project, and for making this task less painful than it might have been. I am grateful to Christopher Manning for sharing the LaTeX macros that resulted in this book design.

I take full credit for all omissions and errors remaining in this book. Please send corrections to kim@cs.williams.edu. I will provide a web site with errata or clarifications at

```
http://www.cs.williams.edu/~kim/FOOLbook.html
```

and through MIT Press at

```
http://mitpress.mit.edu/
```

I give great thanks to my family for their love and support during the long years spent writing this book. Thanks to my colleagues in the Computer Science Department at Williams for their professional support and intellectual stimulation. Finally, thanks to my teachers whose guidance led me to begin this interesting journey. Special thanks are due to H. Jerome Keisler and the late Jon Barwise at the University of Wisconsin, the late Harry Mullikan and Paul Yale at Pomona College, and Shirley Frye and Mike Svaco at Scottsdale Arcadia High School.

Part I

Type Problems in Object-Oriented Languages

1 *Introduction*

It is often stated that object-oriented programming languages are a major improvement over older procedural style languages. If so, why are their static type systems so poor? Some of the static type systems of object-oriented languages are too restrictive, resulting in the need for a plethora of type casts, either checked (as in Java [AGH99]) or unchecked (as in C++ [ES90]). Others allow programs with type errors to be executed. In some of these languages the type errors may be caught at run time (as in the language Beta [KMMPN87]), while in others (like current implementations of Eiffel [Mey92]) the errors may result in run-time crashes.

In this text we will explore the foundations of object-oriented programming languages. Our purpose in examining the formal underpinnings of object-oriented languages is to answer questions like the one in the previous paragraph. This study will help the reader gain deeper insight into the fundamental concepts of these languages. It will help explain why certain features are designed the way they are, as well as provide a tool to help design more expressive, yet statically type-safe, object-oriented languages.

While the first object-oriented language, Simula 67 [BDMN73], was designed and implemented in the mid-60's, and the Smalltalk [GR83] language was first introduced in the early '70's, it wasn't until the advent of C++ in the mid-'80's that a large number of programmers and organizations began adopting object-oriented languages. Even then, many users of C++ simply used it as a "better C" with support for abstraction. However, programmers increasingly adopted pure object-oriented languages like Smalltalk, Eiffel, and, most recently, Java, while an increasing number of C++ programmers write programs in an object-oriented style.

Why has the object-oriented style become so popular? Certainly no small part has been played by the tendency of programmers to jump on the latest "fad" language. However there is real substance behind the reasons for the increasing use of object-oriented languages. There seem to be clear advantages for the object-oriented style in organizing and reusing software components. For example, subtyping and inheritance (notions we will define more carefully later) seem to make it much easier to adapt and reuse existing software components.

However, in many ways the quality of object-oriented programming languages falls short of existing procedural and functional languages. In this text we will focus on two ways in which they fall short – the shortcomings of type systems and the deficiencies in expressiveness of existing object-oriented programming languages.

Based on our years of experience in programming (and teaching programming) in traditional procedural languages such as FORTRAN [Bac81], Pascal [Wir71], C [KR78], Modula-2 [Wir85], and Ada [US 80], as well as functional languages like LISP [MAE+65], Scheme [SS75], ML [MTH90], Miranda [Tur86], and Haskell [HJW92], we are convinced that a strong type system, especially a statically type-safe system, is a very important tool in implementing reliable programs. Thus it would be highly advantageous to provide static type systems for object-oriented languages that are of the same quality as those available for traditional procedural and functional languages, yet make it easy for the programmer to express his or her algorithmic ideas in an object-oriented style.

Unfortunately, commercially available object-oriented languages fall far short of that goal. The static type systems of object-oriented languages tend to be either insecure or more inflexible than one might desire. In some cases the rigidity of the type system leads programmers to rely on type casts (sometimes checked at run time, sometimes not) in order to obtain the expressiveness desired. In other cases, the type systems are too flexible, requiring the run-time system to generate link-time or run-time checks to ensure the integrity of the computation.

1.1   Type systems in programming languages

Type systems in programming languages assign types to all values in a computation. Static type systems also assign type expressions to all expressions of the language. Operations are provided with type information that determines to which types of values they may be applied. For example, a concatenation operator may be restricted to be applied to pairs of strings. An "integer" addition operator may be restricted to be applied only to pairs of integers. A "real" addition operator (which may be represented by the same symbol as the "integer" addition operator) may be restricted to be applied only to pairs of reals. (We treat an overloaded operator symbol or name as referring to multiple operations rather than a single operation with multiple typings.)

Programming languages include primitive data types like integers, reals, booleans, etc., and operations that apply to values of those types. These languages also provide type constructors that allow programmers to build up composite or structured data types (*e.g.*, records or structs, arrays, sets, etc.), as well as providing operations that may construct or be applied to values of these types. In most languages, these more complex types can be named, though their structure is visible and accessible to programmers. While more operations on these types may be designed by the programmer by writing new functions or procedures, these new operations are built from the primitive operations provided by the language. However, any programmer using these structured types may take advantage of the built-in operations to access components of the data structure, by-passing the new operations provided by the type designer. Thus these new type definitions do not appear like predefined types – their structure is visible to all.

ABSTRACT DATA TYPE   The introduction of the notion of *abstract data type* (ADT) [GTW78, Gut77] in the early 1970's, and its introduction in a number of programming languages (*e.g.*, Clu [L+81], Modula-2, and Ada) provided programmers with a mechanism that made it possible to introduce a collection of data type and value definitions, and operations on those definitions, that behaved more like a primitive data type.

ADT's included both a specification and an implementation, which were usually provided separately. The ADT specification provided a name for the type and provided specifications, both type and behavioral, for a collection of operations on the type. The type specification for an operation includes the types of the parameters, if any, and the return type. We will refer to such SIGNATURE   a type specification as the *signature* of the operation. These specifications were usually packaged together, and provided sufficient information for a programmer to write programs that used the type. The ADT implementation provided a representation for the values of the type, typically as a structured data type, and the implementations of the operations, written as procedures and functions that were allowed to access the representation of the data type.

Programmers using ADT's were not allowed access to the implementation of a data type, thus making it easier to replace one implementation of

INFORMATION HIDING   an ADT by another. This *information hiding* was an important feature of the
use of ADT's. Early language mechanisms that provided support for ADT's
included Clu's clusters, Modula-2's modules, and Ada's packages. ML's signatures and structures later provided similar mechanisms.

Object-oriented languages introduced the notions of classes and objects.
Objects contain both state (values) and methods (operations). The main operation provided for objects is sending a *message* to an object. *Classes* provide
both specification and implementation information on objects. Not only are
the names and specifications of methods included in classes, but also representation information for the state and methods. Most object-oriented languages provide mechanisms for allowing the programmer to restrict access
to the representation of the state or methods of objects from clients or subclasses in order to support information hiding.

Some object-oriented languages also allow programmers to provide only
specification information on objects. For example, several languages allow
the programmer to provide pure *abstract* (C++, Java) or *deferred* (Eiffel) classes.
The programmer simply provides method names and signatures, omitting
all mention of the representation of state and implementations of methods.
Java's interfaces, while they may have initially been included to provide support for some aspects of multiple inheritance, provide a clean representation
for this separation of interface and implementation. Several classes with entirely different representations may implement the same interface. A procedure or function whose parameter type is given by an interface can take as
actual parameters objects generated from any class that implements the interface. This promotes a notion of reusability that is essentially independent
of the notions of inheritance and subtyping.

Languages like Ada, Clu, and ML allow the user to define parameterized
types (*e.g.*, Stack(T), Tree(T), etc.). These can be seen as functions that take
types as parameters and return new types. These languages also typically
allow the programmer to define polymorphic functions (functions that take
types as parameters, but return values rather than types). There appears
to be a strong correlation between the increased expressiveness of programming languages and the increasing richness of their type systems.

1.2   Type checking and strongly typed languages

TYPE SYSTEM   *Type systems* for programming languages are typically designed to provide
several important functions. These include:

- Safety: Type checking of programs should prevent (either at compile or run time) the execution of certain illegal operations. In Chapter 13 we go into more detail on which illegal operations type systems are responsible for preventing. For now, we simply provide the examples of attempting to add a string to an integer as a type error, and dividing an integer by zero as a non-type error.

  The first is a type error because that operation should never be applied to two operands, one of which is a string and the other of which is an integer. The second is not a type error because division is an operation that is normally applied to pairs of integers. However, when the operation is applied to certain combinations of values from those types, an error results. Thus, information on the types of the operands is not sufficient to determine whether the operation will be erroneous.

- Optimization: Type checking can provide useful information to a compiler or interpreter. This information can be used to allocate storage for values, select appropriate code to execute (*e.g.*, for overloaded operations), and support various optimizations.

- Documentation: Type annotation (or, to a lesser extent, inference) provides documentation on constructs that make it easier for programmers to determine how the constructs can or should be used. Of course, the programmer should provide more than just type information as documentation, but our experience is that omission of type information significantly impacts the comprehensibility of code.

- Abstraction: The ability to name types, and, even more importantly, the ability to hide the implementation of types, allows (even forces) the programmer to think at a higher level of abstraction in programming. This hiding of details allows more straightforward modeling of the problem domain, while making it possible to change the implementation of a type and its operations without impacting the correctness of programs using the implementation. Of course, an important reason for changing an implementation is to improve some aspect of the behavior of the program, but correctness of the program should be dependent only on the specification of the provided operations.

STRONGLY TYPED
LANGUAGE

Every value generated in a program is associated with a type, either explicitly or implicitly. In a *strongly typed* language, the language implementation is required to provide a type checker that ensures that no type errors will occur at run time. For example, it must check the types of operands in order to ensure that nonsensical operations, like dividing the integer 5 by the string "hello", are not performed. Strongly typed languages may either be dynamically or statically type checked. Dynamic type checking normally occurs during program execution, while static type checking occurs prior to program execution, typically at compile time.[1] Other type-related checks may take place at program link time.

DYNAMICALLY TYPED LANGUAGE

In a *dynamically typed* language like LISP or Scheme, many operations are type checked just before they are performed. Thus the code for a plus operation may have to check the type of its operands just before the addition is performed. If both operands are integers, then an integer addition is performed. If both operands are floating point numbers or one is floating point and the other is an integer, then a floating point addition is performed. However, if one operand is a string and the other is a floating point number, then execution is terminated with an error message. In some languages an exception may be raised, which may either be handled by the program before resuming normal execution or, if there is no handler or no handler can successfully execute, the program terminates.

STATICALLY TYPED LANGUAGE

In a *statically typed* language, every expression of the language is assigned a type at compile time. If the type system can ensure that the value of each expression has a type compatible with the statically assigned type of the expression, then type checking of most operations can be performed at compile time, rather than delayed to run time.

Dynamically typed programming languages can be more expressive and flexible than statically typed languages, because the type checking is postponed until run time. In general, the problem of determining statically for an arbitrary program whether a type error will occur at run time is undecidable,[2] yet it is generally accepted that a static type system should be decidable. As a result, sound static type checkers will rule out some programs as potentially unsafe that would actually execute without a type error.

While the exclusion of safe programs would seem to be a major problem with static type checking, there are many advantages to having a statically type-checked language. These include:

- providing earlier, and usually more accurate, information on programmer errors,

---

1. For convenience, we will refer to static checks as occurring at compile time, even though similar checks take place before execution in interpreted as well as compiled languages.

2. We leave it as an exercise for the more sophisticated reader to show this problem can be reduced to the halting problem. Hint: Have a type error result only if a program that is input as data halts.

- eliminating the need for run-time type checks that can slow program execution and increase program size,

- providing documentation on the interfaces of components (*e.g.*, procedures, functions, and packages or modules), and

- providing extra information that can be used in compiler optimizations.

As a result most modern languages have static type systems.

Procedural languages like Pascal [Wir71], Clu [L+81], Modula-2 [Wir85], and Ada 83 [US 80], and functional languages like ML [HMM86] and Haskell [HJW92] have reasonably safe static typing systems. While some of these languages have a few minor holes in the type system (*e.g.*, variant records in Pascal), ML, Haskell, CLU, and Ada provide fairly secure type systems.

Programmers used to dynamically type-checked languages may worry that the use of a static type system will disallow or restrict the use of programs that can be dynamically determined to be type safe. For example, the static type system of standard Pascal is so inflexible that it will not allow the programmer to write a single sort procedure that will work for integer arrays of different sizes, let alone for arrays of other types like reals or characters. The language C has a similarly restrictive type system, but provides specific mechanisms (type casts) to allow the programmer to bypass the static type system when it gets in the way of the programmer.

However, modern programming languages allow more flexible use of arrays as parameters and often include support for more advanced features, such as parametric polymorphism, that have increased the expressiveness of statically typed languages. Examples of statically type-safe, yet flexible, procedural and functional programming languages include Clu, Modula-2, Ada, ML, and Haskell.

Unfortunately the situation for static type checking in object-oriented languages is not as good. The following is a list of some properties of type-checking systems of some of the more popular object-oriented languages (or the object-oriented portions of hybrid languages).

- Some provide only dynamic type checks.
  Smalltalk

- Some are mainly statically type-safe (if no casts), but inflexible. These languages often require explicit mechanisms to escape from the type system (*e.g.*, unsafe type casts) to overcome deficiencies of the type system.
  C++, Object Pascal

- Some have very flexible static type systems, but the type systems as implemented are not sound.

    Eiffel

- Some are flexible, but need run-time type checks to overcome weaknesses in static typing.

    Beta, Java, Ada95

At the boundary between static and dynamic type systems are several constructs. Here there may be differences of opinion on what features are considered to be part of static type systems and which are part of dynamic systems.

For example, we consider constructs like `typecase` statements, which make explicit tests on the run-time type of a value, to be statically type-safe as long as the execution of such statements cannot give rise to run-time type errors or system-generated exceptions. An example of the use of such a construct in the language Theta [DGLM94] is given below. Assume the identifier x is declared with static type S, and assume that T and U are subtypes of S.

```
typecase x
    when T(t): ... t ...
    when U(u): ... u ...
    others: ... x ...
end;
```

In this statement, if x's run-time type is a subtype of T, the value of x will be denoted by t (which is an identifier with static type T), and the code following the first when clause will be executed. Similarly, the code in the second when clause will be executed (with u denoting the value of x) if the run-time type is a subtype of U, but not of T. Finally, if the run-time type of x fails to be a subtype of any of the types listed in the when clauses, then the code in the others clause will be executed. This is type safe because each of the branches is required to type check correctly.

No run-time type errors can occur, because if x has a type that is not a subtype of the types specified in the when clauses, the code in the others clause will be executed, and it must be type safe for x having static type S.

Eiffel's "reverse assignment" involves an assignment from an expression with static type T to a variable whose static type S is a subtype of T. We consider this to be in the same category as typecase.

Suppose x is declared to have type S, where S is a subtype of T, the static type of exp. Then the statement

```
x ?= exp;
```

will type check. If the run-time type of exp is a subtype of S, the value of exp will be stored in the location corresponding to x. However, if the run-time type of exp fails to be a subtype of S, the value void is assigned to x. Thus in neither case does a run-time type error or system-generated exception occur.

This reverse assignment can be understood as a very restricted form of typecase. We can code the reverse assignment above using typecase as follows:

```
typecase exp
    when S(s): x := s;
    others:    x := void;
end;
```

On the other hand, we treat Java's type cast as not being statically type safe because the failure of a cast raises a run-time exception.[3]

As we shall see later, type restrictions on the redefinition of methods in many object-oriented languages give rise to situations where programmers often feel the need to by-pass the static type system. Some of these type restrictions follow from the need to preserve type safety when redefined methods are used in combination with inherited methods. Other restrictions are due to the desire to have subclasses always generate subtypes. While the introduction of bounded parametric polymorphism has helped loosen some of the rigidities of these languages, programmers of statically typed object-oriented languages are more likely to feel that static type safety gets in their way than programmers in statically typed procedural or functional languages.

As a result, in choosing from existing statically typed object-oriented languages, programmers are faced with unfortunate choices for overcoming the deficiencies of the type systems. They may attempt to program around these deficiencies, use constructs that require dynamic type checking, or use languages that allow run-time type errors to occur.

We make the case in this book that it is possible to define safe statically typed object-oriented languages that are sufficiently expressive to obviate the need for either run-time type checks or ways of escaping the type system. While borderline features like typecase statements or run-time checked

---

3. If Java could somehow guarantee that an instanceof check occurred before every type cast, like typecase statements in some languages, we would consider this to be a statically type-safe operation.

reverse assignments may occasionally be necessary to handle difficult problems with heterogeneous data structures, we prefer to have type systems that allow us to program as naturally as possible, while catching all type errors.

As we shall see in the course of this text, many type problems and rigidities arise in statically typed object-oriented languages because of the conflation of type with class, and with the mismatch of the inheritance hierarchy with subtyping. Whatever the cause, there appears to be much room for improvement in moving toward a combination of better security and greater expressiveness in the type systems.

1.3   Focus on statically typed class-based languages

In this text we explore the foundations of object-oriented languages by paying careful attention to the design of type systems and semantics for object-oriented languages. We will focus particularly on static type systems for class-based object-oriented languages.

There are great advantages to using statically typed languages; for example in helping programmers find and fix errors more efficiently. On the other hand, the restrictions on expressiveness can lead programmers to use languages that are not statically type safe or to find ways of by-passing the type system when it gets in the way. One of the goals of research in this area has been to ameliorate these inherent conflicts by designing language constructs that are both statically type safe and provide increased expressiveness.

Our focus on class-based rather than object-based languages comes from both practical and conceptual considerations. Class-based languages rely on classes that form templates for the generation of new objects. Object-based languages allow programmers to define objects directly, and usually provide mechanisms, for example prototypes, delegation, and cloning operations, for the creation of new objects from old. Like all distinctions in computer science, there is blurring at the edges between this categorization of languages, but the distinctions provided by this categorization are useful. (See Section 7.1.1 for a more detailed description of object-based languages.)

Virtually all popular object-oriented languages (*e.g.*, Simula 67, Smalltalk, Object Pascal, Eiffel, Objective C, C++, Ada95, and Java) are class-based. On the other hand, object-based languages (*e.g.*, Self, Cecil, and Emerald) tend to be research languages or are used by relatively small communities. Of course this popularity is not an indication that class-based languages are necessarily better, but it does suggest that there may be more interest in achieving a better understanding of class-based languages.

There are also conceptual reasons for preferring to analyze class-based languages. In class-based languages, classes and objects separate important concerns. Classes form extensible templates that can be used to create new objects. Objects are the fundamental components of computation, with computation taking place by sending messages to objects. The execution of methods of an object may update its state (instance variables), but no mechanism is provided to update or add methods to existing objects. In class-based languages methods in classes may be updated by using the mechanism of inheritance to create a new subclass with the updated (or added) method. In object-based languages, the methods of objects may be updated in place or (depending on the language) be updated in the creation of a new object based on the original.

In object-based languages, objects essentially play the role of both classes and objects in class-based languages. This causes complications in providing theoretical modeling of these languages, especially in providing support for method update or addition of methods in objects. At this point, it is hard to explain the technical reasons for these difficulties without going into a much more detailed discussion of the modeling of instance variables, methods, and, particularly, the modeling of `self` (written `this` in Java and C++), a keyword representing the object currently executing a method. We will discuss some of these difficulties later in Chapter 7; for now we hope the reader is satisfied with these explanations.

Not all other researchers agree with our views on this topic. For example, Abadi and Cardelli, in their very influential text, *A Theory of Objects* [AC96], argue that objects are more primitive than classes, and that mechanisms other than classes are useful in generating objects with common properties. Moreover they argue that classes are superfluous because they can be defined in terms of objects. This allows them to start with a very simple object calculus and define a variety of mechanisms (including classes) for generating objects. The associated cost is that it is more complex to model their object calculus in terms of the lambda calculus or denotational semantics in such a way as to preserve subtyping. (See Chapter 7 for a comparison.)

1.4   Foundations: A look ahead

We will begin this text by analyzing existing object-oriented programming languages, paying special attention to their type systems and impediments to expressiveness. We explore why type systems for these languages include what may at first seem to be rather arbitrary restrictions, and the consequences of ignoring these restrictions. It will become clear that there are a number of constructions that programmers would like to be able to express in these languages, but that are not currently supported in many existing statically typed object-oriented languages. In some cases, relatively simple extensions to these languages can greatly enhance expressiveness while preserving type-safety (see the discussion in Chapter 4 of the extension, GJ, of Java for one example). In other cases, attempts to add expressiveness have resulted in either type insecurities or the need to add dynamic type checking (see the discussion of Eiffel in the same chapter).

In Chapters 5 and 6 we examine the definitions of two key features of object-oriented languages: subtypes and subclasses. In particular we investigate conditions that guarantee that two types are subtypes. We also look at restrictions necessary to ensure that inherited methods in subclasses remain type correct.

We end the first part of the book with a discussion of different kinds of object-oriented languages (e.g., class-based, object-based, and multi-method languages) and an examination of statically typed object-oriented languages Simula 67, Beta, Java, C++, Smalltalk, Eiffel, and Sather with reference to our model languages and type systems.

In order to support a careful analysis of the type systems and semantics of object-oriented languages, we will introduce a prototypical object-oriented language, $\mathcal{SOOL}$, with a simple type system that is similar to those of class-based object-oriented languages in common use today. After a discussion of subtypes and subclasses (especially with regard to type restrictions on overriding methods), we begin an analysis of the foundations of object-oriented languages by providing a semantics. The semantics will allow us to precisely specify the meaning of these languages, enabling a more careful examination of the rules sufficient to guarantee the type safety of various programming constructs.

There are many alternatives available for providing the semantics of object-oriented languages. A denotational semantics would provide a mathematical specification of meaning. An operational semantics would specify the meaning of programs by providing instructions for an interpreter that would execute programs using a very simple virtual machine. One might also provide an axiomatic semantics that would provide rules for reasoning about programs. While there are advantages to each of these, and in other situations we have been quite happy with the provision of an operational semantics, we have taken a different approach here.

Our semantics provides the meaning of programming constructs by translating them to an extended typed lambda calculus. The main advantage of a typed lambda calculus is its simplicity. The core of the calculus is the representation of functions and function application; concepts that are learned quite early in mathematics courses. While the notation may initially be unfamiliar, the ideas behind the calculus should be familiar to all readers. Also rather than restricting ourselves to a stripped-down, "pure" lambda calculus, we add familiar programming constructs such as records, pairs, and references. We also extend the lambda calculus with less familiar notions, such as parametric polymorphism and existential types, that will help to model parameterized classes and information hiding.

Another advantage of providing a translational semantics based on the lambda calculus is that these calculi have been studied in great detail over the years. As a result, rather than providing very detailed and technically intricate proofs of type soundness and safety, we simply show that our translation preserves types. This will enable us to lift type soundness and safety results from the lambda calculus to our object-oriented language. While soundness and safety proofs are of interest in their own right, our goal here is to provide explanations of typing issues in object-oriented languages to a larger audience. Thus we include only the proofs we feel are most necessary in order to provide convincing evidence that our semantics are correct and that the type system is safe. As a result, we do not hesitate to base our results on systems that are intuitively (as well as provably) safe. We provide pointers to the literature for readers who are interested in complete proofs from first principles.

After the introduction to our extended lambda calculus in the second part of the book (Chapters 8 and 9), we begin the third part of the book with a careful formal definition of our prototypical language, $\mathcal{SOOL}$. In Chapter 11, we begin the task of modeling the semantics of $\mathcal{SOOL}$. While modeling of objects and classes will turn out to be rather straightforward, the modeling of subclasses is surprisingly tricky if we hope to preserve type safety. However, the correct modeling provides an explanation for the difficulties in type checking methods that arise if we wish to guarantee that inherited methods remain type safe in subclasses. As one might hope, our modeling of object-oriented languages will suggest the addition of new constructs to the language (e.g., MyType) as well as to help us understand the type-checking rules of object-oriented languages. This modeling leads into one of the most technical chapters of the text, Chapter 13, in which we prove that the type system is sound by showing that our semantics preserves typing information. We finish this part of the book by adding some common features that were omitted to simplify the original presentation and proof. These include references to methods in the superclass, the handling of null references, more refined information hiding, and multiple inheritance.

In the last part of the book (Chapters 15 through 18) we add desirable features that are not yet included in many statically typed object-oriented languages. These new features include parametric polymorphism (including what is sometimes known as F-bounded polymorphism), and a MyType construct. The combination of these features allows us to overcome many of the expressiveness limitations of existing statically typed object-oriented languages. We end the book with the sketch of a language that includes the MyType construct and drops subtyping for a slightly weaker relation, called matching.

There is much more material that could be included in a text on this subject. For example, we were tempted to include operational semantics for object-oriented languages, and we would have liked to include more material on virtual types and modules. However, our primary goal is to provide in a fairly compact form a good introduction to the concerns in designing safe, yet expressive, object-oriented programming languages. We hope that the following chapters will successfully achieve this goal. After completing this text, the reader should be prepared to go to the research literature to find information on these other topics.

2 *Fundamental Concepts of Object-Oriented Languages*

In this chapter we review the fundamental concepts of object-oriented languages. We assume the reader has some experience with object-oriented languages, so our main purpose here is to establish consistent terminology for the rest of the text.

The concepts of object-oriented languages discussed here include objects, classes, methods, instance variables, dynamic method invocation, subclasses and inheritance, and subtypes. Other features include mechanisms to allow the programmer to refer to the current object and to access methods of its superclass. These concepts are described briefly below. In later chapters we will go into much more detail as to their meanings. For now, we also avoid discussion of most issues involving types. We will devote a substantial amount of attention to typing issues later.

2.1   Objects, classes, and object types

OBJECT

INSTANCE VARIABLE

METHOD

MESSAGE

SHARING SEMANTICS

Objects encapsulate both state and behavior. In particular, they consist of a collection of *instance variables*, representing the state of the object, and a collection of *methods*, representing the behavior that the object is capable of performing. We sometimes refer to instance variables as the *fields* of an object. The methods are routines that are capable of accessing and manipulating the values of the instance variables of the object. When a *message* is sent to an object, the corresponding method of the object is executed. (In C++, instance variables are referred to as *member fields* or variables and methods as *member functions*.)

As is the case in Java and Smalltalk, we will assume that all objects are implicitly references. This results in a *sharing semantics* for assignment. That is, if o and o′ are objects of the same type, execution of the assignment state-

ment, o := o', will result in o referring to the same object as o'.[1] Similarly,
the equality test, o = o', will be true if and only if both have the same reference (*i.e.*, both point to the same object). Also as in Java and Smalltalk, we
will assume that the language implementation is provided with a garbage
collector. Thus programmers do not have to worry about disposing of ob-

NIL   jects when they are no longer needed or accessible. The value nil is used as
a null reference and is considered to be an element of all object types.

CLASS   *Classes* are extensible templates for creating objects, providing initial values for instance variables and the bodies for methods. All objects generated
from the same class share the same methods, but contain separate copies of
the instance variables. New objects can be created from a class by applying

NEW   the new operator to the name of the class.

The following is an example of a class written in the notation to be used
throughout this text.

```
class CellClass {
    x: Integer := 0;

    function get(): Integer is
    { return self.x }

    function set(nuVal: Integer): Void is
    { self.x := nuVal }

    function bump(): Void is
    { self ⇐ set(self ⇐ get()+1) }
}
```

The name of the class is CellClass. It has a single instance variable
named x that holds integer values. When a new object is created by evaluating new CellClass, the initial value of its instance variable x will be
0.

The class contains three methods: get, set, and bump. The method get
takes no parameters and returns an integer. The methods set and bump are
procedures (a function that does not return a value), which is indicated by
a return type of Void. The method set takes a single integer parameter,
nuVal, while bump takes no parameters.

---

1. In this text we will use ":=" for assignment and "=" for the equality operator. While this
differs from the conventions for the languages C, C++, and Java, we find this notation more
sensible in relation to common mathematical usage.

SELF   The keyword self (written this in C++ and Java) is used in method bodies to indicate the object currently executing the method. The "dot" notation is used with self to get access to instance variables of the current object. Thus in the bodies of methods get and set, self.x refers to the instance variable x of the object executing the method.

Adopting notation from Smalltalk, we use the symbol "⇐" to represent sending a message to an object. While most languages don't bother to distinguish notationally between accessing an instance variable and sending a message, they are quite different operations, so we use different symbols. In the body of bump, the message sends self ⇐ set and self ⇐ get indicate that the corresponding methods in the current object should be executed.

In most object-oriented languages, it is possible to omit the prefix self when used in accessing instance variables or performing message sends. For example CellClass could be written:

```
class CellClass {
    x: Integer := 0;

    function get(): Integer is
    { return x }

    function set(nuVal: Integer): Void is
    { x := nuVal }

    function bump(): Void is
    { set(get()+1) }
}
```

In order to keep meanings as clear as possible, we will generally include the prefix self as in the first version of CellClass.

For simplicity, and as an aid to abstraction, we will use the default that instance variables of an object are not accessible from outside of that object's methods. We will also assume that methods are by default publicly accessible from outside of the object.

Later we will introduce notation to allow an object's methods to be hidden from other objects. Obviously we may provide access to an instance variable accessible from outside of the object by writing appropriate "get" and "set" methods that access or update the variable.

In many object-oriented languages, class names are used for three distinct purposes: as a name for the class, as a name for a constructor of the class, and as a name for the type of objects generated from the class. In order to make it easier to describe the different meanings of these three interpretations, as well as to provide better support for abstraction, we choose not to conflate these uses.

For now, we omit discussion of constructors. Instead, we will depend on classes to provide initial values of instance variables when new objects are created with the new operator.[2] However, we do wish to distinguish classes from the types of objects.

We consider types as abstractions that represent sets of values and the operations and relations applicable to them. In order to better support abstraction, and hence later program modification, we believe that object types should not carry implementation information. Instead they should reveal only the names and types (signatures) of the messages that may be sent to them.[3] From this point of view, classes provide too much information to users. The identity of instance variables should not be revealed to the user, nor should hidden methods. The bodies of existing methods should also not be part of the type of an object. To support this degree of abstraction, we provide a new kind of type expression to represent the types of objects.

The type of objects with public methods m_1 of type T_1, up to m_n of type T_n, will be written as `ObjectType` $\{m_1\colon T_1, \ldots, m_n\colon T_n\}$. For example, the type of objects generated by class `CellClass` is:

```
CellType = ObjectType { get: Void → Integer;
                        set: Integer → Void;
                        bump: Void → Void }
```

The notation $A \rightarrow B$ denotes the type of all functions from type A to type B. Thus a function of type $A \rightarrow B$ may be applied to arguments of type A and returns values of type B. We follow Java and C++ in using `Void` in the domain of a function to indicate a parameterless function and, as stated earlier, `Void` in the range is used to indicate a procedure.

Because object types do not mention instance variables, distinct classes that have the same public methods and types can generate objects with the same object types. For example, we can define

---

2. We will see later that we can create functions that provide the initial values of instance variables in classes. This will allow us to more closely model constructors.

3. While it is common in some programming languages to refer to method signatures as though they were distinct from types, we shall find it convenient to refer to all such notations as types.

```
class DimCellClass {
    z: Integer := -1;

    function get(): Integer is
    { return self.z + 1 }

    function set(nuVal: Integer): Void is
    { self.z := nuVal - 1 }

    function bump(): Void is
    { self ⇐ set(self ⇐ get()+1) }
}
```

Class `DimCellClass` has a different instance variable than `CellClass`, and the methods `get` and `set` have bodies that are distinct from those in `CellClass`. However, because the public methods are the same as those in `CellType`, and they have the same types as specified there, `DimCell-Class` also generates objects of type `CellType`. While, in this case, objects generated from `CellClass` and `DimCellClass` exhibit identical observable behaviors, two classes can generate objects of the same type even if the methods result in different behaviors.

The following is a a simple program using these two classes. Notice that the pair // indicates the beginning of a comment, which extends to the end of the line.

```
program CellExample;
... // Definitions of CellClass, DimCellClass,
    // and CellType omitted
var
    c: CellType := nil;        // (1)
{
    c := new CellClass;        // (2)
    c ⇐ set(17);               // (3) set from CellClass
    c ⇐ bump();                // (4)
    writeln(c ⇐ get());        // (5)
    c := new DimCellClass;     // (6)
    c ⇐ set(17);               // (7) set from DimCellClass
    c ⇐ bump();                // (8)
    writeln(c ⇐ get())         // (9)
}
```

The program begins with a `program` statement containing the name of the program. The next several lines should contain the definitions of `CellType`, `CellClass`, and `DimCellClass`, but we have omitted them here to avoid repeating code. Line (1) contains a declaration that the variable c is of type `CellType`.

The main body of a program, like that of a class or method, is enclosed in curly brackets. The `new` expression on line (2) creates a new object from class `CellClass`, which is assigned to variable c. As mentioned earlier, we use `:=` rather than `=` to represent assignment. Lines (3) and (4) send the messages `set(17)` and `bump()` to c, while line (5) prints the value of the cell obtained as the result of sending the message `get()` to c. Because c was generated by class `CellClass`, the actual code executed during these message sends is that of the corresponding methods in `CellClass`.

Line (6) results in c being reassigned a value created from class `DimCell-Class`, with lines (7), (8), and (9) sending the same messages as lines (3), (4), and (5). Because the object held in c is now generated from `DimCellClass`, the code executed during these message sends is now that of the corresponding methods in `DimCellClass`. Executing the above code will result in the number 18 being printed out twice, despite the fact that different method bodies are executed as a result of the method invocations of `set` and `bump` in the first and second half of the listing.

Because c is declared to have type `CellType`, it can be sent the messages `get`, `set`, and `bump`, as they are specified in the type. Objects generated by classes `CellClass` and `DimCellClass` can both be assigned to c because both have public methods with the signatures required by `CellType`.

DYNAMIC METHOD INVOCATION
The mechanism by which the object receiving a message is responsible for knowing which method body to execute is often called *dynamic method invocation*. This facility provides an enormous amount of flexibility for object-oriented programming. It allows a program to send messages to an object of unknown origin as long as the object has a type that guarantees it has a method with the appropriate signature. Thus objects generated by different classes may be used interchangeably and simultaneously as long as they have the same object type.

2.2   Subclasses and inheritance

SUBCLASS
One of the important features of object-oriented languages is the ability to make incremental changes to a class by creating a *subclass* (called a derived

```
class ClrCellClass inherits CellClass modifies set {

    color: ColorType := blue;

    function getColor(): ColorType is
    { return self.color }

    function set(nuVal: int): Void is
    { self.x := nuVal;
      self.color := red }
}

ClrCellType =
    ObjectType { get: Void → Integer;
                 set: Integer → Void;
                 bump: Void → Void;
                 getColor: Void → ColorType
    }
```

Figure 2.1 ClrCellClass defined as a subclass of CellClass.

class in C++). A subclass may be defined from a class by either adding to or modifying the methods and instance variables of the original class. (We will see later that restrictions on the modification of the types of methods and instance variables in subclasses are necessary in order to preserve type
SUPERCLASS safety). If class B is a subclass of C, we say that C is a *superclass* of B.

Figure 2.1 includes an example of a subclass of CellClass that adds color
INHERITANCE to the objects. The *inherits* clause specifies the class from which the new class inherits, while the modifies clause indicates which methods from the superclass will be overridden in the subclass. Because ClrCellClass inherits from CellClass, it automatically has all of the instance variables and methods from CellClass, including both those defined in CellClass and any that were inherited. ClrCellClass adds a new instance variable color of type ColorType with initial value blue. It also adds a new method get-
METHOD OVERRIDE Color, and *overrides* the method set with a new method body that not only updates x, but also sets color to be red. That is, the body of the method set contained in the class definition replaces the inherited body from Cell-

Class. We insist that names of methods that are intended to be overridden
in the subclass be listed in the "modifies" clause as a double-check in order
to ensure that methods are not accidentally overridden. Our type-checking
rules will generate an error if a method is overridden, yet its name is not
listed in the modifies clause.

Because of inheritance, objects generated from ClrCellClass contain the
instance variable x declared in CellClass as well as the new instance variable color. Similarly, they contain methods get and bump as well as the
new getColor and the redefined set. The type of objects generated from
ClrCellClass is ClrCellType.

When new definitions are given to methods in a subclass, it is useful to
be able to refer to the methods of the superclass. For instance, in overriding
a method, one often wishes to apply the method body from the superclass,
and then perform a few more operations before returning from the redefined
SUPER   method. We provide a keyword, super, to provide access to the methods of
the superclass. Using super, we can rewrite the body of set above to be

```
{ super ⇐ set(nuVal);
  self.color := red }
```

While this does not provide enormous savings in this case, in other cases it
can. Moreover it can guarantee that any changes made later to the method
body in the superclass will automatically be carried over to the subclass.

Dynamic method invocation plays an important role during inheritance.
Recall that the body of the bump method in CellClass involves the message send self ⇐ set(...). Inside CellClass, the method set simply
updates the instance variable x. However, inside ClrCellClass, set also
updates color. When bump is inherited in ClrCellClass, the message
send of self ⇐ set(...) now results in invoking the method set of
ClrCellClass. Thus sending a bump message to an object generated from
ClrCellClass will end up *both* incrementing that object's x instance variable, and updating the value of color to be red. (In the terminology of C++,
all methods are *virtual*.)

2.3 Subtypes

SUBTYPE   We say type T is a *subtype* of U, written T <: U, if a value of type T can be
used in any context in which a value of type U is expected. That is, a value
of type T can *masquerade* as an element of type U in all contexts if T <: U. We
SUPERTYPE say U is a *supertype* of T if T is a subtype of U.

SUBTYPE
POLYMORPHISM

Because values may have multiple types in languages supporting subtyping, we say these languages support *subtype polymorphism* (we shall examine other sorts of polymorphism later). If v has type T, subtype polymorphism allows it to be used in any context that expects a value of some type U as long as T is a subtype of U.

Subtyping depends only on the types or interfaces of values, while inheritance depends upon their implementations. In most simple object-oriented languages, the type of objects generated by a subclass is a subtype of objects generated by the superclass. For example, ClrCellType <: CellType. However, we provide examples later that show that if one enriches the language slightly, a class may inherit from another, yet the type of the objects generated by the subclass may not necessarily be a subtype of the type of the objects generated by the superclass.

It is also not necessary to restrict subtypes to those relationships that arise from subclasses. As long as object type T has at least all of the methods of object type U, and the corresponding methods have the same type,[4] then an object of type T can successfully masquerade as an object of type U. For example, the type of objects generated by ClrCellClass is a subtype of the type of objects generated by DimCellClass, even though they are not subclasses.

By separating object types from classes, we hope to make it clearer that subtyping is a relation between types, while subclassing is a relation between classes. The first has to do with public interfaces, while the second has to do with the inheritance of implementations.

STRUCTURAL
SUBTYPING

We remark that we are using *structural subtyping* here. Thus subtyping is determined by the structure of the type rather than its declaration. By contrast, Java requires the programmer to explicitly specify when one type is to be a subtype (*extension* in Java terminology) of another.

In Chapter 5 we examine the subtyping relation very carefully and see that it can allow more variations in object types than we have allowed here. In Chapter 16 we will also define later another relation, *matching*, between object types that is similar to subtyping, but may be even more important in languages with a keyword for the type of self.

---

4. We will loosen this restriction later.

```
class C {
   v: T1 := ...;

   function m(p: T2): T3 is { ... }
}

class SC inherits C modifies v, m {
   v: T1' := ...;

   function m(p: T2'): T3' is { ... }
}
```

Figure 2.2   Covariant and contravariant changes in types.

2.4   Covariant and contravariant changes in types

One of the most confusing things in understanding the type systems of statically typed object-oriented languages has been understanding restrictions on changing the types of methods and instance variables inherited from superclasses when defining subclasses. Most statically typed object-oriented languages allow no changes to types in subclasses. However, as we shall see in the next chapter, this puts real restrictions on the expressiveness of the language. As a result there has been pressure on language designers to allow changes to types.

In Chapter 5 we will see why some restrictions on changing types are necessary in order to preserve type safety. For now, we simply introduce the terminology that will allow us to discuss the issue. Figure 2.2 includes the definitions of a class, C, and its subclass, SC. In the subclass we have changed the type of the instance variable v, and the parameter and return types of method m.

If the types in C are replaced by subtypes in SC (*i.e.*, $T1' <: T1, T2' <: T2$, and $T3' <: T3$), then the changes are referred to as *covariant*. This is the most obvious change to make to types in subclasses. For example, C++ now allows the programmer to make covariant changes in the return types of methods, though it allows no changes to the type of instance variables or the parameters of methods.

COVARIANT

On the other hand, we will see later that we can preserve type safety if we allow the types of parameters of methods to be replaced by supertypes in

CONTRAVARIANT

subclasses. Thus we may allow T2 <: T2'. Replacing a type by a supertype in a subclass is referred to as a *contravariant* change.

The terms covariant and contravariant come from category theory. The simplest way to remember the difference is that *contra*variant changes to types are *contra*dictory to one's intuition.

We will see later that type safety is preserved in subclasses if we allow only covariant changes to the return types of parameters (T3' <: T3), contravariant changes to parameter types (T2 <: T2'), and no changes at all to types of instance variables (T1 = T1').

2.5 Overloading versus overriding methods

OVERLOADED METHOD

Some languages, including both Java and C++, allow programmers to *overload* method names in classes. A method name is overloaded in a context if it is used to represent two or more distinct methods, and where the method represented by the overloaded name is determined by the type or signature of the method.

Look at the following excerpt from the definition of a class Rectangle.

```
class Rectangle {
    ...
    function contains(pt: Point): Boolean is
        { ... }
    function contains(x, y: Integer): Boolean is
        { ... }
}
```

The method name contains is listed twice. The two versions of contains have slightly different signatures as one takes a parameter of type Point while the other takes two parameters of type Integer that represent the coordinates of a point. It is convenient to use the same name for these methods because they represent essentially the same operation, even though the parameter types are different.

As long as their signatures are different, both Java and C++ treat methods with overloaded names as though they had completely different names. In particular, if code is written using these methods, the language processor statically determines what method body is to be executed. Examine the following code fragment:

```
var
   r: Rectangle;
   pt: Point;
   x, y: Integer;
function m(...): ... is {
   ... r ⇐ contains(pt) ... r ⇐ contains(x, y) ...
}
```

The language processor can easily determine that the first invocation corresponds to the first definition of contains in Rectangle, while the second invocation corresponds to the second definition.

Let us compare and contrast overloaded and overridden methods. message sends involving overloaded methods are resolved statically. By contrast, overridden methods always occur in different classes, typically when one of the classes is a subclass of the other. They typically have the same signatures, though some languages allow the overriding method in the subclass to have a signature that is a subtype of the method in the superclass. Message sends involving overridden methods are resolved at run time.

Languages have different rules for when method names may be overloaded. In C++, overloaded methods must be defined in the same class, while in Java, the overloading can happen when a method in a superclass is inherited in a subclass that has a method with the same name, but different signature.

Many programmers believe that overloaded method names make it much easier to understand programs, because they allows the user to reuse names that suggest the operation being performed. For example, in the Rectangle class, both versions of method contains determined whether a particular location, represented alternatively as a Point or as a pair of integer coordinates, was contained in the rectangle.

Moreover, allowing overloading seems to have few consequences for a language, as the language processor automatically renames all overloaded methods with distinct names before runtime.

However, the interaction between overloaded method names with static resolution, and overridden methods with dynamic resolution can result in great confusion as to what methods are called when in a program. We illustrate this with an example.

Class C and subclass SC are defined in Figure 2.3. Class C has an equals method taking a parameter of type CType. Class SC has two equals methods. Thus equals in class SC is overloaded.

```
class C {
    ...

    function equals(other: CType): Boolean is
        { ... }                    // equals 1
}

class SC inherits C modifies equals {
    ...

    function equals(other: CType): Boolean is
        { ... }                    // equals 1

    function equals(other: SCType): Boolean is
        { ... }                    // equals 2
}
```

Figure 2.3   Classes with overridden and overloaded method equals.

The first definition of equals in SC takes a parameter of type CType, overriding the equals method of class C. As a result, the comments label them both with *equals 1*.

The second equals method in class SC takes a parameter of type SC-Type. Because the parameter type is different from the other two definitions of equals, this method is treated as being statically different from the others. As a result, we label it with equals 2.

As usual, let CType and SCType be the types of objects created from those classes. Clearly SCType <: CType.

Let c and c′ be variables with declared type CType, and let sc be a variable with declared type SCType. Consider the following code:

```
c  := new C;
sc := new SC;
c′ := new SC;

c  ⇐ equals(c);
c  ⇐ equals(c′);
```

```
c  ⇐ equals(sc);

c' ⇐ equals(c);
c' ⇐ equals(c');
c' ⇐ equals(sc);

sc ⇐ equals(c);
sc ⇐ equals(c');
sc ⇐ equals(sc);
```

The variable c is assigned an object created from class C and sc is assigned an object created from class SC. Variable c' is also assigned an object created from class SC. This is legal because SCType is a subtype of CType.

The 9 message sends shown above correspond to all possible combinations of receiver and parameter. Which equals method is actually executed as a result of each of the sends? Think carefully about each case before looking at the answers in the next paragraph.

The answer to this question is rather surprising.

- All 3 message sends to c result in the execution of method *equals 1* from class C.

- All 3 message sends to c' result in the execution of method *equals 1* in class SC.

- The first two message sends to sc also result in the execution of method *equals 1* from class SC.

- Only the last message send, sc ⇐equals(sc), results in the execution of method *equals 2* from class SC.

Most people get this wrong, even when they understand the rules for overloading given above. Usually the error is thinking that method *equals 2* is selected for some or all of the message sends to c', and for two or more of the message sends to sc. The key to understanding which method body is selected in these examples is to remember what is resolved statically and what is resolved dynamically.

The overloading of equals is resolved statically. That is, the selection of *equals 1* versus *equals 2* is resolved solely on the static types of the receiver and parameters.

Because the type of both variables c and c' is CType, when the equals message is sent to c or c', the type system examines the methods in class C at compile time to determine if there is an appropriate method `equals`. There is only one method `equals` in `C`, and it has a parameter of type `CType`. That method is appropriate for each of the three actual parameters to `equals`. The actual parameters `c` and `c'` are clearly of the appropriate type. The parameter `sc` is also fine because its type, `SCType`, is a subtype of `CType`. Thus the first 6 method calls are all to *equals 1*.

The first two message sends to `sc` have parameters with static type `CType`. This is an exact match with the signature of *equals 1* in `SC`, so they resolve to that method. The last message send has a parameter of type `SCType`, so its best match is method *equals 2*.

In summary, the first 8 message sends resolve statically to method *equals 1*, while the last resolves to method *equals 2*.

Now all we have to do is figure out which of the first 8 message sends execute the body of *equals 1* from class `C`, and which execute the body from class `SC`. Because we know that all of these resolve statically to method *equals 1*, we determine which version of *equals 1* is executed by determining the class that generated the receiver of the message.

This is now easy because the receiver of the first 3 message sends is a *value* generated from class `C`. Therefore those 3 message sends result in the execution of the body of *equals 1* from class `C`. The receivers of the rest of the message sends are *values* generated from class `SC`. Hence all of those message sends result in the execution of method bodies from class SC.

Exercise 2.5.1 *Suppose that class `SC` did not include the first `equals` method – the one with parameter of type `CType` that overrode the `equals` from class `C`. Determine which of the two remaining method bodies is executed for each of the 9 message sends given above.*

Interestingly, the answer is not the same for C++ and Java because C++ does not allow overloading methods across class boundaries. Look up the rules for each of these languages and determine the correct answer for each. (Hint: The only difference between the two languages with this example is that one or more message sends in C++ result in static type errors.)

We hope that this example provides convincing evidence that the combination of static overloading and dynamic method invocation in object-oriented languages is likely to result in confusion on the part of programmers. While many programmers believe that overloading makes it easier to understand programs, we have seen very experienced programmers working on real code incorrectly believe that one method is being executed, when static resolution of overloading resulted in a different version of the method being selected.

We strongly recommend that object-oriented languages *not* support static overloading of method names. As a result we will not further consider static overloading in the languages discussed in this book.

2.6   Summary

In this chapter we defined the fundamental concepts of object-oriented languages, including classes, objects, methods, messages, and instance variables. We also introduced object types, which include the types of public methods, but do not include the names or types of instance variables.

We also discussed the use of inheritance in the definition of subclasses, and noted its differences from the notions of subtype and subtype polymorphism. We also discussed covariant versus contravariant changes of types that may arise when modifying object types. We shall see later that careful identification of locations in type expressions allowing covariant versus contravariant changes in types is very important in obtaining type safety in object-oriented languages.

Finally we discussed static overloading. As a result of the possible confusion in resolving static overloading and dynamic method invocation, we strongly recommend that programmers avoid using static overloading.

3 *Type Problems in Object-Oriented Languages*

We begin our study of the type systems of object-oriented programming languages by first providing a critique of the type systems of existing statically typed object-oriented programming languages. The reason for providing such a critique is that our goal is not only to describe existing programming languages, but also to use a deep understanding of the object-oriented concepts in order to design better object-oriented languages. While the next few chapters will mainly focus on describing the types and semantics of existing languages, we hope this chapter will give the reader a better insight into the overall goals of this work and provide motivation for the later work on extending the expressiveness of object-oriented languages.

3.1   Type checking object-oriented languages is difficult

The features of object-oriented languages that provide added flexibility, like subtyping and inheritance, also create difficulties in type checking these languages. We provide here a brief overview of some of the typing difficulties that arise from them.

While subtyping is trivial for simple types, defining a correct notion of subtype for more complex types like record, function, and object types can be tricky. In particular, there has been great confusion over what is the proper subtyping rule for functions. Later we explain why the so-called "contravariant" subtyping rule for the types of parameters in function types is correct and why the "covariant" rule may lead to typing errors.

Adding new instance variables and methods to a subclass does not cause typing difficulties, but modifying existing methods may create problems. If the types of parameters or the return type of the modified method differ from those in the corresponding method of the superclass, it might cause type problems.

If the method m being modified was used in a second method n of the superclass, then changes in types in m may destroy the type correctness of n when it is inherited in the subclass. We will see later that considerations involving subtyping can be used to determine which changes in types are guaranteed to preserve type safety.

Another important type-related question that arises with subclasses is determining whether the type of an object generated from a subclass is always a subtype of the type of an object generated from the superclass. While most current object-oriented languages have type systems that ensure this is the case, we will see that it need not hold if the language contains certain features that provide for more flexible constructions of subclasses.

These and other features of object-oriented languages have made it difficult to create statically typed object-oriented programming languages that are both very expressive and type safe. The following enumerates some of the strengths and weaknesses of the type-checking systems of some of the more popular object-oriented languages (or the object-oriented portions of hybrid languages[1]).

- Some show little or no regard for static typing (*e.g.*, Smalltalk).

- Some have relatively inflexible static type systems, requiring type casts to overcome deficiencies of the type system. These type casts may be unchecked, as in C++ and Object Pascal [Tes85], or checked at run time, as in Java.

- Some provide mechanisms like "`typecase`" statements to allow the programmer to instruct the system to check for more refined types than can be determined by the type system (*e.g.*, Modula-3 [CDG+88], Simula 67 [BDMN73], and Beta [KMMPN87]).

- Some allow "reverse" assignments from superclasses to subclasses, which require run-time checks (*e.g.*, Beta, Eiffel [Mey92]).

- Some require that parameters of methods overridden in subclasses have exactly the same types as in the superclasses (*e.g.*, C++, Java, Object Pascal, and Modula-3), resulting in less flexibility than would be desirable, while

---

1. We consider a hybrid language to be one that attempts to support multiple paradigms. C++ and Object Pascal are examples of languages that attempt to support both procedural and object-oriented styles of programming.

others allow *too* much flexibility in changing the types of parameters or instance variables, requiring extra run-time or link-time checks to catch the remaining type errors (*e.g.*, Eiffel and Beta).

Thus all of these languages either require programmers to program around deficiencies of the type system, require run-time type checking, or allow run-time type errors to occur. Thus, there appears to be a lot of room for improvement in moving toward a combination of better security and greater expressiveness in the type systems. In the next section we provide several examples showing problems with current static type systems.

3.2   Simple type systems are lacking in flexibility

Languages like Object Pascal, Modula-3, and C++ arose as object-oriented extensions of imperative programming languages. These languages, as well as Java, have relatively simple and straightforward type systems whose features are similar to those of the procedural languages from which they were derived. In these simple type systems, the programmer has little flexibility in redefining methods in subclasses. They require that a redefined method have exactly the same type as the original method in the superclass. Similarly the types of instance variables may not be changed in subclasses. We refer to type systems that restrict the types of methods and instance variables INVARIANT TYPE in subclasses to be identical to those in superclasses as *invariant* type systems. SYSTEM   Interestingly, in these invariant systems, when a method is inherited or redefined in the subclass, the programmer is often able to deduce more refined types for methods than the language allows to be written. For example the programmer may know that a certain method always returns an object of type DType even though the type system of the program restricts the programmer from writing that type as the return type because it does not allow changes to method types in subclasses. We present examples illustrating this below.

As mentioned earlier, we will find it helpful to keep the notions of class and type separate. The type represents only the public interface of the object (in our case the names and types of all of the methods, but not the instance variables), while the class includes names, types, and initial values for instance variables and names, types, and code for methods.

We will often use the convention in this book of writing CType for the type of objects generated by a class named C or CClass. In Chapter 2, we followed that convention in using `CellType` as the name of the type of objects generated by class `CellClass`.

3.2.1   The need to change return types in subclasses

In our first examples we show that it is useful to be able to modify the return types of methods when the methods are redefined in subclasses (and sometimes even when they are *not*).

In most pure object-oriented languages (*e.g.*, Eiffel, Java, and Smalltalk, as well as the languages we introduce later in this text), all objects are represented as references (*i.e.*, implicit pointers). Thus assignment results in sharing, rather than copying. In these languages, it is useful to have an operation that makes a new copy or clone of an object. A common way of supporting CLONE this is to provide a built-in `clone` method in the top-most class of the object hierarchy (called `Object` in Java), so that all other classes automatically inherit it. For the rest of this chapter we assume that our language has a top-most class named `Object`, and its type is `ObjectType`.

A shallow copy is made by copying the values of instance variables and taking the same suite of methods as the original. If the instance variables hold references to other objects, only the references are copied, not the objects being referred to. Thus if this shallow clone method is applied to the head of a linked list, only the head node is copied while the rest of the list is shared between the new and old lists.

What should be the type of `clone`? When defined in the class `Object`, it seems apparent that it should return a value of type `ObjectType`. However, when this is inherited by a class `CellClass`, we would like it to return a value of type `CellType`. In the invariant type systems, the return type of `clone` remains `ObjectType`, even though the method actually returns a value that is a cell! That is, the semantics of the language does the correct thing, but the type system is not expressive enough to capture that. Instead the programmer must perform a type cast or other operation after the `clone` method has returned in order to allow the system to treat the value as having the proper type!

Often it is desirable to write a `deepClone` method that is based on `clone`. This is typically done by first writing code to send the `clone` message to `self` to make the shallow copy, and then writing code to clone all objects held in the instance variables of the original object.

Suppose we have a class `C` that includes a method `deepClone`, which returns an object of type `CType`. See Figure 3.1. Suppose we now define a sub-

class SC of C that includes a new method, newMeth, as well as a new instance
variable, newVar, holding an object with type newObjType. We assume for
simplicity that newObjType also supports a deepClone method.

We would like to redefine deepClone to clone the contents of this new instance variable after all of the code in the original deepClone method from
C has been executed. (This is a quite common desire in real object-oriented
languages as subclass methods cannot obtain access to private instance variables from the superclass.)

Unfortunately, the rules of the simple type systems require that deep-
Clone for SC also return a CType, just as in C, even though it is obvious that
it actually returns an object of type SCType. While this is not type-unsafe, it
represents an unnecessary loss of information in the type system.

Suppose anSC is a variable of type SCType. If we write (anSC ⇐ deep-
Clone()) ⇐ newMeth(), the type checker will complain, even though
the object resulting from anSC ⇐ deepClone() has the method newMeth.
The problem is that the type system is not aware of this!

In these circumstances, Object Pascal, C++, and Java programmers would
normally be forced to perform a type cast to tell the compiler that the cloned
object has the type SCType. In the case of Object Pascal and C++, the type
cast is unchecked. In Java, it would be checked at run time. Modula-3 programmers would typically use a typecase statement that also performs a
run-time check to get the same effect.

One could attempt working around these deficiencies in the static type
system by making up a new name for the revised deepClone method (e.g.,
SCdeepClone). Unfortunately this would mean that inherited methods that
included a message send of deepClone would call the old deepClone for
C rather than the updated method from SC actually desired.

For example, suppose C includes a method m invoking deepClone as follows

```
function m(): Void is
{ ...
    self ⇐ deepClone()
    ...
}
```

Also suppose class SC is defined as a subclass of C as in Figure 3.1, except
that it adds a new method SCdeepClone that returns a value of type SC-
Type. If sc has type SCType, then sc ⇐ SCdeepClone() will certainly
result in the newly defined clone method being called. However the execu-

```
class C {
  ...

  function deepClone(): CType is
  { self ⇐ clone(); ... }
}

class SC inherits C modifies deepClone {
  newVar: newObjType := nil;

  function newMeth(): Void is
  { ... }

  function setNewVar(newVarVal: newObjType): Void is
  { self.newVar := newVarVal }

  function deepClone(): SCType is
                      // illegal return type change!
                      // Must return CType instead
  var      // local variable declaration
    newClone: SCType := nil;
  {
    newClone := super ⇐ deepClone();
                        // (*) another problem
    newClone ⇐ setNewVar(newVar ⇐ deepClone());
    return newClone
  }
}
```

Figure 3.1   Typing deepClone methods in subclasses.

tion of sc ⇐ m() will result in the execution of the method deepClone from
the superclass rather than the newly defined SCdeepClone that was likely
intended. As a result of calling only the old method, the value in the new instance variable, newVar, will not be cloned, possibly causing problems later
in the program.

Thus the restriction on changing types of methods in subclasses gets in the way of the programmer, even though the run-time system does the right thing. Not surprisingly, we have similar problems even writing down the type of the built-in (shallow) `clone`. In Java, `clone` is simply given a type indicating that it returns an element of the top class, `Object`. The result must then be cast to the appropriate type before anything substantial may be done with it.

In newer versions of C++, it is possible to specialize the return type of methods in subclasses. Thus method `deepClone` in `SC` could be specified to return a value of type `SCType` rather than `CType`. Unfortunately this does not solve all of our problems. First note that the right side of the assignment on line (*) of Figure 3.1 returns a value of type `CType`. Because the type of the variable on the left side is a subtype of `CType`, the assignment is illegal. (A value of the subtype can masquerade as a supertype, not the reverse!) Thus a type cast would have to be inserted to make the assignment legal.

Moreover, suppose class `SC` has a subclass `SSC` that adds new methods, but no new instance variables. As a result, there is no need to override method `deepClone`. However, if it is not overridden then it will continue to return type `SCType` rather than the desired `SSCType`. To get the types right, the programmer would have to override `deepClone` solely to cast the return type of the call of the superclass to the new type.

Thus, allowing covariant changes to the types of methods in subclasses would be helpful, but it would be even more helpful if some way could be found to have them change automatically. In the next section we show that it would also be convenient to be able to change the types of method parameters in subclasses.

3.2.2   Problems with binary methods

BINARY METHODS

Our next class of examples is one that arises surprisingly frequently in practice. The particular typing problem arises in connection with what are often called *binary methods*. Binary methods are methods that have a parameter whose type is intended to be the same as the receiver of the message. Methods involving comparisons, such as `eq`, `lt`, and `gt`, or other familiar binary operations or relations are common examples of such methods (*e.g.*, `someElt` ⇐ `lt(otherElt)`). In procedural languages, these methods would be written as functions that take two parameters (hence the "binary"). However, they are written with single parameters in object-oriented languages because the receiver of the message plays the role of the other parameter. Other compelling examples arise in constructing linked structures (*e.g.*, node $\Leftarrow$ setNext(newNext)).

While it is not difficult to define binary methods when specifying classes from scratch, it is much more problematic for subclasses. Suppose we define class C below with method equals:

```
class C {
    ...
    function equals(other: CType): Boolean is
    { ... }
    ...
}
```

In the example we use our convention that CType is the type of objects generated from class C. If o is generated from class C, the signature of equals requires that the parameter o′ in o.equals(o′) have type CType for the message send to be well-typed.

However, we have problems when we define a subclass SC:

```
class SC inherits C modifies equals {
    ...
    function equals(other: CType): Boolean is
        // Want parameter type to be SCType instead!
    { super ⇐ equals(other);
        ...  // Can't access SC-only features in other
    }

    ...
}
```

Because we are not allowed to change the type of parameters in subclasses, we cannot change the type of CType to SCType, even though that may be what is desired here.

Similarly to our previous example with SCdeepClone, changing the name of the method to newEquals does not help. If there are occurrences of equals in the inherited methods of the superclass, we would like the new method body to be called, but instead the old would be invoked. Overloading the name equals does not help either. Overloading is resolved statically rather than at run time, so the problem of calling the wrong method is no different than using the new name above.

Programmers using languages with invariant type systems sometimes use the following trick of overriding equals in the subclass with a body that casts the argument to the desired type before it is used.

```
class SC' inherits C modifies equals {
   ...
   function equals(other: CType): Boolean is
   var
     otherSC: SCType := nil;
   { otherSC := (SCType)other;     // type cast!
     ...
     return super ⇐ equals(other) & ... }

   ...
}
```

The expression (SCType)other represents casting the expression other to type SCType. However, these casts can fail at run time. This technique requires the programmer to be quite disciplined in adding casts to all overridden versions of binary methods. It also suffers from the twin disadvantages of adding run-time checks to each execution of a method, as well as requiring the programmer to handle the situation where the cast would fail. Clearly it would be a significant advantage both in programming and execution time to be able to check such calls statically.

A second example of the problems with binary methods arises from linked structures. Figure 3.2 contains a definition of the class, Node, which generates objects of type NodeType that form nodes for a singly linked list of integers. In the class there is one instance variable, value, for the value stored in the node, and another, next, to indicate the successor node. There are methods getValue and setValue to get and set the values stored in the node, and methods getNext and setNext to get and set the successor of the node.

Notice that method getNext returns a value of type NodeType, the type of object generated by class Node, while the setNext method takes a parameter of type NodeType. Thus the type NodeType is recursively defined. It is not uncommon to have such recursively-defined types in object-oriented languages.

Suppose we now wish to define a subclass of Node, DoubleNode, which implements doubly linked nodes, while reusing as much as possible the code for methods in Node. Figure 3.3 contains an attempt at defining such a

```
NodeType = ObjectType {
    getValue: Void → Integer;
    setValue: Integer → Void;
    getNext: Void → NodeType;
    setNext: NodeType → Void
}

class Node {
    value: Integer := 0;
    next: NodeType := nil;

    function getValue(): Integer is
    { return self.value }

    function setValue(newValue: Integer): Void is
    { self.value := newValue }

    function getNext(): NodeType is
    { return self.next }

    function setNext(newNext: NodeType): Void is
    { self.next := newNext }
}
```

Figure 3.2   Node class.

subclass, DoubleNode. DoubleNode adds to Node an additional instance variable, previous, as well as new methods to retrieve and set the previous node. If DoubleNodeType is the type of objects generated from the class, then we will want both the next and previous instance variables to have type DoubleNodeType. Similarly, the methods that get and set next or previous nodes should take parameters or return values of type DoubleNodeType rather than NodeType. This is particularly important because we do not want to allow the attachment of a singly linked node to a doubly linked node.[2]

---

2. The method setPrev is not really intended for public use because it only sets one of the two links. Normally it would be given a designation that would indicate this. Because we have not

```
DoubleNodeType = ObjectType {
    getValue: Void → Integer;
    setValue: Integer → Void;
    getNext: Void → NodeType;
    setNext: DoubleNodeType → Void;
    getPrev: Void → DoubleNodeType;
    setPrev: DoubleNodeType → Void
}

class DoubleNode inherits Node modifies setNext {
    previous: DoubleNodeType := nil;

    function getPrev(): DoubleNodeType is
    { return self.previous }

    function setPrev(newPrev: DoubleNodeType): Void is
    { self.previous := newPrev }

    function setNext(newNext: DoubleNodeType): Void is
                    // error - illegal change to parameter type
    { super ⇐ setNext(newNext);
      newNext ⇐ setPrev(self) }
}
```

Figure 3.3   Doubly linked node class — with errors.

Unfortunately, in the simple type system described here, we have no way of changing these types, either automatically or manually, in the subclass. The class DoubleNode defined in the figure illegally changes the parameter type of method setNext in a covariant way. It is also troublesome that method getNext returns type NodeType, while setNext takes a parameter of type DoubleNodeType.

Suppose we create LglDbleNode as a legal subclass of Node. We might write it as shown in Figure 3.4. Problems become apparent when overriding the setNext method. We cannot send a setPrev message to the bare parameter newNext, since its declared type is NodeType rather than LglD-

yet introduced such features, we will ignore that minor point here.

bleNodeType. As a result the programmer must insert a cast to tell the type
checker to treat it as though it has type LglDbleNodeType.

However, if a programmer sends setNext to an object generated from
LglDbleNode with a parameter that is generated from Node, it will not be
picked up statically as an error. Instead the cast will fail at run time.

Even if a variable dn has type LglDbleNodeType, the evaluation of

$$(\text{dn} \; \Leftarrow \; \text{getNext}()) \; \Leftarrow \; \text{getPrev}()$$

will generate a static type error, because the type checker can only predict
that the results of dn ⇐ getNext() will be of type NodeType, not the
more accurate LglDbleNodeType. Thus, even if the programmer has created a list, all of whose nodes are of type LglDbleNodeType, the programmer will still be required to write type casts to get the type checker to accept
the program.

To get the desired types for the instance variable next and the methods
getNext and setNext, we would instead have to define DoubleNode independently of Node, even though much of the code is identical. This is
clearly undesirable.

We do not bother to show the code for an independently defined class, IndDoubleNode, with the same behavior as DoubleNode. We leave it as an
exercise for the reader to write it and notice how similar the code is to that of
Node. However, we show the corresponding object type, IndDoubleNode-
Type, in Figure 3.5. Even such an independent definition has problems.
While we have not yet discussed the rules for determining when object types
are in the subtype relation, the code in Figure 3.5 can be used to show that the
resulting type, IndDoubleNodeType, cannot be a subtype of NodeType.

The function breakit in the figure is well-typed, as setNext takes a
parameter of type NodeType, and the expression new Node as the actual
parameter creates a value of type NodeType.

Suppose IndDoubleNodeType were a subtype of NodeType. If so, and
if dn was a value generated from IndDoubleNode, then breakit(dn)
would be well-typed, as values of type IndDoubleNodeType could masquerade as elements of type NodeType. However, that is not the case!

The execution of node ⇐ setNext(newNode) in the body of breakit
would result in the message send of setPrev to the parameter newNext.
But newNext holds a value that is generated from Node. This would result
in a run-time type error as elements generated from Node have no setPrev
method. This shows that object type IndDoubleNodeType could not be

```
LglDbleNodeType = ObjectType {
    getValue: Void → Integer;
    setValue: Integer → Void;
    getNext: Void → NodeType;
    setNext: NodeType → Void;
    getPrev: Void → LglDbleNodeType;
    setPrev: LglDbleNodeType → Void
}

class LglDbleNode inherits Node modifies setNext {
    previous: LglDbleNodeType := nil;

    function getPrev(): LglDbleNodeType is
    { return self.previous }

    function setPrev(newPrev: LglDbleNodeType): Void is
    { self.previous := newPrev }

    function setNext(newNext: NodeType): Void is
    { super ⇐ setNext(newNext);
      ((LglDbleNodeType)newNext) ⇐ setPrev(self) }
      // cast necessary to recognize setPrev
}
```

Figure 3.4   Legal doubly linked node class — with cast.

a subtype of NodeType, as elements of type IndDoubleNodeType cannot safely masquerade as elements of type NodeType.

This example is particularly troubling in that it seems to be tailor-made for the use of inheritance, but it (i) cannot be written correctly with an invariant type system, and (ii) would result in a type error if the type of objects generated from the desired subclass were a subtype of the type of objects generated from the original class. These problems are not special to the Node example, but arise with all binary methods because of the desire for a covariant change in the parameter type of binary methods.

We will later find a way to add expressiveness to languages in order to allow us to write DoubleNode as a subclass of Node. We will then need to

```
IndDoubleNodeType = ObjectType {
  getValue: Void → Integer;
  setValue: Integer → Void;
  getNext: Void → IndDoubleNodeType;
  setNext: IndDoubleNodeType → Void;
  getPrev: Void → IndDoubleNodeType;
  setPrev: IndDoubleNodeType → Void
}

function breakit(node: NodeType): Void is
{ node ⇐ setNext(new Node) }

var
  n: NodeType
  dn: IndDoubleNodeType
{
  n  := new Node;
  dn := new IndDoubleNode;
  breakit(n);        // No problem
  breakit(dn)        // Run-time error here!
}
```

Figure 3.5 Example showing why `IndDoubleNodeType` cannot be a subtype of `NodeType`.

ensure that the resulting object types are *not* subtypes in order to avoid the second problem.

invariant type systems do have the desirable property that subclasses generate subtypes, but it may be worth losing subtyping in some circumstances if it makes it significantly easier to define desirable subclasses. We will evaluate these trade-offs when we examine the more flexible type system of Eiffel in the next chapter.

3.2.3 Other typing problems

In both of the examples above, the difficulties arose from an attempt to keep return or parameter types the same as those of the object being defined. While this is an extremely important special case, there are other examples

```
class CircleClass {
   center: PointType := nil;
   ...
   function getCenter(): PointType is
   { return self.center }
   ...
}

class ColorCircleClass inherits Circle
                       modifies getCenter {
   color: ColorType := black;
   ...
   function getCenter(): ColorPtType is { ... }
                   // illegal type change in subclass!
   ...
}
```

Figure 3.6 Circle and color circle classes.

where it is desirable to change a type in a subclass in a covariant way. In these examples, the type to be changed may have no relation to the type of objects generated by the classes being defined. Many examples of this phenomenon arise when we have objects with other objects as components.

Figure 3.6 contains the definition of a class, CircleClass, with a get-Center method that returns a point. If we define a subclass that represents a color circle, it would be reasonable to wish to redefine getCenter to return a color point, as in the code in the figure. This would be illegal by the rules on method types in these invariant object-oriented languages. We would like to have a typing system that allows such changes, as long as they are type safe.

Again, however, even if we allowed a change in the return type of get-Center in the subclass, we still have the problem that we cannot change the type of the instance variable center. If center is still of type Point-Type, we will either need to add a type cast (which may fail) to the body of getCenter or we may have to change the body to build a new color point from the color and center instance variables. The latter involves a lot of work each time getCenter is called, and is probably not worth the effort compared to separately returning the values of `center` (as a point) and `color`.

Finally, there likely will be a method `setCenter` in `CircleClass` that takes a parameter of type `PointType`. Even C++ will not allow changing the types of parameters of methods in subclasses, so `setCenter` in `Color-CircleClass` must accept parameters of type `PointType`. Thus if we wish `center` to have type `ColorPtType` in the subclass, we will have to add a dynamic check before assigning the value or live with the possibility that the value could fail to be a color point.

3.3   Summary of typing problems

In this chapter we illustrated several problems with invariant type systems. In each case the difficulty arose from a desire to change the types of methods that are modified in subclasses. However no changes to the types of methods are allowed in invariant type systems.

In order to help alleviate the rigidity in these simple systems, C++ allows changes to the return types of methods in subclasses. This provided some help with overriding `deepClone` and `getCenter` methods, but as we saw above, we are still left with significant problems to be overcome. Moreover, it provides no help in taking care of problems arising in examples involving binary methods, in particular those involved with redefining the type of the instance variable `next` and the parameter type of the method `setNext` in the `DoubleNode` subclass. In Chapter 16 we present a detailed design for an extension to invariant type systems that, when combined with parametric polymorphism, provides one possible solution to all of these problems.

Given these examples, readers may be wondering why statically typed object-oriented languages are so restrictive in not allowing covariant changes to the types of instance variables or the parameters of methods in subclasses. We put off this discussion until after we have discussed the rules for subtyping in chapter 5. For now we content ourselves with the explanation that we are simply examining the restrictions in the most popular existing statically typed object-oriented languages. In the next chapter we examine some more expressive type systems for object-oriented languages that will help overcome these difficulties.

4 Adding Expressiveness to Object-Oriented Languages

In the last chapter, we looked at the limits of expressiveness of statically typed object-oriented languages with invariant typing disciplines. These are languages in which the types of instance variables and methods of a class are not allowed to vary in subclasses. Moreover, we saw that allowing covariant changes to the return types of methods (like C++ does) provided only a small amount of help, as the other restrictions in the language kept us from defining the instance variables and methods in the subclass as directly as we desired.

In this chapter we explore ways of increasing expressiveness provided by some existing object-oriented languages. The languages examined are GJ, an extension to Java supporting parametric polymorphism, and Eiffel, a statically typed object-oriented language that allows a great deal of flexibility in changing the types of methods and instance variables in subclasses.

4.1 GJ

In this section we discuss an extension, GJ [BOSW98], of the object-oriented language Java. Before going into the details of Java, we first present a brief introduction to the notion of polymorphism, and then a short introduction to Java syntax.

4.1.1 Parameterized types and polymorphism

PARAMETERIZED TYPE Many families of types are conveniently expressed using *parameterized types*. A parameterized type is a type expression that takes another type as a parameter. Examples of parameterized types include `array of T`, `stack of T`, tree of T, list of T, etc.[1] Most programming languages include ar-ray as a built-in parameterized type, but only relatively modern program-ming languages like Clu, Ada, ML, Haskell, C++, and Eiffel allow the pro-grammer to define parameterized types or classes.

Many algorithms, for example, sorting, are *generic*, meaning that they de-pend minimally on the type of elements being manipulated. The difference between the code for a quicksort of an array of reals and the quicksort of an array of integers is typically only in the type declarations of variables (and the type of the comparison operator). The actual algorithm is the same in the two cases. The types of these generic operations can be given by parameter-ized types. Thus a generic sort can be applied to a value of type array of T, a generic tail function can be applied to a value of type List of T, etc. Operations that can be applied to values of more than one kind are called polymorphic operations.

In section 2.3 we defined subtype polymorphism. A language supporting *subtype polymorphism* allows values to be given multiple types; in particular, if a value has type T, it also has any supertype of T.

Older languages like Pascal and C force the programmer to create new copies of code in order to handle different instances of generic operations, even though the code is nearly identical. Thus separate copies must be made of the code to perform a quicksort of an array of integers and of an array of reals. In languages with *polymorphic type systems*, one can define param-eterized types and polymorphic operations that operate uniformly on these parameterized types.

POLYMORPHIC TYPE SYSTEM

PARAMETRIC POLYMORPHISM

A language supporting *parametric polymorphism* allows an operation to be applied to arguments of a parameterized family of types. Thus in a language with a parameterized type of the form List of T, a single polymorphic tail function can be applied to any list with type List of T, no matter what type T is.

TEMPLATES

One source of frustration for Java programmers has been its lack of sup-port for parameterized types or classes. By contrast, C++'s *templates* allow programmers to define, for example, a stack template class that can be instan-tiated with the type of element to be held in the stack. While C++'s templates have not been without problems[2], programmers moving from C++ to Java

---

1. These may be thought of more accurately as functions from types to types.
2. Templates are generally not type checked until they are instantiated. Moreover, because C++'s templates are typically compiled into disjoint code segments for each instantiation rather than a single shared code segment, problems arise with code bloat. Support for parameterized types has generally been better in the other cited languages.

have found the lack of support for parameterized classes a major limitation of the language.

The Java extension, GJ (think *Generic Java*[3]), attempts to remedy this omission by adding parameterized classes (types) to Java.[4] The syntax of parameterized classes in GJ is similar to C++'s templates, though the type checking and implementation are quite different.

Later in this section we will describe the extensions to Java and how they increase the expressiveness of the language. However we first take a brief excursion to review Java syntax for those who may not be familiar with it.

4.1.2 Quick review of Java syntax

Java syntax is very similar to C++ syntax, which is itself derived from C syntax. The reader is referred to Gosling and Arnold [AGH99] or any other Java text for more details.

Java's interfaces are similar to the object types we discussed in earlier chapters. Interfaces `PointIfc` and `ColorPointIfc` are given in Figure 4.1. Interfaces include method headers, but not their bodies. Interfaces never include instance variables. All methods listed in interfaces are public by default. An interface may be declared to extend another by adding new methods. Thus `ColorPointIfc` inherits the `move` and `atOrigin` methods from `PointIfc`.

Because `ColorPointIfc` extends `PointIfc`, any value satisfying `ColorPointIfc` may be used in any context that expects a value satisfying `PointIfc`. Thus interface extensions can serve as subtypes in Java.[5]

Figure 4.2 contains two Java class definitions. Note that Java comments begin with `//` and continue until the end of the line. The class `Point` contains two private instance variables, `x` and `y` of type `int`. The next item CONSTRUCTOR listed is a *constructor* that is used to create (or generate) a new object from the class. Evaluating `new Point(7,3)` results in the creation of a `Point` object whose instance variables have values 7 and 3. Finally the class contains two public methods, `move` and `atOrigin`. The method `move` is a procedure

---

3. ..., but not too loud, as the name "Java" is trademarked by Sun Microsystems.
4. GJ or a similar extension of Java supporting parametric polymorphism is likely to be incorporated into Java in the near future. It may already be part of Java by the time you read this.
5. Technically, this is not quite right as subtyping is not fully supported in Java conditional *expressions*. However, for simplicity in the exposition we'll blithely ignore this detail and pretend Java supports subtypes.

```
public interface PointIfc {
    void move(int dx, int dy);
    boolean atOrigin();
}

public interface ColorPointIfc extends PointIfc {
    void setColor(ColorType newColor);
    ...
}
```

Figure 4.1   Point interfaces in Java.

that adds dx and dy to the corresponding instance variables. The method atOrigin returns true if and only if both instance variables are 0.

A class may be declared to implement an interface if it contains every method declared in the interface (and perhaps more). Class Point may legally implement PointIfc because Point includes methods move and atOrigin. Similarly ColorPoint may be declared to implement Color-PointIfc.

Subclasses in Java are defined as *extensions* of their superclasses. In Figure 4.2, ColorPoint is defined as a subclass of Point. An object generated from a subclass can be used in a context expecting a value of the superclass. Thus subclasses can also serve as subtypes.

An object generated from a class SomePoint can be used in a context expecting a value satisfying interface PointIfc only if SomePoint or one of its superclasses is declared to implement either PointIfc or an interface that extends PointIfc. Thus an object generated from either of the classes Point or ColorPoint defined in Figure 4.2 can be used in a context expecting a value satisfying interface PointIfc.

4.1.3   Expressiveness problems in Java

PARAMETERIZED CLASS   A *parameterized class* is a class that takes a type parameter. An example might be a class for a stack that takes a type parameter representing the type of object held in the stack. Parameterized classes have been included in languages like Clu, Ada, and Eiffel, and as templates in C++ (though C++'s implementation is not as robust as those in the other languages).

Java does not currently support parameterized classes. Here is an example

```
public class Point implements PointIfc {
    private int x;  // instance variables
    private int y;

    public Point(int newX, int newY)  // constructor
    {
        x = newX;
        y = newY;
    }

    public void move(int dx, int dy)  // methods
    {
        x = x + dx;
        y = y + dy;
    }

    public boolean atOrigin()
    {
        return (x==0) && (y==0);
    }
}

public class ColorPoint extends Point
                    implements ColorPointIfc {
    private ColorType color;
    ...
    public void setColor(ColorType newColor) {...}
}
```

Figure 4.2   Point class in Java.

where parameterized classes would be useful. Suppose a Java programmer wishes to write programs that use stacks holding different sorts of elements. The programmer could write one class for a stack of strings, another class for a stack of points, and so on, but when the code is examined, it becomes clear that aside from the types of instance variables and methods, the code is exactly the same for each of these classes. It seems unreasonable (and error-prone) for programmers to have to repeatedly write nearly identical code for each type of stack.

One way of working around this omission in Java is to use the class `Object`, which is a superclass of all object types in the language. Programmers can create data structures holding elements of type `Object` (or some other class guaranteed to be a superclass of all classes of elements likely to be used), and take advantage of subtyping to allow the use of objects generated by these other classes in the data structure.[6]

For example, suppose a programmer wants to use the built-in library class `java.util.stack`. Its declaration is similar to:

```
public class Stack extends Vector {
    public void push(Object item){...}
    public Object pop(){...}
    public Object peek(){...}
    public boolean empty(){...}
    public int search(Object o){...}
}
```

Thus the programmer can push and pop elements of type `Object` with the stack. Suppose she wishes to manipulate elements of class `Point` with the stack `myStack`. Creating the stack and inserting items is no problem:

```
Stack myStack = new Stack();
Point aPoint = new Point(2,3);
myStack.push(aPoint);
```

The use of a `Point` as the parameter to `push` is well-typed because `Point` is a subclass (and hence a subtype) of `Object`.

However, suppose we wish to remove the top element from the stack and then send it a `move` message. The static type system believes the result of

---

6. Java allows the use of classes as types, so we shall follow Java in this section and not make a distinction between the two. This causes no difficulties here because subclasses always give rise to subtypes.

evaluating `myStack.pop()` is an element of type `Object` because of the typing of `pop`, even though we know we pushed a `Point` on the stack. Because `Object` does not contain the method `move`, we must first *cast* the element to type `Point` before sending the `move` message:

CAST

```
Point stackPoint = ((Point)(myStack.pop())).move(1,2);
```

Type casts work as follows. Let `exp` be an expression and `SomeType` a class or interface name. A type cast expression, written as `(SomeType)exp`, tells Java to treat the cast expression as if it had class (interface) `SomeType`. Java will check this at run time and raise an exception if the class (interface) of the value of `exp` is not an extension of `SomeType`.

Thus the displayed expression above will raise an exception if the result of `myStack.pop()` is not of class `Point` or one of its subclasses. To avoid the danger of raising an exception, the Java programmer can use the built-in `instanceof` function to determine if the cast will succeed.

It is worse in Java if we wish to put elements of type `int` on the stack, as base types (including `int`) are not object types and hence are not considered subtypes of `Object`. However, Java does provide object types corresponding to each of the base types in the language. For example, the built-in class `Integer` corresponds to `int`. Elements of type `int` can be *wrapped* up as `Integer`'s and used in contexts expecting objects. Thus, to push an integer n on the stack, we must push on the corresponding `Integer` via `myStack.push(new Integer(n))`. Popping off such an element is also painful as you must pop it off, cast it to `Integer`, and then send it the `int-Value()` message before being able to do anything with the value:

```
... ((Integer)(myStack.pop())).intValue() ...
```

There are two major problems with the stack implementation using `Object`:

1. We can't enforce a rule that the stack only hold items of a fixed type.
2. Whenever we remove something from the stack, we must cast it to the type we expect it to be so that we can send messages to it.

Both problems may be overcome by writing specialized stack implementations for each desired type, but reusing library code would clearly be more desirable if we could avoid these problems.

The result of these two problems is ugly code with many casts; leaving the code open to errors if somehow an element of some other type is pushed onto the stack.

4.1.4   GJ's parameterized types

In the GJ extension of Java we can rewrite Stack as:

```
public class Stack<Elt> extends Vector<Elt>{
    public void push(Elt item){...}
    public Elt pop(){...}
    public Elt peek(){...}
    public boolean empty(){...}
    public int search(Elt o){...}
}
```

Here Stack is defined as a parameterized class where Elt is a type variable that can be instantiated to the type of element to be held in the stack. Thus Stack<Point> represents the type of a stack that holds elements of type Point.

We can create and add an element to a stack as follows:

```
Stack<Point> myStack = new Stack<Point>();
Point aPoint = new Point(2,3);
myStack.push(aPoint);
```

Pushing anything other than a Point (or an element of a subclass of Point) onto the stack results in a static type error.

The code for popping a point off the stack and moving it is now much clearer, as we no longer need casts.

```
Point stackPoint = myStack.pop().move(1,2);
```

GJ can also handle more sophisticated examples of parameterized classes in which we wish to restrict the type parameters that can be used.

Suppose we wish to implement a class representing ordered lists. In order to insert an element, we must compare it with other elements in the list. As a result, we should only insert elements of classes that provide the appropriate methods comparing elements:

```
public interface Orderable {
    boolean equal(Orderable other);
    boolean greaterThan(Orderable other);
    boolean lessThan(Orderable other);
}
```

We can then write a class OrderedList as follows:

```
public class OrderedList<Elt implements Orderable>
                                 extends ... {
    public void insert(Elt item){...}
    public Elt removeFirst(){...}
    public boolean empty(){...}
    public int searchFor(Elt o){...}
}
```

In the declaration of OrderedList, the type variable Elt is constrained to implement Orderable. As a result, we are guaranteed that we can send messages equal, greaterThan, and lessThan to expressions of type Elt. Type parameters can be constrained to implement an interface or to extend a class or interface. This variant on polymorphism involving restriction on BOUNDED type variables is called *bounded polymorphism*.
POLYMORPHISM

We can instantiate OrderedList with any class that implements Orderable. This sounds fine, but we soon discover that it is hard to write a class implementing Orderable. The difficulty is that the comparison operators have to take arguments of any other class implementing Orderable.[7] Here is an example of the problem.

```
public class IntOrd implements Orderable {
    protected int value = 0;
    ...
    public boolean greaterThan(Orderable other){
        if (other != null && other instanceof IntOrd){
            return (value > ((IntOrd)other).value)
        } else { ... raise an exception??...}
    }
    ...
}
```

The code for greaterThan is now much more complex than expected or desired. We must cast other to type IntOrd (using instanceof to ensure that the cast is legal) before being able to do anything with it. And what should be done if the instanceof test fails? Returning the value *false* is likely not the appropriate answer; more likely an exception will need to be thrown.

---

7. A similar difficulty arises in Java when attempting to write an implementation of the equals method, which, because it is inherited from Object, must handle any element of type Object as a parameter.

Moreover, one could virtually never use a pre-existing class to instantiate `OrderedList`, because the comparison methods of existing classes are highly unlikely to take parameters of type `Orderable`. Instead they most likely would take parameters of the same type as the class being defined.

For example, the class `IntOrd` defined above would normally be defined instead as `IntOrdBC`, below:

```
public class IntOrdBC {
    protected int value = 0;
    ...
    public boolean greaterThan(IntOrdBC other){
        return (value > other.value);
    }
}
...
}
```

The simple bounded polymorphism illustrated above was first proposed as a programming language construct in the mid-80's by Cardelli and Wegner [CW85]. However, within a few years examples like the above showed that simple bounded quantification was not expressive enough to capture the restrictions on type parameters needed for many important examples that contain *binary methods* (as described in Section 3.2.2).

F-BOUNDED
POLYMORPHISM

A generalized form of parametric polymorphism, *F-bounded polymorphism* [CCH+89], was introduced to handle these more complex cases. This construct has been included in GJ. We illustrate it by example. Rather than defining the interface `Orderable`, we now define a parameterized interface, `OrderableF`:

```
interface OrderableF<T> {
    boolean equal(T other);
    boolean greaterThan(T other);
    boolean lessThan(T other);
}
```

`OrderableF` is a parameterized interface, which may be instantiated with any type (class or interface) `T`. It provides methods for making comparisons with elements of type `T`.

The class `IntOrdBC` above can implement `OrderableF<IntOrdBC>` if we rewrite the header as

```
public class IntOrdBC
        implements OrderableF<IntOrdBC> {
    ...}
```

It implements `OrderableF<IntOrdBC>` because it provides the methods `equal`, `greaterThan`, and `lessThan`, which all take parameters of type `IntOrdBC` and have return type `boolean`.

In general, if class `Elt` implements `OrderableF<Elt>` then it will support comparison operations that take parameters of type `Elt`. This is a sort of recursive constraint in that the constraint on the class `Elt` involves `Elt`. However, there is no technical difficulty in determining if an existing class satisfies such a constraint. One need only check that it has methods of the appropriate types.

Class `OrderedList` can now be rewritten as:

```
public class BPOrderedList<Elt implements
                               OrderableF<Elt>>
                           extends ... {
    public void insert(Elt item){...}
    public Elt removeFirst(){...}
    public boolean empty(){...}
    public int search(Elt o){...}
}
```

The constraint on `Elt` is now somewhat harder to read, but it does state exactly the restrictions necessary to instantiate `BPOrderedList` with a type `Elt`: `Elt` must have methods `equal`, `greaterThan`, and `lessThan`, each of which takes a parameter of type `Elt` and has return type `boolean`.

Because `IntOrdBC` satisfies these constraints, we can instantiate parameterized class `BPOrderedList` with `IntOrdBC`:

```
BPOrderedList<IntOrdBC> ordListSC
                    = new BPOrderedList<IntOrdBC>();
IntOrdBC a = new IntOrdBC();
ordListSC.insert(a);
    ...
```

GJ's addition of F-bounded polymorphism to Java has greatly increased the expressiveness of Java's type system. Whereas earlier one had to use `Object` or another fixed type to represent a whole collection of possible types that could be used in a data structure, we can now instantiate the class to a specific type as long as it satisfies the given constraints.

Unfortunately, F-bounded quantification does not interact well with the subclass or subtype hierarchies in object-oriented languages. The problem is that if a class satisfies an F-bounded constraint, its subclasses will generally not satisfy the constraint. For example, define:

```
public class ExtIntOrdBC extends IntOrdBC {
    ...
    public boolean greaterThan(IntOrdBC other){
        return (value > other.value) && ...
    }
}
    ...
}
```

where as usual we are not allowed to change the type of the method parameter from the superclass.

No matter how few additions or changes are made in the subclass (and even if no methods from the subclass are overridden), `ExtIntOrdBC` will implement `OrderableF<IntOrdBC>`, not `OrderableF<ExtIntOrdBC>`. (We will see later that `OrderableF<ExtIntOrdBC>` also cannot be a subtype of `OrderableF<IntOrdBC>` because of the covariant change to the parameter of `greaterThan`.) As a result the subclass cannot be used with `BPOrderedList`.

The difficulty is that in Java we are not allowed to change the types of method parameters in subclasses. As a result, subclasses do not fit in consistently with the use of F-bounded polymorphism. We will see later that the use of a "`MyType`"-construct and the notion of match-bounded polymorphism gives similar expressiveness as F-bounded polymorphism, but *is* consistent with the subclass relation.

In summary, GJ's addition of F-bounded polymorphism to Java helps to increase the expressiveness of Java and aids the programmer to express type constraints in a readable and type-safe way. While regular bounded polymorphism interacts well with the class hierarchy, F-bounded polymorphism does not.

4.2   Even more flexible typing with Eiffel

The programming language Eiffel [Mey92] was designed in the mid-80's by Bertrand Meyer. It is a statically typed, class-based, object-oriented language that supports multiple inheritance, bounded polymorphism, and run-time testable assertions. Like Java, all objects are implicit references and garbage collection is built in.

The definition of a sample Eiffel class, RATIONAL, is given in Figures 4.3 and 4.4. It represents rational numbers with methods to set, add, and compare rationals. Comments in Eiffel begin with "--" and continue to the end of the line.

This example illustrates several important features of Eiffel. First, it is possible for a class to inherit from multiple classes. Methods in inherited classes can be renamed either for convenience or to resolve name clashes between classes inherited from. Methods that are overridden must be declared to be "redefined". This is required to avoid the problem of having a programmer accidentally override a method in a superclass. It is also possible to change the visibility of inherited methods with a declaration in the inherit clause, though we don't show it here.

Methods listed in the creation section of the class header can be used as constructors. CreateRat is the only creation routine in RATIONAL. If r has type RATIONAL, then !!r.CreateRat will create a new object of type RATIONAL. Instance variables not explicitly initialized are given a default value (e.g., 0 or void, which corresponds to null in Java).

Classes may be parameterized by class (type) variables. The inherited parameterized class ORDEREDPAIR has been specialized to type INTEGER.

Features include both instance variables and methods. A feature clause can be annotated to indicate the visibility of items listed. The default is ALL, the keyword NONE corresponds to Java's private, while you can also list any collection of classes (e.g. "friends") that you wish to be able to have access to particular features. Instance variables can only be made available as read-only outside of the methods of the class. From outside an object it is impossible to distinguish between instance variables and parameterless procedures.

An important part of the Eiffel philosophy is "design by contract". This encourages the program to include assertions indicating what should be true at different points in the program.

In method set, a precondition is given using keyword require and a postcondition is provided using ensure. The class invariant at the bottom of the class is presented with keyword invariant. It is also possible to specify loop invariants and "variants". A variant is an integer expression that is always positive, but that gets closer to zero after each iteration. It is used to help prove termination of the loop. The assertions can be labeled in order to give better error messages when an assertion fails. Determination

```
class RATIONAL
inherit
    ORDEREDPAIR [INTEGER]
        rename  x as n,  y as d -- change feature names
        redefine same    -- method same is redefined
        end
    OTHERCLASS
        redefine ... end
creation
    CreateRat
feature{ALL} -- public features
error: boolean;

CreateRat is -- create a rational
    do
        d := 1
    end; -- Create

set(numer, denom : INTEGER) is  -- set n and d
    require -- precondition
        denom /= 0
    local
        gcd : INTEGER
    do
        n := numer;
        d := denom;
        if d < 0 then
            n := -n;
            d := -d
        end;
        gcd := reduce;   -- see method below
        n := n // gcd;    -- ''//'' is integer division
        d := d // gcd
    ensure  -- postcondition
        d > 0
    end; -- set
```

Figure 4.3   RATIONAL class in Eiffel, part 1.

```
      plus(other : like Current) : like Current is
        local
          sumnum, sumden : INTEGER;
      do
          sumnum := n*other.d + other.n*d;
          sumden := d*other.d;
          !!Result.Create;
          Result.set(sumnum,sumden)
-- returns value of Result automatically
        end; -- plus


      same(other : like Current) : BOOLEAN is
        do  -- override inherited method
        ...
      end;


      ...


feature {NONE} -- private method
    reduce : INTEGER is ...
        end;


invariant d /= 0


end -- RATIONAL
```

Figure 4.4   RATIONAL class in Eiffel, part 2.

of which kinds of assertions are checked at run time is made by setting a
compile-time flag. The default is that preconditions are always checked, but
others are not.

Current is used in Eiffel methods as the name of the object executing the
method. Thus it plays the same role as Java and C++'s this or Smalltalk's
self. If id is a declared identifier, then like id can be used to stand for the
static type of id. Thus the method plus in RATIONAL uses like Current
as the type of the argument and result of the method. If plus is sent to an
object of (static) type RATIONAL, then its actual parameter must also be of

type RATIONAL, and the result will be of type RATIONAL.

If plus is inherited in a subclass, SUBRATIONAL of RATIONAL, then the meaning of like Current will change appropriately. That is, if plus is sent to an object of (static) type SUBRATIONAL, then its actual parameter must also be of type SUBRATIONAL, and the result will be of type SUBRA-TIONAL.

This is very useful and provides great flexibility in creating subclasses. For example, in Figures 4.5 and 4.6 definitions are given of two parameter-ized classes, LINKABLE[G] and a subclass BILINKABLE[G], that are used to create singly and doubly linked nodes. The type parameter G represents the type (class) of the element held in the item field. The classes are slightly simplified versions of classes from the Eiffel structure library.

The type of instance variable right and the parameter of putRight of class LINKABLE[G] are declared to be of type like Current, which means they must be of the same type as Current. Using like Current in method signatures is very useful because the meaning of like Current will be dif-ferent in a subclass from its meaning in the superclass.

Because of the use of like Current in the superclass, elements gener-ated from class BILINKABLE will have both right and left fields hold-ing values of type BILINKABLE. Similarly, the methods putLeft and pu-tRight of an object generated from BILINKABLE will take parameters of type BILINKABLE.

This provides a great deal more flexibility than found in languages with the invariant type discipline. We have seen in Section 3.2.2 how frustrating it is not to be able to write a doubly linked node as a subclass of a singly linked node in languages like Java and C++, so this seems to be a great aid to expressiveness.

But now suppose we write the following routine:

```
trouble(p, q : LINKABLE [RATIONAL] ) is
   do
      p.putRight(q);
      ....
   end
```

Suppose we have declared variables sNode: LINKABLE [RATIONAL] and biNode: BILINKABLE [RATIONAL], and we write:

```
trouble(biNode,sNode)
```

As BILINKABLE[RATIONAL] is a subtype of LINKABLE[RATIONAL] in

```
class LINKABLE [G]

feature{ALL}

    item: G;                    -- value held
    right: like Current;   -- Right neighbor

    putRight (other: like Current) is
            -- Put 'other' to the right of current cell.
        do
            right := other
        ensure
            chained: right = other
        end;

end -- class LINKABLE

class BILINKABLE [G] inherit

        LINKABLE [G]
            redefine
                putRight
            end

feature{ALL} -- Access

    left: like Current;    -- Left neighbor

    putRight (other: like Current) is
            -- Put 'other' to the right of current cell.
        do
            right := other;
            if (other /= Void) then
                other.simplePutLeft (Current)
            end
        end;
```

Figure 4.5   Eiffel classes LINKABLE and BILINKABLE, part 1.

```
    putLeft (other: like Current) is
        -- Put 'other' to the left of current cell.
      do
        left := other;
        if (other /= Void) then
           other.simplePutRight (Current)
        end
      ensure
        chained: left = other
      end;

feature {BILINKABLE}

    simplePutRight (other: like Current) is
        -- set 'right' to 'other'
      do
        right := other
      end;

    simplePutLeft (other: like Current) is
        -- set 'left' to 'other'
      do
        left := other
      end;

invariant

    rightSymmetry:
      (right /= Void) implies (right.left = Current);
    leftSymmetry:
      (left /= Void) implies (left.right = Current)

end -- class BILINKABLE
```

Figure 4.6   Eiffel classes LINKABLE and BILINKABLE, part 2.

Eiffel, this should work. Instead, the program crashes when the code for putRight in BILINKABLE attempts to send the message simplePutLeft to sNode, because sNode has no such method. (*The reader should trace the execution of this code to see exactly how things go wrong.*)

This example shows that implementations of Eiffel are not statically type-safe. In fact, Eiffel allows a number of statically unsafe changes in creating subclasses. One is allowed to replace the type of an instance variable, method parameter, or method result type by a subtype of the one occurring in the superclass. We will see in Chapter 6 that only method result types can be allowed to change in a covariant way if one wishes to guarantee type safety. Eiffel also allows programmers to hide inherited methods in a subclass that were visible in the superclass, creating yet another type insecurity.

This type insecurity has been known since the late 1980's. Bertrand Meyer, the designer of Eiffel, has made various responses to these problems over time. He has consistently claimed that the insecurity is inconsequential because Eiffel users do not write code that would result in this error. That is, while they use features like these, they automatically use them correctly. He also claimed that proposed fixes like eliminating like declarations and instead using bounded polymorphism forced programmers to "plan ahead" too much and would result in programmers having to go back and rewrite superclasses.

After several years of criticism of Eiffel's type problems, Meyer proposed a "system validity check" to ensure that these errors did not occur at run time. Essentially the idea was to perform a conservative "dataflow" analysis at link-time to make sure no unfortunate combinations of types would arise at run time due to interactions of the various classes. None of the Eiffel compiler suppliers ever implemented this check. It is not known why they failed to implement it, but it is likely that either the test was too expensive to run or it ruled out too many useful programs.

Even if this test had worked, programs would have been quite fragile with respect to the test. A program could pass the system validity check, but then the addition of a new class could cause the system validity check to fail due to an unexpected interaction that was only barely related to the new class.

More recently, Meyer proposed an alternative "fix" to Eiffel's static type safety problems called "No polymorphic catcalls". A call is polymorphic if its target can represent objects of more than one type. According to Meyer:

> "A routine is a CAT (Changing Availability or Type) if some redefinition changes its export status or the type of one of its arguments. A call

is a catcall if some redefinition of the routine would make it invalid because of a change of export status or argument type."

His proposal is to ban "catcalls" to expressions that can represent objects of more than one type. Essentially this requires that if the type of a method parameter is changed in a subclass, then you must know the exact type of any object that is a target of the corresponding message.

While a few type-safety problems were found in the original proposal, they have since been fixed. However, it is still not known if implementing this proposal would result in a statically type-safe language. Unfortunately, the proposal seems so restrictive that programmers will not be able to write useful programs that both use the dangerous features and pass this test. At the time this was written, no Eiffel compiler implemented the proposal.

In spite of its static typing problems, Eiffel was quite an advance over existing object-oriented languages. Its "design-by-contract" philosophy, which encourages the use of preconditions and postconditions, may be its most lasting legacy. Like Smalltalk, which is dynamically typed, it also showed how useful certain constructs could be that were not available in other languages.

Eiffel was also one of the first commercially available compilers for object-oriented languages that supported bounded polymorphism. Figure 4.7 includes Eiffel code defining classes similar to those given for GJ in the previous section.

INTORD inherits from the deferred class COMPARING. Deferred classes are like abstract classes in C++ and Java. They need not include code for all of the methods they declare. Classes in which all features are deferred are similar to interfaces in Java. Notice how the use of like Current solves the problems we had before that led us to the use of F-bounded polymorphism in GJ.

We can also use COMPARING as an upper bound for polymorphic classes:

```
class Sorting[T -> COMPARING]
feature
    sort(thearray:ARRAY[T]):ARRAY[T] is
        local  ....
        do
            ......
            ....
            if thearray.item(i).lessThan(thearray.item(j))
            ....
        end;
end -- Sorting
```

```
deferred class COMPARING -- like abstract in Java
feature specification
    lessThan (other: like Current): BOOLEAN is
        deferred;

    greaterThan (other: like Current): BOOLEAN is
        deferred;
end -- class COMPARING

class INTORD inherit COMPARING
feature
    value:INTEGER;
    lessThan (other:like Current) is
        do
            Result := value < other.value
        end;
    ...
end -- class INTORD
```

Figure 4.7 Eiffel version of COMPARING.

The notation "T -> COMPARING" indicates that the type variable T must be a subclass of COMPARING, which means that it must provide the comparison methods that take parameters of type like Current. The fact that COMPARING uses like Current allows the programmer to use regular bounded polymorphism rather than F-bounded polymorphism.

In summary, while Eiffel's static type system does not catch all type errors, and thus is not statically type safe, it does suggest constructs that would be quite useful in other statically typed object-oriented languages. In particular, the use of like Current seems to add a great deal of expressiveness to the language. In Chapter 16 we investigate the possibility of adding a similar MyType construct in a type-safe way.

4.3 Summary

In this chapter we investigated two languages, GJ and Eiffel, each of which offered extensions that increased the expressiveness of the language. Both languages support parametric polymorphism, a feature that appears to be extremely important in designing secure generic data structures. GJ goes further in providing F-bounded polymorphism to support "binary methods" like comparison operators. GJ is statically typed and type-safe.

Eiffel uses the "`like`" construct to describe types. Among other things, this allows the programmer to declare that a type is `like Current`, that is, it is of the same type as the receiver of the message. This construct makes it much easier to define subclasses of classes with binary methods so that these methods have the desired types. Because of the availability of `like Current`, Eiffel also allows the programmer to use ordinary bounded polymorphism to provide the same constraints that require F-bounded polymorphism in GJ.

Unfortunately, this added flexibility in Eiffel results in a statically typed language that is not type-safe (at least in current implementations). However, the constructs introduced in Eiffel seem to be very useful in the cases that require F-bounded polymorphism in GJ. In Chapter 16, we will discuss the addition of type-safe variants of Eiffel's `like` construct.

5 *Understanding Subtypes*

Thus far we have assumed that only object types have subtypes, and that subtypes are formed only by adding new methods to object types. In this chapter we provide some insight into ways that subtyping can be extended to more types, and how the subtyping relation on object types can be made richer.

SUBTYPE

Recall from Chapter 2 that type S is a *subtype* of a type T, written S <: T, if an expression of type S can be used in any context that expects an element of type T. Another way of putting this is that any expression of type S can masquerade as an expression of type T.

This definition can be made more concrete by introducing a rule stating that if S <: T and expression e has type S, then e also has type T. This rule,

SUBSUMPTION RULE

usually termed the *subsumption rule*, provides a mechanism for informing the type checker that an expression of a subtype can masquerade as an element of a supertype.

Subtyping provides added flexibility in constructing legal expressions of a language. Let x be a variable holding values of type T. If e is an expression of type T, then of course x := e is a legal assignment statement.

Now suppose that S is a subtype of T and e′ has type S. Then e′ can masquerade as an element of type T, and hence x := e′ will also be a legal assignment statement. Similarly an actual parameter of type S may be used in a function or procedure call when the corresponding formal parameter's type is declared to be T.

In most pure object-oriented languages, objects are represented as implicit references. Assignment and parameter passing are interpreted as binding new names to existing objects, i.e., as ways of creating sharing. Because elements of a supertype and subtype both take the same amount of space (the space to hold a reference) there is no implementation difficulty in using elements of the subtype in contexts expecting elements of the supertype. The difficulty instead is determining when using an element of another type is logically correct, *i.e.*, all operations expected for the supertype make sense for the subtype.

How can we determine when one type is a subtype of another? A careful theoretical analysis of this topic would take us far afield from the aims of this text into complex issues of domain theory in denotational semantics. Instead we will present intuitive arguments for determining when one type is a subtype of another. The subtyping rules in this section are based on those given by Cardelli [Car88].

5.1   Subtyping for non-object types

Because object types have similarities to records of functions, we begin with examining the simpler cases of subtyping for record and function types, holding off on object types until later in this chapter. We also include a discussion of references (*i.e.*, the types of variables in programming languages) here, in order to prepare for the later discussion of instance variables in objects. This will also be useful in discussing subtyping for arrays and mutable records.

5.1.1   Record types

In order to keep the initial discussion as simple as possible, we deal in this subsection only with immutable (or "read-only") records of the sort found in functional programming languages like ML. While one can create records in a single operation, the only operations that may be applied to existing immutable record values are to extract the values of particular fields. No operations are available to update particular fields of these records. Because the operations do not depend on the order of the fields, we consider record types that differ only in the order of their fields as identical.

An object can be interpreted as a record whose fields include their methods. Because methods may not be updated in objects, the study of immutable records will be important to our understanding of object types. We discuss in Section 5.1.3 the impact of allowing updatable fields.

Records associate values to labels so that the values may be extracted using the name of the label. The type of a record specifies the type of the value corresponding to each label. For example, we can define the record type

SandwichType = {| bread: BreadType; filling: FoodType|}.

An example of an element of type SandwichType is

s: Sandwich := {| bread: BreadType := rye;
                  filling: FoodType := pastrami |}

Because these records are immutable, the only operations available on s are the extraction of values held in the bread and filling fields via expressions s.bread and s.filling.

Suppose that we are given that CheeseType <: FoodType. Let

CheeseSandwichType = {| bread: BreadType;
                        filling: CheeseType;
                        sauce: SauceType |}

and

cs: CheeseSandwich := {| bread: BreadType := white;
                         filling: CheeseType := cheddar;
                         sauce: SauceType := mustard |}

We claim that CheeseSandwichType <: SandwichType.

For elements of CheeseSandwichType to successfully masquerade as elements of SandwichType, expressions of type CheeseSandwichType need to support all of the operations applicable to expressions of type Sand-wichType. Since the only operation available on these records is extracting fields, it is straightforward to show this.

A record cs of type CheeseSandwichType has the bread and filling fields expected of a value of type SandwichType. Moreover, the results of extracting the bread field from values of each of the two sandwich types each have type BreadType. The result of extracting the filling field from a record of type CheeseSandwichType is of type CheeseType, which is not the same as FoodType. However, because CheeseType <: FoodType, it can masquerade as a value of type FoodType.

Thus no matter which label from FoodType is extracted from a value of CheeseSandwichType, the result can masquerade as the corresponding type of SandwichType. Hence CheeseSandwichType is a subtype of SandwichType. The extra fields in CheeseSandwichType are irrelevant as we only need to know that enough fields of the appropriate types are available in order to masquerade as a Sandwich type.

Figure 5.1 illustrates a slightly more abstract version of this argument. In that figure a record r′: {| m: S′; n: T′; p: U′ q: V′ |} is masquerading

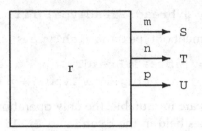 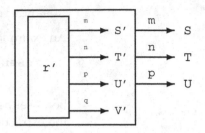

Figure 5.1   A record r: $\{\!\mid m\!:\!S;\,n\!:\!T;\,p\!:\!U \mid\!\}$, and another record r': $\{\!\mid m\!:\!S';\,n\!:\!T';\,p\!:\!U';$ $q\!:\!V' \mid\!\}$ masquerading as an element of type $\{\!\mid m\!:\!S;\,n\!:\!T;\,p\!:\!U \mid\!\}$.

as a record of type $\{\!\mid m\!:\!S;\ n\!:\!T;\ p\!:\!U \mid\!\}$. We illustrate this by placing the figure representing r' inside a box (think costume) which has the same interface as an element of type $\{\!\mid m\!:\!S;\ n\!:\!T;\ p\!:\!U \mid\!\}$.

For the masquerade to be successful, the value of the m field of r', for example, must be able to masquerade as a value of type S. Similarly for the n and p fields. Again, notice that the subtype may have more labeled fields (*e.g.*, the q field) than the supertype, since the extra fields don't get in the way of any of the operations applicable to the supertype.

Thus one record type is a subtype of another if the first has all of the fields of the second (and perhaps more), and the types of the corresponding fields are subtypes. Notice that the ordering of the fields is irrelevant in determining subtyping. We identify record types that are the same up to the ordering of fields.

We write this more formally as follows. Let $\{\!\mid l_i\!:\!T_i \mid\!\}_{1 \leq i \leq n}$ represent the type of a record with labels l_i of type T_i for $1 \leq i \leq n$. Then,

$$\{\!\mid l_j\!:\!T_j \mid\!\}_{1 \leq j \leq n} <: \{\!\mid l_i\!:\!U_i \mid\!\}_{1 \leq i \leq k},\ \textit{if } k \leq n \textit{ and for all } 1 \leq i \leq k, T_i <: U_i.$$

By this definition, `CheeseSandwichType` $<:$ `SandwichType`.

It is sometimes convenient to break up the subtyping for records into two pieces: breadth and depth subtyping rules. One record type is a *breadth subtype* of another if the first has all of the fields of the second (and perhaps more). A record type is a *depth subtype* of another if they have exactly the same fields, but the types of the corresponding fields are subtypes.

Again, the general subtyping rule above is appropriate for record values in which the only operations available are extracting labeled fields. Later we

BREADTH SUBTYPE

DEPTH SUBTYPE

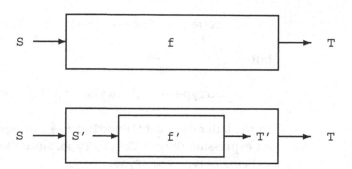

Figure 5.2 A function f: S → T, and another function f′: S′ → T′ masquerading as having type S → T.

discuss how the subtyping rule would change if operations were available to update the fields.

5.1.2 Function types

The proper definition of subtyping for function types has provoked great controversy and confusion, so it is worth a careful look. As discussed earlier, we write S → T for the type of functions that take a parameter of type S and return a result of type T. If (S′ → T′) <: (S → T), then we should be able to use an element of the first functional type in any context in which an element of the second type would type check.

Suppose we have a function f with type S → T. In order to use a function, f′, with type S′ → T′, in place of f, the function f′ must be able to accept an argument of type S and return a value of type T. See Figure 5.2.

To masquerade successfully as a function of type S → T, function f′ must be able to be applied to an argument, s, of type S. Because the domain of f′ is S′, it can be applied to elements of type S as long as S <: S′. In that case, using subsumption, s can be treated as an element of type S′, making f′(s) type-correct.

On the other hand, if the output of f′ has type T′, then T′ <: T will guarantee that the output of f′ can be treated as an element of type T. Summarizing,

$$(S′ → T′) <: (S → T), \quad \text{if } S <: S′ \text{ and } T′ <: T$$

If we assume, as before, that CheeseType <: FoodType, it follows that

$$(\texttt{Integer} \rightarrow \texttt{CheeseType}) \; <: \; (\texttt{Integer} \rightarrow \texttt{FoodType})$$

but

$$(\texttt{FoodType} \rightarrow \texttt{Integer}) \; <: \; (\texttt{CheeseType} \rightarrow \texttt{Integer})$$

In the latter case, if `f'`: `FoodType` $\rightarrow$ `Integer`, then `f'` can be applied to an expression of type `CheeseType`, since that expression can masquerade as being of type `FoodType`.

The reverse is not true, since if `f`: `CheeseType` $\rightarrow$ `Integer`, it may not be possible to apply `f` to an argument of type `FoodType`. The body of `f` may apply an operation that is only defined for expressions of type `CheeseType`. For example, suppose `melt` is a function that can be applied to elements of type `CheeseType`, but not `FoodType`. Then if `melt` is applied to the parameter in the body of `f`, an execution error would arise if the actual parameter was of type `FoodType` and not `CheeseType`.

Procedure types may be subtyped as though they were degenerate function types that always return a default type `Void`.

The subtype ordering of parameter types in function subtyping is the reverse of what might initially have been expected, while the output types of functions are ordered in the expected way. We say that subtyping for parameter types is *contravariant* (*i.e.*, goes the opposite direction of the relation being proved), while the subtyping for result types of functions is *covariant* (*i.e.*, goes in the same direction).

The contravariance for parameter types can be initially confusing, because it is always permissible to replace an actual parameter by another whose type is a subtype of the original. However the key is that in the subtyping rule for function types, it is the function, *not* the actual parameter, which is being replaced.

Let us look at one last example to illustrate why contravariance is appropriate for type changes in the parameter position of functions and procedures. The contravariant rule for procedures tells us that it is possible to replace a procedure, `p`, of type `CheeseType` $\rightarrow$ `Void` by a procedure, `p'`, of type `FoodType` $\rightarrow$ `Void`.

The procedure `p` can be applied to any value, `cheese`, of type `Cheese-Type`. Because `CheeseType` $<:$ `FoodType`, the value `cheese` can masquerade as an element of type `FoodType`. As a result, `p'` can also be applied to the value `cheese`. Thus `p'`, and indeed any procedure of type `FoodType` $\rightarrow$ `Void`, can masquerade as an element of type `CheeseType` $\rightarrow$ `Void`.

5.1.3   Types of variables

Variables holding values of type T have very different properties than simple values of type T. Variables holding values of type T may be the targets (left sides) of assignments, while values of type T may only be the sources (right sides) of such assignments. Obviously, an expression representing a value, *e.g.*, 3, of type integer may not be a target of an assignment statement.

Thus we need to distinguish values of type T from variables holding values of type T. Because variables are sometimes referred to as references, we will denote the type of variables holding values of type T as Ref T. Thus a variable x holding integer values will have type Ref Integer, while the number 17 has type Integer.

Variables in programming languages typically represent two kinds of values. This can be seen by examining the meaning of the statement

        x := x + 1

L-VALUE
R-VALUE

The x on the left side of the assignment represents a location in memory that can hold values, while the x on the right represents the value stored in that location. These values are sometimes referred to as the *l-value* and *r-value* of the variable. The *l*-value (so-called because it is used as the value of variables to the left of an assignment) represents the location of the variable, while the *r*-value (used for variables occurring on the right side of an assignment) represents the value stored in the variable.

To make this distinction clearer as we examine variables, we will use the notation val x to stand for the *r*-value of a variable x, while an unqualified x will represent the *l*-value of the variable. Thus, we would re-write the above assignment as:

        x := val x + 1

In the rest of this subsection we show that the variable (reference) types have only trivial subtypes. We begin as usual with an example.

Suppose once more that CheeseType <: FoodType, apple is a value of type FoodType, fv is a variable with type Ref FoodType, and cheddar is a value of type CheeseType. Then the assignment

        fv := apple

is type-correct because apple has type FoodType. It follows that

        fv := cheddar

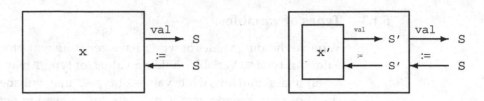

Figure 5.3   A variable x: `Ref S`, and another variable x′: `Ref S′` masquerading as having type `Ref S`.

is also type-correct, because we can always replace a value of type `FoodType` by a value of a subtype. That is, using `cheddar` in a slot expecting a value of type `FoodType` is safe because `CheeseType <: FoodType`.

Suppose `cv` is a variable with type `Ref CheeseType`. We noted above that `fv := apple` is fine, but replacing `fv` by `cv` in the assignment statement to obtain `cv := apple` results in a type error.

For example, suppose again that `melt` is a function that can be applied to cheeses but not general foods like apples. Thus an execution error would result if `melt` were applied to `cv` and it held a value, `apple`, that was not of type `CheeseType`.

Thus it is *not* type-correct to replace a *variable* holding values of a given type by a *variable* holding values of a subtype.

As suggested in the example above, the fact that variables may be the targets of assignments will have a great impact on the subtype properties (or rather the lack of them) of reference types. In particular, the example illustrates that `Ref CheeseType` cannot be a subtype of `Ref FoodType`, even though `CheeseType <: FoodType`.

Suppose we wish variable x′ with type `Ref S′` to masquerade as a variable holding values of type S. See Figure 5.3 for a graphic illustration.

As indicated earlier, a variable x holding values of type S has two values: an *l-value* and an *r-value*, where the latter value is obtained by writing `val` x. Thus two operations are applicable to variables, assignment statements with the variable on the left, and `val` expressions. In the first of these, the variable occurs in a value-receiving context, while in the second it occurs in a value-supplying context.

The second of the two operations is represented in the figure by the arrow labeled "`val`" coming out of the variable (because it supplies a value). If x is a variable with type `Ref S`, then `val` x returns a value of type S.

For a variable x' holding values of type S' to be able to masquerade as a value of type S in all contexts of this kind, we need S' <: S. This should be clear from the right diagram in the figure, where in order for x' to provide a compatible value using the val operator, we need S' <: S.

A value-receiving context is one in which a variable holding values of type S is the target of an assignment, *e.g.*, a statement of the form x := e, for e an expression of type S. This is represented in the figure by an arrow labeled ":=" going into the variable.

In this context we will be interpreting the variable as a reference or location (*i.e.*, the *l*-value) in which to store a value. We have already seen that an assignment x := e is type safe if the type S of e is a subtype of the type declared to be held in the variable x. Thus if we wish to use a variable holding values of type S' in all contexts where the right side of the assignment is a value of type S, we must ensure that S <: S'. Again this should be clear from the right diagram in the figure.

Going back to the example at the beginning of this section, suppose we have an assignment statement,

```
cv := cheddar
```

for cv a variable holding values of type CheeseType and cheddar a value of type CheeseType. If fv is a variable holding values of type FoodType, then we can insert fv in place of cv in the assignment statement, obtaining

```
fv := cheddar
```

Because CheeseType <: FoodType, this assignment is legal. However the assignment cv := apple would *not* be legal.

Thus for a variable holding values of type S' to masquerade as a variable holding values of type S in value-supplying (*r*-value) contexts we must have

$$S' <: S$$

while it can masquerade in value-receiving (*l*-value) contexts only if

$$S <: S'$$

It follows that there are no non-trivial[1] subtypes of variable (reference) types. Thus,

$$Ref\ S' <: Ref\ S,\ \mathit{if}\ S' \simeq S,$$

---

1. A subtype is trivial if it is equivalent to the supertype in the sense that they are each subtypes of each other.

where $S' \simeq S$ abbreviates $S' <: S$ and $S <: S'$. We can think of $\simeq$ as defining an equivalence class of types including such things as pairs of record types that differ only in the order of fields. It is common to ignore the differences between such types and to consider them equivalent.

We can get a deeper understanding of the behavior of reference and function types under subtyping by considering the different roles played by *suppliers* and *receivers* of values. Any slot in a type expression that corresponds to a supplier of values must have subtyping behave covariantly (the same direction as the full type expression), while any slot corresponding to a receiver of values must have contravariant subtyping (the opposite direction).

Thus *l*-values of variables and parameters of functions, both of which are receivers of argument values, behave contravariantly with respect to subtyping. On the other hand, the *r*-values of variables and the results of functions, both of which are suppliers of values, behave covariantly. Because variables have both behaviors, any changes in type must be simultaneously contravariant and covariant. Hence subtypes of reference types must actually be equivalent.

5.1.4   Types of updatable records and arrays

The same analysis as for references can lead us to subtyping rules for updatable records and arrays. An updatable record should support operations of the form `r.l := e`, which results in a record whose `l` field is `e`, while the values of the other fields are unchanged. The simplest way to model this with the constructs introduced so far is to represent an updatable record as an immutable record, each of whose fields represents a reference.[2] Thus the fields represent locations whose values could be updated.

An updatable record with name and age fields would have type

```
PersonInfo = {| name: Ref String; age: Ref Integer |}
```

Thus if `mother` has type `PersonType`, then `mother.name` has type `Ref String`.

Combining the record and reference subtyping rules,

$$\{| \; l_j \!: \text{Ref } T_j |\}_{1 \le j \le n} <: \{| \; l_i \!: \text{Ref } U_i |\}_{1 \le i \le k},$$
$$\textit{if } k \le n \textit{ and for all } 1 \le i \le k, T_i \simeq U_i.$$

---

2. In a real implementation, the locations of the fields would be calculated from the location of the beginning of the record and the size of each field. However this difference has no impact on the subtyping rules.

Thus the subtype has at least the fields of the supertype, but, because the fields can be updated, corresponding fields must have equivalent types. Thus adding fields results in a subtype, but no changes to the types of existing fields is allowed.

Arrays behave analogously to functions. Let

>   ROArray[IndexType] of T

denote a read-only array of elements of type T with subscripts in Index-Type. This data type can be modeled by a function from IndexType to T, as one can think of accessing an array element, A[i], as being similar to applying a function to that index and obtaining the value. As a result, the subtyping rules are similar to those of functions:

$$\text{ROArray[IndexType'] of S'} <: \text{ROArray[IndexType] of S,}$$
$$\textit{if } \text{S'} <: \text{S } \textit{and } \text{IndexType} <: \text{IndexType'}$$

Intuitively, the index types of read-only arrays change contravariantly because, like function parameters, they are value receivers, while the types of elements of the arrays change covariantly because read-only arrays supply values of those types, just like function return types.

Of course, arrays in most programming languages allow individual components to be updated. We can model Array[IndexType] of T by a function from IndexType to Ref T. From function and reference subtyping rules it follows that

$$\text{Array [IndexType'] of S'} <: \text{Array [IndexType] of S}$$
$$\textit{if } \text{S'} \simeq \text{S } \textit{and } \text{IndexType} <: \text{IndexType'}$$

As before, the index types of arrays change contravariantly, but now the types of elements of the arrays are invariant because arrays both supply and receive values of those types.

Java's [AGH99] type rules for array types are not statically type-safe. In Java the type of an array holding elements of type T is written T[].[3] The subtyping rule for array types in Java is

$$\text{S'[]} <: \text{S[], } \textit{if } \text{S'} <: \text{S.}$$

The following Java class will illustrate the problems with this typing rule. Suppose C is a class with a subclass CSub, and suppose the method method-OfCSubOnly() is defined in class CSub, but was not available in C. Now define the class BreakJava below:

---

3. Java array types do not mention the type of subscripts because they are always integers.

```
class BreakJava{
    C v = new C();
    void arrayProb(C[] anArray){
        if (anArray.length > 0)
            anArray[0] = v;                    // ( 2 )
    }

    static void main(String[] args){
        BreakJava bj = new BreakJava();
        CSub paramArray = new CSub[10];
        bj.arrayProb(paramArray);              // ( 1 )
        paramArray[0].methodOfCSubOnly();      // ( 3 )
    }
}
```

The first two lines of the `main` method construct a new instance of the class `BreakJava` and create an array of `CSub` with 10 elements. The message send of `arrayProb` to `bj` at (1) will result in a type error.

The problem is that `paramArray`, an array of elements of type `CSub`, is passed to method `arrayProb` where an array of type `C` was expected. Because of this, the assignment in line (2) of `arrayProb` will result in the assignment of a value `v` from class `C` into an array which is supposed to hold values of type `CSub`. We know that it is illegal to assign a value of a superclass into a variable holding values of the subclass. In fact, if allowed this would result in a run-time error in line (3), which would be executed immediately after the method `arrayProb` finishes executing. Because the value `v` of class `C` was assigned to `paramArray[0]`, the message send of `methodOfCSubOnly()` would fail as elements of class `C` do not support that method.

The correct rule for arrays specified above implies that the message send in line (1) would result in a static type error because `CSub[]` fails to be a subtype of `C[]`.

While the Java designers used an incorrect rule for static checks of subtyping with arrays, they compensated for this by inserting extra dynamic checks. Thus Java would not indicate any type errors at compile time, but it would insert a dynamic check at line (2) because of the assignment to an array parameter. That dynamic check would fail during the execution of the message send `bj.arrayProb(paramArray)` from line (1). The message send at line (3) would never be reached at run time because an exception would have been raised due to the failure of the dynamic check at line (2).

Thus the Java designers compensate for not catching the type error *statically* by performing *dynamic* checks when an individual component of an array is assigned to. Why did they use this obviously faulty subtyping rule, when it results in having to add extra code to assignments to array parameters? While it is necessary for type safety, this extra code in compiled programs is problematic as it results both in increased size of programs and a slowdown in their execution.

One reason the Java designers might have included this faulty rule would be to allow generic sorts (and similar operations) to be written that could pass the static type checker. Java programmers can write sort methods that take elements of type `Comparable[]`, where `Comparable` is an interface supporting a method `compareTo` that returns a negative, zero, or positive `int` depending on whether the receiver is smaller than, equal to, or larger than the parameter. Java's unsafe subtyping rule for arrays allows any array of elements that implement `Comparable` to be passed to such sort methods, even though they are in theory vulnerable to the same errors as illustrated above.

However, the actual code written in these sort routines typically does not create a dynamic type error because it simply reorders elements of the array, rather than assigning brand new values. Thus one result of the decision to give up static type safety by including an "incorrect" subtyping rule for arrays is to make it easier for programmers to write more flexible programs.[4]

As we saw in Section 4.1, parametric polymorphism of the sort introduced in GJ would allow the creation of type-correct generic sorts without the need for this unsafe rule. Thus we can recapture static type safety and maintain expressiveness of the language by introducing a richer type system. We will see other examples of this trade-off in later chapters.

5.2   Object types

While most popular object-oriented languages determine subtyping of object types based on whether the corresponding classes are subclasses, this identification of subclass with subtype is not necessary. In this section we determine subtyping rules for objects that depend only on their public interfaces or object types.

---

4. The reason why this subtyping rule for arrays was included is apparently not as principled. An implementation hack for arrays resulted in a desire for this subtyping rule [Joy98].

The subtyping rules for object types follow from those of records and functions. From the outside, the only operation available on objects is message sending. As a result, object types behave like immutable records. The subtyping rule is:

$$\text{ObjectType} \ \{\!|1_j\!:\!S'_j|\!\}_{1 \leq j \leq n} <: \text{ObjectType} \ \{\!|1_i\!:\!S_i|\!\}_{1 \leq i \leq k},$$
$$\text{if } k \leq n \text{ and for all } 1 \leq i \leq k, S'_i <: S_i.$$

Because the types S'_i and S_i are method types, they are functional types. Suppose $S'_i = T'_i \rightarrow U'_i$ and $S_i = T_i \rightarrow U_i$. Then, by the subtyping rule for function types, $S'_i <: S_i$ if both $T_i <: T'_i$ and $U'_i <: U_i$. That is, object types are subtypes if for every method in the supertype there is a method with the same name in the subtype such that the range types of corresponding methods vary covariantly, and the domain types vary contravariantly.

What is the relation between subclasses and subtypes? Most popular statically typed object-oriented languages allow no changes to method types in subclasses. This clearly implies that the object types generated by a subclass-superclass pair are in the subtype relation. We noted earlier that C++ allows covariant changes to result types in subclasses. By the above, this also results in subtypes.

As we saw in Section 4.2, Eiffel [Mey92] allows covariant changes to both parameter and result types of methods in subclasses. We exhibited an example there showing that this was not type-safe. The subtyping rule given here for object types explains this failure by making it clear that covariant changes to parameter types are *not* statically type safe. The language Sather [Omo91] allows contravariant changes to parameter types and covariant changes to return types in subclasses. Thus it is the most flexible in allowing changes to subclasses so that the resulting object types are in the subtype relation.

While our focus in this section has been on subtyping, a related interesting question is what, if any, restrictions must be placed on changing types of methods in subclasses, even if we don't care whether subclasses generate subtypes. We examine that question in Chapter 6.

5.3   Subtyping for class types

We haven't yet introduced the notion of class types as ways of categorizing classes (just as object types categorize objects). We will do that carefully later. However, it is evident that a class type should include information on the types of instance variables and methods. The reason is that to determine whether we can extend a class with new methods or instance variables, we need to know what methods and instance variables already exist there. If a type of a class is to give us sufficient information about a class to determine whether or not a particular extension is legal, it will need to include that information about methods and instance variables.

Let us use the notation `ClassType(IV, M)` for the type of a class whose instance variables have names and types given by the labels and types of record type `IV`, and whose methods have names and types given by the record type `M`. If all instance variables are invisible from outside of an object generated by a class, then the type of objects generated from a class with type `ClassType(IV, M)` will be `ObjectType M`.

Because most object-oriented languages use class names as types, this notation for class types may look unusual to the reader. We emphasize again that objects have types of the form `ObjectType M`, while classes will now have types of the form `ClassType(IV, M)`.

We can ask whether one class type can be a subtype of another. As before, to determine whether one class type can be a subtype of another we must consider what operations are available on classes. There are only two: creating new objects and extending classes to form subclasses. We will see that in our system there can be no non-trivial subtypes of class types exist, because of the difficulty of masquerading in both of these contexts.

Suppose class `C'` of type `ClassType(IV', M')` is attempting to masquerade as having type `ClassType(IV, M)`. Let us see what constraints on `IV'`, `IV`, `M'`, and `M` follow from this assumption.

Evaluating new `C'` will generate an object of type `ObjectType M'`. If `C'` is to successfully masquerade as an element of type `ClassType(IV, M)` then the type of the expression new `C'`, `ObjectType M'`, must be a subtype of `ObjectType M`. Thus we need $M' <: M$.

Suppose a subclass `SC` is defined by inheritance from `C`:

$$\text{class SC inherits C modifies } l_{i_1}, \ldots, l_{i_m} \{\ldots\}$$

so that `SC` is well-typed with type $\text{ClassType}(IV_{sub}, M_{sub})$ when `C` has type `ClassType(IV,M)`. If the type of `C'` is a subtype of `ClassType(IV,M)`, then `SC` should be well-typed if `C` is replaced by the masquerading `C'`. However, any method `m` of `C` could have been overridden in `SC` with a method of the same type. Because this override must still be legal in the subclass built from `C'`, all methods in `M` must have the same type in `M'` (as otherwise the override would have been illegal).

Similarly, `M'` could have no more methods than `M`. If `M'` had an extra method, m', we could define a subclass of C with an added method m' with an incompatible type from that of m' in M'. If we attempt to define a similar subclass from C', we would get a type error in defining the subclass (presuming that there are any restrictions at all on changing types in subclasses).

Thus if `ClassType(IV',M')` <: `ClassType(IV,M)` then we must have M' $\simeq$ M. Similar arguments on instance variables can be used to show that IV' $\simeq$ IV. Thus there can be no non-trivial subtypes of class types:

$$\texttt{ClassType(IV',M')} <: \texttt{ClassType(IV,M)}, \textit{ if } \texttt{IV'} \simeq \texttt{IV} \textit{ and } \texttt{M'} \simeq \texttt{M}$$

The language discussed so far in this text has no access qualifiers like Java and C++'s private, protected, and public. We will discuss these qualifiers in Section 14.4, where we introduce the names `secret`, `hidden`, and `visible` for access qualifiers whose meanings are similar to Java and C++'s. `Secret` features are not visible outside of the class. That is, they are not visible to subclasses or other objects. Our default for instance variables is that they are `hidden`. This means that they are accessible to subclasses, but not to other objects. In Section 14.4 we assume that class types should not mention `secret` features (i.e., Java's private features). Thus two classes whose `visible` and `hidden` feature names and signatures are the same have the same class type. With this understanding of class types, the claim that there are no non-trivial subtypes for class types remains true.

5.4   Summary

In this chapter, we provided a relatively careful, though informal, analysis of subtyping. The subtyping rules for immutable record types included both *breadth* and *depth* subtyping. That is, a subtype of a record type could include extra labeled fields (breadth) or could replace the type of one of the existing labeled fields by a subtype (depth subtyping).

We addressed the issue of covariance versus contravariance changes in creating subtypes of function types. We discovered that to avoid problems, only covariant changes were allowed to return types and only contravariant changes were allowed to domain types in subtyping function types. Most languages allow no changes to either domain or range types in subtyping function types, though some allow covariant changes in range types. There do not seem to be compelling examples where contravariant changes in domain types are useful.

We emphasize that the rules provided above can be proved mathematically to be safe. Languages that allow covariant changes to both range and domain types (like Eiffel) are not statically type-safe. They either sacrifice type safety altogether or require link or run-time checks to regain type safety.

Reference types (types of variables) allowed no subtyping because elements of these types can both be used as sources of values (*e.g.*, using the `val` construct) and as receivers of values in assignment statements. Subtyping for mutable records and arrays followed naturally from the rules for immutable records, functions, and references. Mutable records allow only breadth subtyping, while arrays only allow contravariant changes to the index types.

Subtyping for object types followed naturally from the rules for immutable records and functions. A subtype of an object type can add new methods (breadth subtyping again) or replace the type of an existing method with a subtype (depth subtyping). By the subtyping rules on function types, one may make contravariant changes to the domain type of the method and covariant changes to the return type. Because instance variables (or hidden methods) do not show up in the public interface of objects, they have no impact on subtyping.

There is no non-trivial subtyping for class types, because of the possibility of conflicts in extending class definitions using inheritance.

We summarize the subtyping rules discussed in this chapter in Figure 5.4. For simplicity we presume that there are no subtype relations involving type constants. (That is, we do not allow `Integer` $<:$ `Real`, for example.)

We have also generalized the subtyping rule for function types to include functions with more than one argument. The domain of a function with multiple arguments is represented as a product or tuple type.

In the next chapter we address the impact of our rules for subtyping on the allowed changes to types of methods and instance variables in defining subclasses.

$Rec <:$ $\{\!| \, l_j : T_j \, |\!\}_{1 \le j \le n} <: \{\!| \, l_i : U_i \, |\!\}_{1 \le i \le k},$
$\qquad\qquad$ *if* $k \le n$ *and for all* $1 \le i \le k$, $T_i <: U_i$.

$Fcn <:$ $(S'_1 \times \ldots \times S'_n \to T') <: (S_1 \times \ldots \times S_n \to T),$
$\qquad\qquad$ *if* $S_i <: S'_i$ *for* $1 \le i \le n$, *and* $T' <: T$.

$Ref <:$ $\texttt{Ref } S' <: \texttt{Ref } S, \textit{if } S' \simeq S.$

$Rec <:$ $\{\!| \, l_j : \texttt{Ref } T_j \, |\!\}_{1 \le j \le n} <: \{\!| \, l_i : \texttt{Ref } U_i \, |\!\}_{1 \le i \le k},$
$\qquad\qquad$ *if* $k \le n$ *and for all* $1 \le i \le k$, $T_i \simeq U_i$.

$Read\text{-}only \; Array <:$ $\texttt{ROArray[IndexType'] of } S' <:$
$\qquad\qquad\qquad\qquad\qquad\quad \texttt{ROArray[IndexType] of } S,$
$\qquad\qquad$ *if* $S' <: S$ *and* $\texttt{IndexType} <: \texttt{IndexType'}$.

$Array <:$ $\texttt{Array[IndexType'] of } S' <: \texttt{Array[IndexType] of } S,$
$\qquad\qquad$ *if* $S' \simeq S$ *and* $\texttt{IndexType} <: \texttt{IndexType'}$.

$Object <:$ $\texttt{ObjectType } \{\!| l_j : S'_j |\!\}_{1 \le j \le n} <: \texttt{ObjectType } \{\!| l_i : S_i |\!\}_{1 \le i \le k},$
$\qquad\qquad$ *if* $k \le n$ *and for all* $1 \le i \le k$, $S'_i <: S_i$.

$Class <:$ $\texttt{ClassType(IV', M')} <: \texttt{ClassType(IV, M)},$
$\qquad\qquad$ *if* $\texttt{IV'} \simeq \texttt{IV}$ *and* $\texttt{M'} \simeq \texttt{M}$

Figure 5.4   Summary of subtyping rules.

6 *Type Restrictions on Subclasses*

There are many circumstances under which we would like to change the types of methods in subclasses. What is it that keeps us from making arbitrary changes to the types of these methods?

In the last chapter we saw that we can create subtypes of object types by adding new methods or by replacing the types of existing methods by subtypes. *A priori*, there seems to be no reason for following these restrictions in creating subclasses if we don't care whether the resulting object type is a subtype of that generated by the superclass. Are any restrictions necessary on changing types of methods or instance variables in subclasses if all we care about is that all of the methods in the subclass are type-safe?

Eiffel allows covariant changes to method return types, method parameter types, and the types of instance variables in subclasses. We saw in Section 4.2 that covariant changes to parameter types break subtyping, but perhaps it is all right to allow these changes if we don't expect the resulting types to be in the subtype relation.

We will see in this chapter that the mutually recursive nature of the methods in classes requires that we do be careful in what changes are allowed to types of instance variables and methods. Interestingly, the restrictions will be similar to those required to preserve subtyping of object types.

6.1 Allowable changes to method types

The main reason for needing restrictions on changes to the types of methods in subclasses is that a method body in a class may call any other method from the class by sending a message to self. Thus, changes to one method may have an impact on both the typing and meaning of another method in the

```
class C {
   function m(s:S): T is  { .... }
   function n(anS:S): U is  {
        ... self ⇐ m(anS) ... }
}

class SC inherits C modifies m {
   function m(s:S'): T' is    // For which S', T' safe?
      { ... }
}
```

Figure 6.1   Changing types of methods in subclasses.

same class. In this section we discuss the changes to method types that are guaranteed *not* to cause typing problems.

Figure 6.1 shows a well-typed class containing methods m and n, where m has type S → T. The body of method n includes a message send of m(anS) to self. We presume that the body of method n will be well-typed if m has type S → T. In particular, we assume that the context in which the message send occurs needs the result to be a value of type T to be type correct.

Suppose we override m in a subclass so that it has type S' → T'. In general, the only way to be sure that the occurrence of self ⇐ m in the body of n is still compatible is to require that S' → T' <: S → T (this is, after all, exactly what the subtype relation guarantees).

Thus we can guarantee type safety when forming subclasses if we restrict ourselves to overriding a method with a new one whose type is a subtype of the type of the original.

Of course it is also technically possible to keep track of which methods are called by other methods and annotate each class with that information. While this would allow more freedom in making changes to some methods, this seems too painful for regular use and may require a data flow analysis of even indirect uses of an object. Hence we state this simpler requirement.

Because methods must be functions or procedures, we can indicate more exactly the changes allowed to types of methods in subclasses. Recall from the previous chapter that subtyping of function types is contravariant in the parameter type and covariant in the result type. Thus, in overriding a method in a subclass, we may replace a result type T by a subtype T' and a parameter type S by a supertype S'.

This flexibility in changing result types is clearly very useful. However, while safe, few compelling examples seem to exist of the value of replacing a parameter type by a supertype. The most likely scenario for changing parameter types would be if the original method had a parameter specification that was needlessly constraining and could thus be easily broadened in the method for the subclass.

In our analysis of message sending outside of the object's methods, given in the previous chapter, we showed that these same restrictions on changing the types of methods in subclasses are sufficient to guarantee that the resulting object types are subtypes. Later we will add more powerful constructs to our language that will result in subclasses sometimes failing to generate subtypes. However, the possibility of mutually recursive definitions of methods will still require us to restrict changes in types of methods to subtypes.

6.2   Instance variable types invariant in subclasses

Unfortunately, we do not have the same flexibility in changing the types of instance variables as we do with methods. Recall from Section 5.1.3 that a variable whose declared type is T is actually a value of type Ref T. As discussed there, reference types have no subtypes because they can be used in either value-receiving (on the left side of :=) or value-supplying positions. As a result, it is not possible to change the types of instance variables in subclasses.

A concrete example of this is given in the following example.

```
class Rect {
    ul: Point := nil;   // upper left corner
    lr: Point := nil;   // lower right corner

    function setUL(newUL: Point): Void is
    { self.ul := newUL }
}

class ColorRect {
    ul: ColorPoint := nil;
    lr: ColorPoint := nil;
    ...
}
```

Suppose the intention is that the redefinitions of `ul` and `lr` in `ColorRect` are to override the corresponding definitions in `Rect` by providing a different type for the instance variables.[1] Unfortunately this change will break the type safety of the inherited method `setUL` as a value of type `Point` may not be assigned to a variable of type `ColorPoint`.

The inability to safely change the types of instance variables minimizes the advantages obtained by being able to make covariant changes to the return types of methods, as we saw in Chapter 3. Later we will expand on the ideas presented in Chapter 4 to increase the expressiveness of the language while retaining type safety.

6.3   Changing visibility

There is one kind of change that can be made to methods in subclasses that we have not yet considered. Rather than changing the types of methods, we can consider changing the visibility of methods.

We have not discussed this earlier because our defaults have been that all methods are visible. We will continue with those defaults until section 14.4, but since most object-oriented languages do allow the programmer to specify degrees of information hiding, we briefly address this question in terms of preserving safety in subclasses.

It is easy to see that taking methods that are hidden inside superclasses and making them more visible in subclasses causes no problems with inherited methods or even in having subclasses generate subtypes. What is more interesting is that, if we do not care whether subclasses generate subtypes, we can also make methods less visible in subclasses.

For the purposes of this discussion, we adopt the terms public, protected, and private from Java [AGH99]. A public method is visible within its class, within all subclasses, and to any object that wishes to send it messages. A protected method is visible within its class and within all subclasses, but objects not of the same class may not send a message that invokes a protected

---

1. If you were to do this in Java, it would instead define new instance variables with the same names as the old instance variables. In other words, references to `ul` in methods inherited from `Rect` would refer to the instance variables defined there, but references to `ul` in new methods or overridden methods in `ColorRect` would refer to the new instance variable. Changes to the old one would have no impact on values of the new one and vice versa. While one might imagine a programmer wanting such behavior, it certainly would be unusual. This is not what we are intending by our redeclaration above.

method. A private method is only visible within the class in which it appears. It is not visible in subclasses or to other objects.

Changing the visibility of a method from public to protected causes no difficulty with inherited methods because public and protected methods are equally visible to inherited methods of the class. Changing the visibility from protected to private also causes no problems. Inherited methods that called the method still have access because their definitions appeared in a class which had access to the method. Of course, if a method body is overridden in a later subclass, it will not be able to access the newly private method. However this does not break any existing code.

Of course, if one hides a previously public method, m, in a subclass SC of C, then SC no longer generates objects whose type is a subtype of the objects generated by C. Objects generated from C can respond to message m, while those generated from SC cannot.

Thus languages that allow method visibility to be restricted do not have problems with type safety of inherited methods. However, they need not generate subtypes.

6.4 Summary

In this chapter we learned that even if we don't care whether or not subclasses generate subtypes, there still need to be restrictions on allowable changes in the types of methods and instance variables in subclasses, if we wish to retain type safety. This is the result of the mutually referential nature of methods and their references to instance variables.

We may only make covariant changes to the return types of methods and contravariant changes to the parameter types of methods. We may make no changes at all to the types of instance variables without raising the possibility of type errors. While allowing covariant changes to return types seems to provide some minor gains in expressiveness, allowing contravariant changes to parameter types doesn't seem to be very useful. For exactly the same reasons as for records, adding new methods and instance variables in subclasses causes no difficulties.

It is interesting that the restrictions on changing method types were exactly those required for subclasses to generate subtypes. Later we will extend the language (using MyType) in such a way that the restrictions for creating type-safe subclasses are not sufficient to guarantee that subclasses generate subtypes.

Thus far we have restricted our attention to class-based object-oriented languages. In the next chapter we will finish our overview of object-oriented languages by taking a quick look at two other related kinds of languages, object-based and multi-method languages.

7 Varieties of Object-Oriented Programming Languages

In this chapter we discuss two other styles of languages that are often discussed as object-oriented languages: object-based and multi-method languages. We also briefly discuss a few interesting features of existing object-oriented languages that distinguish them from the model languages discussed in this book. The goal is to highlight differences in languages that are grouped under the umbrella label of object-oriented languages.

7.1 Multi-methods vs. object-based vs. class-based languages

In this book we focus on class-based languages, but there are other alternatives. In this section we discuss briefly object-based and multi-method styles of languages.

7.1.1 Object-based languages

OBJECT-BASED
LANGUAGE

As discussed in Chapter 2, classes in class-based languages serve as extensible templates for the creation of new objects (though they often serve other purposes as well). *Object-based languages* do not support classes, and thus must provide other mechanisms to create new objects.

In most object-based languages, objects can be constructed directly. Moreover, functions can be defined that, when instantiated with appropriate parameters, return objects that all have the same shape. For example, one might write a function makePoint, taking parameters nx and ny, that, when invoked, returns a Point object whose instance variables are initialized to the values provided as parameters:

```
function makePoint(nx: Integer, ny: Integer): PointType is
{
   return object {
      x: Integer := nx;
      y: Integer := ny;
      function move(dx: Integer, dy: Integer): Void is
      { x := x + dx;
        y := y + dy;
      }
   }
}
```

PROTOTYPE-BASED
LANGUAGE

A *prototype-based language*, a special kind of object-based language, allows the user to generate "prototypical" objects, and then to use these as prototypes to create new objects by cloning. Of course, these clones would not be much more useful than objects generated by functions like `makePoint` above if they did not provide a way of updating features of the cloned objects.

As usual, there is no difficulty in dynamically updating instance variables in the generated objects. However, these languages typically also allow dynamic updates of methods. That is, if a prototype point contains a method `move`, the programmer can replace the `move` method with a new method with the same name. If the language is statically typed, then the new method signature must typically be compatible with that of the original. Because both instance variables and methods can be updated at run time, there is little reason to distinguish between instance variables and methods.[1] As a result we shall use the term feature to refer to either of these.

While clones may update features dynamically, the resulting objects all have the same structure. To add features, as is done with inheritance, a new language mechanism must be provided. Features may be provided either to allow the programmer to *extend* another object or to *delegate* operations to another object.

Extension works much like inheritance in classes. One simply declares that the new object o extends a prototype p and lists the new features. As a result o contains separate copies of the features of p. Thus if p had a field x of type `Integer`, o would also have a field x of type `Integer`. However, changes

---

1. Of course, there may be important distinctions in implementations. Instance variables typically don't involve references to `self`, while methods may use `self`, resulting in a more complex run-time semantics.

to the x field of p would have no impact on the x field of o. This is exactly as one would expect in analogy to what happens when multiple objects are generated from a single class.

Delegation, on the other hand, allows an object to *delegate* certain operations to a surrogate object. For example, suppose again that a prototype p has a field x of type Integer. If a new object o is defined by delegation from p, then any attempt to access the x field of o will actually obtain the value of the x field of p. Also, any change to the x field of p will be visible from o and vice versa.

Thus an object created using delegation retains ties to its prototype parent, while an object created by extension is independent of its parent.

There are advantages and disadvantages to object-based languages. An important argument for object-based languages is that they are conceptually simpler than class-based languages because they avoid having a special syntactic construct – the class – that is only used to generate new objects. Rather than defining a class and then generating objects from it, one can either directly define objects or build them from prototypes by cloning, delegating, or extending. Because of this unification of classes and objects, there is also little need to distinguish methods and fields in the language. Both can be updated at run time, while in a class-based object-oriented language, only instance variables can be updated at run time.

A counter-argument against object-based languages is that, except in the case where only one object of a particular structure is needed, prototypes are typically not used as objects. They are instead created and used like classes. Moreover, an argument can also be made that constructs like Java's anonymous classes [AGH99, GJSB00] are nearly as lightweight (at least syntactically) as directly defining objects.

Moreover, the flexibility provided by allowing dynamic update of methods in objects comes with a price attached in semantic complexity. Because methods may be updated on the fly, it is difficult to reason about object-based languages, as objects with the same structure may have very different behavior. It is typically easy to take into account differences in values of instance variables when reasoning statically about collections of objects generated from the same class. However, when methods may change on the fly, the fact that methods may make calls to other methods through self makes it hard to predict what any of the methods will do.

This semantic complexity also shows up in the difficulty of modeling these languages. The translational semantics provided later in this book is not sufficient to cover the situation where methods may be updated dynamically.

The modeling is not robust enough to allow `self` to refer to different method bodies for the same method name over time.

Abadi and Cardelli [AC96] originally did not believe a translational semantics into the lambda calculus existed for such languages. As a result they developed an *object calculus* to model these languages. However, with Viswanathan [ACV96], they later developed a translational semantics that is somewhat more complex than the one given later in this monograph, but that correctly captures dynamic method update in objects.

OBJECT CALCULUS

The text, *A Theory of Objects* [AC96], by Abadi and Cardelli, is an excellent source of information on the foundations of object-based languages. See especially their Chapter 4 for a discussion of such languages, and the later chapters of the book for a discussion of their object calculus and the translational semantics. The book also discusses how to encode classes in an object-based language.

7.1.2   Multi-method languages

In class-based and object-based languages, the receiver of a message determines which method body is called. In *multi-method languages*, there is no receiver of a message. Method calls look like procedure calls in procedural languages. However, unlike in procedural languages, the selection of method body to be executed depends on the run-time types of the values of one or more of the parameters of the call.

MULTI-METHOD
LANGUAGE

For example, suppose we have a program in a multi-method language that involves both points and color points. The `equal` procedure that we use may depend on the types of both objects being compared:

```
function equal(p1:Point,p2:Point): Boolean is
{ return p1.x = p2.x & p1.y = p2.y }

function equal(p1:ColorPoint,p2:ColorPoint): Boolean is
{ return p1.x = p2.x & p1.y = p2.y
                        & p1.color = p2.color }
```

Assume that `ColorPoint` is a subtype of `Point` and that `pt1` and `pt2` are identifiers declared statically to have type `Point`, but the values of both at run time are of type `Point`. If we evaluate `equal(pt1, pt2)` in a multi-method language, then the first of the two `equal` methods above would be chosen to execute because the choice is based on the run-time types of both parameters. On the other hand, if the values of `pt1` and `pt2` at run time are both of type `ColorPoint` then the multi-method language would choose the second of the two methods to execute, because the parameters are a closer match to the second definition.

Thus there are two key differences between the object-oriented languages discussed to this point and the multi-method languages. First, there is no designated object to serve as the "receiver" of the message. Second, the selection of method body to execute may depend dynamically on the run-time type of more than one of the arguments of the message.

Another way of viewing multi-method languages is that they support *dynamic* method overloading. A language like Java supports *static* overloading by allowing the programmer to provide a class with multiple methods having the same name but different signatures. Thus multiple method bodies may be associated with the same name for a single object. A simple way of understanding overloading is to imagine each method has the types of its parameters appended to the method name. Java then requires these extended names to be unique. Thus Java will not allow two versions of an overloaded method that have exactly the same parameter types.

In Java, when a programmer calls an overloaded method, the compiler determines which version of the method to call based on the name and the static types of the parameters. Of course the actual method body to execute is determined dynamically based on the run-time type of the receiver, but which version (*i.e.,* which extended name for the method) to use is determined statically. In a multi-method language, the selection of which method to execute is determined at run time based on the types of the values of the actual parameters.[2]

Going back to the example above, suppose we evaluate `equal(pt1,pt2)` where at run time `pt1` is a value of type `Point` and `pt2` is a value of type `ColorPoint`. In this case, using the body of the second version of `equal` would not be possible because the first parameter has run-time type `Point`, and hence would not conform to the declaration that the first parameter have type `ColorPoint`. As a result the first method body must be chosen.

In general, multi-method languages search in a predetermined way to find the appropriate "best" match among the available method bodies. In the second example above, where both parameters were actually of type `ColorPoint` at run time, either of the method bodies might have been called,

---

2. Of course in a multi-method language the system may be able to make some decisions on which version of the method to execute based on statically available information as well. If one version has two formal parameters and another has three, that information can be used to eliminate method versions statically.

but the second was a better match because the run-time types were exactly the declared types of the formal parameters.

The first example, where both parameters were `Points`, and the third example, where the first parameter was a `Point` and the second parameter was a `ColorPoint`, were both easy because the types of the actual parameters conformed to only one of the method bodies – the first. In some cases, however, the choice of method body to use is not as obvious as for the three cases we have seen so far.

Suppose we define the following methods:

```
function compare(p1: Point, p2: ColorPoint): Boolean is
{ return ... }

function compare(p1: ColorPoint, p2: Point): Boolean is
{ return ... }
```

A call of `compare(pt1,pt2)` for `pt1` and `pt2`, where both have static type `Point`, would not be statically type safe because there is no `compare` method with signature accepting two values of type `Point`. Instead, there are method bodies corresponding to any call involving one `Point` and one `ColorPoint`. Suppose we write `compare(cpt1, cpt2)`, where `cpt1` and `cpt2` both have type `ColorPoint`. If the two definitions above are the only definitions of `compare`, we now have a problem. If the run-time types of `cpt1` and `cpt2` are `ColorPoint` (or indeed any subtype of `ColorPoint`), it is no longer clear what is the best choice for the method body to be executed. Each method choice matches one of the parameters exactly, but the other parameter is better matched by the other version of the method.

For each method call at run time, multi-method languages generally first determine the set of possible method bodies that might be executed. If there is only one, then there is no problem, otherwise an attempt is made to find the version of the method with the "best" fit. The difficulty arises when there is no clear "best" fit as in the situation described above with `compare`.

Different multi-method languages handle this problem in different ways. Some languages (CLOS [DG87], for example) provide rules to specify which method body is to be chosen when there is more than one match, while others (Cecil [Cha95], for example) require the programmer to disambiguate the calls by inserting one or more new method definitions to resolve the ambiguous cases.

If the first way of handling ambiguities is chosen, the language might specify, for example, that first a best fit among the matching method bodies is found for the first argument , and then for successive arguments. If we were to use this rule, then the call of compare (cpt1, cpt2) would result in the execution of the second method body, because it provides the best match for the first argument.

If the second way of handling ambiguities is chosen, the type system might require the programmer to explicitly add a new method body for the case where both parameters are of type ColorPoint as that eliminates all ambiguities in resolving method calls for compare.

While Java is not a multi-method language, it does complain about overloaded methods that it cannot resolve statically, and insists that the programmer disambiguate such expressions. An example would be a class containing overloaded methods with two parameters whose corresponding types are in opposite subtyping relations like those in the compare methods above.

A major advantage of multi-method languages is in the handling of binary methods. Because there is no designated receiver of the message, all parameter values involved in the computation have equal precedence (aside from orders specified to resolve ambiguities as noted above). Thus if m is desired to be a binary method, programmers can simply ensure that the types for both parameters are the same for all method definitions of m.

For example, our definitions of the method bodies for equal, above, each satisfy the constraint that the types of the two parameters are identical. As can be seen in the examples above, this does not prevent us from calling the equal method with parameters of different types. Thus we could write equal (pt1,pt2), where the value of one of the arguments was of type Point and the other was of type ColorPoint, but we will always have that possibility in languages with subtyping.

We saw that Eiffel also supported binary methods with its like Current construct, but that it was not type safe. In Chapter 16, we introduce a new keyword, MyType, that stands for the type of self. This is similar to Eiffel's like Current, but we will provide static type-checking rules that will ensure that it is safe. Object-oriented languages with MyType and a way of specifying exact types, for example the language $\mathcal{NOOL}$ in Chapter 18, allow the programmer to specify that the type of the parameter is the same as that of the receiver, while also providing the capability of ruling out calls where the value of the actual parameter is a subtype of the formal parameter's static type.

A major disadvantage of multi-method languages compared to the other object-oriented languages is that it is harder to maintain encapsulation and information hiding. When dynamic method selection depends on several parameters that may be of different types, there is no obvious place to keep the multi-method definitions. In ordinary single-dispatch object-oriented languages, method lookup takes place by going to the receiving object to find a method with the same name and signature. In multi-method languages, method lookup takes place first by finding all applicable methods with the same name and then finding the "best" match based on the types of the values at run time.

Thus in single-dispatch languages all methods logically belong with the receiver object (or its class), and the methods typically have access to non-public features of the receiver's object (or class), but not those of its parameters.

In a multi-method language, methods with the same name logically belong together (at least in terms of the lookup strategy). In most cases, multi-methods also need access to non-public features of all parameters used to resolve the method dispatch. This if a multi-method `contains` has parameters of type `Point` and `Circle`, then it may need access to non-public methods and instance variables of both. As a result, it often does not make sense to consider a multi-method as a part of just one class. This also implies that methods outside of a class may need access to features that would normally be hidden outside of that class.

As a result, designers of multi-method languages struggle with modularity issues. Researchers have proposed module systems for multi-methods [CL95], as well as various schemes [Cas97, CM99] for either restricting multi-methods or combining object-oriented programming with multi-methods, but it is not yet clear whether these are sufficient to overcome the difficulties with modularity.

Many variants of multi-method systems exist, including "encapsulated multi-methods", which blend the object-oriented and multi-method styles of programming by retaining the notion of sending a message to an object, but also dynamically resolving overloading in parameters at run time.

Castagna's *Object-Oriented Programming: A unified foundation* [Cas97] is an excellent source of information on the theory of multi-method languages and hybrid systems. CLOS [DG87] and Cecil [Cha95] are interesting examples of multi-method languages.

7.1.3   What languages are truly "object-oriented"?

It seems odd for us to struggle with the definition of object-oriented languages this far into this book. One reason for postponing the discussion until now is that endless arguments have gone on as to which systems deserve the name "object-oriented" languages. Arguments like this have some technical importance, but they often have public relations consequences as well. After all, object-oriented languages are currently "hot", so it is an advantage to have your favorite language classified as object-oriented.

Class-based languages and object-based languages are similar in the way that method bodies are selected at execution time. Object-based languages may be syntactically simpler because they have fewer syntactic constructs. However, we believe objects in object-based languages are semantically more complex, because they play the roles of both classes and objects when compared to class-based languages. In particular, the ability to update methods dynamically in objects seems to require more sophisticated modeling in a translational semantics. Static verification of such programs may also be significantly more complex, because one cannot count on the specification of methods to be the same over the lifetime of an object.

Multi-method languages, while they share the notion of dynamic method dispatch with class-based and object-based languages, organize the lookup of method bodies entirely differently. This results in a quite different semantics for such languages. Moreover, because there is not a receiver of messages specified in a call, the notion of `self` is no longer meaningful. As a result, many prefer not to use the term "object-oriented" for multi-method systems.

An interesting discussion attempting to draw together the two sides of this argument can be found in [Cas95] as well as in Chapter 5 of [Cas97].

Because the use of the term "object-oriented" is so emotionally laden, we prefer not to take sides, but simply to remark that these systems are different. In this text we have chosen to restrict our discussion to class-based languages, so references to object-oriented languages in the rest of this text will refer only to class-based languages. Modeling for object-based languages can be found in [AC96] and for multi-method languages in [Cas97].

7.2   Well-known object-oriented languages

In this section we discuss some interesting features of some well-known object-oriented programming languages. Our focus is on interesting features that are related to their type systems. In particular, we highlight features not covered in the formal models presented in this book.

7.2.1   Simula and Beta

Simula 67 [BDMN73] is generally accepted to be the first object-oriented language. It was defined as an extension of ALGOL 60 to support discrete simulations. It added the notions of objects, classes, inheritance, and dynamic method invocation, but did not support information hiding of either instance variables or methods.

Beta [KMMPN87] was defined later as a modern successor to Simula 67. It uses a very different notation than most object-oriented languages, making it difficult to learn for those not familiar with the language. An important part of the language is the unification of methods and classes into a single construct called a pattern.

An interesting feature of both Simula 67 and Beta is the way that method override is accomplished. Rather than supporting a super construct to allow the programmer to invoke a method from the superclass, instead the programmer includes the keyword inner in the method body. If a new body for the method is given in the subclass, that new body is treated as a replacement for the word inner in the method definition in the superclass. That is, any invocations of the method on an element of the subclass will result in execution of the superclass code that occurs before inner, then execution of the code from the subclass, and then finally execution of the code that follows inner from the superclass.

VIRTUAL CLASS   Beta also supports *virtual classes* (called virtual patterns in the Beta literature). The example in Figure 7.1 gives the flavor of this construct using a syntax similar to that used in this book. To be consistent with our separation of classes from types, our example will use virtual types rather than virtual classes.

The deftype declaration of type variable A in Cell indicates that it may be a subtype of Object. This is not a type parameter to be instantiated. Instead it is a virtual type, whose declaration indicates that A will denote Object in Cell, but that A may be specialized to a subclass of Object in subclasses of Cell. (This use of "virtual" is similar to that of virtual methods in C++, as a feature that may be overridden in subclasses.) Thus in class StringCell, A is further constrained to be String, with the possibility of further specialization in subclasses of StringCell.

Many of the uses of virtual types are similar to those for polymorphic functions. In GJ (or the languages $\mathcal{PSOOL}$ or $\mathcal{PMOOL}$ introduced later), for example, we would write a polymorphic function PolyCell taking a type parameter A, so that Cell and StringCell could be created by applying

```
class Cell {
   deftype A <: Object;
   value:A := null;

   function set(v:A): Void is
   { value := v }

   function get(): A is
   { return value }
}

class StringCell inherits Cell {
   deftype A <: String;
   ...
}
```

Figure 7.1 `Cell` and `StringCell` classes in Beta.

`PolyCell` to the types `Object` and `String`. In using virtual types, we need not write a polymorphic class. The class `Cell` defined above takes the place of both `PolyCell` and `Cell`.

Moreover, because `StringCell` extends `Cell`, and Beta subclasses are assumed to generate subtypes, objects of type `StringCell` may be used in any context expecting values of type `Cell`. By this time, the reader should recognize that this may result in type errors because the parameter of method `set` changes covariantly in moving to the subclass. The designers of Beta realized this, and compensated for this weakness of the static type system by inserting dynamic checks in this circumstance. Thus Beta is type safe by virtue of a combination of static and dynamic type checking.

While the simple example shown above may be easily replaced by a polymorphic class definition, there are other examples where the replacement is not as simple. Figure 7.2 provides a simple example involving mutually recursive types. We assume that `ObserverClass` generates objects of type `Observer`, and `SubjectClass` generates objects of type `Subject`. The mutually recursive definitions of the types `Observer` and `Subject` are written using virtual types.

This is an instance of the Subject-Observer pattern, which is closely re-

```
ObjectType Observer {
    deftype S <: Subject;
    deftype E <: Event;

    function notify(s:S, e:E): Void;
}

ObjectType Subject {
    deftype O <: Observer;
    deftype E <: Event;

    function register(s:S): Void;

    function notifyObservers(e:E): Void;
}

class ObserverClass {
    deftype S <: Subject;
    deftype E <: Event;
    function notify(s:S, e:E): Void is
    { ... }
}

class SubjectClass {
    deftype O <: Observer;
    deftype E <: Event;
    observers:Array of O;
    function register(o:O): Void is
    { ... }
    function notifyObservers(e:E): Void is
    { ... observers[i].notify(self,e) ... }
}
```

Figure 7.2   The Subject-Observer pattern expressed with virtual types.

```
ObjectType WindowObserver { ... }

ObjectType WindowSubject { ... }

class WindowObserverClass {
    deftype S <: WindowSubject;
    deftype E <: WindowEvent;

    function notify(s:S, e:E): Void is    // override
    { super.notify(s,e); ... s.windowMeth() ... }
}

class WindowSubjectClass {
    deftype O <: WindowObserver;
    deftype E <: Event;

    function windowMeth(...): ... is      // new method
    { ... }
}
```

Figure 7.3   Specializing `Subject-Observer` to windows.

lated to the event-handling style for Java 1.1. Observers send a `register` message to a subject so that they can be notified when certain events occur. When an event occurs, the subject executes its `notifyObservers` message to send `notify` messages to each of its registered observers. Clearly `Subject` needs to know about `Observer` and vice versa. In anticipation of specializing these classes, we defined the virtual type `S` to be used in `Observer` and `O` to be used in `Subject`. Virtual type `E` is defined in both classes.

Now suppose we wish to specialize both `SubjectClass` and `ObserverClass` to work with a special type of event from class `WindowEvent`. As illustrated in Figure 7.3, the types `WindowSubject` and `WindowObserver` have simultaneously been specialized from `Subject` and `Observer`.

This usage of virtual types allowed us to simultaneously refine classes and types in ways that would have been extremely awkward without these features. Moreover, as long as we keep objects of type `Subject` interacting only with those of type `Observer`, and objects of type `WindowSubject` interacting only with those of type `WindowObserver`, no type problems result.

However, if we allow objects of type `WindowSubject` to interact with objects of type `Observer`, we get the usual sorts of type insecurities that we have seen before with binary methods. As noted earlier, Beta avoids these problems by including dynamic checks to ensure type safety.

Bruce, Odersky, and Wadler [BOW98] compare the strengths and weaknesses of virtual classes with respect to F-bounded polymorphism. That paper also suggests that many of the uses of virtual classes may be seen to be a mutually recursive generalization of the `MyType` construct introduced in Chapter 16. Bruce and Vanderwaart [BV99] present the design and translational semantics for such a construct. Igarashi and Pierce [IP98] present an alternative semantics using existential types that captures different features of virtual classes.

7.2.2   Java and C++

C++ and Java are two of the most popular statically typed class-based object-oriented languages in use today. C++ is actually a hybrid language that contains features of both procedural and object-oriented languages, while Java is designed to only support an object-oriented style of programming. As a result we will place more emphasis in our discussion on Java.

Java's interfaces are quite similar to the object types discussed in this book. Java and C++ both originally supported the invariant type discipline for subclasses. That is, parameter and return types for overridden methods were required to be the same as for the method in the superclass. C++ later loosened its restrictions to allow covariant changes to return types.

C++ supports multiple inheritance on classes, while Java is restricted to single inheritance on classes. However, Java allows new interfaces to extend multiple existing interfaces. Thus Java's rules for subclasses and subtypes are similar to those presented here. However, both Java and C++ only recognize declared extensions of either classes or interfaces. For example, even if interface B contains all of the methods of interface A (with the same signatures), B will not be recognized as an extension of A unless it is declared to be so in B's definition. Thus subtypes are determined by declaration, rather than structurally as in this text.

Interestingly, Java does not fully support subtyping. The failure arises in conditional expressions of the form `bexp?texp:fexp`. In that expression, `bexp` must have type `Boolean`. If `bexp` is true at run time then the value of `texp` will be returned. Otherwise, the value of `fexp` will be returned.

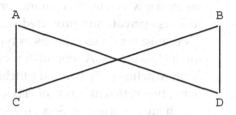

Figure 7.4   Lack of least upper bounds in Java interfaces.

Java type-checking rules require that the types of `texp` and `fexp` either be the same or that one extends the other. For example, suppose that `ColorPoint` and `FatPoint` both extend interface `Point`, with variables `cpt` of type `ColorPoint`, `fpt` of type `FatPoint`, and `pt` of type `Point`. Then the expressions `bexp?pt:pt`, `bexp?pt:cpt`, and `bexp?fpt:pt` are well-typed, but `bexp?fpt:cpt` is not well-typed. Even though Java recognizes that the types of both `fpt` and `cpt` extend `Point`, and using expressions of type `Point` in both branches of the conditional would be fine, the expression with both branches having distinct subtypes of `Point` is not allowed.

The reason for this restriction in Java is that types (interfaces) with an upper bound need not have a least upper bound. For example, suppose interfaces `C` and `D` are both defined to extend both `A` and `B` as in Figure 7.4. Thus each of them contains at least the union of the features declared in `A` and `B`. However if `c` has type `C` and `d` has type `D`, it is not clear what type to assign to `bexp?c:d`. Either type `A` or `B` would be plausible, but there is no reason to prefer one to the other. If the system could synthesize a new interface containing exactly the features of `A` and `B`, and that was declared to extend both, it would be the obvious choice for the type of the conditional. Since that is not possible in Java, the type system is restricted to handle only the simpler cases where the type of one branch extends that of the other.[3]

Java does support subtyping via a subsumption rule in the context of assignment statements and with actual parameters in method calls. As a result, most programmers are unaware that Java does not fully support subtyping.

The visibility rules of Java and C++ are a bit different from those described in this book. Suppose the definition of class `C` includes the declaration of

_____

3. Interestingly, a similar problem arose during the design and implementation of a type system for a functional object-oriented language [BCD+93] in the early 1990's.

method m which takes a parameter c of class C. In the body of m, it is possible to access private and protected variables of the parameter of type C.

Because we do use classes as types in this book, we do not shown how to model this access. A semantics modeling this access to private features is difficult to achieve. Fisher and Mitchell [FM98] show how to obtain this access using two different kinds of classes and by nesting "existential quantifiers", which are discussed in Section 9.3.

7.2.3   Smalltalk

Smalltalk [GR83] can be considered the first pure object-oriented language. It is a dynamically typed language. Therefore there is no need to restrict subtyping to subclasses or vice versa. The only issue is whether a particular object can find a method to handle a given message send at run time.

William Cook published an interesting paper [Coo92] that compared the inheritance graph of classes in the built-in Smalltalk libraries with subtype relations between objects generated by these classes. One of his interesting findings was that there was little correlation between subclass and subtype. He found a significant number of instances in which B was a subclass of A, but that the object type corresponding to A was a subtype of that corresponding to B.

While Smalltalk is an interesting and important object-oriented language, we do not discuss it further here because we are primarily focussing on statically typed languages in this book.

7.2.4   Eiffel and Sather

We presented a rather extensive analysis of Eiffel in Section 4.2. While Eiffel has a very flexible static type system, we showed that it was not sound. While several proposals [Mey92, Mey95a, Coo89b] have been made to "fix" the type system, to our knowledge none of these has yet been implemented in a publicly available compiler.

Sather [Omo91, Omo93] was designed as a more efficient variant of Eiffel. One of the goals of the Sather design was to fix the type insecurities of Eiffel. It accomplished this by only allowing contravariant changes in parameter types in subtypes, and allowing no changes in instance variables. In Sather, inheritance from abstract classes is used to define the subtype hierarchy, while inheritance from concrete classes does not result in subtypes. Thus subtyping and inheritance are somewhat independent.

Both Eiffel and Sather support multiple inheritance and parameterized classes. Multiple inheritance is an essential feature of each. For example, if a method is overridden in a subclass, multiple inheritance must be used if it is desired to call the original version of the method from the superclass.

Eiffel supports "anchor types". Anchor types allow the programmer to declare a type to be "like" that of another identifier. For example, suppose that in class C, x is declared to be an instance variable of type A. Then the expression like x can be used as a type expression within C. Let D be a subclass of C in which the type of x is changed to be of type B (recall that Eiffel allows covariant changes to the types of instance variables). Then all inherited occurrences of like x also change type to B. This construct provides expressiveness similar to Beta's virtual classes.

A special case of this construct is the use in Eiffel of like Current. Current is Eiffel's name for the object we have called self, and that C++ and Java call this. Thus the type like Current is very much like the MyType construct we introduce in Chapter 16.

The uses of anchor types can be replaced by using parameterized types, but this is not as convenient as the use of the anchor types. Unfortunately, the use of anchor types can result in type errors as they can results in covariant changes in parameter and instance variable types in subclasses.

7.3 Summary

In this chapter we discussed different varieties of object-oriented languages, ranging from class-based to object-based to multi-method languages. We also discussed interesting language features from Simula 67, Beta, Java, C++, Smalltalk, Eiffel, and Sather. While several of these have interesting features not discussed earlier, they all share many of the same structures discussed in this book. Interesting work has been done in understanding many of these features using techniques similar to those presented in the rest of this book.

In the next section of the book we will introduce the lambda calculus, a formal language often used for describing the semantics of programming languages. We begin with the simply-typed lambda calculus and build to a higher-order polymorphic lambda calculus supporting bounded parametric polymorphism and a construct known as "existential types", which are useful in modeling information hiding. In the rest of the book we will use the lambda calculus to understand the semantics of object-oriented languages and to verify the soundness of the type systems for these languages.

Historical Notes and References for Section I

Rather than attempting a full-scale history of object-oriented programming languages, we simply sketch some of the more influential events relating to statically-typed object-oriented languages, subtyping, and inheritance that have not already been described in earlier chapters. We postpone most of the discussion of more theoretical work until Section III.

Simula 67 is generally regarded as the first object-oriented programming language. It was designed as an extension of ALGOL 60 with features added to perform discrete simulations. It introduced the notions of class and inheritance, though no information-hiding facilities were provided in the language.

Smalltalk's design was influenced by Simula 67 and LOGO, a language used to teach programming to children. Smalltalk was originally conceived by Alan Kay as the programming language for the Dynabook, a prototype that eventually influenced the design of laptop computers. The idea was that the Dynabook would be easily programmable by the user via a language that supported the use of graphic interfaces, communications to external databases, and audio interfaces. Smalltalk-72 was the first version of the language, while several generations of improvements resulted in Smalltalk-80, the version of the language most commonly described.

Although Smalltalk is dynamically typed, attempts have been made to create statically typed variants. One of the earliest was the system of Borning and Ingalls [BI82]. A very interesting recent effort in designing a type system for Smalltalk resulted in the language Strongtalk [BG93]. The type system includes a type Self, which is similar to (and was influenced by) the MyType construct discussed in Chapter 16. That paper contains references to earlier attempts at providing static type systems for Smalltalk.

By the mid-80's it had become popular to add object-oriented features to more traditional languages. This resulted in hybrid languages like Objective C [Cox86], C++ [Str86, ES90], Object Pascal [Tes85], Modula-3 [CDG+88], Oberon [Wir88], Objective CAML [RV98], and CLOS [DG87].

Eiffel [Mey88, Mey92] was designed in the mid-1980's by Bertrand Meyer as a pure object-oriented language. It has a Pascal-like syntax, though it is not an extension of Pascal. We have already discussed many of the features of Eiffel in Section 4.2. An interesting feature of Eiffel not discussed earlier is its support for design-by-contract, with built-in features that enable run-time checking for preconditions, postconditions, variants, and invariants.

Cook [Coo89b] was one of the earliest to discuss Eiffel's type insecurities. Problems include support for covariant type changes in instance variable and parameter types (including support for indirect changes with the `like` construct) in subclasses, and the ability to hide methods in subclasses. The Eiffel 3 language reference [Mey92] discussed one possible fix – a link-time dataflow analysis of an entire program that determines whether there are possible type insecurities. Several years later, during an invited address at the OOPSLA conference, Meyer [Mey95b] proposed a different solution, termed "No polymorphic catcalls", that he claimed could be implemented with an incremental compiler.

At the time of the publication of this book, we know of no compiler that implements either of these solutions to the type insecurities of Eiffel, though we don't know why. It is possible that they are overly conservative, ruling out too many useful programs that would run without type error. Alternatively, these checks may be too expensive for practical use.

As noted earlier, Sather [Omo91] was a redesign of Eiffel that emphasized efficiency and fixed the problems with type safety. The language Trellis/Owl [SCB+86] seems to be the first language to introduce the `MyType` construct that we introduce in Chapter 16. The language was restricted to ensure that subclasses always gave rise to subtypes. Thus `MyType` was only allowed as the return type of methods. The language Emerald [BHJ+87] was an interesting object-oriented language that supported subtypes but no classes or inheritance. It did include type parameters and a notion similar to F-bounded polymorphism.

Beta [KMMPN87] is a purely object-oriented language that is a successor to Simula 67. Its virtual classes, discussed in Section 7.2.1, provide an alternative (and safe) approach to the flexibility of Eiffel. Beta uses both static and dynamic type checking in order to ensure type safety. When it cannot assure the safety of a section of code statically, it inserts dynamic checks to guarantee the absence of undetected type errors.

The programming language Java was designed to be an object-oriented language. While it shares most of the same syntax with C++, it differs from that language in several ways. Two of the most important are the use of garbage collection and its goal of platform independence. It was described briefly in Section 4.1.2.

The GJ [BOSW98] extension of Java is based on Pizza [OW97], an earlier extension by some of the same authors. An important feature of GJ is its ability to "retrofit" existing classes and interfaces by assigning polymorphic GJ types to existing non-polymorphic Java libraries. It also generates code that can be executed by existing Java Virtual Machine implementations. It is likely that GJ features will be included in a future version of Java. GJ is interesting in that its designers are members of the theoretical programming languages community. Pizza has some features normally found only in functional programming languages.

Other extensions of Java that supported parametric polymorphism were proposed in papers by Myers *et al.* [MBL97], Ageson *et al.* [AFM97], and Bruce and his students [Bru97, Bur98, Fos01]. Extensions to Java incorporating constructs similar to Beta's virtual classes have been proposed by Thorup and Torgersen [Tho97, Tor97, TT97]. Other proposed extensions of Java can be found in recent proceedings of the OOPSLA and ECOOP conferences.

Section 7.1 contained an extensive discussion of object-based and multi-method languages. As noted earlier, Castagna's book, *Object-Oriented Programming: A unified foundation* [Cas97], provides a comprehensive discussion of the theoretical foundations of multi-method languages.

To the earlier discussion we add that David Ungar's language Self [US87, CU89] has been an influential object-based programming language. Partially because it is dynamically typed, it required clever compiler optimizations to run efficiently. The technology developed for this has had a major impact on the implementations of other object-oriented languages, both class-based and object-based. Ungar's former student Craig Chambers [Cha95, CL95, CM99] has been one of the leading proponents of statically typed multi-method programming languages.

Peter Wegner has written a number of papers explaining the concepts of object-oriented programming languages. Two comprehensive surveys are "Dimensions of Object-Oriented Language Design" [Weg87] and "Concepts and Paradigms of Object-Oriented Programming" [Weg90].

There are several influential early theoretical papers on object-oriented programming languages. The first is John Reynold's 1975 paper [Rey75] "User-defined types and procedural data structures as complementary approaches to data abstraction." That paper compared user-defined types (essentially ADT's) with procedural data structures (essentially objects), comparing their advantages and disadvantages. Another early paper is also by Reynolds [Rey80]: "Using Category Theory to Design Implicit Conversions and Generic Operators". That paper discusses implicit conversions of values from one type to another (like those that occur with subtypes) from the point of view of category theory. (A later paper, "An algebraic model of subtype and inheritance" [BW90], by Bruce and Wegner, discussed similar issues in object-oriented languages, using order-sorted algebras rather than category theory.)

Another important early paper is Luca Cardelli's paper [Car88] (originally published as a conference paper in 1984), "A Semantics of Multiple Inheritance". That paper described objects as (recursive) records and carefully set out the rules for subtyping, including both depth (specializing the types of fields of a record) and breadth (adding new fields) subtyping for records, and the correct subtyping rules for function types – covariant in return types and contravariant in parameter types. This paper also presented a type-checking algorithm for languages with subtyping.

The Emerald designers, as well as America [Ame87, AvdL90] and his collaborators, were among the earliest to argue that the subtype and class hierarchies should not be confounded. (Recall that Emerald did not even support inheritance!) The arguments for this separation were also expounded forcefully by the Abel research group at HP Labs in [CHC90]. Cook's analysis [Coo92] of Smalltalk's collection classes provided further evidence of the disconnect between subclasses and subtypes.

Binary methods have long created difficulties for statically typed object-oriented languages. The paper, "On binary methods" [BCC+95], was written by a group of researchers with quite different views on the subject in order to lay out different options for dealing with binary methods. It provides a useful discussion of the problem, and strengths and weaknesses of various attempted solutions. In later chapters we will go into more detail on solutions involving F-bounded polymorphism and MyType.

Part II

Foundations:
The Lambda Calculus

8 Formal Language Descriptions and the Lambda Calculus

How can we be sure that a program is in the legal syntax for a given programming language? How can we be sure that the program will pass through the type checker without error? How do we know whether it will terminate and produce a particular result, run forever, or die with an error? Of course we could submit the program to a compiler for the language in order to answer the first two questions and then run it to obtain the answer to the third, or we could use an interpreter for the language to answer all three questions.

However, that line of reasoning simply begs the question: how do the compiler or interpreter writers know how to handle these issues? Many examples exist of languages where different compilers or interpreters give different answers to these questions for the same programs.

Language designers often try to answer these questions by providing language reference manuals written in discursive style. However, this method leaves open the possibility of ambiguity or other underspecification of the language. A more reliable way of answering these questions is to provide a formal, unambiguous description of the language at hand.

In this chapter we begin our introduction to the formal description of programming languages. We will be interested in careful formal descriptions of language syntax, type-checking rules, and semantics. While the formalism is not difficult, it does require some time to get used to the notation. As a result, in this chapter we focus on a formal description of the *lambda calculus*, a very simple functional language first introduced by Alonzo Church [Chu41] in order to describe notions of computability. Rather than look at the original untyped lambda calculus, we will instead focus on a typed version as this will allow us to exhibit the type-checking rules for the language.

While it may take some effort to learn to read these formal descriptions, the effort in learning to read them will pay off both with more precise and concise descriptions of languages. In particular, we will be able to see precisely what the rules are both for forming type-correct programs and how they will execute.

Aside from our use of the lambda calculus as a simple language in which to apply our formal analysis, our primary use of the lambda calculus will be as a tool to express the semantics of object-oriented languages. We will not attempt to give an in-depth presentation of the lambda calculus, instead presenting only the essentials needed here. Instead interested readers are invited to consult more specialized texts like [Bar84] or [HS86] for a more detailed presentation of the lambda calculus.

We begin this chapter with an introduction to the simply-typed lambda calculus. Because they will be helpful in modeling common features in programming languages, in the second section we add pairs, sums, records, and references. The following chapter adds higher-order features like parametric polymorphism and information hiding via existential types. It also introduces features to support recursive types and expressions as well as subtyping.

As a result, in the next section of the book we will be prepared to use these methods of providing formal descriptions to provide a careful formal definition of a simply-typed object-oriented language, $\mathcal{SOOL}$. Because we will be discussing a language and its translation into enriched forms of the lambda calculus, we will use different fonts for expressions of these languages. We continue to use a teletype-style font for the syntax of object-oriented languages, while we use an italicized font for the expressions of the lambda calculi introduced here.

8.1   The simply-typed lambda calculus

$\Lambda^{\rightarrow}$ In this section we present the simply-typed lambda calculus, written $\Lambda^{\rightarrow}$. In later sections, we add new types and constructs which make it easier to model real languages.

We can think of the typed lambda calculus as an assembly language for functional programming languages. The fundamental constructs of the language only include ways of constructing functions and applying functions to arguments. Because of our concern with typing issues, we will only consider the typed lambda calculus. The only thing that distinguishes the syntax of TYPED LAMBDA   the *typed lambda calculus* from the untyped version is that formal parameters CALCULUS   of functions must be provided with their types.

A first simple example of a function in the typed lambda calculus is the successor function on elements of type *Integer*.[1]

$$\lambda(x\colon Integer).\, x + \underline{1}$$

Functions of the typed lambda calculus are anonymous – that is, they do not have an associated name. The "$\lambda(x\colon Integer)$" indicates the function has a formal parameter x of type *Integer*. Readers familiar with LISP or Scheme will recognize the use of "lambda" to introduce function expressions (the use of lambda in LISP reportedly came from the lambda calculus). Other functional languages may introduce alternative notations such as "$fun(x\colon Integer)$" or "$function(x\colon Integer)$".

The body of the function appears after the period in lambda calculus expressions. The "." notation separating the parameters from function body has low precedence. As a result the function body normally includes as large a subexpression as possible. In the case of the successor function above, the body is $x+\underline{1}$.

We write the type of the successor function as *Integer* → *Integer*. This type describes functions that take an argument of type *Integer* and return an answer of type *Integer*. As in our earlier examples, the type $T \rightarrow U$ represents a function with domain T and range U.

We can apply a function to an argument simply by placing the argument to the right of the function. The argument may be surrounded by parentheses if desired, but this is not necessary. Thus

$$(\lambda(x\colon Integer).\, x + \underline{1})\underline{17}$$

and

$$(\lambda(x\colon Integer).\, x + \underline{1})(\underline{17})$$

both represent the application of the successor function to the number 17. Needless to say, the type of this expression is *Integer*.

The following example is a function which takes two numbers and adds them together:

$$\lambda(x\colon Integer).\, \lambda(y\colon Integer).\, x + y$$

---

1. We assume, at least temporarily, that the lambda calculus contains integer constants and the usual arithmetic functions. Later we will introduce a constant to represent the addition function. We will write constants used in the lambda calculus in the form $\underline{c}$ in order to distinguish them from variables or other expressions of the language.

Because we have written the two λ's successively, this actually represents a function which returns a function, rather than a function which takes two arguments. We can see this more clearly if we insert parentheses:

$$\lambda(x\colon Integer).\,(\lambda(y\colon Integer).\,x + y)$$

With the parentheses inserted, it is clearer that this is a function taking an argument x with type *Integer*, and whose body is

$$\lambda(y\colon Integer).\,x + y$$

In particular, the result of applying this function to the integer constant $\underline{17}$, written

$$(\lambda(x\colon Integer).\,\lambda(y\colon Integer).\,x + y)\underline{17}$$

would be a function of type *Integer* $\rightarrow$ *Integer* that takes an argument, y, and adds $\underline{17}$ to it. We will see later that it evaluates to

$$\lambda(y\colon Integer).\,\underline{17} + y$$

In particular, we must apply the original function to two arguments in succession in order to fully evaluate it:

$$(\lambda(x\colon Integer).\,\lambda(y\colon Integer).\,x + y)(\underline{17})(\underline{13})$$

This expression evaluates to the number 30.

Thus the type of the original function is *Integer* $\rightarrow$ (*Integer* $\rightarrow$ *Integer*). This is the type of functions which take an argument of type *Integer*, and return a function of type *Integer* $\rightarrow$ *Integer*.

That is really all there is to the typed lambda calculus. It contains constants, function definitions, and function applications. In order to specify completely the syntax of the typed lambda calculus, we need a notation to provide a formal description of the language syntax. Let us now introduce the notation to provide a formal description of the language.

The syntax of expressions of a language can be specified by context-free grammars which consist of a set of "productions" of the form:

$$a, b \in Cat ::= exp_1 \mid \ldots \mid exp_n$$

In this definition, *Cat* represents the set of expressions being defined. The expressions to the left indicate typical notation used for representing arbitrary expressions from this set; in this case, "a" and "b". The symbol "$::=$" can be read as "is composed of", while " | " separates alternatives on the right side of the definition. Each of the exp_i on the right side provides a template for the different kinds of elements which are contained in *Cat*. Thus *Cat* consists of expressions in the forms exp_1 through exp_n.

Here is a very simple grammar for non-empty strings of digits:

$$d \in Digit ::= \underline{0} \mid \underline{1} \mid \ldots \mid \underline{9}$$
$$s \in DigString ::= d \mid s\ d$$

A *Digit*, which will typically be written with the identifier *d*, is one of the integer constants representing values between 0 and 9. A *DigString* is either a single digit (the case *d*) or consists of a *DigString* (represented by *s*) followed by a digit.

From the first rule, $\underline{5}$ is a *Digit*. From the first alternative in the second rule, $\underline{5}$ is also a *DigString*. From the second alternative of that rule, $\underline{57}$ is also a *DigString* (because $\underline{5}$ is a *DigString* by the above and $\underline{7}$ is a *Digit* by the first rule). Longer elements of *DigString* can be constructed similarly.

We can use this notation to describe the syntax of the typed lambda calculus. The typed lambda calculus has two sorts of expressions: expressions representing types, and expressions representing typed values of the language. We begin with the definition of type expressions. In defining expressions of the typed lambda calculus we can start with an arbitrary collection, $\mathcal{TC}$, of TYPE EXPRESSION   type constants (which may include *Integer*, *Boolean*, etc.). The set, *Type*, of *type expressions* of the simply-typed lambda calculus, $\Lambda^{\rightarrow}$, is given by:

$$T \in Type ::= C \mid T_1 \rightarrow T_2 \mid (T)$$

where $C \in \mathcal{TC}$. Clearly this definition is parameterized by $\mathcal{TC}$, but for simplicity, we do not show this in the notation *Type*.

This definition states that the set *Type* is composed of (i) type constants *C* from the set $\mathcal{TC}$, (ii) expressions of the form $T_1 \rightarrow T_2$ where T_1 and T_2 are any elements of set *Type*, and (iii) expressions of the form *(T)* for *T* an element of set *Type*. In other words, type expressions are built up from type constants, *C*, by constructing function types, and using parentheses to group type expressions. Typical elements of *Type* include *Integer*, *Boolean*, *Integer* → *Integer*, *Boolean* → (*Integer* → *Integer*), and (*Boolean* → *Integer*) → *Integer*.

When defining the expressions of a typed programming language, we will PRE-EXPRESSION   be careful to distinguish the *pre-expressions* from the *expressions* of the language. The difference is that the pre-expressions are syntactically correct, but may not be typable, while the expressions are those that pass the type checker.

Expressions of the typed lambda calculus can include elements from an arbitrary set of constant expressions, $\mathcal{EC}$. Each of these constants comes with an associated type. For example, $\mathcal{EC}$ might include constants representing integers such as $\underline{0}, \underline{1}, \ldots$, all with type *Integer*; booleans such as $\underline{true}$ and *false*, with type *Boolean*; and operations such as *plus* and $\underline{mult}$ with type *Integer* $\rightarrow$ *Integer* $\rightarrow$ *Integer* (essentially prefix versions of "+" and "*"). We will leave $\mathcal{EC}$ unspecified most of the time, using constant symbols freely where it enhances our examples. As above, we will underline constants of the language to distinguish them.

The collection of pre-expressions of the typed lambda calculus, $\mathcal{TLCE}$, are given with respect to a collection of type constants, $\mathcal{TC}$, a collection of expression identifiers, $\mathcal{EI}$, and expression constants, $\mathcal{EC}$:

$$M, N \in \mathcal{TLCE} ::= c \mid x \mid \lambda(x\!:\!T).\,M \mid M\,N \mid (M)$$

where $x \in \mathcal{EI}$ and $c \in \mathcal{EC}$. As with types, this definition is parameterized by the choice of $\mathcal{TC}$, $\mathcal{EI}$, and $\mathcal{EC}$.

Pre-expressions of $\mathcal{TLCE}$, typically written as M, N, or variants decorated with primes or subscripts, are composed of constants, c, from $\mathcal{EC}$; identifiers, x, from $\mathcal{EI}$; function definitions, $\lambda(x\!:\!T).M$; and function applications, $M\,N$. Also, as with type expressions, any pre-expression, M, may be surrounded by parentheses, (M). All formal parameters in function definitions are associated with a type.

We treat function application as having higher precedence than lambda abstraction. Thus $\lambda(x\!:\!T).\,M\,N$ is equivalent to $\lambda(x\!:\!T).\,(M\,N)$.

In order to complete the specification of expressions of the typed lambda calculus, we need to write down type-checking rules that can be used to determine if a pre-expression is type correct. Expressions being type checked often include identifiers, typically introduced as formal parameters along with their types. In order to type check expressions we need to know what the type is for each identifier.

We use "$\triangleq$" here and later to indicate that an expression to the left of $\triangleq$ is defined by the expression to the right.

Free Identifiers   **Definition 8.1.1** *The collection of* free identifiers *of an expression M, written FI(M), is defined as follows:*

1. $FI(c) \triangleq \emptyset$, *for* $c \in \mathcal{EC}$,

2. $FI(x) \triangleq \{x\}$, *for* $x \in \mathcal{EI}$,

3. $FI(\lambda(x\colon T).\, M) \triangleq FI(M) - \{x\}$,

4. $FI(M\ N) \triangleq FI(M) \cup FI(N)$.

BOUND IDENTIFIERS   When an identifier is used as a formal parameter of a function, its occurrences in the function body are no longer free. Instead we say they are *bound identifiers*. Thus $FI((plus\ x)\ y) = \{x, y\}$, but $FI(\lambda(x\colon Integer).\, (plus\ x)\ y) = \{y\}$. Notice that bound identifiers are supplied with a type when they are declared as formal parameters, but free identifiers are not textually associated with types in the expressions containing them.

Thus the type-checking rules require information about the type s of free identifiers. This information is provided by a *static type environment*, $\mathcal{E}$, which associates types with expression identifiers.

Definition 8.1.2 *A static type environment, $\mathcal{E}$, is a finite set of associations between identifiers and type expressions of the form $x\colon T$, where each x is unique in $\mathcal{E}$ and T is a type. If $x\colon T \in \mathcal{E}$, then we sometimes write $\mathcal{E}(x) = T$.*

TYPE-CHECKING RULES   *Type-checking rules* can be in one of two forms. A rule of the form

$$\mathcal{E} \vdash M\colon T$$

indicates that with the typing of free identifiers given in $\mathcal{E}$, the expression M has type T.

A rule of the form

$$\frac{\mathcal{E}_1 \vdash M_1\colon T_1, \ldots, \mathcal{E}_n \vdash M_n\colon T_n}{\mathcal{E} \vdash M\colon T}$$

indicates that with the typing of free identifiers in $\mathcal{E}$, expression M has type T if the assertions above the horizontal line all hold. Thus the hypotheses of the rule all occur above the horizontal line, while the conclusion is placed below the line.

Now that we have a formalism to express type-checking rules, we can define the set of (legal) expressions of the typed lambda calculus by specifying the rules for determining how to assign types to expressions. The collection EXPRESSION   of *expressions* of the typed lambda calculus with respect to $\mathcal{TC}$ and $\mathcal{EC}$ is the collection of pre-expressions which can be assigned a type by the rules in Figure 8.1.

The intuitive meaning of these rules should be fairly clear. The *Identifier* rule states that if $\mathcal{E}$ indicates that identifier x has type T, then x has that type. The *Constant* rule states that a constant has whatever type is associated with

Identifier	$\mathcal{E} \cup \{x\colon T\} \vdash x\colon T$
Constant	$\mathcal{E} \vdash c\colon C$

where $C \in \mathcal{TC}$ is the pre-assigned type for constant $c \in \mathcal{EC}$.

Function	$\dfrac{\mathcal{E} \cup \{x\colon T\} \vdash M\colon T'}{\mathcal{E} \vdash \lambda(x\colon T).\,M\colon T \to T'}$
Application	$\dfrac{\mathcal{E} \vdash M\colon T \to T', \quad \mathcal{E} \vdash N\colon T}{\mathcal{E} \vdash M\,N\colon T'}$
Parens	$\dfrac{\mathcal{E} \vdash M\colon T}{\mathcal{E} \vdash (M)\colon T}$

Figure 8.1   Typing rules for expressions of the typed lambda calculus.

it in $\mathcal{EC}$. Skipping the *Function* rule momentarily, the *Application* rule states that a function application $M\,N$ has type T' as long as the type of the function, M, is of the form $T \to T'$, and the actual argument, N, has type T, matching the type of the domain of M.

The *Function* rule is the most complex. The idea is that because the formal parameter of the function occurs in the body, the formal parameter and its type need to be added to the environment when type checking the body. Thus if $\lambda(x\colon T).\,M$ is type checked in environment $\mathcal{E}$, then the body, M, should be type checked in the environment $\mathcal{E} \cup \{x\colon T\}$. (Recall that the environment $\mathcal{E} \cup \{x\colon T\}$ is legal only if x does not already occur in $\mathcal{E}$.)

For example, in typing the function $\lambda(x\colon Integer).\,x+\underline{1}$, the body, $x+\underline{1}$, should be type checked in an environment in which x has type *Integer*.

Type-checking rules can also be interpreted algorithmically by reading the rules from the bottom left in a clockwise direction. For example, suppose we wish to type check an expression of the form $M\,N$ under the assumptions in a type environment $\mathcal{E}$. An expression of this form is found on the bottom left of the *Application* rule. Proceed clockwise to the top of the rule and we see that we need to find the types of M and N under $\mathcal{E}$. If the first has type $T \to T'$ and the second has type T (i.e., the domain of the first is the same as the type of the second), then the resulting type of $M\,N$ is T'.

The *Parens* rule simply states that adding parentheses has no effect on the type of an expression. From now on, we will omit type-checking rules for adding parentheses to expressions.

We see how these rules are used to assign types to expressions by looking at a few examples. Let *plus* be the constant with type *Integer* → *Integer* → *Integer* representing addition that was discussed earlier. We wish to determine the type of the expression $\lambda(x: Integer). (plus \ x)x$ in the empty environment $\mathcal{E}_0 = \emptyset$.

In working through this example, we write "??" as the type for expressions whose types have not yet been determined. Thus we start with

$$\mathcal{E}_0 \vdash \lambda(x: Integer). (plus \ x)x: \ ??$$

and use the rules to figure out the appropriate type to replace "??".

By the rule *Function*, to type check this function we must check the body $(plus \ x)x$ in the environment $\mathcal{E}_1 = \{x: Integer\}$:

$$\mathcal{E}_1 \vdash (plus \ x)x: \ ??$$

Because the body is a function application, we type check the function and argument to make sure their types match. Type checking the argument is easy as:

(8.1) $\mathcal{E}_1 \vdash x: Integer$

by rule *Identifier*.

Type-checking *plus x* is a bit more complex, because it is a function application as well. However, by rule *Constant*,

(8.2) $\mathcal{E}_1 \vdash plus: Integer \rightarrow Integer \rightarrow Integer$,

and by rule *Identifier*, we again get $\mathcal{E}_1 \vdash x: Integer$. Because the domain of the type of *plus* and the type of x are the same,

(8.3) $\mathcal{E}_1 \vdash plus \ x: Integer \rightarrow Integer$

by lines 8.2, 8.1, and the *Application* rule.

By another use of the *Application* rule with lines 8.3 and 8.1,

(8.4) $\mathcal{E}_1 \vdash (plus \ x) \ x: Integer$

Finally, by the *Function* rule and line 8.4,

(8.5) $\mathcal{E}_0 \vdash \lambda(x: Integer). (plus \ x)x: Integer \rightarrow Integer$

Now that we have typed this expression, it is easy to see how to type the following expression: $(\lambda(x: Integer). (plus \ x)x)\underline{17}$. Because the type of the function is given in line 8.5 as *Integer → Integer*, and $\mathcal{E}_0 \vdash \underline{17}$: *Integer*, it follows from the *Application* rule that

(8.6) $\mathcal{E}_0 \vdash (\lambda(x: \mathit{Integer}).\, (\underline{\mathit{plus}}\ x)x)\ \underline{17}$: *Integer*

With the above definitions and type-checking rules, we can now determine what are the legal expressions of $\Lambda^{\rightarrow}$, and we can determine their types. However, we do not yet have any information on how to evaluate expressions. That is, our intuitive understanding of function definition and application and the intuitive understanding of the constants used leads us to believe that the result of evaluating $(\lambda(x: \mathit{Integer}).\, (\underline{\mathit{plus}}\ x)\ x)\ \underline{17}$ should give us the value 34. However, we would like to provide formal rules for evaluating these expressions so that there is no ambiguity about how the evaluation takes place or the resulting answer.

SUBSTITUTION

SUBSTITUTION

The formal computation rules of the typed lambda calculus depend on a careful definition of *substitution* in lambda expressions. The (β) "reduction rule" for evaluating lambda expressions given later is formulated in terms of replacing all occurrences of an identifier in an expression by another expression. Rather strange errors can occur if one is not careful in defining such substitutions. As a result we give a precise definition of *substitution* in the lambda calculus.

Definition 8.1.3 *We write [N/x] M to denote the result of replacing all free occurrences of identifier x by N in expression M.*

1. *$[N/x]\, c \triangleq c$, if $c \in \mathcal{EC}$,*

2. *$[N/x]\, x \triangleq N$,*

3. *$[N/x]\, y \triangleq y$, if $y \neq x$,*

4. *$[N/x]\, (L\ M) \triangleq ([N/x]\, L)\, ([N/x]\, M)$,*

5. *$[N/x]\, (\lambda(y: T).\, M) \triangleq \lambda(y: T).\, ([N/x]\, M)$, if $y \neq x$ and $y \notin FI(N)$,*

6. *$[N/x]\, (\lambda(x: T).\, M) \triangleq \lambda(x: T).\, M$.*

The first three rules should be clear: no identifiers exist in constants, so no changes are made; if substituting for an identifier, replace it if the names match, otherwise no changes should be made. The fourth rule simply states that to substitute into a function application, just substitute into the function and its argument.

The last two rules deal with the case of substitution into function definitions. What to do depends on whether or not the identifier being substituted for is the same as the name of the formal parameter. In the last rule, where x is the name of the formal parameter of the function, no replacement is made in the body of the function because all values of x in the body are "bound" by the λ. Looked at from a traditional programming language point of view, the use of x as a formal parameter creates a "hole" in the static scope of the free x, no instance of the free x can occur inside the function.[2] As a result no substitutions should be made.

The fifth rule is similar to the fourth in that if the name of the formal parameter is different from the identifier being substituted for, we just make the substitution in the function body. However, this rule only holds if the name of the formal parameter is not a free identifier in N, the expression being substituted in. Here is an example showing why this restriction is necessary.

Let M be the function $\lambda(y\colon T).\, x + y$, a function which adds the formal parameter to a free identifier, x. Suppose we substitute the expression $y * y$, where y is a free identifier, in place of x. If we blindly apply rule (5), without observing the restriction, then we would obtain $\lambda(y\colon T).\, y * y + y$, an expression which squares the formal parameter and then adds it to itself.

On the other hand, if we had written M as $\lambda(z\colon T).\, x + z$, and then performed the same substitution, we would obtain $\lambda(z\colon T).\, y * y + z$. This is a function which takes a parameter and adds it to the square of the value of the free identifier y.

Thus these two substitutions give quite different results, even though we think of $\lambda(y\colon T).\, x + y$ and $\lambda(z\colon T).\, x + z$ as being essentially the same function. Because the second result is the expected one, the restrictions on rule (5) do not allow the substitution of an expression which includes an identifier which can be "captured" by the formal parameter of the function.

However, this restriction in rule (4) leaves an important gap in the definition of substitution. Substitution of N into the body of a function with formal parameter y is not defined if it results in the capture of a free identifier y occurring in N. However, we can handle this case by formalizing the intuition that functions which differ only in the names of formal parameters may be identified (*i.e.*, treated as being identical).

We can write this identification more formally as

$$\lambda(x\colon T).\, M \equiv \lambda(y\colon T).\, ([y/x]\, M), \text{ if } y \notin FI(M).$$

---

2. See a standard programming languages textbook for details.

Thus $\lambda(x: Integer). (\overline{plus\ x)}\ x)$ will be considered to be the same expression as $\lambda(y: Integer). (\overline{plus\ y)}\ y)$. In the literature these expressions are said to be α-convertible, and the process of changing from the left side to the right is called α-conversion.

The restriction on the new name of the formal parameter is again to avoid capture of free identifiers by the new parameter name. For example, the function $\lambda(x: Integer). (\overline{plus\ x)}\ y)$, where y is the name of a free identifier, is not at all the same as $\lambda(\overline{y: Integer}). (\overline{plus\ y)}\ y)$, the expression obtained by changing the formal parameter name from x to y. The problem occurs because the first y is now captured by the lambda binding of y that occurs at the head of the expression. The first function adds the value of the parameter to a fixed value y, whereas the second doubles the value of the parameter.

The identification of expressions which differ only in the names of formal parameters can overcome the restriction in the next to last case in the definition of $[N/x]\ M$. We fix that case to be

5′. $[N/x]\ (\lambda(y: T). M) \stackrel{\Delta}{=} \lambda(y': T). [N/x]\ M'),\ if\ y \neq x.$

where $y' \stackrel{\Delta}{=} y$ and $M' \stackrel{\Delta}{=} M$ if $y \notin FI(N)$. If $y \in FI(N)$, then let z be a new identifier not occurring in M or N, and let $y' \stackrel{\Delta}{=} z$ and $M' \stackrel{\Delta}{=} [z/y]\ M$.

Thus if there is a danger that a free identifier of N might be bound by making the substitution, we α convert the formal parameter name before making the substitution.

Now we can write down the reduction or evaluation rules for the lambda calculus. Each rule represents a single step in the evaluation of an expression. Rules are written as transformation rules where the expression to the left side of the double arrow is transformed to the expression on the right side. The label over the double arrow is the name of the rule.

REDUCTION RULES   **Definition 8.1.4** *The reduction rules for the typed lambda calculus are given by*

(β) $(\lambda(x: T). M)\ N \stackrel{\beta}{\twoheadrightarrow} [N/x]\ M.$

(η) $\lambda(x: T). (M\ x) \stackrel{\eta}{\twoheadrightarrow} M.$

The β rule is the main computation rule for the lambda calculus. A function applied to an actual parameter results in evaluating the function body where all occurrences of the formal parameter have been replaced by the actual parameter (changing names of free identifiers as necessary to avoid name clashes). For example, $(\lambda(x: Integer). (\underline{plus}\ x)x)\ \underline{17} \stackrel{\beta}{\twoheadrightarrow} (\underline{plus}\ \underline{17})\underline{17}.$ The

β rule allows us to replace all free occurrences of x in the function body by 17.

The η rule is useful in minimizing clutter by reducing expressions formed by applying a function to an identifier and then using that identifier as a function parameter. For example if $f = \lambda(x : Integer). \, (plus \; x)$, then $f \xrightarrow{\eta} plus$. This should be plausible as applying f to a parameter M always results in *plus M* by the β rule.

Other rules (called δ rules, and written with *dred*) may be introduced to take care of evaluating constants and predefined functions (like evaluating arithmetic operations). For example, we could include the rule

$$(plus \; \underline{17}) \; \underline{17} \xrightarrow{\delta} \underline{34}$$

We can write $M \twoheadrightarrow N$ when we don't care to note which of the reduction rules is being applied. The notation $M \twoheadrightarrow^* N$ indicates that N can be derived from M by the application of zero or more reduction steps.

In the lambda calculus one can apply a reduction rule to any subexpression of an expression. For example, if M is a lambda expression, then

$$M \, ((\lambda(x : Integer). \, (plus \; x) \; x) \; \underline{17})$$

first reduces to

$$M \, (plus \; \underline{17}) \underline{17})$$

using β-reduction, and then to

$$M \, \underline{34}$$

using a δ-rule.

SUBJECT REDUCTION The *subject reduction* theorem for the typed lambda calculus is an important result which implies that the type system is consistent with the computation rules. It states that reduction or evaluation of an expression results in a value with the same type as the original expression.

Theorem 8.1.5 *(Subject reduction) Let M be an expression of the typed lambda calculus such that $\mathcal{E} \vdash M : T$. If $M \twoheadrightarrow^* M'$ then $\mathcal{E} \vdash M' : T$.*

The proof of the subject reduction theorem is omitted here, but can be found in any text on the lambda calculus.

A simple consequence of the theorem is that if an expression has type *Integer*, then the subject reduction theorem implies that if reduction of the expression ever terminates, then the final value will be a value of type *Integer*. That is, it will be an integer.

Because the static type system should reflect important statically deter-
minable properties of expression evaluation, a subject reduction theorem is
generally required to show that the type system is reasonable. We will be
interested in proving similar soundness properties of object-oriented languages by translating them into variants of the typed lambda calculus.

NORMAL FORM   An expression is said to be in *normal form* if none of the reduction rules
apply. All expressions of the pure typed lambda calculus with no constants
or δ rules evaluate to a unique normal form. While this form is very convenient, readers who have studied the theory of effectively computable functions will recall that this property implies that the language is actually quite
restricted in its expressiveness.[3] We will increase the expressiveness of the
typed lambda calculus in the following sections by adding new types and
expressions.

We will need a much richer lambda calculus to model object-oriented languages. This richer calculus is needed even for languages like ML and Ada
that support parametric polymorphism. In the next few sections we will
define and provide the type-checking and computation rules for first an extended typed lambda calculus with pairs, records, and references. Then in
Chapter 9 we introduce the polymorphic lambda calculus, an extension of
the typed lambda calculus that includes both parametric polymorphism and
"existential" types.

8.2   Adding pairs, sums, records, and references

In the last section we defined the simply-typed lambda calculus. This calculus included expressions defining functions and applying functions to arguments. While we can encode many language features in the pure lambda
calculus, it is more convenient to extend the syntax to provide a closer match
to real languages. In this section we define an extension of the lambda calcu-
$\Lambda_{rr}^{\rightarrow}$ lus, $\Lambda_{rr}^{\rightarrow}$, which includes tuples, records, sums, and references (variables).

TUPLE TYPE   Ordered tuples are written in the form $\langle a_1, \ldots, a_n \rangle$ and have type $T_1 \times \ldots \times$
T_n where each T_i is the type of the corresponding a_i. Tuple types will be used
to represent the domain of functions taking several parameters.

---

3. The relevant theorem is the following: For any effectively enumerable collection of *total* functions from integers to integers (*i.e.*, functions defined on all integers), there is an effectively
computable function not contained in that collection. Expressions of the typed lambda calculus
represent total functions and can be effectively enumerated. Thus the theorem implies there is
an effectively computable function not contained in the typed lambda calculus.

The projection operations, $proj_i$, extract the *ith* component of a tuple. Thus $proj_i(\langle a_1, \ldots, a_n \rangle) = a_i$.

RECORD TYPE

Records are written in the form $\{| l_1 \colon T_1 \colon = M_1, \ldots, l_n \colon T_n \colon = M_n |\}$. Notice that each labeled field is provided with its type. The type of a record of this form is written as $\{| l_1 \colon T_1; \ldots; l_n \colon T_n |\}$. Dot notation is used to extract the value of a field from a record: $\{| l_1 \colon T_1 \colon = M_1, \ldots, l_n \colon T_n \colon = M_n |\}.l_i = M_i$.

SUM TYPE

A *sum type*, $T_1 + \ldots + T_n$, represents a disjoint union of the types, where each element contains information to indicate which summand it comes from, even if several of the T_i are identical. Suppose M is an expression from a type T_i. The expression $in_i^{T_1, \ldots, T_n}(M)$ injects the value M into the *ith* component of the sum $T_1 + \ldots + T_n$. If M is an expression of type $T_1 + \ldots + T_n$, then an expression of the form

$$case\ M\ of\ x_1 \colon T_1\ then\ E_1 \parallel \ \ldots \ \parallel \ x_n \colon T_n\ then\ E_n$$

represents a statement listing the possible expressions to evaluate depending on which summand M is a part of. Thus if M was created by $in_i^{T_1, \ldots, T_n}(M')$ for some M' of type T_i then evaluating the *case* statement will result in evaluating E_i using M' as the value of x_i.

The expression

$$in_1^{Integer, Integer \rightarrow Integer}(\underline{47})$$

is an expression with type *Integer*+(*Integer* $\rightarrow$ *Integer*). It represents injecting the number 47 into the sum type.

The following function takes elements of the sum type, *Integer*+(*Integer* $\rightarrow$ *Integer*), and uses *case* to compute an integer value. The value depends on whether the element of the sum type arose by injecting an integer or by injecting a function from integers to integers:

$$isFirst = \lambda(y \colon Integer + (Integer \rightarrow Integer)) \, . \, case\ y\ of$$
$$x \colon Integer\ then\ x * \underline{2} \parallel$$
$$f \colon Integer \rightarrow Integer\ then\ f(0)$$

In this example, the parameter y comes from a sum type, the first of whose summands is *Integer*, while the second is the function type, *Integer* $\rightarrow$ *Integer*. If the parameter comes from the first summand, then it must represent an integer, x, and one is added to the value. If it comes from the second summand, then it represents a function from integers to integers, denoted f, and the function is applied to 0. This example shows how the value originally injected in the sum is represented by an identifier in the appropriate branch of the case, and thus can be used in determining the value to be returned.

Note that the *case* expression is a more secure alternative than providing expressions of the form $out_i(M)$. The problem with using an out_i expression is that if, for example, a value was injected into the first summand, but out_i, for some $i \neq 1$ is applied to the resulting value, an error has occurred. To preserve type safety, however, some default value of the appropriate type would have to be returned. The *case* expression appears better because all alternatives must be clearly specified and no default values are necessary.

REFERENCE TYPE   Finally we introduce *reference types* in order to represent updatable variables. If M has type *Ref T*, then we can think of it as denoting a location which can hold a value of type T. The expression *val M* will denote the value stored at that location. In most procedural languages, programmers are not required to distinguish between variables (representing locations) and the values they denote. Instead, the compiler or interpreter automatically selects the appropriate attribute (location or l-value versus value or r-value) based on context without requiring the programmer to annotate the variable. The functional language ML (which supports references) does require the programmer to write $!x$ when the value stored in x is required, while x alone always denotes the location.

null EXPRESSION   The *null* expression is a special constant representing the null reference, a reference that does not point to anything. Evaluating the expression *val null* will always result in an error. If M is a reference, with type *Ref T*, and N has type T, then the expression $M := N$ denotes the assignment of N to M. That is, the value of N is stored in the location denoted by M.

With that informal introduction to the extension, we are ready to define the set of types in $\Lambda_{rr}^{\rightarrow}$.

Definition 8.2.1 *Let $\mathcal{L}$ be an infinite collection of labels, and let $\mathcal{TC}$ be a collection of type constants. The type expressions of $\Lambda_{rr}^{\rightarrow}$ are given by the following grammar:*

$$T \in Type ::= C \mid Void \mid T_1 \rightarrow T_2 \mid T_1 \times \ldots \times T_n \mid T_1 + \ldots + T_n \mid$$
$$\{\!| l_1 : T_1; \ldots; l_n : T_n |\!\} \mid Ref\ T \mid Command$$

where $l_i \in \mathcal{L}$, and, as before, $C \in \mathcal{TC}$ represents type constants (like *Integer*, *Double*, etc.). The type *Void* is the type of zero tuples. It will be used as the return type of commands or statements and as the parameter type for parameterless functions. It will have only one (trivial) value, $\langle \rangle$. The other types represent function types, product (tuple) types, sum (or disjoint union) types, record types, and reference types (the types of variables), as discussed above. The final type, *Command*, represents the type of statements, expressions like assignments that are evaluated simply for their side effects.

We next define the collection of *pre-expressions* of $\Lambda_{rr}^{\rightarrow}$. As before, they are pre-expressions, because the only valid expressions are those which type-check properly:

$$M \in \mathcal{RLCE} ::= x \mid c \mid \langle\rangle \mid \lambda(x\colon T).\,M \mid M\,N \mid \langle M_1, \ldots, M_n \rangle \mid proj_i(M) \mid$$
$$case\;M\;of\;x_1\colon T_1\;then\;E_1 \parallel\;\ldots\;\parallel\;x_n\colon T_n\;then\;E_n \mid$$
$$in_i^{T_1,\ldots,T_n}(M) \mid \{\!| l_1\colon T_1 := M_1, \ldots, l_n\colon T_n := M_n |\!\} \mid M.l_i \mid$$
$$ref\,M \mid null \mid val\,M \mid if\,B\,then\,\{\,M\,\}\,else\,\{\,N\,\} \mid$$
$$nop \mid N := M \mid M;\,N$$

In the above definition, $x \in \mathcal{EI}, c \in \mathcal{EC},$ and $l_i \in \mathcal{L}$. As noted above, the expression "$\langle\rangle$" represents a zero-tuple with type *Void*. The expressions involving function definition and application are familiar from the lambda calculus. The expressions for dealing with tuples, sums, records, and references were introduced above. The expression *if B then { M } else { N }* represents the usual conditional statement, returning either the value of M or N, depending on whether or not B is true.

The last three expressions represent statements. The expression *nop* is a constant that represents a statement that has no effect. The expression $N :=$ M represents an assignment statement, while $M;\,N$ indicates the sequencing of the two statements. Its intended meaning is similar to that of the language ML: do the first statement for the side effect and then return the value of the second. We can sequence as many expressions as we like. Most of the time, all of the expressions in the sequence will have type *Command*, in which case the expressions are evaluated as statements for their side effects, just as in Pascal, C, C++, and Java.

We could have added other expressions to the language such as various loop constructs; however it will be most convenient to work with a small language. We will add recursion later, which will provide the necessary expressive power to model real programming languages.

As before, the type-checking rules for these expressions require information about the types of free identifiers in an expression, provided through a static type environment, $\mathcal{E}$. The type-checking rules for expressions of $\Lambda_{rr}^{\rightarrow}$ are given in Figures 8.2 and 8.3.

As we observed earlier, these rules can be read algorithmically by starting with the bottom left side and proceeding clockwise around the rule. Thus to find the type of a pre-expression of the form $M.l_i$ with respect to a static type assignment $\mathcal{E}$, first find the type of M. If it is of the form $\{\!| l_1\colon T_1; \ldots; l_n\colon T_n |\!\}$,

Identifier $$\mathcal{E} \cup \{x\colon T\} \vdash x\colon T$$

Constant $$\mathcal{E} \vdash c\colon N$$

Void $$\mathcal{E} \vdash \langle\rangle\colon Void$$

Function $$\frac{\mathcal{E} \cup \{x\colon S\} \vdash M\colon T}{\mathcal{E} \vdash \lambda(x\colon S).\, M\colon S \to T}$$

Application $$\frac{\mathcal{E} \vdash M\colon S \to T, \qquad \mathcal{E} \vdash N\colon S}{\mathcal{E} \vdash M\,N\colon T}$$

Tuple $$\frac{\mathcal{E} \vdash M_i\colon T_i, \ \ \text{for all } 1 \le i \le n}{\mathcal{E} \vdash \langle M_1, \ldots, M_n \rangle\colon T_1 \times \ldots \times T_n}$$

Projection $$\frac{\mathcal{E} \vdash M\colon T_1 \times \ldots \times T_n}{\mathcal{E} \vdash proj_i(M)\colon T_i} \ \text{for all } 1 \le i \le n$$

Sum $$\frac{\mathcal{E} \vdash M\colon T_i, \ \ \text{for some } 1 \le i \le n}{\mathcal{E} \vdash in_i^{T_1,\ldots,T_n}(M)\colon T_1 + \ldots + T_n}$$

Case $$\frac{\begin{array}{c}\mathcal{E} \vdash M\colon T_1 + \ldots + T_n, \\ \mathcal{E} \cup \{x_i\colon T_i\} \vdash E_i\colon U, \ \ \text{for all } 1 \le i \le n\end{array}}{\mathcal{E} \vdash case\ M\ of\ x_1\colon T_1\ then\ E_1 \ \| \ \ldots \ \| \ x_n\colon T_n\ then\ E_n\colon U}$$

Record $$\frac{\mathcal{E} \vdash M_i\colon T_i, \ \ \text{for all } 1 \le i \le n}{\mathcal{E} \vdash \{\!| \, l_1\colon T_1 := M_1, \ldots, l_n\colon T_n := M_n \, |\!\}\colon \{\!| \, l_1\colon T_1; \ldots; l_n\colon T_n \, |\!\}}$$

Selection $$\frac{\mathcal{E} \vdash M\colon \{\!| \, l_1\colon T_1; \ldots; l_n\colon T_n \, |\!\}}{\mathcal{E} \vdash M.l_i\colon T_i} \ \text{for all } 1 \le i \le n$$

Figure 8.2   Type-checking rules for $\Lambda_{rr}^{\rightarrow}$, part 1.

Reference
$$\frac{\mathcal{E} \vdash M : T}{\mathcal{E} \vdash ref\, M : Ref\, T}$$

Null
$$\mathcal{E} \vdash null : Ref\, T, \ \ for\ any\ type\ T$$

Value
$$\frac{\mathcal{E} \vdash M : Ref\, T}{\mathcal{E} \vdash val\, M : T}$$

No op
$$\mathcal{E} \vdash nop : Command$$

Assignment
$$\frac{\mathcal{E} \vdash N : Ref\, T, \quad \mathcal{E} \vdash M : T}{\mathcal{E} \vdash N := M : Command}$$

Conditional
$$\frac{\mathcal{E} \vdash B : Boolean, \quad \mathcal{E} \vdash M : T, \quad \mathcal{E} \vdash N : T}{\mathcal{E} \vdash if\, B\, then\, \{\, M\, \}\, else\, \{\, N\, \} : T}$$

Sequencing
$$\frac{\mathcal{E} \vdash M : S, \quad \mathcal{E} \vdash N : T}{\mathcal{E} \vdash M; N : T}$$

Figure 8.3 Type-checking rules for $\Lambda_{rr}^{\rightarrow}$, part 2.

then the type of $M.l_i$ is T_i. Otherwise no rule applies and the type-checking algorithm fails.

The *case* and *if-then-else* expressions require that the types of the branches all be the same type. This way a result of the same type is returned no matter which branch is selected.

If we have a sequence of two or more statements, the *Sequencing* rule indicates that the type of the sequence is the type of the last expression. Normally, all statements in the sequence will have type *Command*, but we also allow more general types.

The collection of expressions of $\Lambda_{rr}^{\rightarrow}$ with respect to $\mathcal{E}$ is the set of preexpressions that can be assigned types with respect to the type-assignment axioms and rules.

We will sometimes find it convenient to use certain abbreviations in writing expressions of the lambda calculus. Two important abbreviations have to do with writing *n-ary functions* and *let expressions*. For each of these abbreviations, we will provide the corresponding derived typing rule.

n-ARY FUNCTIONS
LET EXPRESSIONS

We will find it convenient to write

$$\lambda(id_1\colon T_1, \ldots, id_n\colon T_n).\, M$$

as an abbreviation for

$$\lambda(arg\colon T_1 \times \ldots \times T_n).\, [proj_i(arg)/id_i]_{i=1,\ldots,n}\, M.$$

Thus an n-ary function is an abbreviation for a function of a single argument that takes an n-tuple. When expanded, each of the individual parameters is replaced by an appropriate projection from the n-tuple. For example

$$\lambda(x\colon Integer, y\colon Integer).\, plus\ x\ y$$

abbreviates

$$\lambda(p\colon Integer \times Integer).\, plus\ (proj_1(p))\ (proj_2(p))$$

The derived typing rule for n-ary functions is

$$n\text{-}ary\ Function \qquad \frac{\mathcal{E} \cup \{id_1\colon T_1, \ldots, id_n\colon T_n\} \vdash M\colon U}{\mathcal{E} \vdash \lambda(id_1\colon T_1, \ldots, id_n\colon T_n).\, M\colon T_1 \times \ldots \times T_n \to U}$$

We will write *let* $x\colon T = M$ *in* N *end* as an abbreviation for $(\lambda(x\colon T).\, N)\ M$. Thus, introducing an identifier for an expression is modelled by writing a function with that identifier as the parameter, and then applying the function to the intended value for the identifier. The β-rule verifies our intuition that let-expressions allow us to use the identifier to stand for the appropriate expression.

We have the following derived typing rule for let expressions:

$$Let \qquad \frac{\mathcal{E} \cup \{x\colon T\} \vdash N\colon S, \qquad \mathcal{E} \vdash M\colon T}{\mathcal{E} \vdash let\ x\colon T = M\ in\ N\ end\colon S}$$

We leave it as an exercise for the reader to verify that the typing rules for n-ary functions and let expressions are derivable from the other typing rules when the abbreviations are expanded.

Along with the β and η conversion rules from the last section, there are now similar rules for expressions of the new types introduced here. Some of these rules can be found in Figure 8.4.

At this point we warn the reader that, because of the addition of assignment statements, the reduction rules provided in the figure are not sufficient

$$\beta \qquad\qquad (\lambda(x\colon T).\,M)N \twoheadrightarrow [N/x]\,M$$

$$\eta \qquad\qquad \lambda(x\colon T).\,(M\,x) \twoheadrightarrow M$$

$$\pi \qquad\qquad proj_i(\langle M_1,\dots,M_n\rangle) \twoheadrightarrow M_i$$

$$\sigma \qquad case\,(inj_i^{T_1,\dots,T_n}(M))\,of\,x_1\colon T_1\,then\,E_1\;\|\;\dots\;\|\;x_n\colon T_n\,then\,E_n \twoheadrightarrow$$
$$[M/x_i]\,E_i,\,for\;1\le i\le n.$$

$$\xi \qquad\quad \{\!|\,l_1\colon T_1 = M_1,\dots,l_n\colon T_n = M_n\,|\!\}.l_i \twoheadrightarrow M_i,\,for\;1\le i\le n.$$

$$\rho \qquad\qquad (val\,(ref\,M)) \twoheadrightarrow M$$

$$true \qquad\qquad if\,true\,then\,M\,else\,N \twoheadrightarrow M$$

$$false \qquad\qquad if\,false\,then\,M\,else\,N \twoheadrightarrow M$$

$$\chi \qquad\qquad (x\colon = M;\,val\,x) \twoheadrightarrow M$$

Figure 8.4   Computation rules for $\Lambda_{rr}^{\rightarrow}$.

to perform the computations that one would normally expect an interpreter for this language to perform. The problem is that we have not provided an explicit representation of memory. Consider the following example

$$let\;\; x\colon Ref\,Integer = ref\,\underline{5}\;in$$
$$let\;\; y\colon Ref\,Integer = ref\,\underline{2}\;in$$
$$x\colon = val\,x + \underline{1};\,y\colon = val\,x - \underline{2};\,val\,x$$
$$end$$
$$end$$

where we use the *let* clause abbreviation just introduced. None of the computation rules apply to the sequence of expressions in the body of the let clauses because the assignment to y is between the assignment to x and the *val x* expression. Yet it is clear that the entire expression should evaluate to 6.

If we were interested in writing an interpreter, we could write computation rules that are based on taking the triple of an expression, an environment representing the current values of identifiers (where the value of a variable would be a location in memory), and an expression representing the values held in memory. Evaluating an expression would result in a pair consisting of the value of the expression and the new memory configuration obtained after evaluating the expression.

Because the intuition behind the evaluation of such expressions should be clear, we do not bother to write down the formal computation rules, but instead leave that as an exercise for the reader. Thus the computation rules provided so far, as well as those to come, should be treated as a very incomplete set of computation rules that are provided only to give intuition for the meaning of expressions.

8.3   Summary

In this chapter we introduced formal notations for describing the syntax of a language and a set of type-checking rules. We applied this notation to describe the typed lambda calculus, including extensions to add tuples, sums, records, and references (variables).

We will use the lambda calculus to describe the meaning of the constructs of object-oriented languages. However, we need more advanced features in order to describe some of the special features of object-oriented languages like objects, classes, subclasses, and information hiding. We introduce the polymorphic lambda calculus in the next chapter in order to more accurately model these features. We also introduce mechanisms to define recursive functions and types.

9 *The Polymorphic Lambda Calculus*

In the previous chapter we introduced a version of the lambda calculus with type and value expressions similar to those in most common functional programming languages, including simple imperative features. We wish to use the lambda calculus to explain object-oriented language constructs. However, the version of the lambda calculus introduced so far is not adequate to model these constructs. To model these features it will be necessary to add to the lambda calculus expressions supporting parametric polymorphism, existential types (to model information hiding), and the definition of recursive functions and types.

Λ_{rr}^{P} The polymorphic lambda calculus, Λ_{rr}^{P}, extends the typed lambda calculus with pairs, records, and references, $\Lambda_{rr}^{\rightarrow}$, defined in the previous section. It adds functions that are parameterized over types, as well as a mechanism to hide type information in an expression. We begin with parametric polymorphism, and then add support for recursion and information hiding. Finally we extend the polymorphic lambda calculus to $\Lambda_{<:}^{P}$, which supports subtyping and bounded polymorphism.

9.1 Parameterized types and polymorphism

Polymorphic functions are functions that operate uniformly on values of different types. These functions typically are defined to work with parameterized types, like *Stack(T)*, *Tree(T)*, *Array of T*, etc. As can be seen from these examples, parameterized types typically represent structured collections of values. The parameter T typically indicates the type of values stored in the structure.

PARAMETERIZED TYPE   We begin by examining *parameterized types*. Parameterized types can best be modeled as functions from types to types. But rather than restricting ourselves only to functions from types to types, we will add higher-order functions on types as well. These will be classified by a *kind* structure that is, in many ways, quite similar to the types that categorize expressions. However, the kinds will categorize functions from types to types.

The simplest kind is $\star$, representing the kind of all types, while more complex kind s are built up by defining functions from kinds to kinds.

$$\kappa \in \text{\textit{Kind}} ::= \ \star \ | \ \kappa \Rightarrow \kappa'$$

The kind $\star \Rightarrow \star$ thus represents functions from $\star$ to $\star$, like *Tree* and *Stack*. We use the double arrow for function kinds to distinguish them from function types. Higher kinds represent more complex functions involving types. For example, $(\star \Rightarrow \star) \Rightarrow \star$ represents the kind of functions that take a function from types to types and return a type. We will presume that function kinds, like types, associate from the right. That is, $\star \Rightarrow \star \Rightarrow \star$ will be treated as being the same as $\star \Rightarrow (\star \Rightarrow \star)$.

The elements that are classified by kinds are called *type constructors* or simply *constructors*. Let $\mathcal{CI}$ be a collection of constructor identifiers, each labelled with its kind, where $\mathcal{CI}$ contains an infinite number of identifiers for each kind. Let $\mathcal{CC}$ be a collection of constructor constants, where again each element is associated with a constructor.

Definition 9.1.1 *Let $\mathcal{L}$ be an infinite collection of labels, and let $\mathcal{CC}$ be a collection of type constants. The type constructor pre-expressions of Λ^P_{rr} are given by the following grammar.*

$$\mu, \nu \in \text{\textit{Constructor}} ::= v^\kappa \ | \ c^\kappa \ | \ \text{\textit{Void}} \ | \ \mu \to \nu \ | \ \mu_1 \times \ldots \times \mu_n \ |$$
$$\mu_1 + \ldots + \mu_n \ | \ \{\!| l_1 : \mu_1; \ldots; l_n : \mu_n |\!\} \ | \ \text{\textit{Ref}} \ \mu \ |$$
$$\text{\textit{Command}} \ | \ \lambda v^\kappa . \mu \ | \ \mu \, \nu$$

where $v^\kappa \in \mathcal{CI}$, $c^\kappa \in \mathcal{CC}$, and $l_i \in \mathcal{L}$.

The constructor pre-expressions include all of the type expressions introduced in the previous chapter, but include more expressions dealing with constructors of higher kinds.

Type constructor identifiers are labeled with their kinds. Thus $v^\star$ is an identifier representing types, while $v^{\star \Rightarrow \star}$ is an identifier representing a function from types to types. For notational simplicity, we will usually omit the $\star$ as a superscript for type identifiers, and simply write t, u, t', or t_i. We will do the same for constructor constants of kind $\star$ (*i.e.*, type constants).

If $\mathcal{CI}$ is non-empty, the system includes type constructor constants. For example rather than thinking of $\to$ and $\times$ as operators, we could consider them as type constructor constants, each of which has kind $\star \Rightarrow \star \Rightarrow \star$. However, we will prefer to continue to treat them as type operators.

Type constructor pre-expressions of kind $\star$ (*i.e.*, type expressions) can be built up as in the last chapter to form function, record, sum, product, and reference types. The type constructor pre-expressions also include the types Void and Command.

Functions from kinds to kinds are written in the form $\lambda v^{\kappa}.\mu$, where μ is a type constructor. The application of a constructor function to an argument of the appropriate kind is written in the form $\mu \nu$, where μ and ν are constructors.

We will write kind assignments to constructors in the form "$\mu :: \kappa$". kind assignments do not depend on "static kind environments", unlike the type-checking rules that depended on static type environments. The reason is that all of the constructor identifiers are provided with kinds. kind checking

TYPE CONSTRUCTOR
EXPRESSION

is straightforward. The rules can be found in Figure 9.1. The *type constructor expressions* are the type constructor pre-expressions that can be assigned a kind by the kinding rules.

Constructor identifiers are assigned the kind in their label. *Void* and *Command* have kind $\star$. That is, they are types. The kinding rules assign kind $\star$ to expressions built up from types using $\to$, sums, products, records, and reference types. Notice these expressions are not well-kinded if any of the components fail to have kind $\star$.

Function expressions result in higher kinds, while applications of constructors of kind $\mu \Rightarrow \nu$ to type constructors of kind μ result in constructors of kind ν.

This figure also includes a "congruence rule" for simplifying constructor applications. A congruence rule indicates when one object may be treated as being the same as another. In particular, if two constructors are congruent, then if one is substituted for the other in any constructor then the new constructor will be congruent with the old. In combination with a forthcoming typing rule, this will allow us to simplify constructor applications appearing in expressions to be type-checked.

A simple example of a constructor with kind $\star \Rightarrow \star$ is *Pair* $= \lambda t.(t \times t)$. (Recall that we usually drop the kind from type variables.) This is a function that takes a type as an argument and returns the product of the type with itself. Thus, *Pair(Integer)* = *Integer* $\times$ *Integer* and *Pair(Boolean)* = *Boolean* $\times$ *Boolean*.

AppPair $= \lambda t. \lambda u.((t \times (t \to u)) \to u)$ is an example of a constructor with kind $\star \Rightarrow \star \Rightarrow \star$. This constructor can be applied to two successive type

$$c^\kappa :: \kappa$$

$$v^\kappa :: \kappa$$

$$Void :: \star$$

$$Command :: \star$$

$$\frac{\mu :: \star \qquad \nu :: \star}{\mu \to \nu :: \star}$$

$$\frac{\mu_1 :: \star, \ldots, \qquad \mu_n :: \star}{\mu_1 \times \ldots \times \mu_n :: \star}$$

$$\frac{\mu_1 :: \star, \ldots, \qquad \mu_n :: \star}{\mu_1 + \ldots + \mu_n :: \star}$$

$$\frac{\mu_1 :: \star, \ldots, \qquad \mu_n :: \star}{\{\!| l_1 : \mu_1; \ldots; l_n : \mu_n |\!\} :: \star}$$

$$\frac{\mu :: \star}{Ref\, \mu :: \star}$$

$$\frac{\mu :: \kappa'}{\lambda v^\kappa . \mu :: \kappa \Rightarrow \kappa'}$$

$$\frac{\mu :: \kappa \Rightarrow \kappa', \qquad \nu :: \kappa}{\mu\, \nu :: \kappa'}$$

$$\frac{\nu :: \kappa}{(\lambda v^\kappa . \mu)\nu \cong [\nu / v^\kappa]\mu}$$

Figure 9.1   Kind checking and equivalence rules.

expressions. For example, *AppPair(Integer)(Boolean)* = ((*Integer* × (*Integer* → *Boolean*)) → *Boolean*).

Because we will be adding constructs over the next few sections, we will not bother to repeat in our new definitions the constructs introduced in previous sections of this chapter. Instead we will indicate their omission by the use of "...".

In order to introduce polymorphic functions, we first enrich our type system by adding an expression representing the type of a polymorphic function. This will be added as a type constructor with kind $\star$.

$$\mu, \nu \in Constructor ::= \; \dots \; | \; \forall v^{\kappa}.T$$

The constructor expression $\forall v^{\kappa}.T$, where v^{κ} may occur in T, represents the type of a function that takes a *type constructor* with kind κ and returns a *value* of type T. Because of the use of the universal quantifier in the notation for UNIVERSAL TYPE polymorphic types, these are called *universal types*.

The kinding rule for this constructor is:

$$\frac{T :: \star}{\forall v^{\kappa}.T :: \star}$$

For example, a polymorphic function that takes a type identifier, t, and then a value, x, of type t, returning the pair $\langle x, x \rangle$ will have type $\forall t.\, t \rightarrow Pair(t)$, where *Pair* is the constructor introduced earlier.

In order to avoid notational overhead, from now on we will identify types with type constructors of kind $\star$, treating the type constructors as containing all of the types in $\Lambda_{rr}^{\rightarrow}$. Similarly the expressions of the polymorphic lambda calculus, Λ_{rr}^{P} include all expressions of $\Lambda_{rr}^{\rightarrow}$.

We now add two new pre-expressions to our language to represent polymorphic function construction and polymorphic function application:

$$M \in \mathcal{PLCE} ::= \; \dots \; | \; \Lambda v^{\kappa}.M \; | \; M[\mu]$$

The notation $\mathcal{PLCE}$ stands for the set of polymorphic lambda calculus (pre-)expressions.

The first expression in the definition is a polymorphic function taking a parameter of kind κ (we use capital Λ to distinguish polymorphic functions that take types to *values* from constructor functions that take types to *types*). The second represents the application of a polymorphic function to a constructor parameter of the appropriate kind. As above, when the kind of the

PolyFunction
$$\frac{\mathcal{E} \vdash M \colon T}{\mathcal{E} \vdash \Lambda v^\kappa . M \colon \forall v^\kappa . T}$$

PolyApplication
$$\frac{\mathcal{E} \vdash M \colon \forall v^\kappa . T, \ \mu \colon \colon \kappa}{\mathcal{E} \vdash M[\mu] \colon [\mu / v^\kappa] T}$$

Congruence
$$\frac{\mathcal{E} \vdash M \colon T, \qquad T \cong T'}{\mathcal{E} \vdash M \colon T'}$$

Figure 9.2   New type-checking and congruence rules in Λ_{rr}^P.

parameter is $\star$, we will omit the kind superscript and write $\Lambda t . M$ rather than the more accurate $\Lambda t^\star . M$.

Continuing our example above, we write the polymorphic function that takes a value of type t and returns a pair with that value duplicated as follows:

$$polyPair = \Lambda t . \lambda(x \colon t) . \langle x, x \rangle$$

The reader should be sure to understand why the Λt is used in this definition (to indicate a polymorphic function that returns a value) and the λt was used in the earlier definition of *Pair* (a function that returns a type rather than a value).

The type-checking rules for these new expressions are given in Figure 9.2. The first two rules are similar to those for regular functions. The main twist is that, after the application of a polymorphic function, M, to a constructor expression, μ, the type of the result is obtained by replacing all occurrences of the type identifier t in the polymorphic type by μ.

Exercise 9.1.2 *Extend Definition 8.1.1 to define the set of free identifiers (regular and type constructor) for an expression M.*

Exercise 9.1.3 *Extend Definition 8.1.3 and define substitution for type constructor identifiers.*

Using type-checking rule *PolyFunction* we can show the type of the expression *polyPair* defined above is $\forall t . (t \to t \times t)$. By the *PolyApplication* typing rule, the type of *polyPair* [*Integer*] will be *Integer* $\to$ *Integer* $\times$ *Integer*.

We also add a *Congruence* rule that ensures that if an expression has a type S, then it can also be assigned any other type congruent to S.

As before, we will find it convenient to use *let* expressions as abbreviations. We will write *let $v^\kappa = \mu$ in M end* as an abbreviation for $[v^\kappa/\mu]\,M$. The derived typing rule for this let expression on types is:

TypeLet
$$\frac{\mathcal{E} \vdash ([v^\kappa/\mu]\,M)\colon S \qquad \mu\colon\colon \kappa}{\mathcal{E} \vdash \mathit{let}\ v^\kappa = \mu\ \mathit{in}\ M\ \mathit{end}\colon S}$$

We are unable to treat this as an abbreviation for a type application because the type information will generally be used in typing the rest of the expression. For example, the expression

let t = Integer in let x: t = 7 in x + 2 end end

may only be type checked properly if it is known that t stands for `Integer` at the time the declaration is checked. This was not necessary for regular let expressions as the value was not needed in type-checking.

Again we will identify type constructors and polymorphic functions that differ only by the name of the formal parameter. Rewriting rules analogous to β and η are added to the calculus.

$\pi\beta$ $\qquad (\Lambda v^\kappa.\,M)\,[\mu] \twoheadrightarrow [\mu/v^\kappa]M$, if no free identifier of μ is bound in M.

$\pi\eta$ $\qquad\qquad\qquad\qquad\qquad \Lambda v^\kappa.\,(M\,[v^\kappa]) \twoheadrightarrow M$

In Section 9.4 we further enrich the polymorphic lambda calculus to support bounded polymorphism. However, we will first discuss recursion and existential types.

9.2   Recursive expressions and types

Recursive functions and procedures are supported in almost all modern programming languages. Just as we have provided λ-notation to provide the description of anonymous functions, we would like to do the same for recursive functions. This seems difficult since the essence of a recursive definition is that the definition uses the name of the function. However, there is a standard way of working around this difficulty using what are known as

FIXED-POINT   *fixed-point operators.*
OPERATORS
A common example of a recursively defined function is the factorial function:

fact(n: Integer) $\triangleq$ if n = $\underline{0}$ then $\underline{1}$ else n * fact(n-$\underline{1}$)

or, more accurately,

$$fact \triangleq \lambda(n: Integer). \, if \ n = \underline{0} \ then \ \underline{1} \ else \ n * fact(n\text{-}\underline{1})$$

If we think of the above as an equation to be solved for *fact*, it is apparent that we need to find a function, *f*, that, when substituted for *fact* on the right side of the equation, results in exactly the same function as *f*. We can formalize this by writing the following higher-order function definition:

$$G \triangleq \lambda(f: Integer \rightarrow Integer). \, \lambda(n: Integer). \, if \ n = \underline{0} \ then \ \underline{1} \ else \ n * f(n\text{-}\underline{1})$$

We can apply *G* to any function from integers to integers. For example, $G(\lambda(n: Integer). \, \underline{0})$ results in a function that returns $\underline{1}$ when applied to $\underline{0}$, and $\underline{0}$ for all other input values. (*Try it!*)

However, if *fact* is defined above, then

$$G(fact) = \lambda(n: Integer). \, if \ n = \underline{0} \ then \ \underline{1} \ else \ n * fact(n\text{-}\underline{1}) = fact$$

Thus we can change our point of view and say that what we are really looking for is a function f_0 such that $G(f_0) = f_0$.

FIXED POINT   An expression *e* is a *fixed point* of a function *G* if $G(e) = e$. Because *G* applied
GENERATOR   to *fact* returns itself, *fact* is a fixed point of *G*. We call *G* a *generator* of the fixed point.

We can use the information that *fact* is a fixed point of *G* in order to compute the value when *fact* is applied to a number. The key is that any occurrence of *fact* may be replaced by *G(fact)*. Thus we compute

$$
\begin{aligned}
fact(\underline{2}) \ &= \ G(fact)(\underline{2}) \\
&= \ (\lambda(n: Integer). \, if \ n = \underline{0} \ then \ \underline{1} \ else \ n * fact(n\text{-}\underline{1}))(\underline{2}) \\
&= \ if \, \underline{2} = \underline{0} \ then \ \underline{1} \ else \ \underline{2} * fact(\underline{2} - \underline{1}) \\
&= \ if \, false \ then \ \underline{1} \ else \ \underline{2} * fact(\underline{2} - \underline{1}) \\
&= \ \underline{2} * fact(\underline{1}) \\
&= \ \underline{2} * G(fact)(\underline{1}) \\
&= \ \underline{2} * (if \, \underline{1} = \underline{0} \ then \ \underline{1} \ else \ \underline{1} * fact(\underline{1} - \underline{1})) \\
&= \ \underline{2} * (if \, false \ then \ \underline{1} \ else \ \underline{1} * fact(\underline{1} - \underline{1})) \\
&= \ \underline{2} * (\underline{1} * fact(\underline{0})) \\
&= \ \underline{2} * (\underline{1} * G(fact)(\underline{0})) \\
&= \ \underline{2} * (\underline{1} * (if \, \underline{0} = \underline{0} \ then \ \underline{1} \ else \ \underline{0} * fact(\underline{0} - \underline{1}))) \\
&= \ \underline{2} * (\underline{1} * (if \, true \ then \ \underline{1} \ else \ \underline{0} * fact(\underline{0} - \underline{1}))) \\
&= \ \underline{2} * (\underline{1} * \underline{1}) \\
&= \ \underline{2}
\end{aligned}
$$

We can generalize this construction so that, given a recursive definition of a function *f*, we can define a higher-order function like *G* above, so that *G(f)* = *f*. We can then use the fact that *f* is a fixed point to compute the values of the function.

Unfortunately, there are some recursive function definitions that do not result in values when expanded as above. For example, the recursive function definitions:

$$f \triangleq \lambda(n\colon Integer).\, f(n) + \underline{1}$$

and

$$g \triangleq \lambda(n\colon Integer).\, g(n + \underline{1})$$

are everywhere undefined, though for very different reasons.

These non-convergent function definitions will be handled by introducing

PARTIAL FUNCTIONS   *partial functions*. We interpret the function type $T \to U$ as the set of partial functions from *T* to *U*. That is, they represent the functions whose domain is a *subset* of *T*.

We introduce a special constant *fix* to represent a polymorphic fixed point operator. It is applied first to a type *T*, and then to a higher-order function, *H*, with type $T \to T$. the result will be a value of type *T* that is a fixed point of *H*.[1]

Thus in the above example defining the factorial function,

$$fact \triangleq \underline{fix}\,[Integer \to Integer](G)$$

results in a function of type $Integer \to Integer$.

The corresponding typing rule is:

FixElt $\emptyset \vdash \underline{fix}\colon \forall t.\,(t \to t) \to t$

In this rule, *t* represents the type of the function being defined, so is generally itself a function type.

We also add the following computation rule. If *G* has type $t \to t$, then:

μ*Elt* $\underline{fix}\,[t](G) \twoheadrightarrow G(\underline{fix}\,[t]G)$

This is exactly the computation rule used earlier in order to compute *fact*($\underline{2}$). If $f = \underline{fix}\,[t]\,(G)$, the step of replacing *f* by *G(f)* is often termed *unrolling* the

---

1. Though we won't provide the details here, we intend *fix* to provide what is usually called the *least* fixed point, as that will correspond to the computation rule.

recursive definition. As in the example above, unrolling the definition typically results in an expression headed by a lambda that can be used in a β reduction to make progress in the computation.

Many of the types of interest to programmers are also defined recursively. A common example is lists, where the definition of a list of integers might be given as

$$IntList \triangleq Void + Integer \times IntList$$

That is, an element from *IntList* is either an empty tuple or is the pair of an integer with an element from *IntList*. Examples of elements of this type include $\langle\rangle$, $\langle\underline{17}, \langle\rangle\rangle$, $\langle\underline{2}, \langle\underline{17}, \langle\rangle\rangle\rangle$, and $\langle\underline{47}, \langle\underline{2}, \langle\underline{17}, \langle\rangle\rangle\rangle\rangle$.

We can also define parameterized recursive types using functions from types to types:

$$List(t) = Void + t \times List(t)$$

or, more accurately,

$$List \triangleq \lambda t. \, (Void + t \times List(t))$$

We introduce a new operator, *Fix*, on type constructors in order to create fixed points of functions from kinds to kinds, just as *fix* creates fixed points of regular functions. We could make *Fix* polymorphic on kinds, but that would require us to make our kind language more complex. We will avoid that by treating *Fix* similarly to $\rightarrow$, that is, as an operator used in creating new constructor expressions. The kinding rule for *Fix* is as follows:

$$\frac{\mu :: \kappa \Rightarrow \kappa}{Fix(\mu) :: \kappa}$$

Thus if

$$\nu = \lambda(IL :: \star). \, (Void + Integer \times IL)$$

then $Fix(\nu)$ is a type that will be equivalent to the recursively defined type *IntList* above.

We can define the parameterized type function *List* similarly by defining

$$\nu' = \lambda(L :: \star \Rightarrow \star). \, \lambda t. \, (Void + t \times L(t))$$

and letting $List = Fix(\nu')$.

As with regular recursive functions, we can also unfold recursively defined types. We will treat recursively defined type constructors (i.e., those defined using *Fix*) as being congruent to their unfoldings:

Fold/Unfold $$\frac{\mu :: \kappa \Rightarrow \kappa}{Fix(\mu) \cong \mu(Fix(\mu))}$$

While we do not bother to write the explicit rules here, we treat $\cong$ as a true congruence relation, so that if we replace a constructor μ in ν by $\mu' \cong \mu$ to obtain ν', then $\nu' \cong \nu$.

The *Congruence* typing rule from Figure 9.2 allows us to replace recursive types in the type-checking rules by their foldings or unfoldings.

We will now use recursive definitions freely when working with the polymorphic lambda calculus, with the understanding that we can formalize all definitions as shown in this section.

9.3   Information hiding and existential types

Sometimes we wish to use abstraction to hide information outside of a particular context. This is one of the main reasons for defining modules in programming languages, but information hiding is also of great importance in the use of object-oriented languages. For example, we will generally want to restrict instance variables from being visible outside of an object.

A traditional example of information hiding is when we want to have defined expressions and types treated as though they are built-in primitives. For example, it is possible to define a type and operations in the polymorphic lambda calculus that behave like the booleans.

Expressions representing true and false can be defined as follows:

$$\underline{True} \triangleq \Lambda t.\, \lambda(y\colon t).\, \lambda(n\colon t).\, y$$
$$\underline{False} \triangleq \Lambda t.\, \lambda(y\colon t).\, \lambda(n\colon t).\, n$$

They both have type $\forall t.\, t \to t \to t$, a type we can think of as an abbreviation for *Boolean*.

Conditional expressions can be defined as follows:

$$\underline{IfThenElse} \triangleq \Lambda u.\, \lambda(b\colon \forall t.\, t \to t \to t).\, \lambda(M\colon u).\, \lambda(N\colon u).\, b\,[u]M\,N$$

with type $\forall u.\, (\forall t.\, t \to t \to t) \to u \to u \to u$. The type parameter u in the definition of *IfThenElse* determines the result type of the conditional expression.

With these definitions, it is easy to see that if M and N both have type T, then *IfThenElse* $[T]\,\underline{True}\,M\,N \twoheadrightarrow M$ and *IfThenElse* $[T]\,\underline{False}\,M\,N \twoheadrightarrow N$.

Exercise 9.3.1 *Define $\underline{not}$ in the polymorphic lambda calculus. Show that $\underline{not}(\underline{True})$ reduces to $\underline{False}$ and that $\underline{not}(\underline{False})$ reduces to $\underline{True}$. Define $\underline{and}$ and $\underline{or}$ and show that they behave appropriately. All three of these are most easily defined using the definitions of $\underline{True}$, $\underline{False}$, and IfThenElse.*

Exercise 9.3.2 *Define expressions in the polymorphic lambda calculus for each of the integers, $\underline{n}$ as*

$$\underline{n} \stackrel{\Delta}{=} \Lambda t.\, \lambda(f\colon t{\to}t).\, \lambda(x\colon t).\, f^{(n)}(x)$$

where $f^{(n)}$ represents applying the function f a total of n times. What is the type of integers? Write functions $\underline{Plus}$ and $\underline{Mult}$ and show they have the appropriate behaviors when applied to encodings of integers. Subtraction is much more difficult to define, and requires a very clever encoding.

Because all of these expressions are definable, and expressions for the integers as well, we could go ahead and use them informally, knowing that the informal expressions can be replaced by the corresponding formal expressions. However, we have earlier added the types *Integer* and *Boolean*, as well as an *if-then-else* expression to our language. Why did we do introduce these as constants and operators if it is possible to define these expressions?

One reason for introducing these as primitives rather than just using the expressions is that it is painful, for example, to have to write down the type $\forall t.\, t \to t \to t$ whenever we have a boolean parameter or variable. We would prefer to be able to just write down a name *Boolean*, and not have to worry about the actual definition. Similarly for the expressions representing $\underline{True}$, $\underline{False}$, and conditionals.

EXISTENTIAL TYPE   One solution to this problem is to introduce *existential types*, which will allow us to hide certain types and definitions, while providing sufficient typing information that we can use the expressions and types. For instance we can write the type

$$BoolSpec \stackrel{\Delta}{=} \exists Bool.\{\!| \; True\colon Bool;$$
$$False\colon Bool;$$
$$IfThenElse\colon \forall u.\, Bool \to u \to u \to u \;|\!\}$$

that provides the specification of a package representing booleans. The specification includes a hidden type *Bool*, exported features *True* and *False* with type *Bool*, and polymorphic operation *IfThenElse* that takes a type parameter u, a value of type *Bool*, two values of type u, and returns a value of type u.

The idea is that users should be able to see this specification and understand how to use the components of a package satisfying the specification without knowing what the implementation type, *Bool*, of the package really is. (Of course, the typing information only provides information on how the elements of this specification can be used without generating type errors. Further semantic specifications would need to be given to ensure that the components behave as one would expect with booleans.)

We should be able to package up the definitions of the boolean expressions given above to satisfy *BoolSpec* if we let the implementation of *Bool* be the type $\forall t. t \rightarrow t \rightarrow t$. After all, if we let *Bool* stand for that type then the earlier definitions of *True*, *False*, and *IfThenElse* all have the types specified in *BoolSpec*.

We could just put all of these definitions in a record, but then the user could take advantage of the details of the implementation to perform operations we had not intended. For example *True* could be treated as a function and applied to *Integer*, *7*, and *15*. Another problem with making the implementations of these expressions available to the programmer is that we might later want to change the implementations, for example to get more efficiency or extra behaviors. If the user took advantage of the implementation of these expressions then changing the implementation would likely cause problems throughout the code that was using it.

The reasons just given are the classic reasons for the introduction of abstract data types (ADT's) in programming languages. The formal mechanism for supporting this kind of information hiding is the introduction of existential types.

Thus we add existential type expressions to our collection of constructor expressions:

$$\mu, \nu \in Constructor ::= \ldots \mid \exists v^\kappa. T$$

The constructor expression $\exists v^\kappa. T$, where v^κ may occur in T, represents the type of a package specification that hides the representation of a type constructor (represented by v^κ) and exports components with type T. As usual, we do not bother to write a superscript on constructor identifiers with kind $\star$.

The kinding rule for this constructor is:

$$\frac{T :: \star}{\exists v^\kappa. T :: \star}$$

The following expressions provide operations to pack up and open existentials:

$$M \in \mathcal{PLCE} ::= \ldots \mid pack \langle \mu, M \rangle \ as \ \exists v^\kappa. T \mid open \ M \ as \ \langle v^\kappa, x \rangle \ in \ N$$

The first expression takes a value, M, and creates a packed version of existential type by hiding certain occurrences of construction expression, μ, and replacing them with the constructor identifier, v^κ. After replacing appropriate occurrences of μ in the type of M by v^κ, the resulting type is given by T.

The second expression "opens" an existential, revealing that it is composed of a pair of a type constructor and value, and uses the given type and value names in the expression N. While *open* provides names v^κ and x for the hidden type and the value abstracted, it does not provide any information about the actual representation of the type or expression.

Returning to our example of creating a package representing boolean values, we can use the pack expression along with the definitions in the previous subsection to define

$$BoolPack \triangleq pack \langle \forall t.\, t \rightarrow t \rightarrow t,$$
$$\{\!| \ True = \Lambda t.\, \lambda(y\colon t).\, \lambda(n\colon t).\, y$$
$$False = \Lambda t.\, \lambda(y\colon t).\, \lambda(n\colon t).\, n$$
$$IfThenElse = \Lambda u.\, \lambda(b\colon \forall t.\, t \rightarrow t \rightarrow t).$$
$$\lambda(M\colon u).\, \lambda(N\colon u).\, b\,[u]M\,N$$
$$|\!\} \ \rangle$$

as *BoolSpec*,

where we omitted the type information in the record of values to reduce the clutter in the expression. All of the details of the implementation of the type *Boolean* are now hidden inside *BoolPack*, whose type will be *BoolSpec*. The pack expression takes the type *Boolean* and the record of implementations of the values and implementations and converts them to a value of existential type. The components are no longer directly accessible now that they have been packed.

We can use *BoolPack* as follows:

$$open \ BoolPack \ as \ \langle Bool, BOps \rangle \ in$$
$$let \ \ bval\colon Bool = BOps.True \ in$$
$$\ldots BOps.IfThenElse\,[Integer](bval)(\underline{3})(\underline{17}) \ldots$$
$$end$$

Thus we only get access by opening the package and referring to the components through the record whose name, *BOps*, and type, *Bool* are provided in the open expression. We know *Bops.IfThenElse* is legal because the existential type *BoolSpec* guarantees that the implementation has a field *IfThenElse* with type $\forall u.\, Bool \rightarrow u \rightarrow u \rightarrow u$. As a result we are guaranteed that the type of *BOps.IfThenElse*[*Integer*](*bval*)(\underline{3})(\underline{17}) is *Integer*.

Pack
$$\frac{\mathcal{E} \vdash M\colon [\mu/v^\kappa]T \qquad \mu\colon\colon\kappa}{\mathcal{E} \vdash pack\ \langle \mu, M \rangle\ as\ \exists v^\kappa.\,T\colon \exists v^\kappa.\,T}$$

Open
$$\frac{\mathcal{E} \vdash M\colon \exists v^\kappa.\,T, \qquad \mathcal{E} \cup \{x\colon T\} \vdash N\colon S}{\mathcal{E} \vdash open\ M\ as\ \langle v^\kappa, x \rangle\ in\ N\colon S}$$

where v^κ does not appear in S

Figure 9.3   Type-checking rules for existentials in Λ_{rr}^P.

The typing rules in Figure 9.3 are a bit more complex than the earlier ones. The first rule is relatively straightforward. One can simply replace as many occurrences of μ as one would like in the type of M by a constructor identifier, and report the packed version of the element as being of an existential type. The body of the *pack* is type checked using the knowledge of the constructor, μ, but the final type uses the constructor identifier. Clearly *BoolPack* has type *BoolSpec* by this rule.

The second rule is a bit more subtle. The expression M is of an existential type, so it has been packed as a pair. The *open* expression reveals the pair that can be used in N. However, statically N doesn't have access to the exact type of the value x in the pair. Thus we need to be able to determine the type of N without knowing anything about the constructor identifier v^κ, aside from the fact that it represents a constructor of kind κ and that the type of x is T. The side condition on the rule ensures that the constructor v^κ does not escape from the scope of the "open" expression. This is essential both because we want the type to remain hidden, and because outside the expression, v^κ is a free constructor identifier with no meaning associated with it.

For example, the earlier expression that opens and uses *BoolPack* is well-typed using this rule as long as the expression surrounded by the *open* clause has a type that does not mention *Bool*. For example, it could be a statement (with type *Command*) or return an integer value. However if it returned a value of type *Bool* we would not know what to do with it as the identifier Bool is introduced only as part of the open expression and has no meaning outside of that expression.

Computation with existentials is relatively straightforward. If you first pack something and then open it, it is as though you used it directly in a let statement. Thus,

o $open\ (pack\ \langle \mu, M \rangle\ as\ \exists v^\kappa.\,T)\ as\ \langle u^\kappa, x \rangle\ in\ N \twoheadrightarrow [M/x][\mu/u^\kappa]N$

As usual we identify existential types and *open* expressions that differ only in the names of bound constructor identifiers.

We can relate this to our example using *BoolPack*. In that example, *BoolPack* was opened and the *IfThenElse* component was applied to the type *Integer*, *bval*, and the integers 3 and 17. By the computation rule, opening *BoolPack* allows access to the hidden type and the definitions of all of the components. Thus the computation using *IfThenElse* proceeds just as if we hadn't hidden the type and component values.

Existential types are a suitable mechanism for defining abstract data types (ADT's). In our example above, as with other abstract data types, values of existential type provide enough hooks that they can be used without knowing anything about the hidden implementation.

9.4   Adding subtypes to the polymorphic lambda calculus

In Chapter 5 we presented the intuition behind subtyping rules for standard type constructors. In this section we add subtypes to the polymorphic lambda calculus to form the bounded polymorphic lambda calculus, $\Lambda^P_{<:}$, and formalize the rules for subtypes.

We will use subtyping in the bounded polymorphic lambda calculus in two ways. First, we shall use a "subsumption" rule to allow us to treat a value of a type as if it were a value of any of its supertypes. Second, we will use subtyping to constrain type and other constructor identifiers in polymorphic functions. For example, if we are defining a routine to calculate areas, we will only wish to apply it to records containing height and width fields. We will be able to constrain the function in this way with bounded polymorphism.

Let *TwoD* = {|*height*: *Integer*; *width*: *Integer*|}. Then we can define

$$Area = \Lambda(R <: TwoD). \lambda(obj: R). obj.height * obj.width$$

The restriction on type identifier *R* guarantees than any record with that type has *height* and *width* fields of type *Integer*, and thus the operations of extracting fields will succeed.

We define the types and expressions of the language first. Then we will define the subtyping rules, and finally the type-checking rules of this extended calculus. Because we have added types and expressions many times in this chapter, and this will be our final extension of the lambda calculus, we will provide complete definitions rather than just indicating incremental changes.

$$\frac{T::\star \qquad \mu::\kappa}{\exists (v^\kappa <: \mu).\,T::\star}$$

$$\frac{T::\star \qquad \mu::\kappa}{\forall (v^\kappa <: \mu).\,T::\star}$$

Figure 9.4 Kind checking rules for bounded polymorphic and existential types.

We will not make changes to the kinds, so we do not bother to repeat those definitions from Section 9.1. We will assume that the constructor constants include *Fix*, introduced in Section 9.2 to generate recursive types, which has kind $(\star \Rightarrow \star) \Rightarrow \star$.

Definition 9.4.1 *Let $\mathcal{L}$ be an infinite collection of labels, and let $\mathcal{CC}$ be a collection of type constructor constants. The type constructor pre-expressions of Λ_{rr}^P are given by the following grammar.*

$$\mu, \nu \in Constructor ::= v^\kappa \mid c^\kappa \mid Void \mid \mu \to \nu \mid \mu_1 \times \ldots \times \mu_n \mid$$
$$\mu_1 + \ldots + \mu_n \mid \{\!| l_1\!:\mu_1; \ldots; l_n\!:\mu_n |\!\} \mid Ref\,\mu \mid$$
$$Command \mid \lambda v^\kappa.\mu \mid \mu \nu \mid$$
$$\forall v^\kappa.T \mid \exists v^\kappa.T \mid \forall (v^\kappa <: \mu).T \mid \exists (v^\kappa <: \mu).T$$

where $v^\kappa \in \mathcal{CI}$, $c^\kappa \in \mathcal{CC}$, and $l_i \in \mathcal{L}$.

All but the last two type forms were introduced earlier. The last two are variations of the universal and existential types, where now the constructor identifiers are bounded by other constructors of the same kind as the bound identifier. The intuition is that the bound constructor identifiers represent constructors that are in the subtype relation to the given bounds.

The kinding rules for the new bounded polymorphic and existential types are given in Figure 9.4. We do not repeat the kinding rules for the other constructors given earlier in this chapter.

The expressions of the full language are given below:

$$M \in \mathcal{PLCE} ::= x \mid c \mid \langle\rangle \mid \lambda(x\colon T).\,M \mid M\,N \mid \langle M_1, \ldots, M_n\rangle \mid proj_i(M) \mid$$

$$case\ M\ of\ x_1\colon T_1\ then\ E_1 \parallel\ \ldots\ \parallel x_n\colon T_n\ then\ E_n \mid$$

$$in_i^{T_1,\ldots,T_n}(M) \mid \{\!|\,l_1\colon T_1 = M_1, \ldots, l_n\colon T_n = M_n\,|\!\} \mid M.l_i \mid$$

$$ref\ M \mid null \mid val\ M \mid nop \mid N := M \mid$$

$$if\ B\ then\ \{\ M\ \}\ else\ \{\ N\ \} \mid M;\ N \mid$$

$$\Lambda v^\kappa.\,M \mid \Lambda(v^\kappa <: \mu).\,M \mid M\,[\mu] \mid$$

$$pack\ \langle \mu, M\rangle\ as\ \exists v^\kappa.\,T \mid pack\ \langle \mu, M\rangle\ as\ \exists(v^\kappa <: \nu).\,T \mid$$

$$open\ M\ as\ \langle v^\kappa, x\rangle\ in\ N$$

We assume that the constants of $\mathcal{PLCE}$ include the constant *fix* with type $\forall t.\,(t \to t) \to t$, which was introduced in Section 9.2 to support recursive definitions. Notice that we have added two new expressions representing the formation of bounded polymorphic functions and of existential packages with bounded existential types.

The axioms and rules for type-checking expressions of $\Lambda_{<:}^P$, as well as those for $<:$, are given with respect to a set, $\mathcal{C}$, of simple type constraints, that provide information about type identifiers. For example, in type-checking the body of the function *Area* defined earlier, we will need to use the fact that the type identifier R is a subtype of record type *TwoD*.

SIMPLE TYPE
CONSTRAINTS
CONSTRAINT SYSTEM

Definition 9.4.2 *Relations of the form $v^\kappa <: \mu$, where v^κ is a type constructor identifier and μ is a constructor expression of kind κ, are said to be* simple type constraints. *A* constraint system *is defined as follows:*

1. *The empty set, $\emptyset$, is a type constraint system.*

2. *If $\mathcal{C}$ is a type constraint system, and v^κ is a constructor identifier that does not appear in $\mathcal{C}$, then $\mathcal{C} \cup \{v^\kappa <: \mu\}$ is a type constraint system.*

Before collecting together all of the type-checking rules for the bounded polymorphic lambda calculus, we write down the rules for subtyping in Figures 9.5 and 9.6. Because types may involve type identifiers, the subtyping relations may depend on a constraint system, $\mathcal{C}$.

The rules *Reflex* $_{<:}$ and *Transitivity* $_{<:}$ are very natural for a partial ordering. Rule *Identifier* $_{<:}$ simply allows one to infer any constraint contained in the type constraint system.

Rules *Function* $_{<:}$ and *Record* $_{<:}$ reflect our earlier discussion of subtyping in Chapter 5. Function subtyping is covariant in the return type and contravariant in the parameter type. Record subtyping allows both breadth

$$Reflex_{<:} \qquad \frac{\mu :: \kappa}{\mathcal{C} \vdash \mu <: \mu}$$

$$Transitivity_{<:} \qquad \frac{\mathcal{C} \vdash S <: T, \qquad \mathcal{C} \vdash T <: U}{\mathcal{C} \vdash S <: U}$$

$$Identifier_{<:} \qquad \mathcal{C} \cup \{v^\kappa <: \mu\} \vdash v^\kappa <: \mu$$

$$Function_{<:} \qquad \frac{\mathcal{C} \vdash S <: S', \qquad \mathcal{C} \vdash T' <: T}{\mathcal{C} \vdash S' \to T' <: S \to T}$$

$$Product_{<:} \qquad \frac{\mathcal{C} \vdash S_i <: T_i, \text{ for } 1 \leq i \leq n}{\mathcal{C} \vdash S_1 \times \ldots \times S_n \times \ldots \times S_{n+m} <: T_1 \times \ldots \times T_n}$$

$$Sum_{<:} \qquad \frac{\mathcal{C} \vdash S_i <: T_i, \text{ for } 1 \leq i \leq n}{\mathcal{C} \vdash S_1 + \ldots + S_n <: T_1 + \ldots + T_n + \ldots + T_{n+m}}$$

$$Record_{<:} \qquad \frac{\mathcal{C} \vdash S_i <: T_i, \text{ for } 1 \leq i \leq n}{\mathcal{C} \vdash \{\!| l_1 \colon S_1; \ldots; l_n \colon S_n; \ldots; l_{n+m} \colon S_{n+m} |\!\} <: \{\!| l_1 \colon T_1; \ldots; l_n \colon T_n |\!\}}$$

$$Poly_{<:} \qquad \frac{\mathcal{C} \vdash S <: T}{\mathcal{C} \vdash \forall v^\kappa . S <: \forall v^\kappa . T}$$

$$BdPoly_{<:} \qquad \frac{\mathcal{C} \cup \{w^\kappa <: \mu\} \vdash S <: T}{\mathcal{C} \vdash \forall (v^\kappa <: \mu). S <: \forall (v^\kappa <: \mu). T}$$

$$Exist_{<:} \qquad \frac{\mathcal{C} \vdash S <: T}{\mathcal{C} \vdash \exists v^\kappa . S <: \exists v^\kappa . T}$$

$$BdExist_{<:} \qquad \frac{\mathcal{C} \cup \{w^\kappa <: \mu\} \vdash S <: T}{\mathcal{C} \vdash \exists (v^\kappa <: \mu). S <: \exists (v^\kappa <: \mu). T}$$

Figure 9.5 Subtyping rules for $\Lambda^P_{<:}$: Part 1.

$ConstructorFcns_{<:}$
$$\frac{\mathcal{C} \vdash \mu' <: \mu}{\mathcal{C} \vdash \lambda v^{\kappa}.\,\mu' <: \lambda v^{\kappa}.\,\mu}$$

$ConstructorApp_{<:}$
$$\frac{\mu :: \kappa \Rightarrow \kappa', \qquad \nu :: \kappa', \qquad \mathcal{C} \vdash \mu' <: \mu}{\mathcal{C} \vdash \mu'\nu <: \mu\nu}$$

$Cong_{<:}$
$$\frac{S \cong S', \qquad T \cong T', \qquad \mathcal{C} \vdash S <: T}{\mathcal{C} \vdash S' <: T'}$$

$Fix_{<:}$
$$\frac{\mathcal{C} \cup \{v'^{\kappa} <: v^{\kappa}\} \vdash \mu'(v'^{\kappa}) <: \mu(v^{\kappa})}{\mathcal{C} \vdash Fix(\mu') <: Fix(\mu)}$$

Figure 9.6   Subtyping rules for $\Lambda_{<:}^{P}$: Part 2.

and depth subtyping by supporting both the addition of more fields and subtyping of individual fields. Products behave like records whose fields are accessed by the $proj_i$ operations. Width and depth subtyping are supported by rule $Product_{<:}$. The order of tuple components is significant because slots are accessed by location rather than name.

The rule $Sum_{<:}$ for sums is new. It asserts that an element of type $S_1 + \ldots + S_n$ can masquerade as having type $T_1 + \ldots + T_n + \ldots + T_{n+m}$. The only operation applicable to an element of a sum type is the *case* statement. For an expression M to successfully masquerade as having type $T_1 + \ldots + T_n + \ldots + T_{n+m}$ in a *case* statement (having $m+n$ alternatives) it is only necessary that each summand in the type of M match one of the alternatives in the case statement. Hence the actual type of M may involve fewer summands than expected in the case statement. Because the order of the summands is important in the interpretation of the case statement, the summands of the type of M must be subtypes of the corresponding summands.

The subtyping rules for polymorphic and bounded polymorphic types, $Poly_{<:}$ and $BdPoly_{<:}$, are simplifications of the rule $Function_{<:}$ in that they allow covariant changes to the return type, but no change to the bound on the type identifier in bounded polymorphic types. Similarly, the rules for existential and bounded existential types, $Exist_{<:}$ and $BdExist_{<:}$, indicate that these types are also covariant in the result type.

It is possible to generalize the rules $BdPoly_{<:}$ and $BdExist_{<:}$ to allow changes in the polymorphic bounds (contravariant in the first case and covariant in the second), but subtyping, and hence type checking, becomes undecidable [Pie94]. As a result we will work with this more restricted set of subtyping rules.

The four rules in Figure 9.6 define subtyping (or *subconstructoring?*) for higher-order type constructors and for fixed points. Rule *ConstructorFcns* $_{<:}$ allows subtyping of constructor functions if the result types change covariantly.

The rule *ConstructorApp* $_{<:}$ has the results of constructor function applications be subtypes as long as the functions are subtypes and the arguments are the same. It might seem that we could also allow the arguments to vary in a covariant way, but that would not be sound.

Suppose $\mu = \lambda t. t \to t$, $\nu = S$, and $\nu' = S'$ for some $S' <: S$. Then $\mu \nu' = S' \to S'$, which is *not* a subtype of $\mu \nu = S \to S$ (or vice versa). Without knowing extra information about type functions (*e.g.*, without knowing they are covariant in their type parameter), one may not make deductions about subtyping when the actual parameters are subtypes. In practice, it is unusual for type functions to be either covariant or contravariant in their parameters, so we do not pursue this kind of rule further.

Recall that $\cong$ is used to relate recursive types and their unfoldings in Section 9.2. The *Cong* $_{<:}$ rule allows one to substitute congruent types in a subtype relationship. In particular, if recursive types are subtypes, then so are their recursive unfoldings.

The last rule allows us to determine when two recursive types are subtypes of each other. This rule is the most complex to understand of all.

One might expect to be able to show that if $C \vdash \mu' <: \mu$, that would be sufficient to show that $C \vdash Fix(\mu') <: Fix(\mu)$. But that is false. Let

$$\mu \triangleq \lambda t. \{\!|m: t \to Boolean|\!\}$$

and

$$\mu' \triangleq \lambda t. \{\!|x: Integer; m: t \to Boolean|\!\}.$$

Clearly $\mu' <: \mu$. However, we show that $S' = Fix(\mu')$ is *not* a subtype of $S = Fix(\mu)$. Define

$$s': S' = \{\!|x: Integer = 0; m: S' \to Boolean = \lambda(u: S'). (u.x = 0) |\!\},$$

and

$$s: S = \{\!|m: S' \to Boolean = \lambda(u: S). true|\!\},$$

and

$$f \triangleq \lambda(v: S). v.m(s).$$

Suppose, in order to find a contradiction, that $C \vdash S' <: S$. By the fact that values of subtypes can masquerade as supertypes (supported more formally by the *Subsumption* rule later in this section), it follows that $C \vdash s': S$, and $f(s')$ is well-typed. But $f(s') = s'.m(s) = (s.x = 0)$, and s has no x field. Thus the assumption that $C \vdash S' <: S$ must be false. This shows that the intuitive subtyping rule for recursive types is not correct. We need the stronger assumption given in rule *Fix $<:$* to obtain correct conclusions.[2]

While verifying the correctness of this rule would take us too far afield, we present the following intuition, which may be helpful. If we hope to show that

$$C \vdash S' = Fix(\mu') <: Fix(\mu) = S,$$

then we will need

$$C \vdash S' \cong \mu'(S') <: \mu(S) \cong S.$$

If the hypothesis of the *Fix $<:$* rule holds, then we already know that

$$C \cup \{v'^{\kappa} <: v^{\kappa}\} \vdash \mu'(v'^{\kappa}) <: \mu(v^{\kappa}).$$

As a result, if $C \vdash S' <: S$, it will follow from the hypothesis of the rule that $C \vdash \mu'(S') <: \mu(S)$. That is, if $C \vdash S' <: S$, then the unfoldings of S' and S are also in the subtyping relation.

Of course, this is not a proof – the implications go the wrong direction! Rather it shows that a possible proof by contradiction fails to reveal a contradiction. Instead one can treat this as a plausibility argument. An actual proof of correctness would require either a co-inductive proof or arguments using infinite trees [AC93], neither of which we wish to pursue.

Stronger rules are possible for subtyping with recursive types. However, we will only need this one rule for our work with object-oriented languages.

The typing rules for expressions in Figures 9.7 and 9.8 are a straightforward extension of those given earlier. The main difference between these and the earlier type-checking rules is the inclusion of C as an added hypothesis for type-checking. This is necessary in order to type-check the new expressions in Figure 9.9.

The only difference between type-checking bounded polymorphic functions and regular (unbounded) polymorphic functions is that with bounded polymorphism we type-check the body under the assumption (added to C) that the type parameter is constrained by the bound of the type identifier.

---

2. The alert reader will notice the similarity of this argument to the failure of subtyping with binary methods in Eiffel.

Similarly when applying a bounded polymorphic function, we must ensure that the actual type parameter is a subtype of the upper bound expressed in the type.

Bounded existentials are handled similarly to bounded polymorphic functions. We must ensure the hidden type is a subtype of the declared bound before packing the expression into one whose type is a bounded existential. When unpacking such an expression, one can count on the fact that the hidden type is bounded above by the upper bound included in the type.

SUBSUMPTION   The *subsumption* rule states that if an expression has a type S, then it also has as type any supertype of S. Another way of stating this is that an element of a type can successfully masquerade as an element of any supertype. This rule provides the formal justification of subtype polymorphism.

Computation rules for the bounded polymorphic and existential expressions are similar to those for their unbounded counterparts in Section 9.1 and 9.3. Their formulation is left as an exercise for the reader. It is possible to show a *subject reduction theorem* for this calculus (see [Pie02]):

Theorem 9.4.3 *Suppose* $\mathcal{C}, \mathcal{E} \vdash M: T$ *and* $M \twoheadrightarrow^* M'$. *Then* $\mathcal{C}, \mathcal{E} \vdash M': S$ *for some* S *such that* $\mathcal{C} \vdash S <: T$.

In essence, this theorem states that computation preserves types. One might think that computation might not result in a subtype, but consider the following simple example:

$$(\lambda(x: T). x)(y) \twoheadrightarrow y$$

Suppose $y: S$, where $\mathcal{C} \vdash S <: T$. It is easy to see that the left side has type T because the function has type $T \to T$ and the type of y can be promoted to T by subsumption. It is easy to see that the expression cannot have a smaller type because subsumption applied to the function can only result in a larger return type. On the other hand, the result of the computation, y, has type S. Thus evaluating an expression can result in a value whose minimum type is a subtype of the original.

Constructing semantic models of the bounded polymorphic lambda calculus and proving subject-reduction is non-trivial and beyond the scope of this text. For our purposes it is sufficient to understand the syntax, type-checking, and some of the computation rules for this extended typed lambda calculus. We hope the reader will accept that the typing and computation rules discussed in this chapter are intuitive and that the subject-reduction theorem is plausible. See the references for suggestions as to where to find the details of these developments.

identifier	$\mathcal{C}, \mathcal{E} \cup \{x\colon T\} \vdash x\colon T$
Constant	$\mathcal{C}, \mathcal{E} \vdash c\colon N$
Void	$\mathcal{C}, \mathcal{E} \vdash \langle \rangle\colon Void$

Function
$$\frac{\mathcal{C}, \mathcal{E} \cup \{x\colon S\} \vdash M\colon T}{\mathcal{C}, \mathcal{E} \vdash \lambda(x\colon S).\, M\colon S \rightarrow T}$$

FuncApp
$$\frac{\mathcal{C}, \mathcal{E} \vdash M\colon S \rightarrow T, \qquad \mathcal{C}, \mathcal{E} \vdash N\colon S}{\mathcal{C}, \mathcal{E} \vdash M\, N\colon T}$$

Product
$$\frac{\mathcal{C}, \mathcal{E} \vdash M_i\colon T_i, \; for \; 1 \leq i \leq n}{\mathcal{C}, \mathcal{E} \vdash \langle M_1, \ldots, M_n \rangle\colon T_1 \times \ldots \times T_n}$$

Proj
$$\frac{\mathcal{C}, \mathcal{E} \vdash M\colon T_1 \times \ldots \times T_n}{\mathcal{C}, \mathcal{E} \vdash proj_i(M)\colon T_i} for \; 1 \leq i \leq n$$

Sum
$$\frac{\mathcal{C}, \mathcal{E} \vdash M\colon T_i}{\mathcal{C}, \mathcal{E} \vdash in_i^{T_1, \ldots, T_n}(M)\colon T_1 + \ldots + T_n} for \; 1 \leq i \leq n$$

Case
$$\frac{\mathcal{C}, \mathcal{E} \vdash M\colon T_1 + \ldots + T_n, \quad \mathcal{C}, \mathcal{E} \cup \{x_i\colon T_i\} \vdash E_i\colon U, \; for \; 1 \leq i \leq n}{\mathcal{C}, \mathcal{E} \vdash case \; M \; of \; x_1\colon T_1 \; then \; E_1 \; \| \; \ldots \; \| \; x_n\colon T_n \; then \; E_n\colon U}$$

Record
$$\frac{\mathcal{C}, \mathcal{E} \vdash M_i\colon T_i, \; for \; 1 \leq i \leq n}{\mathcal{C}, \mathcal{E} \vdash \{\!| l_1\colon T_1 = M_1, \ldots, l_n\colon T_n = M_n |\!\}\colon \{\!| l_1\colon T_1; \ldots; l_n\colon T_n |\!\}}$$

Selection
$$\frac{\mathcal{C}, \mathcal{E} \vdash M\colon \{\!| l_1\colon T_1; \ldots; l_n\colon T_n |\!\}}{\mathcal{C}, \mathcal{E} \vdash M.l_i\colon T_i}, \; for \; 1 \leq i \leq n$$

Figure 9.7   Type-checking rules for $\Lambda_{\leq:}^{P}$, part 1: revised rules.

Reference	$$\dfrac{\mathcal{C}, \mathcal{E} \vdash M \colon T}{\mathcal{C}, \mathcal{E} \vdash \mathit{ref}\, M \colon \mathit{Ref}\, T}$$
Null	$$\mathcal{E} \vdash \mathit{null} \colon \mathit{Ref}\, T$$
Value	$$\dfrac{\mathcal{C}, \mathcal{E} \vdash M \colon \mathit{Ref}\, T}{\mathcal{C}, \mathcal{E} \vdash \mathit{val}\, M \colon T}$$
Assignment	$$\dfrac{\mathcal{C}, \mathcal{E} \vdash N \colon \mathit{Ref}\, T, \quad \mathcal{C}, \mathcal{E} \vdash M \colon T}{\mathcal{C}, \mathcal{E} \vdash N \colon= M \colon \mathit{Command}}$$
Conditional	$$\dfrac{\mathcal{C}, \mathcal{E} \vdash B \colon \mathit{Boolean}, \quad \mathcal{C}, \mathcal{E} \vdash M \colon T, \quad \mathcal{C}, \mathcal{E} \vdash N \colon T}{\mathcal{C}, \mathcal{E} \vdash \mathit{if}\, B\, \mathit{then}\, \{\, M\, \}\, \mathit{else}\, \{\, N\, \} \colon T}$$
Sequencing	$$\dfrac{\mathcal{C}, \mathcal{E} \vdash M \colon S, \quad \mathcal{C}, \mathcal{E} \vdash N \colon T}{\mathcal{C}, \mathcal{E} \vdash M ; N \colon T}$$
PolyFunc	$$\dfrac{\mathcal{C}, \mathcal{E} \vdash M \colon T}{\mathcal{C}, \mathcal{E} \vdash \Lambda v^{\kappa}. M \colon \forall v^{\kappa}. T}$$
PolyApp	$$\dfrac{\mathcal{C}, \mathcal{E} \vdash M \colon \forall v^{\kappa}. T, \quad \mu \colon\colon \kappa}{\mathcal{C}, \mathcal{E} \vdash M[\mu] \colon [\mu / v^{\kappa}] T}$$
Pack	$$\dfrac{\mathcal{C}, \mathcal{E} \vdash M \colon [\mu / v^{\kappa}] T, \quad \mu \colon\colon \kappa}{\mathcal{C}, \mathcal{E} \vdash \mathit{pack}\, \langle \mu, M \rangle\, \mathit{as}\, \exists v^{\kappa}. T \colon \exists v^{\kappa}. T}$$
Unpack	$$\dfrac{\mathcal{C}, \mathcal{E} \vdash M \colon \exists v^{\kappa}. T, \quad \mathcal{C}, \mathcal{E} \cup \{x \colon T\} \vdash N \colon S}{\mathcal{C}, \mathcal{E} \vdash \mathit{open}\, M\, \mathit{as}\, \langle v^{\kappa}, x \rangle\, \mathit{in}\, N \colon S}$$

where v^{κ} does not appear in S

Figure 9.8 Type-checking rules for $\Lambda_{<:}^{P}$, part 2: revised rules.

9.5 Summary

We have now completed the preliminary background material needed to understand the semantics of object-oriented languages. In the next chapter we use the machinery we have built up here to explain objects and classes. We will use pairs and records to represent objects as a pair of the records of meth-

BdPolyFunc
$$\frac{\mathcal{C} \cup \{v^\kappa <: \mu\}, \mathcal{E} \vdash M: T, \qquad \mu::\kappa}{\mathcal{C}, \mathcal{E} \vdash \Lambda(v^\kappa <: \mu). M: \forall(v^\kappa <: \mu). T}$$

BdPolyApp
$$\frac{\mathcal{C}, \mathcal{E} \vdash M: \forall(v^\kappa <: \mu). T, \qquad \mathcal{C} \vdash \mu' <: \mu}{\mathcal{C}, \mathcal{E} \vdash M[\mu']: [\mu'/v^\kappa]T}$$

BdPack
$$\frac{\mathcal{C}, \mathcal{E} \vdash M: [\mu/v^\kappa]T, \qquad \mathcal{C} \vdash \mu <: \nu}{\mathcal{C}, \mathcal{E} \vdash pack \langle \mu, M \rangle \ as \ \exists(v^\kappa <: \nu). T: \exists(v^\kappa <: \nu). T}$$

BdUnpack
$$\frac{\begin{array}{c} \mathcal{C}, \mathcal{E} \vdash M: \exists(v^\kappa <: \mu). T, \\ \mathcal{C} \cup \{v^\kappa <: \mu\}, \mathcal{E} \cup \{x: T\} \vdash N: S \end{array}}{\mathcal{C}, \mathcal{E} \vdash open \ M \ as \ \langle v^\kappa, x \rangle \ in \ N: S}$$

where v^κ does not appear in S

Subsumption
$$\frac{\mathcal{C}, \mathcal{E} \vdash M: S, \qquad \mathcal{C} \vdash S <: T}{\mathcal{C}, \mathcal{E} \vdash M: T}$$

Congruence
$$\frac{\mathcal{E} \vdash M: T, \qquad T \cong T'}{\mathcal{E} \vdash M: T'}$$

Figure 9.9   Type-checking rules for $\Lambda^P_{<:}$, part 3: new rules.

ods and instance variables. Existential types will be used to hide the record of instance variables outside of the methods of an object, and bounded polymorphic functions in turn will be critical in ensuring that methods defined in a class can safely be inherited in subclasses.

Historical Notes and References for Section II

Alonzo Church developed the untyped lambda calculus in the 1930's to aid in the study of mathematical logic [Chu32], and in order to define computable functions [Chu36, Chu41]. Church's student Kleene discovered the remarkable expressiveness of the untyped lambda calculus, proving in 1936 [Kle36] that the collection of functions from natural numbers to natural numbers definable in the untyped lambda calculus was the same as that definable from recursive functions. A year later, Turing [Tur37] proved that these sets were the same as the set of Turing machine computable functions.

The typed lambda calculus [Chu40, Hen50] was introduced several years later as a restriction of the untyped lambda calculus. However, as a result of research into the solution of recursive domain equations in the 1970's, the simply typed lambda calculus with recursive types and terms is now typically seen as more general, with the untyped lambda calculus treated as a special case whose models satisfy a particular domain equation. See Mitchell [Mit96] or Gunter's [Gun92] texts for details. We follow the modern approach here by working with the typed lambda calculus. Good references on the lambda calculus include the books and articles of Hindley [Hin97], Hindley and Seldin [HS86] and Barendregt [Bar84, Bar92]. The recent text [Pie02] by Pierce is an excellent reference for the kinds of extensions of the lambda calculus discussed here. Pierce's survey article, "Foundational Calculi for programming languages" [Pie97] provides a short introduction to both the lambda calculus and the pi calculus.

Interest in using the lambda calculus to model high level programming languages was spurred by the work of Landin [Lan65, Lan66] and Strachey [Str67] in the 1960's. Initially there was some skepticism as to the soundness of the untyped lambda calculus because of the lack of models for its use in denotational semantics, but work by Scott [Sco76] and others showed that both the untyped lambda calculus and the typed lambda calculus with recursive domain equations had very rich sets of models.

The polymorphic lambda calculus, sometimes referred to as second-order lambda calculus or System F, was invented independently by Girard [Gir71, Gir86] and Reynolds [Rey74]. They came to this system through two different viewpoints, Girard through a study of the proof theory of mathematical logic, and Reynolds from a programming languages perspective. McCracken [McC79], building on results of Scott, produced the first model of the polymorphic lambda calculus.

MacQueen, Plotkin, and Sethi invented the ideal model [MPS86] for the implicit polymorphic lambda calculus. This model is useful in understanding languages like ML in which the system infers polymorphic types for untyped terms rather than having types declared as part of the language syntax. The importance of this model is that subtyping in these languages could be interpreted as subsets of ideals. While ideal models are not sound for the explicitly typed polymorphic lambda calculus, they did provide an important semantic understanding of the notion of subtype.

While existential types were included in Girard's System F, Mitchell and Plotkin's paper, "Abstract types have existential types" [MP88], was the first to tie these types to programming language constructs. While the initial application was to model information hiding and abstract data types, we will see later that they are extremely useful in modeling objects with instance variables.

Cardelli and Wegner's paper, "On understanding types, data abstraction, and polymorphism" [CW85], introduced bounded polymorphism to better model object-oriented programming languages. Mitchell's 1984 paper, "Coercion and type inference" [Mit84], used a prenex form of bounded polymorphism for type inference with a restricted form of subtyping.

Mitchell's 1984 paper, "Coercion and type inference" [Mit84], also contained suggestions that bounded polymorphism would be necessary for type inference to obtain most general types.

HP Lab's Abel group along with Mitchell [CCH+89] were among the first to notice that many of the applications of bounded polymorphism (especially those involving binary methods) required an extension to F-bounded polymorphism. The designers of Emerald also recognized this problem, providing similar mechanisms.

The first models of bounded polymorphic lambda calculus were by Bruce and Longo [BL90] and by Breazu-Tannen *et al.* [BTCGS91]. In each case subtyping was not modeled by subset of the interpretation of types, but instead by particular kinds of mappings from the interpretation of a subtype to the interpretation of the supertype.

In their paper, Bruce and Longo extended the definition of the bounded second-order lambda calculus by generalizing the definition of the subtyping relation on bounded polymorphic types to allow contravariant changes in type bounds. While the models were sound, it turned out that this extension destroyed the decidability of subtyping, as Pierce showed in his paper, "Bounded quantification is undecidable" [Pie94]. Both subtyping and type checking for Cardelli and Wegner's original version of the language are decidable. As a result, the original version is generally used even though subtyping of bounded polymorphic types is more restricted than is strictly necessary. Most models for the bounded polymorphic lambda calculus are easily extended to handle F-bounded polymorphism.

Amadio and Cardelli provided the first careful theoretical analysis of subtyping rules for recursive types. Kozen *et al.* [KPS93] provided a more efficient algorithm for deciding subtyping. A recent tutorial, "Recursive Subtyping Revealed" [GLP00], provides a more modern, coinductive treatment of recursive types.

Part III

Formal Descriptions of Object-Oriented Languages

10 $\mathcal{SOOL}$, a Simple Object-Oriented Language

$\mathcal{SOOL}$

In the last two chapters we introduced the formal notation necessary in order to specify programming languages. Now we are ready to present the formal specification of a simple object-oriented programming language, $\mathcal{SOOL}$, in terms of the formal notation of $\Lambda^P_{<:}$. The language $\mathcal{SOOL}$ is intended to share the core features of most statically typed class-based object-oriented programming languages. It is essentially the same language used in the examples in the earlier chapters of this book. It does not include the extensions discussed in Chapter 4. These will be added in Part IV, starting with Chapter 15.

Analyzing this language and its extensions will be the focus of most of the remaining chapters of this text. We will first carefully give formal specifications of the syntax, type-checking rules, and semantics of the $\mathcal{SOOL}$. With that specification complete we will be able to prove that the type system is sound.

In order to make it simpler to write down semantics and type-checking rules for our language, the syntax for the language will be somewhat more cluttered than most common object-oriented languages. However, we will also introduce abbreviations which provide a more friendly and familiar programming style. One can imagine the early steps of a compiler expanding the code from the language with abbreviations to the full language.

10.1 Informal description and example

An early example of the programming notation introduced in Chapter 2 was the program repeated in Figure 10.1. That will be a valid class definition in our language with abbreviations (as will the version that drops all of the "`self.`" subexpressions), but the formal language specification will define

```
class CellClass {
   x: Integer = 0;

   function get(): Integer is
   { return self.x }

   function set(nuVal: Integer): Void is
   { self.x := nuVal }

   function bump(): Void is
   { self ⇐ set(self ⇐ get()+1) }
}
```

Figure 10.1   Cell class.

a more verbose version of the language which allows function and classes to be defined as "anonymous" expressions. That is, similar to the way the lambda calculus allows one to define unnamed function expressions using the lambda notation, we will be able to write down unnamed expressions that represent functions and classes.

In Figure 10.2, CellClass is shown as written in the fully expanded language. We explain the changes in notation between the two versions below.

In the fully expanded language we will adopt some of the notation of the lambda calculus with references described in Section 5.1.3. Types of the form Ref T are reference types, denoting the types of variables holding values of type T. An expression with type Integer (*e.g.*, 3+7) denotes an integer value, while an expression x of type Ref Integer denotes an updatable variable holding values of type Integer.

An expression of the form ref e denotes a reference or location holding the value of e. These expressions are used to initialize variables. If x is declared to be a variable of type T with initial value e in the abbreviated language, then x will be defined as a constant with type Ref T and value ref e in the expanded language.

We will use the val qualifier to distinguish between the value of a variable as a location (*e.g.*, as used on the left side of assignment statements) and the value stored in the variable (*e.g.*, as used on the right side of expressions). Thus if x is an integer variable (identifier with type Ref Integer), we will

```
CellClass = class ({|
        x: Ref Integer = ref 0
    |}, {|
        get: Void → Integer =
                function(v: Void): Integer is {
            return val self.x };

        set: Integer → Command =
                function(nuVal: Integer): Command is {
            self.x := nuVal;
            return nop };

        bump: Void → Command =
                function(v: Void): Command is {
            self ⇐ set(self ⇐ get()+1);
            return nop }
    |})
```

Figure 10.2   CellClass in the fully expanded language.

write

```
    x := (val x) + 1;
```

rather than the more usual x := x + 1.

We will generally not bother to include the Ref types, ref expressions, and val qualifiers in example code, but we will use them in formal specifications in order to distinguish variables of type T from values of type T and the two kinds of values of variables. Having these distinctions show up in the language will make it significantly easier to write type-checking rules and semantics for $\mathcal{SOOL}$.

In order to avoid having to distinguish between functions and procedures in the semantics, the expanded language will represent procedures as functions which return a value nop of type Command, the type of commands. The expression nop stands for a command which does nothing. In the abbreviated language, we will allow return nop to be omitted.

Because of this convention, the return type of procedures will also be given as Command, the type of all other statements, rather than the Void we have been using in the abbreviated language. While this differs from the conventions used in C-style syntax, it is helpful to distinguish between a function which takes a default value () of type Void, and a procedure whose return type indicates that it is executed to change the state of the computer.

Invoking a parameterless method involves applying it to (). In order to make method definitions and invocations more uniform, parameterless methods will be considered to be abbreviations for methods which take a new (and unused) parameter of type Void. Because () has type Void, this will work smoothly with our type-checking rules.

Other differences between the original and the non-abbreviated version of the notation for class definitions are that names of classes and methods are separated from the expressions that define them, and method names are provided with their types. One reason for specifying this somewhat more verbose version of the language is that it will allow us to have anonymous class and function expressions.

The method get in Figure 10.2 illustrates these differences. The method name with its signature (typing) occurs before the equals sign. After the equals sign is the definition of the anonymous function represented by get.

Another change is that the collections of instance variables and methods are grouped together using the symbols "{|" and "|}". These symbols are chosen to be distinct from the curly brackets used to enclose sequences of statements. As we will see in the formal specification, records are not considered expressions or types of *SOOL*. However, notation representing classes as being composed of a record of instance variable declarations and another record of method definitions will make it easier to specify type-checking rules.

These changes are included to make the formal syntax more uniform and allow us to write fewer formal rules for grammar, type checking rules, and semantics. It should be clear that it is easy to automatically translate a program in the abbreviated language into one of the expanded language. Again, all formal specification will be of the expanded language.

10.2　Syntax and type-checking rules

In this section we will provide formal specifications of the syntax and type-checking rules for our simple language, *SOOL*. Later on we will add more constructs to the language to increase its expressiveness. The expressions of *SOOL* are limited to those which type check correctly. As with the typed lambda calculus, we will introduce these expressions in two steps. In this section we provide the syntactic specification of pre-expressions of the language, some examples, and then the type checking rules. The legal expressions of the language will be comprised of those pre-expressions which can be assigned a type via the type-checking rules.

10.2.1 Syntax of types and expressions

The syntax of $\mathcal{SOOL}$ types and expressions will be given by a context-free grammar. Because expressions contain type expressions, we begin by specifying the syntax of types.

Syntax of types

The definition of type expressions will be built from a collection of built-in types (or type constants), $\mathcal{TC}$. We assume that $\mathcal{TC}$ contains at least the type constants `Integer` for the set of integers, `Real` for the real numbers, `Boolean` for the booleans, `Character` for the characters, `String` for the strings, `Void` for a type with only a single value, written (), and `Command` for the type of statements or commands. When convenient, we will assume $\mathcal{TC}$ has other built-in types.

Definition 10.2.1 *The set,* $\mathcal{TYPE}_{\mathcal{SOOL}}(\mathcal{TC}, \mathcal{L}, \mathcal{TI})$, *of type expressions of* $\mathcal{SOOL}$ *over a set* $\mathcal{TC}$ *of type constants, a set* $\mathcal{L}$ *of record labels, and a set* $\mathcal{TI}$ *of type identifiers is given by the following context-free grammar (where we assume* $t \in \mathcal{TI}$, $C \in \mathcal{TC}$, $1_i \in \mathcal{L}$, *and* $T, T_i \in \mathcal{TYPE}_{\mathcal{SOOL}}(\mathcal{TC}, \mathcal{L}, \mathcal{TI})$ *):*

$$
\begin{aligned}
T \in \text{Type} \ ::= \ & C \mid t \mid T_1 \times \ldots \times T_n \to T_{n+1} \mid \text{Ref } T \mid \\
& \text{ObjectType } RT \mid \text{VisObjectType}(RT_i, RT_m) \mid \\
& \text{ClassType}(RT_i, RT_m) \\
RT \in \text{RType} \ ::= \ & \{\!| \ 1_1 \colon T_1; \ldots; 1_n \colon T_n \ |\!\}
\end{aligned}
$$

Items generated by `RType` are not themselves considered legal types of $\mathcal{SOOL}$. Instead these record types are used only to build up legal object and class types. Record types consist of a list of labels and their associated types.

Types of the form $T_1 \times \ldots \times T_n \to T_{n+1}$ are function types, denoting functions which take n arguments of types T_1 through T_n and return a value of type T_{n+1}. Object types are provided with a record type that specifies the names and types of methods.

As discussed earlier, types of the form `Ref T` are reference types, denoting the types of variables holding values of type `T`. An expression with type Integer (*e.g.*, 3+7) denotes an integer value, while an expression x of type Ref Integer denotes an updatable variable holding values of type Integer.

Types of the form ObjectType M are the types of objects with method names and types given by the record type M. (We often use identifiers M and IV to represent record types, where M is used as the type of the record of methods in a class or object, while IV is used as the type of the record of instance variables.) The names and types of instance variables are not visible in object types.

The keyword self provides access to both the instance variables and methods of the object. As a result, we need a type for self that includes the names and types of instance variables, reflecting the fact that they are visible or accessible via self. Thus the type of self will be a "visible" object type rather than ObjectType M. Types of the form VisObjectType(IV^{ref}, M) are introduced explicitly to serve as the types of self. In definitions of this form, IV^{ref} will represent the type of the record of instance variables (all of which will be references), whereas M will represent the type of the record of methods (all of which will be functions).

We have so far only encountered class types briefly in Section 5.3, where we discussed the lack of subtyping between class types. Class types are normally not explicitly written in programs of *SOOL*. However, because we will support class expressions, it is possible to have variables that hold class values or to pass class expressions as parameters to functions.

While objects hide their record of instance variables, the instance variables will be visible in classes, as they may be used in subclasses. (Thus our instance variables behave like protected members of Java or C++, and are visible in subclasses.) Thus the types of instance variables must be specified in class types.

In a class type of the form ClassType(IV, M), IV is the record type specifying the names and types of the initial values of instance variables, while M specifies the names and types of the methods. Notice the difference between the types in visible object types and class types. In the former, IV^{ref} represents the type of the record of instance *variables*. That is, it is a record of reference types. In class types, IV represents the type of a record of *initial values* of instance variables. Typically these will not be explicit references.

Syntax of expressions

The syntax of *SOOL* programs is given by a context-free grammar. Rather than specifying all of the built-in constants and pre-defined functions of the language, we will simply assume that there is a collection, $\mathcal{EC}$, of such expressions. This will allow us to introduce such built-in expressions as needed rather than give a complete specification now. We also assume a collection, $\mathcal{L}$, of labels (used for method and instance variable names), and a set, $\mathcal{EI}$, of expression identifiers.

Definition 10.2.2 *The pre-expressions, $\mathcal{PEXP}_{SOOL}(\mathcal{EC}, \mathcal{L}, \mathcal{EI})$, of $SOOL$ over a set $\mathcal{EC}$ of expression constants, a set $\mathcal{L}$ of labels, and a set $\mathcal{EI}$ of identifier names, is given by the following context-free grammar (where we assume* $\text{id} \in \mathcal{EI}$, $\text{t} \in \mathcal{TI}$, $\text{c} \in \mathcal{EC}$, $\text{l}_i, \text{m}_i \in \mathcal{L}$, *and* $\text{T}, \text{T}_i \in \mathcal{TYPE}_{SOOL}(\mathcal{TC}, \mathcal{L}, \mathcal{TI})$ *):*

$$
\begin{array}{lll}
\text{Prog} & ::= \text{Program id; Blk.} \\
\text{Blk} \in \text{Block} & ::= \text{TDs CDs}\,\{\,\text{S return E}\,\} \\
\text{TDs} \in \text{TDefs} & ::= \epsilon \mid \text{type TDL} \\
\text{TDL} \in \text{TDefLst} & ::= \text{t = T} \mid \text{t = T; TDL} \\
\text{CDs} \in \text{CDefs} & ::= \epsilon \mid \text{const CDL} \\
\text{CDL} \in \text{CDefLst} & ::= \text{id: T = E} \mid \text{id: T = E; CDL} \\
\text{E} \in \text{Exp} & ::= \text{id} \mid \text{c} \mid \text{nil} \mid () \mid \text{val E} \mid \text{ref E} \mid \text{E}(\text{E}_1, \ldots, \text{E}_n) \mid \\
& \quad \text{function}(\text{id}_1 : \text{T}_1, \ldots, \text{id}_n : \text{T}_n) : \text{T}_{n+1} \text{ is Blk} \mid \\
& \quad \text{class}(\text{R}_i, \text{R}_m) \mid \text{new E} \mid \text{E} \Leftarrow \text{m} \mid \text{E.l} \mid \\
& \quad \text{class inherits E modifies } \text{l}_{j_1}, \ldots, \text{l}_{j_m}\,(\text{R}_i, \text{R}_m) \\
\text{R} \in \text{Rec} & ::= \{\!|\ \text{l}_1 : \text{T}_1 = \text{E}_1; \ldots; \text{l}_n : \text{T}_n = \text{E}_n\ |\!\} \\
\text{S} \in \text{Stmt} & ::= \text{nop} \mid \text{id} := \text{E} \mid \text{if E then}\,\{\,\text{S}_1\,\}\,\text{else}\,\{\,\text{S}_2\,\} \mid \\
& \quad \text{while E do}\,\{\,\text{S}\,\} \mid \text{S}_1; \text{S}_2
\end{array}
$$

A program in $SOOL$ consists of a Program statement with the name of the program, followed by a block. The block consists of a list of type and constant definitions (which include definitions of functions and classes), and finally by a statement and return expression surrounded by curly brackets. For programs, the block will be the main program and will return the default value nop. In function bodies, the return value can be any expression of the appropriate type.

The symbol ϵ indicates that a construct may be replaced by an empty string. In other words, the ϵ in type and constant definitions indicates that these constructs are optional.

Expressions in $SOOL$ consist of identifiers, constants, the keyword nil, val expressions, ref expressions, function applications, function expressions, class expressions, new expressions (for creating new objects), message sends, extracting a labeled field, and subclass expressions. The keyword nil represents an uninitialized object.

We have already discussed `ref` and `val` expressions. As stated earlier, if `x` is declared to be a variable of type `T` in the abbreviated language, then `x` will be defined as a constant with type `Ref T` in the expanded language. It will be initialized with an appropriate default value for the type. If `T` is an object type then it will be initialized with `nil`. Variables of number types will be initialized to the zero value of the type, characters to the "NUL" character, and strings to the empty string. Functions will be initialized to functions returning the default value of the result type.

For example, a variable declaration of the form

```
x: Integer;
```

will be transformed into the constant definition

```
x: Ref Integer = ref 0;
```

Thus `x` is initialized to be a reference to a location that initially holds `0`.

Assignment statements can update the value held (referred to) by `x`, but do not change the reference (location) itself. Hence it may be included in with the other constant definitions.

Function applications consist of a function expression followed by the list of actual parameters. Function expressions contain a list of formal parameters and their types, the return type (which is `Command` for procedures), and the function body.

Class expressions contain a record of initial values of instance variables and a record of method definitions. Subclass expressions differ from class expressions by including the superclass and a list of methods that are to be overridden by the subclass. "New" expressions contain the class that is used as a template to generate a new object.

Message sends include the target object and the name of the message. Recall that we use $\Leftarrow$ to distinguish message sends from accesses to instance variables, which use the "." notation. Sending a message to `nil` should result in a run-time error. Labelled field projection normally appears only in the bodies of method expressions. It typically appears in the form `self.x`, where `x` is the name of an instance variable of the class.

The statements of the language include `nop`, assignment statements, if-then-else expressions, while loops, and sequencing of statements. The expression `nop` represents a statement that has no effect (a "no op" or "skip").

Two keywords of the language do not appear in the grammar above. They are `self`, a name for the object currently executing a method, and `close`, a function used to convert the type of `self` in order to hide the instance variables. We do not introduce them as constants because they may appear only inside method definitions, and cannot be assigned types independently of those contexts. In particular their meanings will vary depending on the context. To be consistent with our type-checking rules presented below, these keywords will instead be introduced as "bound" identifiers. The type of `self` will always be the "visible" object type generated by the class definition that contains it. Recall this is necessary so that access is allowed to instance variables.

We have not yet discussed the `close` keyword. Its sole purpose is to convert objects of type `VisObjectType(IV`^{ref}`,M)` to type `ObjectType M` once we no longer need access to instance variables. If the value of `self` is provided outside of the class definition, either by returning it from a method or using it as a parameter in another method, the instance variables should no longer be accessible. In particular, we do not wish to have either the return type or the parameter type of a method be a visible object type that includes the types of instance variables.

Thus, before passing `self` as a parameter or returning it from a method, we will apply `close` in order to convert it to an object type. As with `val`, the abbreviated form of the language will not require the programmer to insert applications of `close`, instead they will automatically be inserted where needed.

10.2.2   Examples

Figure 10.3 contains a very simple example of a complete program in $\mathcal{SOOL}$. It defines a `Point` class, creates an object from `Point`, and moves it. It uses the syntax abbreviations that allow the program to look more like it was written in a typical object-oriented language. Notice that we do not require the section headings `type` and `const`, and variable declarations are written in a form similar to those found in most languages.

If we remove all of the abbreviations, we get the program in Figure 10.4. For this program, the syntax is defined exactly by the context-free grammar given in the previous section.

We have not yet discussed constructors for classes. We will omit constructors in $\mathcal{SOOL}$, replacing them by functions that return classes. In the language with abbreviations we will write these as parameterized classes, but these can be replaced with functions returning classes.

In Figure 10.5, a variation of the program `PointExample` from Figure

```
Program PointExample;

    PointType = ObjectType {
        move: Integer × Integer → Command;
        getx: Void → Integer;
        gety: Void → Integer
    };

    class Point {
        x: Integer = 0;
        y: Integer = 0;
        function move(dx: Integer, dy: Integer): Command is
        {
            x := x + dx;
            y := y + dy }
        function getx(): Integer is { return x }
        function gety(): Integer is { return y }
    };

    pt: PointType;

{
    pt := new Point;
    pt ⇐ move(3,2)
}
```

Figure 10.3   `PointExample` program in language with abbreviations.

10.3 illustrates the use of parameterized classes. The class `PPoint` takes two integers as parameters. The two integer parameters are used to initialize the instance variables x and y.

In Figure 10.6 we remove the abbreviations to reveal the parameterized class to be a function returning a class. In the assignment to `pt` in the main program, the application of `PPoint` to the arguments 2 and 7 has higher priority than the new operator.

```
Program PointExample;
type
   PointType = ObjectType {|
      move: Integer × Integer → Command;
      getx: Void → Integer;
      gety: Void → Integer
   |};
   PtClassType = ClassType ({|
      x: Integer;
      y: Integer
   |}, {|
      move: Integer × Integer → Command;
      getx: Void → Integer;
      gety: Void → Integer
   |});
const
   Point: PtClassType = class ({|
      x: Integer = 0;
      y: Integer = 0;
   |}, {|
      move: Integer × Integer → Command =
         function(dx: Integer, dy: Integer): Command is {
            self.x := (val self.x) + dx;
            self.y := (val self.y) + dy;
            return nop };
      getx: Void → Integer = function(): Integer is {
            return val self.x };
      gety: Void → Integer = function(): Integer is {
            return val self.y };
   |});
   pt: Ref PointType = ref nil;
{
   pt := new Point;
   pt ⇐ move(3,2);
   return nop
}
```

Figure 10.4 PointExample program in language without abbreviations.

```
Program PPointExample;

...

class PPoint(x0: Integer, y0: Integer) {
    x: Integer = x0;
    y: Integer = y0;
    ...
};

pt: PointType;
{
    pt := new PPoint(2,7);
    pt ⇐ move(3,2)
}
```

Figure 10.5   Parameterized Point class in language with abbreviations.

10.2.3   Type-checking rules

Most programming languages do not provide explicit formal rules for statically type-checking programs to the programmer. Instead they are typically implicit in the language definition and then in the code of compilers. However, these rules are not difficult to formulate. As in the typed lambda calculus, the type-checking rules can be given inductively based on the productions of the context-free grammar that generates the language. In this section we provide the formal type-checking rules for $\mathcal{SOOL}$.

As in the typed lambda calculus, the type checking rules require information about the types of free identifiers in an expression and information about the meaning of type identifiers. The static type environment $\mathcal{E}$ associates expression identifiers with types.

Definition 10.2.3 *A static type environment, $\mathcal{E}$, is a finite set of associations between identifiers and type expressions of the form* x: T, *where each* x *is unique in $\mathcal{E}$ and* T *is a type. If the relation* x: T $\in \mathcal{E}$, *then we sometimes write* $\mathcal{E}(x)$ = T.

An important difference between $\mathcal{SOOL}$ and the typed lambda calculus is that $\mathcal{SOOL}$ can include type definitions. These definitions are recorded

```
Program PPointExample;

type
    ...

const

    PPoint: Integer × Integer → PtClassType =
        function(x0: Integer, y0: Integer): PtClassType is {
            return class ({|
                            x: Integer = x0;
                            y: Integer = y0;
                       |}, {|
                            ...
                       |}) }


    pt: Ref PointType = ref nil;

{
    pt := new PPoint(2,7);
    pt ⇐ move(3,2);
    return nop
}
```

Figure 10.6 Parameterized Point class in language without abbreviations.

for type checking purposes in a type constraint system that associates type identifiers with their definitions. That way the identifiers can be replaced by their definitions wherever necessary.

Definition 10.2.4 *Relations of the form* t = T, *where* t *is a type identifier and* T *is a type expression, are said to be* type definitions. *A type constraint system,* $\mathcal{C}$, *is defined as follows:*

TYPE CONSTRAINT
SYSTEM

1. *The empty set,* $\emptyset$, *is a type constraint system.*

2. *If* $\mathcal{C}$ *is a type constraint system and* t *is a type identifier that does not appear in* $\mathcal{C}$ *or* T, *then* $\mathcal{C} \cup \{t = T\}$ *is a type constraint system.*

For example, in type checking the body of the program `PointExample`, $\mathcal{C}$ would contain type definitions for both `PointType` and `PtClassType`.

Recall that a type constraint system for the polymorphic lambda calculus kept track of subtyping assumptions rather than type definitions. We retain the same name here because we will add subtyping definitions to type constraint systems when we add polymorphism to the language.

The function $\mathcal{C}(\mathtt{T})$ returns the type expression formed by replacing all type identifiers in `T` by their definitions in $\mathcal{C}$ (recursively, if necessary).

$\mathcal{C}(\mathtt{T})$ **Definition 10.2.5** $\mathcal{C}(\mathtt{T})$, *for* `T` *a type expression, is defined inductively as follows:*

1. *If* `t` *is a type identifier, then* $\mathcal{C}(\mathtt{t}) = \mathcal{C}(\mathtt{T})$ *if* $(\mathtt{t} = \mathtt{T}) \in \mathcal{C}$, *otherwise* $\mathcal{C}(\mathtt{t}) = \mathtt{t}$.

2. *If* `C` *is a type constant, then* $\mathcal{C}(\mathtt{C}) = \mathtt{C}$.

3. $\mathcal{C}(\mathtt{T}_1 \times \ldots \times \mathtt{T}_n \to \mathtt{T}_{n+1}) = \mathcal{C}(\mathtt{T}_1) \times \ldots \times \mathcal{C}(\mathtt{T}_n) \to \mathcal{C}(\mathtt{T}_{n+1})$.

4. $\mathcal{C}(\mathtt{Ref\,T}) = \mathtt{Ref}\,\mathcal{C}(\mathtt{T})$.

5. $\mathcal{C}(\mathtt{ObjectType\,RT}) = \mathtt{ObjectType}\,\mathcal{C}(\mathtt{RT})$.

6. $\mathcal{C}(\mathtt{VisObjectType\,(RT_i, RT_m)}) = \mathtt{VisObjectType}\,(\mathcal{C}(\mathtt{RT_i}), \mathcal{C}(\mathtt{RT_m}))$.

7. $\mathcal{C}(\mathtt{ClassType\,(RT_i, RT_m)}) = \mathtt{ClassType}\,(\mathcal{C}(\mathtt{RT_i}), \mathcal{C}(\mathtt{RT_m}))$.

8. $\mathcal{C}(\{\!| \mathtt{l}_1 \colon \mathtt{T}_1; \ldots; \mathtt{l}_n \colon \mathtt{T}_n |\!\}) = \{\!| \mathtt{l}_1 \colon \mathcal{C}(\mathtt{T}_1); \ldots; \mathtt{l}_n \colon \mathcal{C}(\mathtt{T}_n) |\!\}$

The function $\mathcal{C}(\mathtt{T})$ is guaranteed to terminate because the restrictions in clause (2) of the definition of $\mathcal{C}$ rule out recursive (or mutually recursive) type definitions. If all free identifiers of `T` are contained in the domain of $\mathcal{C}$, then $\mathcal{C}(\mathtt{T})$ will be a type expression with no free identifiers. A recursive definition is necessary because type definitions occurring later in a program may use type identifiers defined earlier.

We begin by introducing rules that process declarations. Processing a type or constant definition or variable declaration results in adding type information about the new identifiers introduced into the type constraint system, $\mathcal{C}$, or type environment, $\mathcal{E}$.

JUDGEMENT   The symbol $\diamond$ is used to separate a declaration in $\mathcal{SOOL}$ from the resulting constraint system and type environment. A *judgement* of the form $\mathcal{C}, \mathcal{E} \vdash$ `Dec` $\diamond \; \mathcal{C}', \mathcal{E}'$ asserts that, under the assumptions in $\mathcal{C}$ and $\mathcal{E}$, processing the declaration `Dec` results in an enhanced type constraint system, $\mathcal{C}'$, and type environment, $\mathcal{E}'$. This notation makes it clear that the result of processing a declaration is changes to the type constraint system and type environment.

The processing rules for declarations are written similarly to the type-checking rules for the lambda calculus given in Chapter 8:

AxiomName $\qquad\qquad\qquad \mathcal{C}, \mathcal{E} \vdash \text{Dec} \diamond \mathcal{C}', \mathcal{E}'$

if the rule is not dependent on hypotheses, or

$$\textit{RuleName} \quad \frac{\mathcal{C}, \mathcal{E} \vdash \text{Dec}_1 \diamond \mathcal{C}_1, \mathcal{E}_1, \ldots, \mathcal{C}_{n-1}, \mathcal{E}_{n-1} \vdash \text{Dec}_n \diamond \mathcal{C}_n, \mathcal{E}_n}{\mathcal{C}, \mathcal{E} \vdash \text{Dec} \diamond \mathcal{C}_n, \mathcal{E}_n},$$

where the conclusion is written below the line, and the hypotheses are above the line. Typically, the expressions appearing in judgements above the line in rules are subexpressions of the expressions appearing in judgements below the line.

We read the rules starting from the bottom and then proceeding from left to right across the top. For example, the sample rule can be read as stating, "from the type assumptions in $\mathcal{C}$ and $\mathcal{E}$, processing Dec results in a richer collection of type assumptions $\mathcal{C}_n, \mathcal{E}_n$, if processing Dec_1 from $\mathcal{C}$ and $\mathcal{E}$ results in $\mathcal{C}_1, \mathcal{E}_1, \ldots$, and processing Dec_n from $\mathcal{C}_{n-1}, \mathcal{E}_{n-1}$ results in $\mathcal{C}_n, \mathcal{E}_n$."

The type-checking rules for declarations can be found in Figure 10.7. They are relatively straightforward. By rule *TypeDef*, processing a type definition results in adding the definition to $\mathcal{C}$, but no changes to the type environment, $\mathcal{E}$. In contrast, rule *ConstDef* indicates that processing a constant declaration results in adding the constant name and its type to the type environment, but no change to the type constraint system, $\mathcal{C}$. A list of type or constant declarations is processed by processing the first declaration to get an enriched type environment, and then processing the rest of the declarations recursively to get the final type environment.

Type-checking rules for non-declarations are written similarly. A judgement of the form $\mathcal{C}, \mathcal{E} \vdash \text{exp}: \text{T}$ asserts that, under the type assumptions in $\mathcal{C}, \mathcal{E}$, the expression exp has type T. We introduce a special notation to make writing type-checking rules easier. If RType is a record type of the form $\{\!|x_1: T_1; \ldots; x_n: T_n|\!\}$, we let $\text{RType}^{ref} = \{\!|x_1: \text{Ref } T_1; \ldots; x_n: \text{Ref } T_n|\!\}$.

We will give type-checking rules for each of the other syntactic categories of $\mathcal{SOOL}$. We start by providing the type-checking rules for expressions in Figure 10.8.

Most of these rules are straightforward. By rule *Identifier*, an identifier can be deduced to have the type that is specified for it in the type environment,

TypeSec
$$\frac{\mathcal{C}, \mathcal{E} \vdash \texttt{TDefLst} \diamond \mathcal{C}', \mathcal{E}'}{\mathcal{C}, \mathcal{E} \vdash \texttt{type TDefLst} \diamond \mathcal{C}', \mathcal{E}'}$$

TypeDefLst
$$\frac{\mathcal{C}, \mathcal{E} \vdash \texttt{t} = \texttt{T} \diamond \mathcal{C}_1, \mathcal{E}_1 \quad \mathcal{C}_1, \mathcal{E}_1 \vdash \texttt{TDefLst} \diamond \mathcal{C}_2, \mathcal{E}_2}{\mathcal{C}, \mathcal{E} \vdash \texttt{t} = \texttt{T}; \texttt{TDefLst} \diamond \mathcal{C}_2, \mathcal{E}_2}$$

TypeDef
$$\mathcal{C}, \mathcal{E} \vdash \texttt{t} = \texttt{T} \diamond \mathcal{C} \cup \{\texttt{t} = \texttt{T}\}, \mathcal{E} \quad \textit{if } \texttt{t} \notin dom(\mathcal{C})$$

ConstSec
$$\frac{\mathcal{C}, \mathcal{E} \vdash \texttt{CDefLst} \diamond \mathcal{C}', \mathcal{E}'}{\mathcal{C}, \mathcal{E} \vdash \texttt{const CDefLst} \diamond \mathcal{C}', \mathcal{E}'}$$

ConstDefList
$$\frac{\mathcal{C}, \mathcal{E} \vdash \texttt{id}: \texttt{T} = \texttt{E} \diamond \mathcal{C}, \mathcal{E}_1 \quad \mathcal{C}, \mathcal{E}_1 \vdash \texttt{CDefLst} \diamond \mathcal{C}, \mathcal{E}_2}{\mathcal{C}, \mathcal{E} \vdash \texttt{id}: \texttt{T} = \texttt{E}; \texttt{CDefLst} \diamond \mathcal{C}, \mathcal{E}_2}$$

ConstDef
$$\frac{\mathcal{C}, \mathcal{E} \vdash \texttt{E}: \texttt{T} \quad \texttt{id} \notin dom(\mathcal{E})}{\mathcal{C}, \mathcal{E} \vdash \texttt{id}: \texttt{T} = \texttt{E} \diamond \mathcal{C}, \mathcal{E} \cup \{\texttt{id}: \texttt{T}\}}$$

Figure 10.7   Type checking rules for declarations.

$\mathcal{E}$. In reporting the type of the identifier, all of the type identifiers in the type are replaced by their definitions in $\mathcal{C}$. This is done by writing the resulting type as $\mathcal{C}(\texttt{T})$. Because all user-introduced names will be replaced by their definitions during type-checking, *SOOL* uses structural rather than name equivalence of types [Lou93].

By rule *Const*, built-in constants are assigned the type that is provided in the language definition. The expression () is the only value of type Void. The expression nil is unusual in that it can have any object type. Which type it is assigned will depend on context. If E has type T, then ref E is a reference to E, and hence has type Ref T. If E has type Ref T, *i.e.*, is a variable holding values of type T, then val E has type T.

Type checking function definitions is only a bit more complicated. By the *Function* rule, a function has type $\texttt{T}_1 \times \ldots \times \texttt{T}_n \rightarrow \texttt{T}_{n+1}$ iff the body has type $\texttt{T}_{n+1}$ under the added assumptions (in $\mathcal{E}$) that the parameters have types $\texttt{T}_1$ through $\texttt{T}_n$. The assumption on the types of formal parameters is necessary since the function body may involve the formal parameters. Similarly if a function has type $\texttt{T}_1 \times \ldots \times \texttt{T}_n \rightarrow \texttt{T}_{n+1}$, and the actual parameters have types $\texttt{T}_1$ through $\texttt{T}_n$, the *Application* rule indicates that the result of applying the function to the actual parameters has type $\texttt{T}_{n+1}$.

Identifier $\qquad\qquad \mathcal{C}, \mathcal{E} \cup \{\text{id}: \text{T}\} \vdash \text{id}: \mathcal{C}(\text{T})$

Constant $\qquad\qquad\qquad \mathcal{C}, \mathcal{E} \vdash \text{c}: \text{C}$

where C is the pre-assigned type for built-in constant c.

Void $\qquad\qquad\qquad \mathcal{C}, \mathcal{E} \vdash (): \text{Void}$

Nil $\qquad\qquad\qquad \mathcal{C}, \mathcal{E} \vdash \text{nil}: \text{ObjectType M}$

Value $\qquad\qquad \dfrac{\mathcal{C}, \mathcal{E} \vdash \text{E}: \text{Ref T}}{\mathcal{C}, \mathcal{E} \vdash \text{val E}: \text{T}}$

Function $\quad \dfrac{\mathcal{C}, \mathcal{E} \cup \{\text{id}_1: \text{T}_1, \ldots, \text{id}_n: \text{T}_n\} \vdash \text{Block}: \text{T}_{n+1}}{\mathcal{C}, \mathcal{E} \vdash \text{function}(\text{id}_1: \text{T}_1, \ldots, \text{id}_n: \text{T}_n): \text{T}_{n+1} \text{ is Block}:}$
$$\text{T}_1 \times \ldots \times \text{T}_n \to \text{T}_{n+1}$$

Application $\dfrac{\mathcal{C}, \mathcal{E} \vdash \text{E}: \text{T}_1 \times \ldots \times \text{T}_n \to \text{T}_{n+1}, \ \mathcal{C}, \mathcal{E} \vdash \text{E}_1: \text{T}_1, \ldots, \mathcal{C}, \mathcal{E} \vdash \text{E}_n: \text{T}_n}{\mathcal{C}, \mathcal{E} \vdash \text{E}(\text{E}_1, \ldots, \text{E}_n): \text{T}_{n+1}}$

Reference $\qquad\qquad \dfrac{\mathcal{C}, \mathcal{E} \vdash \text{E}: \text{T}}{\mathcal{C}, \mathcal{E} \vdash \text{ref E}: \text{Ref T}}$

Class $\qquad \dfrac{\mathcal{C}, \mathcal{E} \vdash \text{inst}: \text{IV}, \qquad \mathcal{C}', \mathcal{E}' \vdash \text{meth}: \text{M}}{\mathcal{C}, \mathcal{E} \vdash \text{class}(\text{inst}, \text{meth}): \text{ClassType}(\text{IV}, \text{M})}$

where

- $\mathcal{C}' = \mathcal{C} \cup \{\text{SelfType} = \text{VisObjectType}(\text{IV}^{ref}, \text{M})\}$,

- $\mathcal{E}' = \mathcal{E} \cup \{\text{self}: \text{SelfType}, \text{close}: \text{SelfType} \to \text{ObjectType M}\}$, and

- SelfType does not occur in IV or M.

New $\qquad\qquad \dfrac{\mathcal{C}, \mathcal{E} \vdash \text{E}: \text{ClassType}(\text{IV}, \text{M})}{\mathcal{C}, \mathcal{E} \vdash \text{new E}: \text{ObjectType M}}$

Message $\qquad \dfrac{\mathcal{C}, \mathcal{E} \vdash \text{E}: \text{ObjectType} \ \{\!|\text{m}_1: \text{T}_1, \ldots, \text{m}_n: \text{T}_n|\!\}}{\mathcal{C}, \mathcal{E} \vdash \text{E} \Leftarrow \text{m}_i: \text{T}_i}$

Figure 10.8 Type-checking rules for expressions of $\mathcal{SOOL}$, part 1.

The type checking of classes is more challenging. A class of the form class(inst, meth) has type ClassType(IV, M), if two conditions hold. First, the record of instance variables, inst, must have type IV. Second, the record of methods, meth, must have type M.

There is a complication, however. Because method bodies may contain occurrences of self, we need to type check methods in a context that allows us to assign a type to all expressions involving self. We assign the type Self-Type to self, where SelfType = VisObjectType(IV^{ref}, M). Recall that the type expression IV^{ref} represents a record type formed from IV by adding Ref before the type of each field type. That is, if IV = $\{l_1: T_1; \ldots; l_n: T_n\}$, then $IV^{ref} = \{l_1: \text{Ref } T_1; \ldots; l_n: \text{Ref } T_n\}$.

While inst with type IV is the record of initial *values* of instance variables, the type SelfType of self includes the types of the instance *variables* themselves. That is, if x is an instance variable and the class contains an initial value of x of type T, then the corresponding type in the visible object type is Ref T.

Because self will be assigned type SelfType in $\mathcal{E}$, we will be able to type check expressions involving sending messages to self and extracting instance values from self inside the bodies of methods. (The type checking rules for these operations will be introduced in the next figure.) As discussed earlier, close is introduced as a function to convert values (like self) from SelfType to ObjectType M. Its typing is inserted into $\mathcal{E}'$ in order to type check the bodies of methods.

Applying rule *Class* to type check a class definition requires that we know the types of the instance variables and methods *before* we begin type checking, because this information must be added to $\mathcal{C}$ and $\mathcal{E}$ when type checking methods of the class. Our syntax for classes ensures that each instance variable and method definition inside a class does appear with its type information, so no difficulties arise with having to guess what these types might be if inst and meth are written as record expressions. However it is possible that inst or meth could be provided in some other way, *e.g.*, as a formal parameter or the value of a variable, so that we only know a type, rather than the most explicit type.

For example, we might only have partial information on the instance variables or methods in type-checking an expression. Suppose m is a method that is never referenced in any of the other methods of the class, and let M' be the type of the record consisting of all of the methods of the class aside from m. We could then type check the methods under the assumption that Self-Type= VisObjectType(IV^{ref}, M') rather than VisObjectType(IV^{ref}, M).

If the type checking succeeds, then the resulting type of the class would be `ClassType(IV,M')` rather than `ClassType(IV,M)`.

Of course the type of objects generated from the class with this typing would be `ObjectType M' <: ObjectType M`. Thus there is little advantage to obtaining a weaker type for the class. As a result, a type-checking algorithm will normally deduce the most specific type possible for the class. Most languages do not allow a programmer to pass a record of methods or even an individual method into a class. Thus this issue rarely arises.

Finally, note the restriction that `SelfType` may not occur in the types of either instance variables or methods. "Visible object types" are not really part of *SOOL*, they are simply introduced as an aid in type-checking programs. As a result it may not appear explicitly anywhere in a program, though it is used when type checking expressions involving `self`.

Expressions of the form `new E` generate new objects from a class. The new object has an object type with methods corresponding to those given in the class type of `E`. By rules *Message*, a message send has the type of the corresponding method of the object type.

The type-checking rules for subclasses, records, and blocks are given in Figure 10.9.

The type-checking rule for subclasses is longer than any we have seen so far, but it is simpler than it may first appear. Recall from Chapter 6 that a subclass may add new instance variables and methods, but that the types of instance variables may not be changed, and that the types of overridden methods may only be replaced by subtypes. Thus parameters may only change in a contravariant way, and return types in a covariant way.

As a result, to type-check the expression

$$\text{class inherits E modifies } l_{i_1}, \ldots, l_{i_m}(\text{inst}, \text{meth}),$$

we must first determine the type of superclass, `E`, the new instance variables in `inst`, and the new methods in `meth`. We also must ensure that the names of the new instance variables do not overlap with those of `E`, and that if any of the new method names overlap with those of `E`, then the new types in the subclass will be subtypes of those for the superclass `E`. (We do not bother to check whether instance variable and method identifiers overlap since they are referred to in different ways.)

If the type of the subclass is expected to be `ClassType(IV,M)`, then we determine the types of the new methods under the assumption that the type of `self` is `SelfType = VisObjectType(IV`^{ref}`,M)`, and that the type of `close` is `SelfType → ObjectType M`, as with the type checking rule for classes.

Subclass

$$\frac{\mathcal{C}, \mathcal{E} \vdash \text{E: ClassType} (\text{IV}_{sup}, \text{M}_{sup}), \quad \mathcal{C}, \mathcal{E} \vdash \text{inst: IV}_{sub}, \quad \mathcal{C}', \mathcal{E}' \vdash \text{meth: M}_{sub}}{\mathcal{C}, \mathcal{E} \vdash \text{class inherits E modifies } 1_{i_1}, \ldots, 1_{i_m} \quad (\text{inst}, \text{meth}): \text{ClassType} (\text{IV}, \text{M})}$$

where

- $\text{IV} = \text{IV}_{sup} \oplus \text{IV}_{sub}$ and $\text{M} = \text{M}_{sup} \oplus \text{M}_{sub}$,

- there is no overlap in the labels occurring in IV_{sup} and IV_{sub},

- the overlapping labels in M_{sup} and M_{sub} are exactly $1_{i_1}, \ldots, 1_{i_m}$, and the type of each 1_{i_j} in M_{sub} is a subtype of the type of the same label in M_{sup},

- $\mathcal{C}' = \mathcal{C} \cup \{\text{SelfType} = \text{VisObjectType} (\text{IV}^{ref}, \text{M})\}$,

- $\mathcal{E}' = \mathcal{E} \cup \{\text{self: SelfType, close: SelfType} \rightarrow \text{ObjectType M}\}$, and

- SelfType does not occur in IV or M.

Inst Vble

$$\frac{\mathcal{C}, \mathcal{E} \vdash \text{E: VisObjectType} (\text{IVR}, \text{M})}{\mathcal{C}, \mathcal{E} \vdash \text{E.1}_k: \text{T}_k}$$

where $\text{IVR} = \{\! | \, 1_1: \text{T}_1, \ldots, 1_n: \text{T}_n \, | \!\}$ and $1 \leq k \leq n$.

VisObj Message

$$\frac{\mathcal{C}, \mathcal{E} \vdash \text{E: VisObjectType} (\text{IVR}, \text{M})}{\mathcal{C}, \mathcal{E} \vdash \text{E} \Leftarrow \text{m}_j: \text{U}_j}$$

where $\text{M} = \{\! | \, \text{m}_1: \text{U}_1, \ldots, \text{m}_k: \text{U}_k \, | \!\}$ and $1 \leq j \leq k$.

Record

$$\frac{\mathcal{C}, \mathcal{E} \vdash \text{E}_i: \text{T}_i, \; \textit{for } 1 \leq i \leq n}{\mathcal{C}, \mathcal{E} \vdash \{\! | \, 1_1: \text{T}_1 = \text{E}_1, \ldots, 1_n: \text{T}_n = \text{E}_n | \!\}: \{\! | \, 1_1: \text{T}_1, \ldots, 1_n: \text{T}_n | \!\}}$$

Block

$$\frac{\mathcal{C}, \mathcal{E} \vdash \text{TDefs} \diamond \mathcal{C}_1, \mathcal{E}, \; \mathcal{C}_1, \mathcal{E} \vdash \text{CDefs} \diamond \mathcal{C}_1, \mathcal{E}_1, \quad \mathcal{C}_1, \mathcal{E}_1 \vdash \text{S: Command}, \; \mathcal{C}_1, \mathcal{E}_1 \vdash \text{E: T}}{\mathcal{C}, \mathcal{E} \vdash \text{TDefs CDefs} \{ \text{S return E;} \}: \text{T}}$$

where T does not contain any type identifiers defined in TDefs.

Type Abbrev

$$\frac{\mathcal{C}, \mathcal{E} \vdash \text{E: } \mathcal{C}(T)}{\mathcal{C}, \mathcal{E} \vdash \text{E: T}}$$

Figure 10.9   Type-checking rules for expressions of *SOOL*, part 2.

The notation $R \oplus R'$ represents the combination of two record types. The result is a record type with all of the fields of both record types. If there are overlapping labels, then the type associated with each such label in the result is the corresponding type from R'. Thus we can think of $\oplus$ as a right dominant operation that combines record types.

The next two rules provide type-checking rules for message sends and instance variable extraction from elements of type `VisObjectType(IVR,M)`. Recall that the type of `self` in type checking methods in classes and subclasses is of the form `VisObjectType(IVR,M)`. The result of extracting an instance variable has the same type as the corresponding field of the type of the record of instance variables. The type checking rule for message sends to visible object types is essentially the same as for object types and is based only on the type of the methods.

The type of a record, `E`, is determined by the types associated with the individual fields. Notice that record expressions include type expressions along with the values for each field.

A block consists of the declarations and body of either a program or function. By rule *Block*, it is type checked by processing the declarations to obtain a new type environment, which is then used to type check the body and return expression. The body should be a statement, and the type of the return expression determines the type of the block. The type of the block should not involve any local type definitions as they will not be visible outside of the scope of the block.

By using the rule *Identifier*, we end up typing expressions by first removing all user-introduced type identifiers. That is, when $x:T$ is included in $\mathcal{E}$, we assigned x the type $\mathcal{C}(T)$ rather than just `T`. However, as a convenience, we would also like to report the types of expressions with type expressions that use these abbreviations. By rule *Type Abbrev*, we can provide an expression with a type expression involving abbreviations once we determine that the expression has the type obtained by removing the abbreviations.

Figure 10.10 contains type-checking rules for statements. Recall that well-typed statements have type `Command`.

The special constant, nop, is a command, by rule *No Op*. By rule *Assn*, an assignment statement is well-typed if the type of the left side is a reference to the type of the expression appearing on the right side. `If-then-else` and `while` statements are well-typed if the guard expressions have type `Boolean` and the component statements are themselves well-typed. Individual statements in statement lists should be well-typed. However, unlike the lambda calculus, we do not allow non-statements, *i.e.*, expressions with

No Op $\mathcal{C}, \mathcal{E} \vdash$ nop: Command

Assn $\dfrac{\mathcal{C}, \mathcal{E} \vdash \text{id: Ref T}, \qquad \mathcal{C}, \mathcal{E} \vdash \text{E: T}}{\mathcal{C}, \mathcal{E} \vdash \text{id}:= \text{E: Command}}$

Cond $\dfrac{\mathcal{C}, \mathcal{E} \vdash \text{E: Boolean}, \\ \mathcal{C}, \mathcal{E} \vdash \text{S}_1\text{: Command}, \qquad \mathcal{C}, \mathcal{E} \vdash \text{S}_2\text{: Command}}{\mathcal{C}, \mathcal{E} \vdash \text{if E then } \{ \text{S}_1 \} \text{ else } \{ \text{S}_2 \}\text{: Command}}$

While $\dfrac{\mathcal{C}, \mathcal{E} \vdash \text{E: Boolean}, \qquad \mathcal{C}, \mathcal{E} \vdash \text{S: Command}}{\mathcal{C}, \mathcal{E} \vdash \text{while E do } \{ \text{S} \}\text{: Command}}$

StmtList $\dfrac{\mathcal{C}, \mathcal{E} \vdash \text{S}_1\text{: Command}, \qquad \mathcal{C}, \mathcal{E} \vdash \text{S}_2\text{: Command}}{\mathcal{C}, \mathcal{E} \vdash \text{S}_1\text{; S}_2\text{: Command}}$

Program $\dfrac{\mathcal{C}, \mathcal{E} \vdash \text{Block: Command}}{\mathcal{C}, \mathcal{E} \vdash \text{Program id; Block. : Command}}$

Figure 10.10   Type-checking rules for statements of *SOOL*.

type different from Command, to occur in statement lists. Finally, a program is well-typed if the block it contains is well-typed.

We have now defined type-checking rules for the complete language, but we have not yet mentioned subtyping. Rather than using the very simple invariant subtyping rules used in Java and early versions of C++, we instead use the more general rules discussed in Chapter 5. The *SOOL* subtyping rules can be found in Figure 10.11.

Because $\mathcal{C}$ does not contain subtyping assumptions, we need $\mathcal{C}$ only to expand user-defined type definitions. Rule *TypeDef* $_{<:}$ specifies that to determine if two types are subtypes under the assumptions in $\mathcal{C}$, simply expand the type definitions and determine whether the expanded types are subtypes using no assumptions.

The remaining subtyping rules make no direct use of $\mathcal{C}$. Rule *Reflex* $_{<:}$ specifies that a type is always a subtype of itself, while rule *Trans* $_{<:}$ asserts that subtyping is closed under transitivity. Subtyping for functions is covariant in the argument type and contravariant in the argument types by rule *Function* $_{<:}$, just as we would expect based on our earlier discussions of subtyping for function types in Section 5.1.2.

$$TypeDef_{<:} \qquad \frac{\emptyset \vdash \mathcal{C}(\mathtt{S}) <: \mathcal{C}(\mathtt{T})}{\mathcal{C} \vdash \mathtt{S} <: \mathtt{T}}$$

$$Reflex_{<:} \qquad \mathcal{C} \vdash \mathtt{S} <: \mathtt{S}$$

$$Trans_{<:} \qquad \frac{\mathcal{C} \vdash \mathtt{S} <: \mathtt{T}, \qquad \mathcal{C} \vdash \mathtt{T} <: \mathtt{U}}{\mathcal{C} \vdash \mathtt{S} <: \mathtt{U}}$$

$$Function_{<:} \qquad \frac{\mathcal{C} \vdash \mathtt{T}_i <: \mathtt{S}_i, \textit{ for } 1 \le i \le n, \quad \mathcal{C} \vdash \mathtt{S}_{n+1} <: \mathtt{T}_{n+1}}{\mathcal{C} \vdash \mathtt{S}_1 \times \ldots \times \mathtt{S}_n \to \mathtt{S}_{n+1} <: \mathtt{T}_1 \times \ldots \times \mathtt{T}_n \to \mathtt{T}_{n+1}}$$

$$Record_{<:} \qquad \frac{m \le n \textit{ and } \mathcal{C} \vdash \mathtt{S}_i <: \mathtt{T}_i \textit{ for all } 1 \le i \le m}{\mathcal{C} \vdash \{\!| \mathtt{l}_1 \colon \mathtt{S}_1, \ldots, \mathtt{l}_n \colon \mathtt{S}_n |\!\} <: \{\!| \mathtt{l}_1 \colon \mathtt{T}_1, \ldots, \mathtt{l}_m \colon \mathtt{T}_m |\!\}}$$

$$Object_{<:} \qquad \frac{\mathcal{C} \vdash \mathtt{RType'} <: \mathtt{RType}}{\mathcal{C} \vdash \mathtt{ObjectType~RType'} <: \mathtt{ObjectType~RType}}$$

$$Subsumption \qquad \frac{\mathcal{C}, \mathcal{E} \vdash \mathtt{E} \colon \mathtt{S}, \qquad \mathcal{C} \vdash \mathtt{S} <: \mathtt{T}}{\mathcal{C}, \mathcal{E} \vdash \mathtt{E} \colon \mathtt{T}}$$

Figure 10.11   Subtyping rules for $\mathcal{SOOL}$.

Rule *Record* $_{<:}$ indicates that record subtyping includes both width and depth subtyping. Finally, rule *Object* $_{<:}$ specifies that two object types are subtypes if the types of their records of methods are subtypes.

The last rule, *Subsumption*, is actually a type-checking rule rather than a subtyping rule. It states that if an expression has a type, then it can also be assigned any supertype of that type. In Chapter 2 we defined types Color-CellType and CellType where ColorCellType <: CellType. If colorCell has type ColorCellType, then by the *Subsumption* rule it also has type CellType.

10.2.4   A type checking example

In the previous section we presented a number of formal type-checking rules for $\mathcal{SOOL}$. In this section we present an example showing how these rules can be used to type-check $\mathcal{SOOL}$ programs. At the end of the section we include a brief discussion of how the type-checking rules can be used to create a type-checking algorithm for $\mathcal{SOOL}$.

We show how to use the type-checking rules by verifying that the program `PointExample` in Figure 10.4 is type-correct. We start with the program as a whole, and with a type constraint system and type environment, $\mathcal{C}_0, \mathcal{E}_0$, that are both empty.

It follows from the *Program* rule in Figure 10.10 that the program as a whole is well-typed iff its block has type `Command`. Looking back at Figure 10.9, we see that a block is type-checked by processing the type and constant definitions to get an enriched type constraint system and type environment. Then the body of the block is type-checked to make sure that it is well-typed. Finally the type of the entire block is the type of the return expression. In this case the return expression is nop, which by rule *No Op* has type `Command`. Thus the block as a whole will be well-typed if we can first successfully type-check the constant definitions to obtain an enriched type environment, and then can use that enriched type environment to ensure the body of the block is well-typed.

There are two type definitions in the program. By the type-checking rules, both `PointType` with its definition, and `PtClassType` with its definition are added to $\mathcal{C}_0$, resulting in

$$\mathcal{C}_1 = \mathcal{C}_0 \cup \{\texttt{PointType} = \texttt{ObjectType} \ \{\!| \dots |\!\},$$
$$\texttt{PtClassType} = \texttt{ClassType}\,(\dots)\}$$

There are only two constant definitions in the program. The first is of the constant `Point`, which is defined to be a class of type `PtClassType`. We must show that the class expression in Figure 10.12 has type `PtClassType`:

For simplicity, we will use the abbreviations:

$$\texttt{PIV} \ = \{\!| \ \texttt{x: Integer; y: Integer} \ |\!\}$$
$$\texttt{PIVR} = \{\!| \ \texttt{x: Ref Integer; y: Ref Integer} \ |\!\}$$
$$\texttt{PM} \ \ = \{\!| \ \texttt{move: Integer} \times \texttt{Integer} \to \texttt{Command};$$
$$\texttt{getx: Void} \to \texttt{Integer};$$
$$\texttt{gety: Void} \to \texttt{Integer} \ |\!\}$$

We begin by showing that

$$\mathcal{C}_1, \mathcal{E}_0 \vdash \{\!| \ \texttt{x: Integer} = 0; \ \texttt{y: Integer} = 0 \ |\!\}: \texttt{PIV}.$$

```
class ({|
    x: Integer = 0;
    y: Integer = 0;
|}, {|
    move: Integer × Integer → Command =
          function(dx: Integer, dy: Integer): Command is
    { self.x := (val self.x) + dx;
      self.y := (val self.y) + dy;
      return nop};

    getx: Void → Integer =
       function(): Integer is
    { return val self.x };

    gety: Void → Integer = function(): Integer is
    { return val self.y };
|});
```

Figure 10.12   Class definition from `PointExample`.

But this is easy as the *Constant* rule implies that $C_1, \mathcal{E}_0 \vdash 0$: `Integer`.[1] The desired typing of the record of instance variables follows from rule *Record*.

We must next show that the record of methods in `Point` has the type `PM` under the type assumption

$$\mathcal{E}_1 = \mathcal{E}_0 \cup \{\texttt{self: SelfType, close: SelfType} \to \texttt{ObjectType PM}\}$$

and type constraint system

$$C_2 = C_1 \cup \{\texttt{SelfType} = \texttt{VisObjectType(PIVR, PM)}\}.$$

By the *Record* rule, it is sufficient to show that each individual method has the appropriate type. We will only type check the move method, as the others are similar, but simpler.

We must show that the function expression,

```
function(dx: Integer, dy: Integer): Command is {
```

---

1. We did not list all constants of the language in $\mathcal{EC}$, but instead assume familiar constants (like numerals) have the obvious types.

```
self.x := (val self.x) + dx;
self.y := (val self.y) + dy;
return nop }
```

has type `Integer` × `Integer` → `Command` under assumption $C_2, \mathcal{E}_1$.

We type check the function using the *Function* rule by checking the body under type constraint C_2 and type assumption

$$\mathcal{E}_2 = \mathcal{E}_1 \cup \{\text{dx: Integer}, \text{dy: Integer}\}.$$

The first line of the function is an assignment. By rule *Inst Vble* and the assumption on the type of `self` in $\mathcal{E}_2$, it follows that

$$C_2, \mathcal{E}_2 \vdash \text{self.x: Ref Integer}.$$

By the *Value* rule, the type of `val self.x` is `Integer`. The type of `dx` is also `Integer` by the *Identifier* rule, because `dx: Integer` is in $\mathcal{E}_2$.

At this point we must cheat a bit since we did not include a type-checking rule for operations like "+". The operation "+" should actually be written as a prefix function `Plus` with type `Integer`×`Integer`→`Integer`. Then `val self.x + dx` abbreviates `Plus(val self.x, dx)`, which, by the *Application* rule, has type `Integer`. Now the *Assignment* rule allows us to infer from $C_2, \mathcal{E}_2$ that statement

```
self.x := (val self.x) + dx;
```

has type `Command`, because the left side has type `Ref Integer`, and the right side has type `Integer`. Showing the other assignment statement has type `Command` is similar. By the rule *StmtList*, the sequence of the two assignments also has type `Command`.

The expression `nop` has type `Command` by rule *No Op*, so by rule *Block* the whole function body has type `Command` when typed with respect to $C_2, \mathcal{E}_2$. By rule *Function*, the function expression associated with method `move` has type `Integer` × `Integer` → `Command` when typed with $C_2, \mathcal{E}_1$.

Similar arguments show that the other two method bodies have the desired types using the assumptions in $C_2, \mathcal{E}_1$. Hence the record of methods has type `PM` under $C_2, \mathcal{E}_1$. Finally the *Class* rule implies that the entire `Point` body has type `PtClassType`. By rule *ConstDef*,

$$\mathcal{E}_3 = \mathcal{E}_0 \cup \{\text{Point: PtClassType}\}$$

results from processing the definition of `PointClass`, starting with $C_1, \mathcal{E}_0$.

The other definition in the program is

```
pt: Ref PointType = ref nil;
```

By rule *Nil*, nil can be assigned type PointType (this is the one place where we use information about context in type checking). By rule *Reference*, ref nil has type Ref PointType. Therefore by rule *ConstDef*,

$$\mathcal{E}_4 = \mathcal{E}_3 \cup \{\text{pt: Ref PointType}\}$$

results from processing the definition of pt, starting with $\mathcal{C}_1, \mathcal{E}_3$.

By rules *ConstSec* and *ConstDefList* and the results of processing the two constant definitions above, processing the const section of the program results in static type environment $\mathcal{E}_4$. We use this environment along with $\mathcal{C}_1$ to type check the body of the program.

The first assignment statement is well-typed because new Point has type PointType by the *New* rule. The message send of pt $\Leftarrow$ move has type Integer $\times$ Integer $\rightarrow$ Command by rule *Message*, and, by rule *Application*, pt $\Leftarrow$ move(3,2) has type Command. As before, nop has type Command by rule *No Op*. Combining rules *StmtList* and *Block*, it follows that the block consisting of the program declarations and code has type Command. Thus by rule *Program*, the entire program is well-typed.

As the description above shows, type checking a program is fairly mechanical. All constants are declared with their types, so we need only verify that the definitions are of the appropriate types. The expressions representing class and function definitions include sufficient type information in the expressions that the type can be extracted from the expression. For classes (and subclasses) this information can be extracted from the types of the record of instance variables and the record of methods. The types of individual components of records are included in record expressions, so all necessary type information can be extracted from those subexpressions. Then it is only required to check that the subexpressions have the appropriate types.

Most of the other expressions have types that can be simply composed from the types of their subexpressions. For example, the type of a function application will always be the return type of the function, the type of an expression of the form val E is obtained by stripping the Ref off of the type of E, etc. Identifiers' types can be found in the type environment and constants' types are predefined.

That really leaves only nil expressions as problematic. Their types may depend on the context, as with the definition of pt in the sample program. There it was necessary to look at the type declared with the constant in order to determine which type nil should be assigned (it was PointType). We could get around this by creating a new type, Bottom, which is a subtype of all object types, and give nil type Bottom. The *Subsumption* rule could then be used to promote the type of nil to whatever object type is needed in the context. We will forgo adding this new type and simply presume enough information is available from context to allow us to infer an appropriate type for nil.

10.3   Summary

In this chapter we provided a formal definition of the language *SOOL* via a context-free grammar and type-checking rules. As noted earlier, we will usually use an abbreviated version of the language that is closer to existing common object-oriented languages, as it will be easy to algorithmically convert from the simplified language to the stricter formal language.

Simply providing a formal language definition and type-checking rules does not guarantee that a statically typed language is type-safe. For example, how do we know that at run time an expression of some type T will actually hold a value of type T? How do we know that all message sends at run time will be to objects that have methods that can execute in response to the message?

We will address such questions after we have defined the semantics of *SOOL*. In the next chapter, we begin our investigation of a translational semantics for *SOOL*.

11 A Simple Translational Semantics of Objects and Classes

In this chapter we provide a first approximation to the semantics of an object-oriented language via a translation into the language $\Lambda^P_{<:}$. We will see that our first simple translation works well through the definition of classes, but fails to work with subclasses. Nevertheless, it provides a useful first step toward a correct definition. In the next chapter we show how to modify this translation in order to model subclasses correctly.

In this and the following sections we will use the language $\mathcal{SOOL}$ introduced in the last chapter as our source language. We will use the fully expanded language, rather than the abbreviated version, both because it matches the formal description of syntax and type-checking rules given in the last chapter, and because it will be easier to translate.

As discussed earlier, we will presume that all instance variables are hidden from clients (*protected* in Java and C++ notation) and all methods are visible (*public*). In Section 14.4 we will refine the notation, type-checking rules, and semantics so that we can allow the hiding of selected methods as well.

11.1 Representing objects at runtime

Before launching into a description of the formal translation from $\mathcal{SOOL}$ to $\Lambda^P_{<:}$, we discuss the representation of objects in real object-oriented systems.

One possible representation for objects is as pairs of a record of instance variables and a record of methods. We illustrate this with an object generated by class CellClass from Figure 10.2 in the last chapter. The record of instance variables for the object has a single field, which represents a location to hold the value of the instance variable x. The record of methods has fields for each of the methods, get, set, and bump. In these methods, references to `self.x` would be replaced by the address of the slot in the record holding the value of `x`.

Specializing the methods to directly access the instance variables provides for more efficient access to these instance variables in methods. However, it results in great waste of space in class-based systems, as a separate copy of each method must be created for each object existing at runtime because each method has been specialized to only reference its own instance variables. Such a representation may make sense for a delegation-based object-oriented system, but, because of the space inefficiencies, it is not used in implementations of any major class-based languages that we know of. Instead, only one copy of the methods of a class is created, and it is shared by all objects generated by the class. In this case, a convenient representation for objects is as a record of its instance variables along with a pointer to the method suite of the object. Access to the record of instance variables from a method body is obtained by an indirect access of one sort or another.

In our formal representation, we will provide access to instance variables inside method bodies by requiring the record of instance variables to be passed as a parameter to the methods. This could be done in two ways. One might add an extra parameter representing the record of instance variables to each method of the class. Alternatively, we could parameterize the entire record of methods by the record of instance variables. From a formal point of view, these are essentially equivalent. We will choose the second of these for notational simplicity. It might be interesting to investigate which choice would provide the best average execution-time efficiency.

In the next section we present our "implementation" of objects by providing a translation from $\mathcal{SOOL}$ into $\Lambda_{<:}^P$. That translation results in a representation of objects as pairs. The first component of the pair is a record of instance variables. The second component is a function that takes a record of instance variables as a parameter, and returns the message suite specialized to that record of instance variables. (*See details below.*) While our objects will actually contain the parameterized method suites as part of the object representation, it should be clear that these functions are identical for all objects created from the same class, and hence they could be stored in a central location (*e.g.*, with the class) and accessed via references from the object.

As suggested earlier, it would be possible to specialize the method suite to each particular object, essentially by compiling into the method suite the references to each instance variable. However, we prefer the representation where the method suites for all objects created from a given class are identical, and thus can be shared.

$$\mathcal{T}_C[\![\mathtt{C}]\!] \triangleq C$$

$$\mathcal{T}_C[\![\mathtt{t}]\!] \triangleq \begin{cases} \mathtt{t} & \text{if } \mathcal{C}(\mathtt{t}) = \mathtt{t} \\ \mathcal{T}_C[\![\mathcal{C}(\mathtt{t})]\!] & \text{otherwise} \end{cases}$$

$$\mathcal{T}_C[\![\mathtt{T_1} \times \ldots \times \mathtt{T_n} \to \mathtt{T_{n+1}}]\!] \triangleq \mathcal{T}_C[\![\mathtt{T_1}]\!] \times \ldots \times \mathcal{T}_C[\![\mathtt{T_n}]\!] \to \mathcal{T}_C[\![\mathtt{T_{n+1}}]\!]$$

$$\mathcal{T}_C[\![\mathtt{Ref\ T}]\!] \triangleq Ref\ \mathcal{T}_C[\![\mathtt{T}]\!]$$

$$\mathcal{T}_C[\![\{\!| \mathtt{l_1} \colon \mathtt{T_1}; \ldots; \mathtt{l_n} \colon \mathtt{T_n} |\!\}]\!] \triangleq \{\!| \mathtt{l_1} \colon \mathcal{T}_C[\![\mathtt{T_1}]\!]; \ldots; \mathtt{l_n} \colon \mathcal{T}_C[\![\mathtt{T_n}]\!] |\!\}$$

$$\mathcal{T}_C[\![\mathtt{VisObjectType(IVR,M)}]\!] \triangleq \mathcal{T}_C[\![\mathtt{IVR}]\!] \times (\mathcal{T}_C[\![\mathtt{IVR}]\!] \to \mathcal{T}_C[\![\mathtt{M}]\!])$$

$$\mathcal{T}_C[\![\mathtt{ObjectType\ M}]\!] \triangleq \exists Y.\, Y \times (Y \to \mathcal{T}_C[\![\mathtt{M}]\!])$$

Figure 11.1   Translation of types of $\mathcal{SOOL}$ to types in $\Lambda^P_{<:}$.

11.2   Modeling $\mathcal{SOOL}$ types in $\Lambda^P_{<:}$

In this section we provide a formal mapping from $\mathcal{SOOL}$ types to $\Lambda^P_{<:}$ types in which the representation of objects corresponds to the implementations described in the previous section. The translation function, denoted $\mathcal{T}_C[\![\ ]\!]$, will provide the translation of both types and expressions of the language $\mathcal{SOOL}$ to types and expressions of $\Lambda^P_{<:}$. We include the type constraint $\mathcal{C}$ as a subscript, because the translation may involve type variables that should be replaced by the translations of their definitions in $\mathcal{C}$. The translation of types is given in Figure 11.1.

Constant types are translated to fixed types in $\Lambda^P_{<:}$ with no free type identifiers. For example we could let $\mathcal{T}_C[\![\mathtt{Integer}]\!] \triangleq Integer$, where $Integer$ is the type of $\Lambda^P_{<:}$ representing the collection of integers, and $\mathcal{T}_C[\![\mathtt{Void}]\!] \triangleq Void$.

Because $\Lambda^P_{<:}$ includes both product and function types, the function types of $\mathcal{SOOL}$ are translated by translating the component types and then combining them using the corresponding type constructors in $\Lambda^P_{<:}$. Record types of $\mathcal{SOOL}$ are similarly translated by creating the corresponding record types in $\Lambda^P_{<:}$, replacing the types of fields by their translations using $\mathcal{T}_C[\![\ ]\!]$.

To simplify notation in the definition of object types, we introduce the following abbreviations. If $\mathtt{IV} = \{\mathtt{l_1} \colon \mathtt{T_1}; \ldots; \mathtt{l_n} \colon \mathtt{T_n}\}$, let $\mathtt{IV}^{ref} = \{\mathtt{l_1} \colon \mathtt{Ref\ T_1}; \ldots; \mathtt{l_n} \colon \mathtt{Ref\ T_n}\}$. Similarly, if $\mathtt{inst} = \{\mathtt{l_1} \colon \mathtt{T_1} := \mathtt{E_1}; \ldots; \mathtt{l_n} \colon \mathtt{T_n} := \mathtt{E_n}\}$, then let $\mathtt{inst}^{ref} = \{\mathtt{l_1} \colon \mathtt{Ref\ T_1} := \mathtt{ref\ E_1}; \ldots; \mathtt{l_n} \colon \mathtt{Ref\ T_n} := \mathtt{ref\ E_n}\}$. This notation is useful because classes will provide only the initial values of instance variables, while objects will contain variables that are initialized to those values.

Thus if IV is the type of the record of initial values given by a class, IV^{ref} will be the type of the actual record of instance variables for objects generated by that class.

The types in Figure 11.1 include the type VisObjectType(IVR,M) that was introduced in the last chapter. Again, think of VisObjectType(IVR, M) as presenting the view of an object as seen from the "inside", with both the instance variables and methods accessible.

As described earlier, we represent objects as pairs in which the first component is the record of instance variables and the second component is a function taking the record of instance variables and returning the record of methods that access these instance variables. Let IVR be the type of the record of instance variables of an object and let M be the type of the record of methods of the same object. As presented in Figure 11.1, the translation of VisObjectType(IVR, M) is obtained by using $\mathcal{T}_C[\![\ ]\!]$ to translate the types IVR and M, and then creating the type of pairs whose first component has type $\mathcal{T}_C[\![\text{IVR}]\!]$ and whose second component has type $\mathcal{T}_C[\![\text{IVR}]\!] \to \mathcal{T}_C[\![\text{M}]\!]$. Note that if IV is the type of the record of initial values for instance variables in a class and M is the type of its methods, then the internal view of objects built from the class will have type VisObjectType(IV^{ref}, M). Thus we replace the IV in the class definition by IV^{ref} in the actual object.

With this representation we can obtain access to instance variables of an object by accessing the appropriate field of the first component of the pair representing the object. We obtain access to a method of the object by first applying the second component of the pair (the parameterized methods) to the first (the record of instance variables). Now that the record of methods has been provided access to the instance variables, it is only necessary to select the appropriate method.

We illustrate the translation with the example of objects generated from the class CellClass. The type of the values of instance variables in objects generated from CellClass is

$$\text{CellIV} \triangleq \{\!| \ x\colon \text{Integer} \ |\!\}$$

while the type of the record of methods is

$$\text{CellM} \triangleq \{\!| \ \text{get}\colon \text{Void} \to \text{Integer};$$
$$\text{set}\colon \text{Integer} \to \text{Void};$$
$$\text{bump}\colon \text{Void} \to \text{Void} \ |\!\}$$

The type of x in CellIV is Integer rather than Ref Integer because it refers only to the values stored in the instance variables. The references will be added in forming the meaning of the object type.

Because `CellIV` and `CellM` include only non-object types, their translations are simple. Let *CellIV* $\triangleq \mathcal{T}_C[\![$`CellIV`$]\!]$, *RfCellIV* $\triangleq \mathcal{T}_C[\![$`CellIV`$^{ref}]\!]$ and *CellM* $\triangleq \mathcal{T}_C[\![$`CellM`$]\!]$. Then

$$CellIV = \{\!|\; x\colon Integer|\!\},$$

$$RfCellIV = \{\!|\; x\colon Ref\,Integer|\!\},$$

and

$$CellM = \{\!|\; get\colon Void \to Integer;$$
$$set\colon Integer \to Void;$$
$$bump\colon Void \to Void|\!\}$$

The types of instance variables in the translations have been converted to the corresponding reference types. The structures of the original and translated types of methods are identical, with base types like `Void` and `Integer` of $\mathcal{SOOL}$ replaced by the corresponding types, *Void* and *Integer*, of $\Lambda^P_{<:}$.

It follows that

$$\mathcal{T}_C[\![\texttt{VisObjectType}(\texttt{CellIV}^{ref},\texttt{CellM})]\!] = RfCellIV \times (RfCellIV \to CellM).$$

We will use the following abbreviation to simplify writing the interpretations of visible object types:

$$VisObj\,(IV, M) \triangleq IV \times (IV \to M)$$

Thus we can now write

$$\mathcal{T}_C[\![\texttt{VisObjectType}(\texttt{CellIV}^{ref},\texttt{CellM})]\!] = VisObj\,(RfCellIV, CellM).$$

If o has type $\mathcal{T}_C[\![\texttt{VisObjectType}(\texttt{CellIV}^{ref},\texttt{CellM})]\!]$, then *inst* $\triangleq proj_1(o)$ represents the record of instance variables of o, while *inst.x* returns (the location of) instance variable x of o. The expression *methfun* $\triangleq proj_2(o)$ represents the function which takes a record of instance variables and returns the suite of methods that use that record of instance variables. Thus *methfun(o)* represents the method suite instantiated with o. As a result, *methfun(o).bump$\langle\rangle$* extracts the method body of bump and applies it to $\langle\rangle$, providing a command that increases the value of instance variable x of o by 1.

This leaves us with only the translation of `ObjectType` M in Figure 11.1 left to explain. Recall that the difference between `VisObjectType(IVR,`

M) and `ObjectType` M is that instance variables should not be accessible in values of type `ObjectType` M. If the type of the object were to include the type of the instance variables, then clients could get access to the instance variables of the object.

In particular, we would like it to be possible for several distinct classes (*e.g.*, with different collections of instance variables) to generate objects with the same type. Thus it is important that the type of instance variables *not* appear in object types.

We introduced existential types exactly so that we could hide this sort of information. Thus the only change we need to make to our representation of `VisObjectType(IVR, M)` is to hide the type of the instance variables by using an existential type as shown in the definition in Figure 11.1. Using the abbreviation introduced above,

$$\mathcal{T}_C[\![\texttt{VisObjectType}(\texttt{CellIV}^{ref}, \texttt{CellM})]\!] = VisObj\,(RfCellIV, CellM)$$

while

$$\mathcal{T}_C[\![\texttt{ObjectType CellM}]\!] = \exists Y.\,VisObj\,(Y, CellM).$$

Intuitively, the object type admits to the fact that the type of the record of instance variables occurs in the representation of the object type, but it does not reveal exactly what that type is.

We can transform objects from a visible object type into a regular object type by applying the function *closeobj*, which, when provided with the translations of the types `IVR` and `M` of the record of instance variables and methods, takes values of type $\mathcal{T}_C[\![\texttt{VisObjectType}(\texttt{IVR},\texttt{M})]\!]$ to values of type $\mathcal{T}_C[\![\texttt{ObjectType M}]\!]$ by "packing" the value to hide the type of the record of instance variables:

closeobj

$$closeobj \triangleq \Lambda IVR.\,\Lambda M.\,\lambda(vo\colon IVR \times (IVR \to M)).$$
$$pack\ \langle IVR, vo\rangle\ as\ \exists Y.\,Y \times (Y \to M)$$

Thus *closeobj* is a polymorphic function of type

$$closeobj\colon \forall IVR.\,\forall M.\,(IVR \times (IVR \to M)) \to (\exists Y.\,(Y \times (Y \to M))).$$

or, equivalently,

$$closeobj\colon \forall IVR.\,\forall M.\,VisObj\,(IVR, M) \to (\exists Y.\,VisObj\,(Y, M)).$$

Going back to our example, the type of objects generated by `CellClass` will be `CellType` $\triangleq$ `ObjectType CellM`, and

$$\mathcal{T}_C[\![\texttt{CellType}]\!] = \exists Y.\,Y \times (Y \to CellM).$$

Sending messages to values of object type is now just slightly more work than with visible types. We must first "open" the existential before applying the second component to the first and then extracting the appropriate method. We show more details in the next section.

The observant reader will have noticed that we have not yet provided a translation for class types. We will postpone all discussions of classes and their types until later in this chapter.

We end this section with the observation that our translation of $SOOL$ types into $\Lambda^P_{<:}$ types preserves subtyping.

Theorem 11.2.1 *If* S *and* T *are types in* $SOOL$ *such that* $C \vdash$ S $<:$ T*, then* $\emptyset \vdash$ $\mathcal{T}_C[\![$S$]\!] <: \mathcal{T}_C[\![T]\!]$ *in* $\Lambda^P_{<:}$.

Proof.   Most cases are trivial because nearly all of the types of $SOOL$ translate directly into similar types in $\Lambda^P_{<:}$. The use of type abbreviations goes through because the abbreviations are removed by the definition of the translation of type identifiers. The only other interesting case is for object types, as visible object types have no non-trivial subtypes.

Suppose $C \vdash$ ObjectType M$'$ $<:$ ObjectType M. By the subtyping rules for $SOOL$ this can only occur if $C \vdash$ M$'$ $<:$ M. By induction on the subtyping derivation, $\emptyset \vdash \mathcal{T}_C[\![M'$ $]\!] <: \mathcal{T}_C[\![M]\!]$. By the function and product type subtyping rules of $\Lambda^P_{<:}$, it follows that $\emptyset \vdash Y \times (Y \to \mathcal{T}_C[\![M'$ $]\!]) <: Y \times (Y \to \mathcal{T}_C[\![M]\!])$. Finally, by rule *Exist* $_{<:}$,

$$\emptyset \vdash \exists Y. Y \times (Y \to \mathcal{T}_C[\![M'$ $]\!]) <: \exists Y. Y \times (Y \to \mathcal{T}_C[\![M]\!]).$$

■

11.3   Modeling $SOOL$ expressions in $\Lambda^P_{<:}$

In this section we provide translations of most of the expressions and statements of $SOOL$ into $\Lambda^P_{<:}$. We will see later that the translations of classes and subclasses depend on the types of some of these expressions. As a result, our translation is actually based on the typing of the expressions, rather than just the expressions themselves. If $C, \mathcal{E} \vdash$ E: T then we write $\mathcal{T}_C[\![C, \mathcal{E} \vdash$ E: T$]\!]$ to represent the translation of that typing of the expression.

Two different typings of an expression may result in two different translations of the expression. Of more concern, because the translation actually depends on the actual typing derivation of a type for an expression, it appears that two different derivations of the same type for an expression may result in two different translations, even though they both have the same final type. Thus $\mathcal{T}_\mathcal{C}[\![\mathcal{C}, \mathcal{E} \vdash \text{E: T}]\!]$ may not be well-defined if two different derivations of $\mathcal{C}, \mathcal{E} \vdash \text{E: T}$ result in different translations. As a result it appears we should write $\mathcal{T}_\mathcal{C}[\![\mathcal{D}, \mathcal{C}, \mathcal{E} \vdash \text{E: T}]\!]$, where $\mathcal{D}$ is a derivation of the typing, instead.

However, we will see in Section 13.2, that with only very slight restrictions on $\mathcal{SOOL}$ to ensure that classes have unique types, the translation will be independent of the actual typing derivation. The reader can check that all of the translations given in this section may easily be shown to be independent of the type of the expression, let alone its typing derivation, though that will change in the next section when we introduce the translation of classes. In order to reflect that dependency we will write $\mathcal{T}_\mathcal{C}[\![\mathcal{C}, \mathcal{E} \vdash \text{E: T}]\!]$ for the translation from $\mathcal{SOOL}$ to $\Lambda^P_{<:}$.

We postpone the translations of the `class`, `subclass` and `new` expressions until later. See Figure 11.2 for the translations of the typings of other $\mathcal{SOOL}$ expressions.

The translation of non-object-oriented expressions is relatively straightforward. Identifiers of $\mathcal{SOOL}$ are translated to corresponding identifiers of $\Lambda^P_{<:}$. Constants are translated into *closed* expressions of $\Lambda^P_{<:}$ of the appropriate type. (An expression is closed if it has no free identifiers.) For example, the constant 2 of $\mathcal{SOOL}$ could be translated to the expression $\underline{2}$ of $\Lambda^P_{<:}$. Application of a function to n arguments is translated as the application of the translated function to an n-tuple of the translated arguments. Similarly for the definition of a function of n arguments. Translation of `val`, `ref`, and `record` expressions is straightforward. We postpone the discussion of `nil` until Section 14.2.

Translation of the blocks that form the bodies of functions and also form the main program is a bit tricky because blocks introduce new type and constant definitions. We use the *let* expressions introduced as abbreviations in Chapters 8 and 9 to make the translation more readable. Type definitions are translated into type *let* expressions introducing the appropriate names for the translations of the type definitions. Similarly, regular *let* expressions bind names for constant expressions in the $\mathcal{SOOL}$ program. All of these are used in the translation of the body of the `Block`.

If we did not use the *let* expressions, the definition would have to be given in the following, less readable, style:

$$\mathcal{T}_C[\![\mathcal{C}, \mathcal{E} \vdash \texttt{id: T}]\!] \triangleq id$$

$$\mathcal{T}_C[\![\mathcal{C}, \mathcal{E} \vdash \texttt{c: T}]\!] \triangleq c$$

$$\mathcal{T}_C[\![\mathcal{C}, \mathcal{E} \vdash \texttt{(): Void}]\!] \triangleq \langle\rangle$$

$$\mathcal{T}_C[\![\mathcal{C}, \mathcal{E} \vdash \texttt{val E: Ref T}]\!] \triangleq val\ \mathcal{T}_C[\![\mathcal{C}, \mathcal{E} \vdash \texttt{E: T}]\!]$$

$$\mathcal{T}_C[\![\mathcal{C}, \mathcal{E} \vdash \texttt{ref E: Ref T}]\!] \triangleq ref\ \mathcal{T}_C[\![\mathcal{C}, \mathcal{E} \vdash \texttt{E: T}]\!]$$

$$\mathcal{T}_C[\![\mathcal{C}, \mathcal{E} \vdash \texttt{E(E}_1, \ldots, \texttt{E}_n\texttt{): T}]\!] \triangleq \mathcal{T}_C[\![\mathcal{C}, \mathcal{E} \vdash \texttt{E: T}_1 \times \ldots \times \texttt{T}_n \to \texttt{T}]\!]$$
$$(\langle \mathcal{T}_C[\![\mathcal{C}, \mathcal{E} \vdash \texttt{E}_1\texttt{: T}_1]\!], \ldots, \mathcal{T}_C[\![\mathcal{C}, \mathcal{E} \vdash \texttt{E}_n\texttt{: T}_n]\!]\rangle)$$

$$\mathcal{T}_C[\![\mathcal{C}, \mathcal{E} \vdash \texttt{function(id}_1\texttt{: T}_1, \ldots, \texttt{id}_n\texttt{: T}_n\texttt{):T is Block:}$$
$$\texttt{T}_1 \times \ldots \times \texttt{T}_n \to \texttt{T}]\!] \triangleq$$
$$\lambda(\langle id_1\colon \mathcal{T}_C[\![\texttt{T}_1]\!], \ldots, id_n\colon \mathcal{T}_C[\![\texttt{T}_n]\!]\rangle). \mathcal{T}_C[\![\mathcal{C}, \mathcal{E}' \vdash \texttt{Block: T}]\!]$$
$$\text{where } \mathcal{E}' = \mathcal{E} \cup \{\texttt{id}_1\texttt{: T}_1, \ldots, \texttt{id}_n\texttt{: T}_n\}$$

$$\mathcal{T}_C[\![\mathcal{C}, \mathcal{E} \vdash \{\!| \texttt{ l}_1\texttt{: T}_1 = \texttt{E}_1; \ldots; \texttt{l}_n\texttt{: T}_n = \texttt{E}_n |\!\}\texttt{: } \{\!| \texttt{ l}_1\texttt{: T}_1; \ldots; \texttt{l}_n\texttt{: T}_n |\!\}]\!] \triangleq$$
$$\{\!| \texttt{ l}_1\texttt{: } \mathcal{T}_C[\![\texttt{T}_1]\!] = \mathcal{T}_C[\![\mathcal{C}, \mathcal{E} \vdash \texttt{E}_1\texttt{: T}_1]\!]; \ldots; \texttt{l}_n\texttt{: } \mathcal{T}_C[\![\texttt{T}_n]\!] = \mathcal{T}_C[\![\mathcal{C}, \mathcal{E} \vdash \texttt{E}_n\texttt{: T}_n]\!] |\!\}$$

$$\mathcal{T}_C[\![\mathcal{C}, \mathcal{E} \vdash \texttt{Block: T}]\!] \triangleq let\ t_1 = \mathcal{T}_C[\![\texttt{T}_1]\!]\ in\ \ldots\ let\ t_n = \mathcal{T}_C[\![\texttt{T}_n]\!]\ in$$
$$let\ id_1\colon \mathcal{T}_C[\![\texttt{U}_1]\!] = \mathcal{T}_C[\![\mathcal{C}, \mathcal{E} \vdash \texttt{E}_1\texttt{: U}_1]\!]\ in\ \ldots$$
$$let\ id_k\colon \mathcal{T}_C[\![\texttt{U}_k]\!] = \mathcal{T}_C[\![\mathcal{C}, \mathcal{E} \vdash \texttt{E}_k\texttt{: U}_k]\!]\ in$$
$$\mathcal{T}_C[\![\mathcal{C}, \mathcal{E} \vdash \texttt{S: Command}]\!]; \mathcal{T}_C[\![\mathcal{C}, \mathcal{E} \vdash \texttt{E: T}]\!]\ end\ \ldots\ end$$
$$\text{where } \texttt{Block is}\ \ \texttt{type t}_1 = \texttt{T}_1; \ldots; \texttt{t}_n = \texttt{T}_n$$
$$\texttt{const id}_1\texttt{: U}_1 = \texttt{E}_1; \ldots; \texttt{id}_k\texttt{: U}_k = \texttt{E}_k$$
$$\{\ \texttt{S return E}\ \}$$

$$\mathcal{T}_C[\![\mathcal{C}, \mathcal{E} \vdash \texttt{E} \Leftarrow \texttt{m}_i\texttt{: T}_i]\!] \triangleq (proj_2(\mathcal{T}_C[\![\mathcal{C}, \mathcal{E} \vdash \texttt{E: T}]\!])(proj_1(\mathcal{T}_C[\![\mathcal{C}, \mathcal{E} \vdash \texttt{E: T}]\!]))).m$$
$$\text{where } \texttt{T} = \texttt{VisObjectType}(\texttt{IVR}, \texttt{ObjectType } \{\!| \texttt{m}_1\texttt{: T}_1, \ldots, \texttt{m}_n\texttt{: T}_n |\!\})$$

$$\mathcal{T}_C[\![\mathcal{C}, \mathcal{E} \vdash \texttt{E} \Leftarrow \texttt{m}_i\texttt{: T}_i]\!] \triangleq open\ \mathcal{T}_C[\![\mathcal{C}, \mathcal{E} \vdash \texttt{E: T}]\!]\ as\ \langle IR, vo\rangle$$
$$in\ (proj_2(vo)(proj_1(vo))).m$$
$$\text{where } \texttt{T} = \texttt{ObjectType } \{\!| \texttt{m}_1\texttt{: T}_1, \ldots, \texttt{m}_n\texttt{: T}_n |\!\}$$

$$\mathcal{T}_C[\![\mathcal{C}, \mathcal{E} \vdash \texttt{E.l}_k\texttt{: T}_k]\!] \triangleq proj_1(\mathcal{T}_C[\![\mathcal{C}, \mathcal{E} \vdash \texttt{E: VisObjectType}(\texttt{IVR}, \texttt{M})]\!]).l$$
$$\text{where } \texttt{IVR} = \{\!| \texttt{ l}_1\texttt{: T}_1, \ldots, \texttt{l}_n\texttt{: T}_n |\!\} \text{ and } 1 \le k \le n.$$

Figure 11.2   Translation of selected expressions of $\mathcal{SOOL}$ to expressions in $\Lambda^P_{<:}$.

$$\mathcal{T}_C[\![\mathcal{C}, \mathcal{E} \vdash \texttt{Block: T}]\!] \triangleq (\Lambda t_1 \dots \Lambda t_n \cdot (\lambda(id_1 \colon \mathcal{T}_C[\![\texttt{U}_1]\!]) \dots ; \lambda(id_k \colon \mathcal{T}_C[\![\texttt{U}_k]\!]) \cdot$$
$$\mathcal{T}_C[\![\mathcal{C}, \mathcal{E} \vdash \texttt{S: Command}]\!]; \mathcal{T}_C[\![\mathcal{C}, \mathcal{E} \vdash \texttt{E: T}]\!])$$
$$[\mathcal{T}_C[\![\texttt{T}_1]\!]] \dots [\mathcal{T}_C[\![\texttt{T}_n]\!]] (\mathcal{T}_C[\![\mathcal{C}, \mathcal{E} \vdash \texttt{E}_1 \colon \texttt{U}_1]\!]) \dots (\mathcal{T}_C[\![\mathcal{C}, \mathcal{E} \vdash \texttt{E}_k \colon \texttt{U}_k]\!])$$
$$\text{where } \texttt{Block} = \texttt{type } \texttt{t}_1 = \texttt{T}_1; \dots; \texttt{t}_n = \texttt{T}_n$$
$$\texttt{const } \texttt{id}_1 \colon \texttt{U}_1 := \texttt{E}_1; \dots; \texttt{id}_k \colon \texttt{U}_k := \texttt{E}_k$$
$$\{ \texttt{ S; return E } \}$$

Using the rule *TypeLet* in Section 9.1, it can be shown that handling the type definitions by the use of type parameters is equivalent to adding expressions of the form $t_i = \mathcal{T}_C[\![\texttt{T}_i]\!]$ to $\mathcal{C}$.

Translation of message sends depends on the type of the receiver. Suppose first that the receiver has a type of the form `VisObjectType(IV,M)` (*e.g.*, it is `self`). Recall from the previous section that the translation of this type is of the form $IV \times (IV \to M)$. To send a message to an object with this type, simply apply the second component (the method suite) of the object to the first component (the record of instance variables), and then extract the appropriate method.

Suppose, on the other hand, that the receiver has a type of the form `ObjectType M`. The translation of this type is of the form $\exists Y. Y \times (Y \to M)$. Therefore, to send a message to an object of this type, the object must first be opened before performing the same operations as the earlier case (*i.e.*, applying the second component to the first component and then extracting the appropriate method).[1]

Extraction of instance variables is obtained simply by extracting the appropriate field of the first component of the object (recall that instance variables are only available in values with type of the form `VisObjectType(IVR,M)`).

Because the translation of expressions is by induction on the type derivations, we must also include a translation corresponding to the application of the subsumption rule to promote the type of an expression from a subtype to a supertype. This is completely trivial as it simply gives the expression with supertype exactly the same type as the same expression with the subtype.

The translation of statements of $\mathcal{SOOL}$ is given in Figure 11.3. The translation of `if-then-else`, assignment, and sequencing expressions are trivial. Translations of programs are obtained as the translations of their blocks. The

---

1. We could have used slightly different syntax for these two types of definitions in order to avoid having the translation depend on the type of the receiver. For example, it would be easy to have the type-checker generate different notations for the internal representations of expressions. However, we decided the distinction was not worth the effort here.

$$\mathcal{T_C}[\![\mathcal{C}, \mathcal{E} \vdash \texttt{if E then } \{S_1\} \texttt{ else } \{S_2\} \texttt{: Command}]\!] \triangleq$$
$$\textit{if } \mathcal{T_C}[\![\mathcal{C}, \mathcal{E} \vdash \texttt{E: Boolean}]\!] \textit{ then } \{\mathcal{T_C}[\![\mathcal{C}, \mathcal{E} \vdash S_1 \texttt{: Command}]\!]\}$$
$$\textit{else } \{\mathcal{T_C}[\![\mathcal{C}, \mathcal{E} \vdash S_2 \texttt{: Command}]\!]\}$$

$$\mathcal{T_C}[\![\mathcal{C}, \mathcal{E} \vdash \texttt{E: T}]\!] \triangleq \mathcal{T_C}[\![\mathcal{C}, \mathcal{E} \vdash \texttt{E: S}]\!]$$
where $\mathcal{C} \vdash \texttt{S} <: \texttt{T}$.

$$\mathcal{T_C}[\![\mathcal{C}, \mathcal{E} \vdash \texttt{id}:= \texttt{E: Command}]\!] \triangleq \textit{id}:= \mathcal{T_C}[\![\mathcal{C}, \mathcal{E} \vdash \texttt{E: T}]\!]$$
where $\mathcal{C}, \mathcal{E} \vdash \texttt{id: Ref T}$

$$\mathcal{T_C}[\![\mathcal{C}, \mathcal{E} \vdash \texttt{while E do } \{S\} \texttt{: Command}]\!] \triangleq \textit{fix}\,[\textit{Command}](\lambda(w\text{: } \textit{Command}).$$
$$\textit{if } \mathcal{T_C}[\![\mathcal{C}, \mathcal{E} \vdash \texttt{E: Command}]\!] \textit{ then } \{\mathcal{T_C}[\![\mathcal{C}, \overline{\mathcal{E}} \vdash \texttt{S: Command}]\!]; w\} \textit{ else } \{\textit{nop}\}$$

$$\mathcal{T_C}[\![\mathcal{C}, \mathcal{E} \vdash S_1; S_2 \texttt{: Command}]\!] \triangleq \mathcal{T_C}[\![\mathcal{C}, \mathcal{E} \vdash S_1 \texttt{: Command}]\!];$$
$$\mathcal{T_C}[\![\mathcal{C}, \mathcal{E} \vdash S_2 \texttt{: Command}]\!]$$

$$\mathcal{T_C}[\![\mathcal{C}, \mathcal{E} \vdash \texttt{Program id; Block.: Command}]\!] \triangleq$$
$$\mathcal{T_C}[\![\mathcal{C}, \mathcal{E} \vdash \texttt{Block: Command}]\!]$$

Figure 11.3   Translation of more expressions and statements of $\mathcal{SOOL}$ to expressions in $\Lambda^P_{<:}$.

use of subtyping in deriving the type of an expression has no effect on its translation.

While statements are interpreted recursively. Using w as an abbreviation for while E do { S }, it is easy to see that w is equivalent to if E then { S; w } else { nop}. We saw earlier that recursive definitions can be interpreted as fixed points. Thus the meaning of the while loop in Figure 11.3 is defined as the fixed point of the function taking parameter w and returning the meaning defined in terms of *if-then-else*. Because the fixed point will be a statement (and hence an expression of type *Command*), we apply $\textit{fix}\,[\textit{Command}]$ to interpret the recursion.

At this point we could show that the translations of types and expressions given so far preserve typing. However, we will postpone the proof of this until after we have completed the translations of classes and subclasses.

However to provide some assurance that our translations so far are reasonable, we look at an example using class CellClass example. Examination of the translations shows that if expression o has type ObjectType CellM, then the translation $\mathcal{T_C}[\![\mathcal{C}, \mathcal{E} \vdash \texttt{o} \Leftarrow \texttt{set(7: Command)}]\!]$ will have type *Com-*

mand and $\mathcal{T}_C[\![\mathcal{C}, \mathcal{E} \vdash \mathrm{o} \Leftarrow \mathrm{get}(): \mathrm{Integer}]\!]$ will have type *Integer*. These are exactly the translations of the types of the original expressions in $\mathcal{SOOL}$.

11.4   Modeling classes — first try

While we now know how to represent objects, we have not yet talked about how to represent classes or how classes can be used to create objects. An important part of modeling classes is to figure out how to use the initial values of instance variables and methods provided in the class in order to create the "visible" objects, which can then be packed up to hide the instance variables. Using the initial values of instance variables is pretty straightforward, but getting the methods in proper form will be a bit more difficult. In this section we present a first approximation to translating classes. Later we will see that this translation will need to be refined in order to handle subclasses properly.

The bodies of methods in classes may refer to the keyword `self`, which represents the receiver of the message. This keyword may be understood as an extra parameter of these messages. We expect that when we instantiate new objects using the class, `self` will be resolved as a fixed point representing the object being defined. As we have seen in our `CellClass` example, `self` provides access both to the instance variables and methods of the object. Thus we type check method bodies assuming that the type of `self` is `VisObjectType(IV`^{ref}`, M)`.[2]

We translate the class as a pair:

$$\mathcal{T}_C[\![\mathcal{C}.\mathcal{E} \vdash \mathrm{class(inst, meth): ClassType(IV, M)}]\!] \triangleq$$
$$\langle \mathcal{T}_C[\![\mathcal{C}, \mathcal{E} \vdash \mathrm{inst: IV}]\!], methfun \rangle,$$

---

2. Later on, we will see that a somewhat more general type for `self` is better, but this will be fine for now.

where

$$\textit{methfun} = \lambda(\textit{self}: \textit{VisObj}\,(\textit{IVR}, M)).$$
$$\textbf{let}\ \textit{close}: \textit{VisObj}\,(\textit{IVR}, M) \to (\exists Y.\,\textit{VisObj}\,(Y, M))$$
$$= \textit{closeobj}\,[\textit{IVR}]\,[M]$$
$$\textbf{in}\ \mathcal{T}_{C'}\,[\![\mathcal{C}', \mathcal{E}' \vdash \texttt{meth}\colon \texttt{M}]\!],$$
$$\mathcal{C}' = \mathcal{C} \cup \{\texttt{SelfType} = \texttt{VisObjectType}\,(\texttt{IV}^{\textit{ref}}, \texttt{M})\}$$
$$\mathcal{E}' = \mathcal{E} \cup \{\texttt{self}\colon \texttt{SelfType}, \texttt{close}\colon \texttt{SelfType} \to \texttt{ObjectType M}\}$$
$$\textit{IVR} = \mathcal{T}_C\,[\![\texttt{IV}^{\textit{ref}}]\!], \text{ and}$$
$$M = \mathcal{T}_C\,[\![\texttt{M}]\!].$$

In this translation, `self` is translated as a parameter to the method suite, while *close* is translated as the function that takes elements of type $\mathcal{T}_C\,[\![\texttt{VisObjectType}\,(\texttt{IV}^{\textit{ref}}, \texttt{M})]\!] = \textit{VisObj}\,(\textit{IVR}, M)$ and transforms them to elements of type $\mathcal{T}_C\,[\![\texttt{ObjectType M}]\!] = \exists Y.\,\textit{VisObj}\,(Y, M)$ by packing them up as existentials.

The translation of the type of a class is given by:

$$\mathcal{T}_C\,[\![\texttt{ClassType}\,(\texttt{IV}, \texttt{M})]\!] =$$
$$\mathcal{T}_C\,[\![\texttt{IV}]\!] \times (\mathcal{T}_C\,[\![\texttt{VisObjectType}\,(\texttt{IV}^{\textit{ref}}, \texttt{M})]\!] \to \mathcal{T}_C\,[\![\texttt{M}]\!]).$$

The initial values of the instance variables have type $\mathcal{T}_C\,[\![\texttt{IV}]\!]$, while the translation of the visual object type involves type $\mathcal{T}_C\,[\![\texttt{IV}^{\textit{ref}}]\!]$ because it includes variables rather than just values.

In order to translate a new expression, which creates an object from the class, it appears that all we need to do is to create a record of references to the initial values of instance variables given in the class, and create a pair of this record of instance variables and of the method suite from the class. However, we have one problem. The method suite for objects takes only the record of instance variables (of type $\mathcal{T}_C\,[\![\texttt{IV}^{\textit{ref}}]\!]$) as a parameter,[3] while the method suite for classes takes an entire object of type $\mathcal{T}_C\,[\![\texttt{VisObjectType}\,(\texttt{IV}^{\textit{ref}}, \texttt{M})]\!]$ as a parameter. That is, the method suite for objects has type $\mathcal{T}_C\,[\![\texttt{IV}^{\textit{ref}}]\!] \to \mathcal{T}_C\,[\![\texttt{M}]\!]$, while the method suite for classes has type $\mathcal{T}_C\,[\![\texttt{VisObjectType}\,(\texttt{IV}^{\textit{ref}}, \texttt{M})]\!] \to \mathcal{T}_C\,[\![\texttt{M}]\!]$.

This difference is important because subclasses might override the definition of a method. As a result, we would not like to have the meanings of

---

3. Actually, this is only for "visible objects", those with type $\texttt{VisObjectType}\,(\texttt{IV}^{\textit{ref}}, \texttt{M})$, as the type of instance variables for object types has been hidden with an existential quantifier. However, we will need to go through the stage of representing the object as a "visible object", before "packing" it up with the existential.

methods frozen to be their definitions in the class. We need to leave open the possibility that the meaning of self ⇐ m will be different in a subclass than in the class. Because methods are parameterized by self in classes, this happens naturally when self changes. On the other hand, methods cannot be overridden in objects, so it makes sense to freeze the meaning of methods when creating objects. Thus the methods of objects take only the record of instance variables as a parameter rather than all of self.

We must resolve this (deliberate) inconsistency in representations by converting methods in classes to a different form in objects so that the meanings of the methods are fixed. (Recall we could have also fixed the location of instance variables in methods of the objects, but we chose to share methods between all objects of the same class. As a result instance variables must be supplied to methods when sending messages.)

We will start with *methfun*, the record of methods parameterized by *self*, and then transform this into a function *methfun'* that is parameterized by only the record, *inst*, of instance variables. We will accomplish this by replacing all occurrences of *self* in the method bodies by the pair $\langle inst, \text{methfun}' \rangle$. Because we will be defining methfun' in terms of itself, *methfun'* will be defined recursively using fixed points.

Let C be an expression with type ClassType(IV,M). Let

$$methfun = proj_2(\mathcal{T}_C[\![\mathcal{C}, \mathcal{E} \vdash \text{C: ClassType(IV, M)}]\!])$$

be the translation of the method suite from C. By the translation of class types, the type of *methfun* will be $\mathcal{T}_C[\![\text{VisObjectType(IV}^{ref}, \text{M)}]\!] \to \mathcal{T}_C[\![\text{M}]\!]$. We now create *methfun'* with the desired type $\mathcal{T}_C[\![\text{IV}^{ref}]\!] \to \mathcal{T}_C[\![\text{M}]\!]$ as follows:

$$methfun'(inst': \mathcal{T}_C[\![\text{IV}^{ref}]\!]) = methfun(\langle inst', methfun' \rangle)$$

or equivalently,

$$methfun' = \lambda(inst': \mathcal{T}_C[\![\text{IV}^{ref}]\!]).\, methfun(\langle inst', methfun' \rangle).$$

Notice that the pair $\langle inst', methfun' \rangle$ thus replaces all occurrences of *self* in the body of the methods. We can write this definition more formally with a fixed point to capture the recursive definition, but it is even less readable! The formal definition is:

$$methfun' = \underline{fix}\,[\mathcal{T}_C[\![\text{IV}^{ref}]\!] \to \mathcal{T}_C[\![\text{M}]\!]]\lambda(fm: \mathcal{T}_C[\![\text{IV}^{ref}]\!] \to \mathcal{T}_C[\![\text{M}]\!]).$$
$$\lambda(inst': \mathcal{T}_C[\![\text{IV}^{ref}]\!]).\, methfun(\langle inst', fm \rangle).$$

Creating the record of instance variables is straightforward. If

$$inst \stackrel{\Delta}{=} proj_1(\mathcal{T}_C[\![\mathcal{C}, \mathcal{E} \vdash \text{C: ClassType(IV,M)}]\!]): \{\!| \, l_1: T_1; \ldots; l_n: T_n |\!\}$$

then

$$inst^{ref} = \{\!| \, l_1: Ref\,T_1 = ref\,inst.l_1; \ldots; l_n: Ref\,T_n = ref\,inst.l_n |\!\}$$

Now we have all the pieces necessary to create a new object from a class:

$$\mathcal{T}_C[\![\mathcal{C}, \mathcal{E} \vdash \text{new C: ObjectType M}]\!] \stackrel{\Delta}{=} closeobj\,[IVR][M]\langle inst^{ref}, methfun'\rangle$$
where
$$c \stackrel{\Delta}{=} \mathcal{T}_C[\![\mathcal{C}, \mathcal{E} \vdash \text{C: ClassType(IV,M)}]\!]$$
$$IVR = \mathcal{T}_C[\![\text{IV}^{ref}]\!]$$
$$M = \mathcal{T}_C[\![\text{M}]\!]$$
$$inst = proj_1(c),$$
$$methfun = proj_2(c),$$

$inst^{ref}$ is formed by adding refs to all fields of *inst* as above, and
$$methfun' = \underline{fix}\,[IVR \rightarrow M]\lambda(fm: IVR \rightarrow M).$$
$$\lambda(inst': IVR).methfun(\langle inst', fm\rangle).$$

To make this construction more concrete we provide the translation for `CellClass`. From the definition, we see that

```
inst = {| x: Integer = 0 |}: CellIV
```

and

```
meth = {| get: Void → Integer =
            function(v: Void): Integer is {
               return val self.x };

         set: Integer → Command =
            function(nuVal: Integer): Command is {
               self.x := nuVal;
               return nop };

         bump: Void → Command =
            function(v: Void): Command is {
               self ⇐ set(self ⇐ get()+1);
               return nop }
      |}: CellM
```

The class `CellClass` will be represented by `class(inst,meth)` for `inst` and `meth` defined above.

Recall from Section 11.2 the definitions of *CellIV*, *RfCellIV*, and *CellM*. The translations of the instance variables, *inst* $\triangleq \mathcal{T}_C[\![\mathcal{C}, \mathcal{E} \vdash \text{inst: CellIV}]\!]$, and the method suite, *methfun* $\triangleq \lambda(self: VisObj\,(IVR, M)).\,\mathcal{T}_C[\![\mathcal{C}, \mathcal{E} \vdash \text{meth: CellM}]\!]$, are straightforward:

$$inst \quad = \{\!| \ x: Integer = 0 |\!\}: CellIV,$$

$$methfun = \lambda(self: VisObj\,(IVR, M)).$$
$$\{\!| \ get = \lambda(v: Void).\ val\ self.x;$$
$$set = \lambda(nuVal: Integer).\ self.x := nuVal;$$
$$bump = \lambda(v: Void).\ self \Leftarrow set(self \Leftarrow get\langle\rangle + \underline{1})$$
$$|\!\} : CellM.$$

To improve readability, we wrote expressions of the form *self* $\Leftarrow m$ in the definition of *bump* as abbreviations for $proj_2(self)(proj_1(self)).m$. Technically the body of *bump* should be written as

$$proj_2(self)(proj_1(self)).set(proj_2(self)(proj_1(self)).get\langle\rangle + \underline{1}),$$

but that is virtually unreadable! As a result, we will continue to use the abbreviation with "$\Leftarrow$" to make the expressions more readable.

Using these expressions, we can construct the interpretation of `Cell-Class`:

$$\mathcal{T}_C[\![\emptyset, \emptyset \vdash \text{CellClass: ClassType}\,(\text{CellIV}, \text{CellM})]\!] = \langle inst, methfun \rangle$$

Let's now examine what happens when we create a new object from class `CellClass`. We begin by creating a record of locations holding the initial values obtained from the class.

$$inst^{ref} \triangleq \{\!| \ x: Ref\ Integer = ref\ \underline{0} \ |\!\}: RfCellIV.$$

Next we rewrite the method suite, *methfun*, by fixing the method suite of *self* to be exactly the methods in *methfun*. This is accomplished by replacing all occurrences of *self* by $\langle ir, methfun' \rangle$, where *methfun'* is the new method suite being defined, and *ir* is a parameter of *methfun'* representing the record of instance variables of the associated object.

$$methfun' \triangleq \lambda(ir: RfCellIV).$$
$$\{\!| \; get = \lambda(v: Void).\; val\; proj_i(\langle ir, methfun'\rangle).x;$$
$$set = \lambda(nuVal: Integer).\; proj_i(\langle ir, methfun'\rangle).x := nuVal;$$
$$bump = \lambda(v: Void).\; \langle ir, methfun'\rangle \Leftarrow set(\langle ir, methfun'\rangle \Leftarrow get\langle\rangle + \underline{1} \;|\!\}$$

where we have used "$\Leftarrow$" as an abbreviation as above. Then *methfun'* has type *RfCellIV* → *CellM*.

The new object generated by class `CellClass` can be obtained by evaluating

$$closeobj\; [RfCellIV]\; [CellM]\langle inst^{ref}, methfun'\rangle.$$

To get a better sense of the meaning of the method suite, *methfun'*, of this new object, we simplify the method bodies a bit further. Using the definitions and simplifying, we get

$$methfun' = \lambda(ir: RfCellIV).$$
$$\{\!| \; get = \lambda(v: Void).\; val\; ir.x;$$
$$set = \lambda(nuVal: Integer).\; ir.x := nuVal;$$
$$bump = \lambda(v: Void).\; methfun'(ir).set(methfun'(ir).get\langle\rangle + \underline{1} \;|\!\}$$

Of course, we could go further in simplifying the code for *bump*, replacing expressions of the form *methfun'(ir).m* by their definitions. If we do this then the body of *bump* becomes:

$$bump = \lambda(v: Void).\; ir.x := val\; ir.x + \underline{1}$$

just as expected.

Exercise 11.4.1 *Translate and then evaluate* o $\Leftarrow$ bump(), *where* o *is an object of type* ObjectType CellM *that was created through a call of* new CellClass *and whose* x *instance variable currently has value* 47. *Recall that you must open the existential before sending the message (and that opening a packed element gives you access to the details of its innards - see the computation rule at the end of Section 9.3).*

The translations discussed in this section are collected in Figure 11.4.

In the next section we investigate problems with using this representation for defining subclasses.

$$\mathcal{T}_C [\![\mathcal{C}.\mathcal{E} \vdash \texttt{class(inst,meth): ClassType(IV,M)}]\!] \triangleq$$

$$\langle \mathcal{T}_C [\![\mathcal{C}, \mathcal{E} \vdash \texttt{inst: IV}]\!], \mathit{methfun} \rangle,$$

where

$\mathit{methfun} = \lambda(\mathit{self}: \mathit{VisObj}(\mathit{IVR}, M)).$

$\qquad \text{let } \mathit{close}: \mathit{VisObj}(\mathit{IVR}, M) \to (\exists Y. \mathit{VisObj}(Y, M))$

$\qquad\qquad = \mathit{closeobj}[\mathit{IVR}][M]$

$\qquad \text{in } \mathcal{T}_{C'} [\![\mathcal{C}', \mathcal{E}' \vdash \texttt{meth: M}]\!],$

$\mathcal{C}' = \mathcal{C} \cup \{\texttt{SelfType} = \texttt{VisObjectType}(\texttt{IV}^{\mathit{ref}}, \texttt{M})\}$

$\mathcal{E}' = \mathcal{E} \cup \{\texttt{self: SelfType, close: SelfType} \to \texttt{ObjectType M}\}$

$\mathit{IVR} = \mathcal{T}_C [\![\texttt{IV}^{\mathit{ref}}]\!],$ and

$M = \mathcal{T}_C [\![\texttt{M}]\!].$

$$\mathcal{T}_C [\![\mathcal{C}, \mathcal{E} \vdash \texttt{new C: ObjectType M}]\!] \triangleq \mathit{closeobj}[\mathit{IR}][M]\langle \mathit{inst}^{\mathit{ref}}, \mathit{methfun}' \rangle$$

where

$c \triangleq \mathcal{T}_C [\![\mathcal{C}, \mathcal{E} \vdash \texttt{C: ClassType(IV,M)}]\!]$

$\mathit{IR} = \mathcal{T}_C [\![\texttt{IV}^{\mathit{ref}}]\!]$

$M = \mathcal{T}_C [\![\texttt{M}]\!]$

$\mathit{inst} = \mathit{proj}_1(c),$

$\mathit{methfun} = \mathit{proj}_2(c),$

$\mathit{inst}^{\mathit{ref}}$ is formed by adding refs to all fields of inst, and

$\mathit{methfun}' = \underline{\mathit{fix}}\,[\mathit{IR} \to M]\lambda(\mathit{fm}: \mathit{IR} \to M).\lambda(\mathit{inst}': \mathit{IR}).\mathit{methfun}(\langle \mathit{inst}', \mathit{fm} \rangle).$

Figure 11.4   Translation of `class` and `new` expressions of $\mathcal{SOOL}$ to expressions in $\Lambda^P_{<:}$.

11.5   Problems with modeling subclasses

Now that we have presented the encoding of classes, we investigate how to encode subclasses. Subclasses can add new instance variables and methods as well as override methods from the superclass. Recall from Chapter 6 that in defining subclasses, no changes are allowed to the types of instance variables from the superclass, while types of methods of the superclass may be replaced by subtypes in the subclass definition.

We begin by using the simple encoding of the last section and then seeing where we run into trouble. Recall that

$$\texttt{class inherits C modifies } \texttt{m}_{j_1}, \ldots, \texttt{m}_{j_k}(\texttt{inst,meth})$$

represents a subclass formed by inheriting the instance variables and methods from C and then adding the instance variables and methods from inst and meth. The methods overridden are named in the list $m_{j_1}, \ldots, m_{j_k}$.

If a method in C is redefined in meth, then the type-checking rules require that the redefined method have a type that is a subtype of the original. As an example, suppose C = class (inst$_{sup}$, meth$_{sup}$), and thus has encoding

$$\mathcal{T}_C[\![\mathcal{C}, \mathcal{E} \vdash \text{C: ClassType} (\text{IV}_{sup}, \text{M}_{sup})]\!] =$$
$$\langle \mathcal{T}_C[\![\mathcal{C}, \mathcal{E} \vdash \text{inst}_{sup}: \text{IV}_{sup}]\!], \text{methfun}_{sup}\rangle,$$

where

$methfun_{sup} = \lambda(self\text{: } VisObj\,(IV^{ref}_{sup}, M_{sup})).$
   $let\ close\text{: } VisObj\,(IV^{ref}_{sup}, M_{sup}) \rightarrow (\exists Y.\ VisObj\,(Y, M_{sup}))$
    $= closeobj\,[IV^{ref}_{sup}]\,[M_{sup}]$
   $in\ \mathcal{T}_{C'}[\![\mathcal{C'}, \mathcal{E'} \vdash \text{meth}_{sup}: M_{sup}]\!],$
  $\mathcal{C'} = \mathcal{C} \cup \{\text{SelfType} = \text{VisObjectType}\,(IV^{ref}_{sup}, M_{sup})\}$
  $\mathcal{E'} = \mathcal{E} \cup \{\text{self: SelfType},$
    $\text{close: SelfType} \rightarrow \text{ObjectType } M_{sup}\}$
 $IV^{ref}_{sup} = \mathcal{T}_C[\![\text{IV}^{ref}_{sup}]\!],\ \text{and}$
 $M_{sup} = \mathcal{T}_C[\![\text{M}_{sup}]\!].$

Let inst$_{all}$ = inst$_{sup}\oplus$ inst have type IV, where $\oplus$ is right dominant record combination, as usual. Similarly, let meth$_{all}$ = meth$_{sup}\oplus$ meth have type M. Mimicking the encoding of classes from the previous section, one would anticipate that we could encode the subclass as follows:[4]

$$\mathcal{T}_C[\![\text{class inherits C modifies } m_{j_1}, \ldots, m_{j_k}(\text{inst, meth})]\!] =$$
$$\langle \mathcal{T}_C[\![\mathcal{C}, \mathcal{E} \vdash \text{inst}_{all}: \text{IV}]\!], \text{methfun}_{all}\rangle,$$

where

$methfun_{all} = \lambda(self\text{: } VisObj\,(IV^{ref}, M)).$
   $let\ close\text{: } VisObj\,(IV^{ref}, M) \rightarrow (\exists Y.\ VisObj\,(Y, M))$
    $= closeobj\,[IV^{ref}]\,[M]$
   $in\ \mathcal{T}_{C'}[\![\mathcal{C'}, \mathcal{E'} \vdash \text{meth}_{all}: M]\!],$
  $\mathcal{C'} = \mathcal{C} \cup \{\text{SelfType} = \text{VisObjectType}\,(IV^{ref}, M)\}$
  $\mathcal{E'} = \mathcal{E} \cup \{\text{self: SelfType},$
    $\text{close: SelfType} \rightarrow \text{ObjectType } M\}$
 $IV^{ref} = \mathcal{T}_C[\![\text{IV}^{ref}_{sup}]\!],\ \text{and}$
  $M = \mathcal{T}_C[\![\text{M}]\!].$

---

4. We leave off the typing information in expressions to be translated for the rest of this chapter to reduce clutter.

Unfortunately, this simple encoding will not work for subclasses because of typing problems with inherited methods.

The problem is that when we type-checked the methods of `meth`, we assumed that the type of `self` was `VisObjectType(IV`$_{sup}^{ref}$`, M`$_{sup}$`)`, whereas now we are using the inherited methods in a context where the type of `self` is `VisObjectType(IV`^{ref}`, M)`. This would be fine if `self` having type `VisObjectType(IV`^{ref}`, M)` implied that it had type `VisObjectType(IV`$_{sup}^{ref}$`, M`$_{sup}$`)`, *i.e.*, if

$$\mathcal{T_C}[\![\texttt{VisObjectType}(\texttt{IV}^{ref},\texttt{M})]\!] <: \mathcal{T_C}[\![\texttt{VisObjectType}(\texttt{IV}_{sup}^{ref},\texttt{M}_{sup})]\!],$$

but that is NOT the case.

Recall that

$$\mathcal{T_C}[\![\texttt{VisObjectType}(\texttt{IV}^{ref},\texttt{M})]\!] = \mathcal{T_C}[\![\texttt{IV}^{ref}]\!] \times (\mathcal{T_C}[\![\texttt{IV}^{ref}]\!] \rightarrow \mathcal{T_C}[\![\texttt{M}]\!])$$

Thus for

$$\mathcal{T_C}[\![\texttt{VisObjectType}(\texttt{IV}^{ref},\texttt{M})]\!] <: \mathcal{T_C}[\![\texttt{VisObjectType}(\texttt{IV}_{sup}^{ref},\texttt{M}_{sup})]\!],$$

we will need

$$\mathcal{T_C}[\![\texttt{IV}^{ref}]\!] <: \mathcal{T_C}[\![\texttt{IV}_{sup}^{ref}]\!],$$

and

$$\mathcal{T_C}[\![\texttt{IV}^{ref}]\!] \rightarrow \mathcal{T_C}[\![\texttt{M}]\!] <: \mathcal{T_C}[\![\texttt{IV}_{sup}^{ref}]\!] \rightarrow \mathcal{T_C}[\![\texttt{M}_{sup}]\!].$$

The first is no problem since `IV`^{ref} is simply an extension of `IV`$_{sup}^{ref}$, and hence $\mathcal{T_C}[\![\texttt{IV}^{ref}]\!] <: \mathcal{T_C}[\![\texttt{IV}_{sup}^{ref}]\!]$. However, recall that subtyping for function types is covariant in the return type and contravariant in the domain type. The return types are in the subtype relation, as `M` is an extension of `M`$_{sup}$, but the domains change in a covariant way, rather than contravariant. That is, we need $\mathcal{T_C}[\![\texttt{IV}_{sup}^{ref}]\!] <: \mathcal{T_C}[\![\texttt{IV}^{ref}]\!]$ for the function types to be subtypes, but we have the reverse. The result is that the methods in `meth` may not be type safe when used in a context in which `self` has type `VisObjectType(IV`^{ref}`,M)`.

Let's look at an example showing what can go wrong when you use a parameter, `self`, of type `VisObjectType(IV`^{ref}`,M)` in a context that is type-correct when `self` has type `VisObjectType(IV`$_{sup}^{ref}$`,M`$_{sup}$`)`.

Let `oself` be a record of type `IV`$_{sup}^{ref}$` = {|j : Ref Integer |}`, and define class `C` to be:

```
class ({|
   j: Integer = 0
|}, {|
   m: Void → Integer = function(v: Void): Integer is
       { return ⟨oself, snd(self)⟩ ⇐ n() };
   n: Void → Integer = function(v: Void): Integer is
       { return val self.j }
|})
```

Of course you normally can't treat self as a pair in object-oriented languages or use a projection function, snd to grab the second component of a pair, but we will be loose with the syntax in order to express the problem in a simple way.

Let $oself \triangleq \mathcal{T}_C[\![oself]\!]$. Then the following is the translation of C:[5]

$$\langle\{| j: Integer = 0 |\},$$
$$\lambda(self: \mathcal{T}_C[\![\text{VisObjectType}(\text{IV}_{sup}^{ref}, \text{M}_{sup})]\!]).$$
$$\{| m: Void \rightarrow Integer = \lambda(v: Void). \{\langle oself, proj_2(self)\rangle \Leftarrow n\langle\rangle\};$$
$$n: Void \rightarrow Integer = \lambda(v: Void). \{val\ self.j\}$$
$$|\}\rangle$$

The method m of $\mathcal{T}_C[\![C]\!]$ builds a new object, $\langle oself, proj_2(self)\rangle$, with type $\mathcal{T}_C[\![\text{VisObjectType}(\text{IV}_{sup}^{ref}, \text{M}_{sup})]\!]$, by replacing the first component of $self$ by $oself$, and then sends it the message n. In other words, when method n is executed, it is with self interpreted by this new object whose instance variables are now represented by $oself$. All the method n of C does is to return the value of the instance variable j. This is no problem at all when n is called from m, as $oself$ has a field j of type *Ref Integer*.

Now define subclass SC of C as follows:

```
class inherits C modifies n ({|
       k: Integer = 0
|}, {|
   n: Void → Integer = function(v: Void): Integer is
       { return val self.k }
|})
```

---

5. We omit the *let* clause introducing *close* because it does not occur in the translation of the methods. We will also omit it in the translation of SC.

The translation of SC is

$$\langle \{\!| \ j\colon Integer = 0; k\colon Integer = 0 \ |\}\!,$$
$$\lambda(self\colon \ \mathcal{T}_C[\![\texttt{VisObjectType}(\texttt{IV}^{ref}_{sup}, \texttt{M}_{sup})]\!]).$$
$$\{\!| \ m\colon Void \to Integer = \lambda(v\colon Void). \ \{\langle oself, proj_2(self)\rangle \Leftarrow n\langle\rangle\};$$
$$n\colon Void \to Integer = \lambda(v\colon Void). \ \{val \ self.k\}$$
$$|\}\rangle$$

But now a problem arises when method m is sent to an object generated from class SC. Since m is not overridden, the inherited code is run, resulting in sending a message n to an object whose method suite is the same (i.e., the full method suite of self), but whose instance variables have been replaced by oself (which has no k field). Thus when the evaluation of method n results in an attempt to access self.k, an error will result.

Exercise 11.5.1 *Write out the translation of classes C and SC in detail, evaluate the expression* new SC *to get an object, and then send that object the message* m *in order to show that a type error results.*

What does this imply about the type-safety of languages like Java and C++? Luckily, not very much, as no object-oriented language would actually allow one to write a method like m above. That is fortunate, for if it were legal, virtually all existing statically typed languages would allow type errors. The stumbling block to writing such a method is that object-oriented languages do not allow you to take apart self and then build a new object with a different collection of instance variables.

In fact we can only generate type errors with our encoding if we allow the methods to refer to the record of instance variables as a whole. If we only are allowed to access individual instance variables and methods of self, no errors result. In particular, the typing rules for classes and subclasses in $\mathcal{SOOL}$ given in Section 10.2.3 *are correct* in that any $\mathcal{SOOL}$ program that passes the type checker is guaranteed not to have type errors at run time. The problem that has arisen here is that our encoding of classes and subclasses in $\Lambda^P_{<:}$ is not type-safe, because extra operations are available in $\Lambda^P_{<:}$ that do not correspond to operations in $\mathcal{SOOL}$.

As a result, we could try to create a restricted version of the typed lambda calculus used here that disallows the updates that caused the problems, and then try to prove the correctness of our translation. However, it is quite difficult to restrict manipulations of *self* in the translation without also restricting other useful constructs in our underlying lambda calculus. Thus, rather than restricting the underlying calculus, in the next chapter we will instead modify the type-checking rules and translation of classes so that it will be type safe no matter what manipulations of *self* are made in the method bodies.

11.6 Summary

In this chapter we presented a translation of $\mathcal{SOOL}$ into $\Lambda_{<:}^P$. The translation of non-object-oriented features was straightforward, and our translation of classes resulted in reasonable, though somewhat complex, definitions of the translations of new C and E $\Leftarrow$m. Unfortunately, we found that the translation of classes does not extend properly to subclasses. As a result, in the next chapter we introduce a more careful type-checking rule and translation of classes that will support the correct definition of subclasses.

12 *Improved Semantics for Classes*

We need to rethink the translation of classes from first principles in order to overcome the difficulties encountered in trying to translate subclasses. A problem whose solution will lead us to the correct definition of translation is that we type checked the methods under the assumption that the type of self was the same as the (visible) type of the objects generated by the class. Yet, these methods may be inherited in subclasses that generate objects having more instance variables and methods (let alone the fact that existing methods may be overridden). It's no wonder that we got into trouble!

12.1 (Re-)Defining classes

If the methods in classes are to be inherited in subclasses without any danger of encountering new errors, then it seems obvious that they should be type checked under the assumption that they may be inherited in any subclass of the class being defined. Of course, at the time we are defining a class, we have no idea what subclasses may later be defined.

In Chapter 6 we investigated what changes are allowed in the types of instance variables and methods in order to preserve type safety in subclasses. These restrictions were reflected in the $\mathcal{SOOL}$ type-checking rule, *Subclass*. That rule implies that if class C has type ClassType(IV, M) and C' is a subclass with type ClassType(IV', M'), then it is necessary to have IV'^{ref} <: IV^{ref} and M' <: M to ensure that inherited methods will be type correct in the subclass.

We can use this to write type-checking rules for subclasses in such a way that inherited methods will be guaranteed to be type-safe in subclasses. As before, let inst of type IV be the record of initial values of instance variables for a class, and let meth of type M be the record of method bodies (which may include the keyword `self`). The new type-checking rules for classes and subclasses can be found in Figure 12.1.

The new type-checking rules use a generalization of the type constraint system $\mathcal{C}$ that supports adding type identifiers with their bounds. While $\mathcal{SOOL}$ does not support bounded polymorphism[1], the type constraint systems are required for type checking. They keep track of the requirements that ensure that the type of `self` can be the type of objects generated in any subclass of the class being type checked. In particular the definition of $\mathcal{C}'$ in the new rule *Class* adds to $\mathcal{C}$ two subtyping constraints that correspond to the restrictions on the types of the records of instance variables and methods in subclasses.

Definition 12.1.1 *Relations of the form* `t = T` *and* `t <: T`, *where* `t` *is a type identifier and* `T` *is a type expression are said to be* type constraints. *A type constraint system is defined as follows:*

1. *The empty set, $\emptyset$, is a type constraint system.*

2. *If $\mathcal{C}$ is a type constraint system and* `t` *is a type identifier that does not appear in $\mathcal{C}$ or* `T`, *then $\mathcal{C} \cup \{t = T\}$ is a type constraint system.*

3. *If $\mathcal{C}$ is a type constraint system and* `t` *is a type identifier that does not appear in $\mathcal{C}$, then $\mathcal{C} \cup \{t <: T\}$ is a type constraint system.*

We define the function $\mathcal{C}(T)$ as in Definition 10.2.5 to be the result of replacing all type identifiers by their definitions in $\mathcal{C}$. If `t` is included in $\mathcal{C}$ with a subtype bound rather than a definition, then $\mathcal{C}(t) = t$.

With this new definition of type constraint system we must add one new rule to our subtyping rules to cover the case of type identifiers introduced with a subtyping bound:

Identifier <: $\mathcal{C} \vdash t <: \mathcal{C}(T),\ \textit{if}\ (t <: T) \in \mathcal{C}$

This rule simply states that if $\mathcal{C}$ contains a type identifier, `t`, with a bound, then we may deduce that `t` has that bound (where we expand all abbreviations introduced in $\mathcal{C}$).

We now examine the new type-checking rules for classes and subclasses. As before, when type checking the methods of a class, `self` will have type

---

1. Later, we will introduce an extension of $\mathcal{SOOL}$, $\mathcal{PSOOL}$, that will support bounded polymorphism.

Class
$$\frac{\mathcal{C}, \mathcal{E} \vdash \text{inst: IV}, \quad \mathcal{C}', \mathcal{E}' \vdash \text{meth: M}}{\mathcal{C}, \mathcal{E} \vdash \text{class (inst, meth): ClassType (IV, M)}}$$

where

- $\mathcal{C}' = \mathcal{C} \cup \{\, \text{M}' <: \text{M}, \text{IVR}' <: \text{IV}^{ref},$
  $\text{SelfType} = \text{VisObjectType (IVR}', \text{M}')\},$

- $\mathcal{E}' = \mathcal{E} \cup \{\, \text{self: SelfType}, \text{close: SelfType} \rightarrow \text{ObjectType M}'\},$
  and

- SelfType does not occur in IV or M.

Subclass
$$\begin{array}{c} \mathcal{C}, \mathcal{E} \vdash \text{E: ClassType (IV}_{sup}, \text{M}_{sup}), \\ \mathcal{C}, \mathcal{E} \vdash \text{inst: IV}_{sub}, \qquad \mathcal{C}', \mathcal{E}' \vdash \text{meth: M}_{sub}, \\ \mathcal{C} \vdash \text{T}'_{i_j} <: \text{T}_{i_j} \text{ for } 1 \leq j \leq m \\ \hline \mathcal{C}, \mathcal{E} \vdash \text{class inherits E modifies } \text{l}_{i_1}, \ldots, \text{l}_{i_m} \\ \text{(inst, meth): ClassType (IV, M)} \end{array}$$

where

- $\text{IV} = \text{IV}_{sup} \oplus \text{IV}_{sub},$

- $\text{M} = \text{M}_{sup} \oplus \text{M}_{sub},$

- there is no overlap in the labels occurring in IV_{sup} and IV_{sub}, and

- the overlapping labels in M_{sup} and M_{sub} are exactly $\text{l}_{i_1}, \ldots, \text{l}_{i_m}$.

- The type of l_{i_j} in M_{sub} is T'_{i_j}, while the corresponding type in M_{sup} is T_{i_j}.

- $\mathcal{C}' = \mathcal{C} \cup \{\, \text{M}' <: \text{M}, \text{IVR}' <: \text{IV}^{ref},$
  $\text{SelfType} = \text{VisObjectType (IVR}', \text{M}')\},$ and

- $\mathcal{E}' = \mathcal{E} \cup \{\, \text{self: SelfType}, \text{close: SelfType} \rightarrow \text{ObjectType M}'\}$

- SelfType does not occur in IV or M.

Figure 12.1   Revised type-checking rules for classes and subclasses.

SelfType. However, we may not assume that SelfType= VisObject-Type(IV^{ref}, M). Instead we may only assume that it has type VisObject-Type(IVR', M'), where all we know about IVR' and M' is that they are sub-types of the corresponding types IV^{ref} and M from the class. Notice that this does allow us to infer that self has all the instance variables and methods of the class, but it may have more of each, and the types of the methods may be subtypes of those in M.

These are exactly the conditions that hold for subclasses. Thus if we type check the methods of classes under these assumptions, then we are guaranteed that they will type check for the types corresponding to any subclass. In particular, if the initial values of the instance variables and the methods were found to be type correct in the superclass, they should remain correct in any subclass.[2]

The same argument shows that type checking subclasses under the weaker conditions on SelfType in rule *Subclass* will ensure that methods inherited in further subclasses will remain type correct.

These more general type-checking rules for classes and subclasses will require more general rules for message sending and instance variable accesses. The problem is that when we try to type check self.l and self $\Leftarrow$ m inside methods of a class, we only know the type of self is SelfType = VisObject-Type(IVR', M'), and, rather than having specific information about the fields and types of IVR' and M', we only know that they are subtypes of IV^{ref} and M. Thus we need type-checking rules that will allow us to type message sends and instance variable accesses when we only know information about the supertype of the records of instance variables and methods.

The new rules for message sending and instance variable access can be found in Figure 12.2. We take advantage of subtyping to simplify the statement of the rules by having the supertype in each case contain only a single field. Of course if

$$\mathcal{C} \vdash M <: \texttt{ObjectType } \{\!| \ m_1 \colon T_1 ; \ldots ; m_n\, T_n \ |\!\},$$

then we can also deduce

$$\mathcal{C} \vdash \texttt{ObjectType } \{\!| \ m_1 \colon T_1 ; \ldots ; m_n\, T_n \ |\!\} <: \texttt{ObjectType } \{\!| \ m_i \colon T_i \ |\!\}$$

for whichever method m_i is of interest, and hence deduce

$$\mathcal{C} \vdash M <: \texttt{ObjectType } \{\!| \ m_i \colon T_i \ |\!\},$$

---

2. We give a formal proof of this in Section 13.1.

$$\textit{Message} \quad \frac{\mathcal{C}, \mathcal{E} \vdash \texttt{E: M}, \quad \mathcal{C} \vdash \texttt{M} <: \texttt{ObjectType} \; \{\!\mid \texttt{m: T} \mid\!\}}{\mathcal{C}, \mathcal{E} \vdash \texttt{E} \Leftarrow \texttt{m: T}}$$

$$\textit{Inst Vble} \quad \frac{\mathcal{C}, \mathcal{E} \vdash \texttt{E: VisObjectType(IVR, M)}, \quad \mathcal{C} \vdash \texttt{IVR} <: \{\!\mid \texttt{l: T} \mid\!\}}{\mathcal{C}, \mathcal{E} \vdash \texttt{E.l: T}}$$

$$\textit{VisObj Message} \quad \frac{\mathcal{C}, \mathcal{E} \vdash \texttt{E: VisObjectType(IVR, M)}, \quad \mathcal{C} \vdash \texttt{M} <: \{\!\mid \texttt{m: T} \mid\!\}}{\mathcal{C}, \mathcal{E} \vdash \texttt{E} \Leftarrow \texttt{m: T}}$$

Figure 12.2   Revised type-checking rules for messages and instance variables.

and apply the type-checking rule.

At this point these more general rules are mainly necessary for objects whose types are of the form `VisObjectType(IVR,M)`. However we run into a similar problem in type checking if `close(self)`, which has type `Object-Type M'`, is the receiver of a message. While we could just use subtyping to promote the type to `ObjectType M`, we include the more general type-checking rule for elements of regular object types as well.

We now use the new type-checking rules to guide the definition of the translation of classes. The new translation of classes and their types, provided in Figure 12.3, explicitly takes into consideration that the methods should work for any subclass. It does this by parameterizing the translation of the class by types extending the method and instance variable types.

Just as we type checked instance variables using $\mathcal{C}$, and methods using $\mathcal{C}'$, we translate the instance variables of the class using $\mathcal{C}$ and the methods using $\mathcal{C}'$. The record of initial values of instance variables still has type IV, but the parameter $self$ to the method suite now has type $VisObj\,(IVR', M')$. When $IVR' = \mathcal{T}_\mathcal{C}[\![\texttt{IV}^{ref}]\!]$ and $M' = \mathcal{T}_\mathcal{C}[\![\texttt{M}]\!]$, the methods will be typed appropriately for objects generated from a class C. But we can also instantiate the type identifiers with types corresponding to any subclass of C.

Of course, we must modify the translation of the type of a class similarly. The new translation for class types as a polymorphic type is also given in Figure 12.3.

The translation of expressions that create new objects from classes, shown in Figure 12.4, now just takes one more step from the procedure given for our previous encoding. First apply the translation of the class to the translation of the type of its record of methods, M, and to the translation, $\mathcal{T}_\mathcal{C}[\![\texttt{IV}^{ref}]\!]$, of

$$\mathcal{T_C}[\![\mathcal{C}, \mathcal{E} \vdash \texttt{class(inst, meth)}: \texttt{ClassType(IV, M)}]\!] \triangleq$$
$$\Lambda(M' <: \mathcal{T_C}[\![\texttt{M}]\!]).\, \Lambda(IVR' <: \mathcal{T_C}[\![\texttt{IV}^{ref}]\!]).\, \langle \mathcal{T_C}[\![\mathcal{C}, \mathcal{E} \vdash \texttt{inst: IV}]\!], methfun \rangle,$$

where

$$methfun = \lambda(self: VisObj\,(IVR', M')).$$
$$let\ close: VisObj\,(IVR', M') \to (\exists Y.\, VisObj\,(Y, M'))$$
$$= closeobj\,[IVR']\,[M']$$
$$in\ \mathcal{T_{C'}}[\![\mathcal{C}', \mathcal{E}' \vdash \texttt{meth: M}]\!],$$
$$\mathcal{C}' = \mathcal{C} \cup \{M' <: M, IVR' <: IV^{ref},$$
$$\qquad\qquad \texttt{SelfType} = \texttt{VisObjectType}(IVR', M')\},$$
$$\mathcal{E}' = \mathcal{E} \cup \{\texttt{self: SelfType, close: SelfType} \to \texttt{ObjectType M}'\}$$

$$\mathcal{T_C}[\![\texttt{ClassType(IV, M)}]\!] \triangleq \forall(M' <: \mathcal{T_C}[\![\texttt{M}]\!]).\, \forall(IVR' <: \mathcal{T_C}[\![\texttt{IV}^{ref}]\!]).$$
$$\mathcal{T_C}[\![\texttt{IV}]\!] \times (VisObj\,(IVR', M') \to \mathcal{T_C}[\![\texttt{M}]\!]).$$

Figure 12.3 New translation of classes and class types.

the type $\texttt{IV}^{ref}$ of its record of instance variables, and then proceed exactly as before.

With the new translation for classes, the translation of the problem code from the last chapter that broke subtyping will no longer type check properly. While it might be more compelling to show that the untranslated code doesn't type check, that is impossible because we have written that code using pairs and projection, neither of which is legal in $\mathcal{SOOL}$. As a result we will be satisfied by showing that the translation no longer type checks.

Here is the troublesome example again:

```
class ( {|
   j: Integer = 0
|}, {|
   m: Void → Integer = function(v: Void): Integer is
      { return ⟨oself, snd(self)⟩ ⇐ n() };
   n: Void → Integer = function(v: Void): Integer is
      { return val self.j }
|})
```

where $\texttt{oself}$ has type $\texttt{IV}^{ref} = \{\texttt{j: Ref Integer}\}$

$$\mathcal{T}_C [\![\mathcal{C}, \mathcal{E} \vdash \texttt{new}\; \texttt{C: ObjectType}\; \texttt{M}]\!] \triangleq \textit{closeobj}\,[IVR]\,[M]\langle \textit{inst}^{\textit{ref}}, \textit{methfun}'\rangle$$

where

$$c \triangleq \mathcal{T}_C [\![\mathcal{C}, \mathcal{E} \vdash \texttt{C: ClassType}\,(\texttt{IV}, \texttt{M})]\!]\,[M]\,[IVR]$$
$$IVR = \mathcal{T}_C [\![\texttt{IV}^{\textit{ref}}]\!]$$
$$M = \mathcal{T}_C [\![\texttt{M}]\!]$$
$$\textit{inst} = \textit{proj}_1(c),$$
$$\textit{methfun} = \textit{proj}_2(c),$$

$\textit{inst}^{\textit{ref}}$ is formed by adding refs to all fields of $\textit{inst}$, and

$$\textit{methfun}' = \underline{\textit{fix}}\,[IVR \rightarrow M]\lambda(\textit{fm}: IVR \rightarrow M).$$
$$\lambda(\textit{inst}': IVR).\textit{methfun}(\langle \textit{inst}', \textit{fm}\rangle).$$

Figure 12.4   New translation of new expressions.

The translation is

$$\forall M' <: \mathcal{T}_C [\![\texttt{M}]\!].\,\forall IVR' <: \mathcal{T}_C [\![\texttt{IV}^{\textit{ref}}]\!].$$
$$\langle \{\!|\; j: \textit{Integer} = \underline{0}\; |\!\},$$
$$\lambda(\textit{self}: \textit{VisObj}\,(IVR', M')).$$
$$\{\!|\; m: \textit{Void} \rightarrow \textit{Integer} = \lambda(v: \textit{Void}).\; \{\langle \textit{oself}, \textit{proj}_2(\textit{self})\rangle \Leftarrow n\langle\rangle\};$$
$$n: \textit{Void} \rightarrow \textit{Integer} = \lambda(v: \textit{Void}).\; \{\textit{val self.j}\}$$
$$|\!\}\rangle$$

where $\textit{oself} \triangleq \mathcal{T}_C [\![\mathcal{C}, \mathcal{E} \vdash \texttt{oself: IV}^{\textit{ref}}]\!]$.

If we eliminate the use of the abbreviation $\Leftarrow$ in the body of method m, it becomes:

$$\lambda(v: \textit{Void}).\; \{(\textit{proj}_2(\textit{self})(\textit{oself})).n\langle\rangle\}$$

Because we may only assume that the type of $\textit{self}$ is $\textit{VisObj}\,(IVR', M') = IVR' \times (IVR' \rightarrow M')$, the application of $\textit{proj}_2(\textit{self})$ to $\textit{oself}$ is not type correct. The function has type $IVR' \rightarrow M'$ while the argument has type $\texttt{IV}^{\textit{ref}}$. The problem is that we only know $IVR' <: \mathcal{T}_C [\![\texttt{IV}^{\textit{ref}}]\!]$. For the application of $\textit{proj}_2(\textit{self})$ to $\textit{oself}$ to be correct, we need the type of $\textit{oself}$ to be a subtype of the domain of the function, i.e., for $\mathcal{T}_C [\![\texttt{IV}^{\textit{ref}}]\!] <: IVR'$. Because we only know the reverse, we cannot send the message n to this pair. The translation of class C will not type check, and hence is illegal.

The fact that (the translation of) this counterexample has been ruled out should give us some confidence that we are on the right track with our translation. We should also gain confidence because the type-checking rules explicitly take into consideration the possibility of being inherited into sub-classes. The translation for classes and subclasses also follows the type-checking rules closely. In the next chapter we prove that this confidence is indeed warranted.

12.2   A correct subclass encoding

With more confidence in our refined type-checking rules and translation for classes, let us proceed to redefine the translation of subclasses and provide some assurance that the translated expression is type safe. A formal proof that the translation preserves types will be given in Section 13.1.

Suppose the class C has type $\texttt{ClassType}(\texttt{IV}_{sup}, \texttt{M}_{sup})$, and let $\texttt{C}_{sub} \triangleq \texttt{class}$ $\texttt{inherits C modifies } l_{i_1},\dots, l_{i_m} \ (\texttt{inst}, \texttt{meth})$ be a subclass with type $\texttt{ClassType}(\texttt{IV},\texttt{M})$. As before, we assume that new and old instance vari-ables have no overlap, and if a method in C is redefined in $\texttt{meth}$, then the redefined method must have a type that is a subtype of the original.

We will use notation similar to that of the type-checking rule for sub-classes. Let $\texttt{IV}_{sub}$ be the type of $\texttt{inst}$ and $\texttt{M}_{sub}$ be the type of $\texttt{meth}$. Let $\texttt{IV} = \texttt{IV}_{sup} \oplus \texttt{IV}_{sub}$ and $\texttt{M} = \texttt{M}_{sup} \oplus \texttt{M}_{sub}$.

The translation of subclasses is given in Figure 12.5. It generalizes the pre-vious translation by adding type parameters M' and IV', just as we did for classes.

The definition of *methfun*$_{all}$ is the only questionable part of the definition because it is where the old methods are combined with the new. We argue in-formally that the application of *methfun*$_{sup}$ to *self* in the definition of *methfun*$_{all}$ is type correct.

We expect $\mathcal{T_C}[\![\mathcal{C}, \mathcal{E} \vdash \texttt{C: ClassType}(\texttt{IV}_{sup}, \texttt{M}_{sup})]\!]$ to have type:[3]

$$\forall(M' <: \mathcal{T_C}[\![\texttt{M}_{sup}]\!]).\, \forall(IVR' <: \mathcal{T_C}[\![\texttt{IV}_{sup}^{ref}]\!]).$$
$$\mathcal{T_C}[\![\texttt{IV}_{sup}]\!] \times (\textit{VisObj}\,(IVR',M') \to \mathcal{T_C}[\![\texttt{M}_{sup}]\!])$$

From this we see that *methfun*$_{sup}$ has type $\textit{VisObj}\,(IVR', M') \to \mathcal{T_C}[\![\texttt{M}_{sup}]\!]$ under the assumptions that $IVR' <: \mathcal{T_C}[\![\texttt{IV}_{sup}^{ref}]\!]$ and $M' <: \mathcal{T_C}[\![\texttt{M}_{sup}]\!]$.

In the subclass translation, these inherited methods are applied to *self*, which has type $\textit{VisObj}\,(IVR', M')$, where $IVR' <: \mathcal{T_C}[\![\texttt{IV}^{ref}]\!]$ and $M' <: \mathcal{T_C}[\![\texttt{M}]\!]$. However, because we are defining a subclass of C, $\mathcal{T_C}[\![\texttt{IV}^{ref}]\!] <: \mathcal{T_C}[\![\texttt{IV}_{sup}^{ref}]\!]$ and $\mathcal{T_C}[\![\texttt{M}]\!] <: \mathcal{T_C}[\![\texttt{M}_{sup}]\!]$.[4] By transitivity, it follows that $IVR' <: \mathcal{T_C}[\![\texttt{IV}^{ref}]\!]$ and

---

3. We prove this in Section 13.1.
4. Again, these will follow from the results in Section 13.1.

$\mathcal{T}_C[\![\,\mathcal{C}, \mathcal{E} \vdash \texttt{class inherits C modifies } \texttt{l}_{i_1}, \ldots, \texttt{l}_{i_m} \,(\texttt{inst}, \texttt{meth})\text{:}$
$$\texttt{ClassType}\,(\texttt{IV}, \texttt{M}) \triangleq$$
$$\Lambda(M' <: \mathcal{T}_C[\![\texttt{M}]\!]).\,\Lambda(IVR' <: \mathcal{T}_C[\![\texttt{IV}^{ref}]\!]).\langle inst_{all}, methfun_{all}\rangle,$$

where

$c = \mathcal{T}_C[\![\mathcal{C}, \mathcal{E} \vdash \texttt{C: ClassType}\,(\texttt{IV}_{sup}, \texttt{M}_{sup})]\!]\,[M']\,[IVR']$

$inst_{sup} = proj_1(c)$

$methfun_{sup} = proj_2(c)$

$inst_{all} = inst_{sup} \oplus \mathcal{T}_C[\![\mathcal{C}, \mathcal{E} \vdash \texttt{inst: IV}_{sub}]\!]$

$methfun_{all} = \lambda(self\text{: } VisObj\,(IVR', M')).$

    let $close\text{: } VisObj\,(IVR', M') \to (\exists Y.\,VisObj\,(Y, M'))$

        $= closeobj\,[IVR']\,[M']$

    in $methfun_{sup}(self) \oplus \mathcal{T}_{C'}[\![\mathcal{C}', \mathcal{E}' \vdash \texttt{meth: M}_{sub}]\!]$,

$\mathcal{C}' = \mathcal{C} \cup \{M' <: \texttt{M}, IVR' <: \texttt{IV}^{ref},$

        $\texttt{SelfType} = \texttt{VisObjectType}\,(IVR', M')\},$

$\mathcal{E}' = \mathcal{E} \cup \{\texttt{self: SelfType}, \texttt{close: SelfType} \to \texttt{ObjectType M}\}$

Figure 12.5 New translation of subclasses.

$M' <: \mathcal{T}_C[\![\texttt{M}_{sup}]\!]$, so the application of $methfun_{sup}$ to $self$ should be type safe.

12.3 Summary and a look ahead

The final translations of all types and expressions of $\mathcal{SOOL}$ are summarized in Figures 12.6, 12.7, 12.8, and 12.9. The major difference between the translation of classes and subclasses presented here versus those given in the previous chapter is that the classes are polymorphic, parameterized by the types of methods and instance variables that might arise in subclasses. As a result, methods take a *self* parameter whose type is *not* that of objects generated from the class, but instead from some possible subclass (which one depends on the instantiations of the type parameters).

The constraints on the type parameters, *IVR'* and *M'*, in the subclass type-checking rules and translation are stronger than those in the superclass, so any method that type checks under the original, weaker assumptions, is guaranteed to type check under the stricter assumptions in the subclass. As a result, we have now succeeded in modeling objects, classes, and subclasses

$$\mathcal{T}_{\mathcal{C}}[\![\texttt{C}]\!] \triangleq C$$

$$\mathcal{T}_{\mathcal{C}}[\![\texttt{t}]\!] \triangleq \begin{cases} t & \text{if } \mathcal{C}(\texttt{t}) = \texttt{t} \\ \mathcal{T}_{\mathcal{C}}[\![\mathcal{C}(\texttt{t})]\!] & \text{otherwise} \end{cases}$$

$$\mathcal{T}_{\mathcal{C}}[\![\texttt{T}_1 \times \ldots \times \texttt{T}_n \to \texttt{T}_{n+1}]\!] \triangleq \mathcal{T}_{\mathcal{C}}[\![\texttt{T}_1]\!] \times \ldots \times \mathcal{T}_{\mathcal{C}}[\![\texttt{T}_n]\!] \to \mathcal{T}_{\mathcal{C}}[\![\texttt{T}_{n+1}]\!]$$

$$\mathcal{T}_{\mathcal{C}}[\![\texttt{Ref T}]\!] \triangleq \textit{Ref } \mathcal{T}_{\mathcal{C}}[\![\texttt{T}]\!]$$

$$\mathcal{T}_{\mathcal{C}}[\![\{\!| \texttt{l}_1 \colon \texttt{T}_1; \ldots; \texttt{l}_n \colon \texttt{T}_n |\!\}]\!] \triangleq \{\!| \texttt{l}_1 \colon \mathcal{T}_{\mathcal{C}}[\![\texttt{T}_1]\!]; \ldots; \texttt{l}_n \colon \mathcal{T}_{\mathcal{C}}[\![\texttt{T}_n]\!] |\!\}$$

$$\mathcal{T}_{\mathcal{C}}[\![\texttt{VisObjectType}(\texttt{IVR}, \texttt{M})]\!] \triangleq \mathcal{T}_{\mathcal{C}}[\![\texttt{IVR}]\!] \times (\mathcal{T}_{\mathcal{C}}[\![\texttt{IVR}]\!] \to \mathcal{T}_{\mathcal{C}}[\![\texttt{M}]\!])$$

$$\mathcal{T}_{\mathcal{C}}[\![\texttt{ObjectType M}]\!] \triangleq \exists Y.\, Y \times (Y \to \mathcal{T}_{\mathcal{C}}[\![\texttt{M}]\!])$$

$$\mathcal{T}_{\mathcal{C}}[\![\texttt{ClassType}(\texttt{IV}, \texttt{M})]\!] \triangleq \forall (M' <: \mathcal{T}_{\mathcal{C}}[\![\texttt{M}]\!]).\, \forall (IVR' <: \mathcal{T}_{\mathcal{C}}[\![\texttt{IV}^{ref}]\!]).$$
$$\mathcal{T}_{\mathcal{C}}[\![\texttt{IV}]\!] \times (\textit{VisObj}\,(IVR', M') \to \mathcal{T}_{\mathcal{C}}[\![\texttt{M}]\!])$$

Figure 12.6   Final translation of types of $\mathcal{SOOL}$ to types in $\Lambda^P_{<:}$.

in such a way that inherited methods will remain type correct if they were type correct in the superclass.

In the next chapter, we prove the soundness of our translation by showing that if an expression of $\mathcal{SOOL}$ is well-typed, then its translation in $\Lambda^P_{<:}$ is also well-typed, with a type which is the translation of the type of the original $\mathcal{SOOL}$ expression. The proof is long and quite technical, but provides confidence that our translation makes sense.

Before proceeding to this proof, we pause to look ahead to topics to be discussed in succeeding chapters. First, there are some details that we left out of our typing rules and translations that we have yet to address. These include how to handle calls to superclasses, the typing and translation of nil, and handling of errors. They will be addressed in Chapter 14.

It may be surprising that the translation of classes required moving to a language which included bounded polymorphism. However, this reflects the complexity of subclasses and inheritance. But as a result, we will find in Chapter 15 that adding F-bounded polymorphism to $\mathcal{SOOL}$ requires no new technical tools. The added complexity necessary to model classes is sufficient to handle the translation of F-bounded polymorphism.

Also in Chapter 14, we discuss some subtle points which arise in the typing of self. While these are easily handled with the use of close and the *Subsumption* rule, they end up giving a less accurate typing of self than might be desired. This weakness in the typing system suggests the addition

$$\mathcal{T}_C[\![\mathcal{C}, \mathcal{E} \vdash \texttt{id: T}]\!] \triangleq id$$

$$\mathcal{T}_C[\![\mathcal{C}, \mathcal{E} \vdash \texttt{c: T}]\!] \triangleq c$$

$$\mathcal{T}_C[\![\mathcal{C}, \mathcal{E} \vdash \texttt{(): Void}]\!] \triangleq \langle\rangle$$

$$\mathcal{T}_C[\![\mathcal{C}, \mathcal{E} \vdash \texttt{val E: Ref T}]\!] \triangleq val\ \mathcal{T}_C[\![\mathcal{C}, \mathcal{E} \vdash \texttt{E: T}]\!]$$

$$\mathcal{T}_C[\![\mathcal{C}, \mathcal{E} \vdash \texttt{ref E: Ref T}]\!] \triangleq ref\ \mathcal{T}_C[\![\mathcal{C}, \mathcal{E} \vdash \texttt{E: T}]\!]$$

$$\mathcal{T}_C[\![\mathcal{C}, \mathcal{E} \vdash \texttt{E(E}_1\texttt{,} \ldots \texttt{, E}_n\texttt{): T}]\!] \triangleq \mathcal{T}_C[\![\mathcal{C}, \mathcal{E} \vdash \texttt{E: T}_1 \times \ldots \times \texttt{T}_n \rightarrow \texttt{T}]\!]$$
$$(\langle \mathcal{T}_C[\![\mathcal{C}, \mathcal{E} \vdash \texttt{E}_1\texttt{: T}_1]\!], \ldots, \mathcal{T}_C[\![\mathcal{C}, \mathcal{E} \vdash \texttt{E}_n\texttt{: T}_n]\!]\rangle)$$

$$\mathcal{T}_C[\![\mathcal{C}, \mathcal{E} \vdash \texttt{function(id}_1\texttt{: T}_1\texttt{,} \ldots \texttt{, id}_n\texttt{: T}_n\texttt{): T is Block:}$$
$$\texttt{T}_1 \times \ldots \times \texttt{T}_n \rightarrow \texttt{T}]\!] \triangleq$$
$$\lambda(\langle id_1\texttt{: } \mathcal{T}_C[\![\texttt{T}_1]\!], \ldots, id_n\texttt{: } \mathcal{T}_C[\![\texttt{T}_n]\!]\rangle).\mathcal{T}_C[\![\mathcal{C}, \mathcal{E}' \vdash \texttt{Block: T}]\!]$$
$$\text{where } \mathcal{E}' = \mathcal{E} \cup \{\texttt{id}_1\texttt{: T}_1, \ldots, \texttt{id}_n\texttt{: T}_n\}$$

$$\mathcal{T}_C[\![\mathcal{C}, \mathcal{E} \vdash \{\!| \texttt{l}_1\texttt{: T}_1 = \texttt{E}_1\texttt{;} \ldots \texttt{; l}_n\texttt{: T}_n = \texttt{E}_n |\!\}\texttt{: } \{\!| \texttt{l}_1\texttt{: T}_1\texttt{;} \ldots \texttt{; l}_n\texttt{: T}_n |\!\}]\!] \triangleq$$
$$\{\!| \, l_1\texttt{: } \mathcal{T}_C[\![\texttt{T}_1]\!] = \mathcal{T}_C[\![\mathcal{C}, \mathcal{E} \vdash \texttt{E}_1\texttt{: T}_1]\!]\texttt{;} \ldots \texttt{; } l_n\texttt{: } \mathcal{T}_C[\![\texttt{T}_n]\!] = \mathcal{T}_C[\![\mathcal{C}, \mathcal{E} \vdash \texttt{E}_n\texttt{: T}_n]\!] \,|\!\}$$

$$\mathcal{T}_C[\![\mathcal{C}, \mathcal{E} \vdash \texttt{Block: T}]\!] \triangleq let\ t_1 = \mathcal{T}_C[\![\texttt{T}_1]\!]\ in\ \ldots\ let\ t_n = \mathcal{T}_C[\![\texttt{T}_n]\!]\ in$$
$$let\ id_1\texttt{: } \mathcal{T}_C[\![\texttt{U}_1]\!] = \mathcal{T}_C[\![\mathcal{C}, \mathcal{E} \vdash \texttt{E}_1\texttt{: T}]\!]\ in\ \ldots$$
$$let\ id_k\texttt{: } \mathcal{T}_C[\![\texttt{U}_k]\!] = \mathcal{T}_C[\![\mathcal{C}, \mathcal{E} \vdash \texttt{E}_k\texttt{: T}]\!]\ in$$
$$\mathcal{T}_C[\![\mathcal{C}, \mathcal{E} \vdash \texttt{S: Command}]\!]\texttt{;} \mathcal{T}_C[\![\mathcal{C}, \mathcal{E} \vdash \texttt{E: T}]\!]\ end\ \ldots\ end$$
$$\text{where Block is } \quad \texttt{type t}_1 = \texttt{T}_1\texttt{;} \ldots \texttt{; t}_n = \texttt{T}_n$$
$$\texttt{const id}_1\texttt{: U}_1 = \texttt{E}_1\texttt{;} \ldots \texttt{; id}_k\texttt{: U}_k = \texttt{E}_k$$
$$\{ \texttt{ S return E } \}$$

$$\mathcal{T}_C[\![\mathcal{C}, \mathcal{E} \vdash \texttt{E} \Leftarrow \texttt{m}_i\texttt{: T}_i]\!] \triangleq (proj_2(\mathcal{T}_C[\![\mathcal{C}, \mathcal{E} \vdash \texttt{E: T}]\!]) (proj_1(\mathcal{T}_C[\![\mathcal{C}, \mathcal{E} \vdash \texttt{E: T}]\!]))).m$$
$$\text{where } \texttt{T} = \texttt{VisObjectType(IVR, ObjectType } \{\!| \texttt{m}_1\texttt{: T}_1, \ldots, \texttt{m}_n\texttt{: T}_n |\!\})$$

$$\mathcal{T}_C[\![\mathcal{C}, \mathcal{E} \vdash \texttt{E} \Leftarrow \texttt{m}_i\texttt{: T}_i]\!] \triangleq open\ \mathcal{T}_C[\![\mathcal{C}, \mathcal{E} \vdash \texttt{E: T}]\!]\ as\ \langle IR, vo\rangle$$
$$in\ (proj_2(vo)(proj_1(vo))).m$$
$$\text{where } \texttt{T} = \texttt{ObjectType } \{\!| \texttt{m}_1\texttt{: T}_1, \ldots, \texttt{m}_n\texttt{: T}_n |\!\}$$

$$\mathcal{T}_C[\![\mathcal{C}, \mathcal{E} \vdash \texttt{E.l}_k\texttt{: T}_k]\!] \triangleq proj_1(\mathcal{T}_C[\![\mathcal{C}, \mathcal{E} \vdash \texttt{E: VisObjectType(IVR, M)}]\!]).l$$
$$\text{where } \texttt{IVR} = \{\!| \texttt{l}_1\texttt{: T}_1, \ldots, \texttt{l}_n\texttt{: T}_n |\!\} \text{ and } 1 \leq k \leq n.$$

$$\mathcal{T}_C[\![\mathcal{C}, \mathcal{E} \vdash \texttt{E: T}]\!] \triangleq \mathcal{T}_C[\![\mathcal{C}, \mathcal{E} \vdash \texttt{E: S}]\!]$$
$$\text{where } \mathcal{C} \vdash \texttt{S} <: \texttt{T}$$

Figure 12.7 Translation of selected expressions of $\mathcal{SOOL}$ to expressions in $\Lambda^P_{<:}$.

$\mathcal{T}_{\mathcal{C}}[\![\,\mathcal{C}, \mathcal{E} \vdash \text{class(inst,meth)}: \text{ClassType}\,(\text{IV}, \text{M})]\!] \triangleq$
$\quad \Lambda(M' <: \mathcal{T}_{\mathcal{C}}[\![\text{M}]\!]).\, \Lambda(IVR' <: \mathcal{T}_{\mathcal{C}}[\![\text{IV}^{ref}]\!]).\langle \mathcal{T}_{\mathcal{C}}[\![\,\mathcal{C}, \mathcal{E} \vdash \text{inst: IV}]\!], methfun\rangle,$

where

$\quad methfun = \lambda(self: VisObj\,(IVR', M')).$
$\qquad\qquad\qquad\quad let\ close: VisObj\,(IVR', M') \rightarrow (\exists Y.\, VisObj\,(Y, M'))$
$\qquad\qquad\qquad\qquad = closeobj\,[IVR']\,[M']$
$\qquad\qquad\qquad\quad in\ \mathcal{T}_{\mathcal{C}'}[\![\,\mathcal{C}', \mathcal{E}' \vdash \text{meth: M}]\!],$
$\quad \mathcal{C}' = \mathcal{C} \cup \{M' <: \text{M}, IVR' <: \text{IV}^{ref},$
$\qquad\qquad\quad\ \text{SelfType} = \text{VisObjectType}\,(IVR', M')\},$
$\quad \mathcal{E}' = \mathcal{E} \cup \{\text{self: SelfType, close: SelfType} \rightarrow \text{ObjectType M}'\}$

$\mathcal{T}_{\mathcal{C}}[\![\,\mathcal{C}, \mathcal{E} \vdash \text{class inherits C modifies } \text{l}_{i_1},\dots,\text{l}_{i_m}\,(\text{inst,meth}):$
$\qquad\qquad\qquad\qquad\qquad\qquad\qquad \text{ClassType}\,(\text{IV}, \text{M}) \triangleq$
$\qquad\qquad\quad \Lambda(M' <: \mathcal{T}_{\mathcal{C}}[\![\text{M}]\!]).\, \Lambda(IVR' <: \mathcal{T}_{\mathcal{C}}[\![\text{IV}^{ref}]\!]).\langle inst_{all}, methfun_{all}\rangle,$

where

$\quad c = \mathcal{T}_{\mathcal{C}}[\![\,\mathcal{C}, \mathcal{E} \vdash \text{C: ClassType}\,(\text{IV}_{sup}, \text{M}_{sup})]\!]\,[M']\,[IVR']$
$\quad inst_{sup} = proj_1(c)$
$\quad methfun_{sup} = proj_2(c)$
$\quad inst_{all} = inst_{sup} \oplus \mathcal{T}_{\mathcal{C}}[\![\,\mathcal{C}, \mathcal{E} \vdash \text{inst: IV}_{sub}]\!]$
$\quad methfun_{all} = \lambda(self: VisObj\,(IVR', M')).$
$\qquad\qquad\qquad\quad let\ close: VisObj\,(IVR', M') \rightarrow (\exists Y.\, VisObj\,(Y, M'))$
$\qquad\qquad\qquad\qquad = closeobj\,[IVR']\,[M']$
$\qquad\qquad\qquad\quad in\ methfun_{sup}(self) \oplus \mathcal{T}_{\mathcal{C}'}[\![\,\mathcal{C}', \mathcal{E}' \vdash \text{meth: M}_{sub}]\!],$
$\quad \mathcal{C}' = \mathcal{C} \cup \{M' <: \text{M}, IVR' <: \text{IV}^{ref},$
$\qquad\qquad\quad\ \text{SelfType} = \text{VisObjectType}\,(IVR', M')\},$
$\quad \mathcal{E}' = \mathcal{E} \cup \{\text{self: SelfType, close: SelfType} \rightarrow \text{ObjectType M}\}$

$\mathcal{T}_{\mathcal{C}}[\![\,\mathcal{C}, \mathcal{E} \vdash \text{new C: ObjectType M}]\!] \triangleq closeobj\,[IVR]\,[M]\langle inst^{ref}, methfun'\rangle$
$\quad$ where

$\qquad c \triangleq \mathcal{T}_{\mathcal{C}}[\![\,\mathcal{C}, \mathcal{E} \vdash \text{C: ClassType}\,(\text{IV}, \text{M})]\!]\,[M]\,[IVR]$
$\qquad IVR = \mathcal{T}_{\mathcal{C}}[\![\text{IV}^{ref}]\!], M = \mathcal{T}_{\mathcal{C}}[\![\text{M}]\!]$
$\qquad inst = proj_1(c), methfun = proj_2(c),$
$\qquad inst^{ref}$ is formed by adding refs to all fields of $inst$, and
$\qquad methfun' = \underline{fix}\,[IVR \rightarrow M]\lambda(fm: IVR \rightarrow M).$
$\qquad\qquad\qquad\qquad\qquad\qquad \lambda(inst': IVR).methfun(\langle inst', fm\rangle).$

Figure 12.8   Final translation of expressions of $\mathcal{SOOL}$ to $\Lambda^{P}_{<:}$. Part 2.

$$\mathcal{T_C}[\![\mathcal{C}, \mathcal{E} \vdash \texttt{id:} = \texttt{E: Command}]\!] \triangleq id := \mathcal{T_C}[\![\mathcal{C}, \mathcal{E} \vdash \texttt{E: T}]\!]$$
$$\text{where } \mathcal{C}, \mathcal{E} \vdash \texttt{id: Ref T}$$

$$\mathcal{T_C}[\![\mathcal{C}, \mathcal{E} \vdash \texttt{while E do } \{\texttt{S}\}\texttt{: Command}]\!] \triangleq \underline{fix}\,[Command](\lambda(w\text{: } Command).$$
$$\text{if } \mathcal{T_C}[\![\mathcal{C}, \mathcal{E} \vdash \texttt{E: Boolean}]\!]\ then\ \{\mathcal{T_C}[\![\mathcal{C}, \overline{\mathcal{E}} \vdash \texttt{S: Command}]\!]; w\}\ else\ \{nop\}$$

$$\mathcal{T_C}[\![\mathcal{C}, \mathcal{E} \vdash \texttt{if E then } \{\texttt{S}_1\} \texttt{ else } \{\texttt{S}_2\}\texttt{: Command}]\!] \triangleq$$
$$\qquad\qquad if\ \mathcal{T_C}[\![\texttt{E: Boolean}]\!]\ then\ \{\mathcal{T_C}[\![\mathcal{C}, \mathcal{E} \vdash \texttt{S}_1\texttt{: Command}]\!]\}$$
$$\qquad\qquad\qquad else\ \{\mathcal{T_C}[\![\mathcal{C}, \mathcal{E} \vdash \texttt{S}_2\texttt{: Command}]\!]\}$$

$$\mathcal{T_C}[\![\mathcal{C}, \mathcal{E} \vdash \texttt{S}_1\texttt{; S}_2\texttt{: Command}]\!] \triangleq \mathcal{T_C}[\![\mathcal{C}, \mathcal{E} \vdash \texttt{S}_1\texttt{: Command}]\!];$$
$$\qquad\qquad\qquad\qquad\qquad \mathcal{T_C}[\![\mathcal{C}, \mathcal{E} \vdash \texttt{S}_2\texttt{: Command}]\!]$$

$$\mathcal{T_C}[\![\mathcal{C}, \mathcal{E} \vdash \texttt{Program id; Block.: Command}]\!] \triangleq$$
$$\qquad\qquad\qquad\qquad \mathcal{T_C}[\![\mathcal{C}, \mathcal{E} \vdash \texttt{Block: Command}]\!]$$

Figure 12.9   Translation of statements of $\mathcal{SOOL}$ to expressions in $\Lambda^P_{<:}$.

of a type safe MyType construct similar to that of Eiffel's unsafe like Cur-rent expression, which was discussed in Section 4.2. The reason for this addition is to provide more accurate typing of self, especially when it is used in methods inherited in subclasses.

Perhaps surprisingly, we only need to make minor changes to the encoding introduced to this point in order to model MyType. Moreover, the encoding suggests safe type-checking rules for programs using this construct. How-ever, it will turn out that MyType interferes with the possibility of subtypes. Instead a different, though similar, relation, called matching, will work more uniformly than subtyping in languages with MyType.

We will come back and discuss these extensions to $\mathcal{SOOL}$ in future chap-ters, but in the next chapter we dig deep into the technical details in proving the soundness of our translation.

13 *SOOL's Type System Is Safe (and Sound)*

Why bother to have a static type system for a programming language unless it guarantees some safety properties in the run-time behavior of a language? After all, one of the main reasons for having a static type system is to uncover errors as early as possible. In this chapter we investigate whether type-checking rules can guarantee the absence of certain run-time errors.

In this chapter we show that $SOOL$'s static type-checking rules are safe in the sense that they are sufficient to rule out run-time type errors. We do this by providing careful mathematical proofs of the soundness of our translation.

For example, we will show that if types S and T of $SOOL$ are in the subtype relation, then so are their translations. Similarly, if expression M of $SOOL$ has type S, then the translation of M has a type that is the translation of S. In Section 13.3 we discuss type errors and type safety in more detail and use the fact that $\Lambda^P_{<:}$ has a statically safe type system in order to deduce the extremely important result that $SOOL$'s type system is also safe. We finish the chapter with a brief discussion of general run-time errors.

The reader who is less interested in the mathematical proofs may find it easier to skip the detailed proofs in the first section of this chapter on a first reading, returning to them later. However, we strongly recommend that the rest of the chapter not be skipped. The discussion of errors and type safety highlights the goals of the formal analysis in this book.

13.1 The translation of $SOOL$ to $\Lambda^P_{<:}$ is sound

SOUND — We say that a translation of $SOOL$ to $\Lambda^P_{<:}$ is *sound* if the translation of well-typed expressions of $SOOL$ are well-typed, and the types of the translated expressions are the translations of the types of the original $SOOL$ expressions. That is, the translation is sound if the translation function $\mathcal{T}_C[\![\,]\!]$ preserves typing. We will first show that if two types of $\mathcal{SOOL}$ are subtypes, then their translations are subtypes in $\Lambda^P_{<:}$. We will then show that if $\mathcal{C}, \mathcal{E} \vdash$ E: T in $\mathcal{SOOL}$ then its translation, $\mathcal{T}_C[\![\mathcal{C}, \mathcal{E} \vdash$ E: T$]\!]$, will have type $\mathcal{T}_C[\![\text{T}]\!]$ via a translation of the typing derivation in $\mathcal{SOOL}$ to a typing derivation in $\Lambda^P_{<:}$.

Before getting started on the proofs of soundness we first need some definitions and technical lemmas about the translations with respect to different type constraint systems. These results will be used in the proof of the soundness of the translation.

Because typing judgements depend on a collection of assumptions on type variables, we must translate the assumptions as well.

Definition 13.1.1 *If $\mathcal{C}$ is a type constraint system and $\mathcal{E}$ is a static type environment for $\mathcal{SOOL}$, then let $\mathcal{T}_C[\![\mathcal{E}]\!] = \{x\colon \mathcal{T}_C[\![\text{T}]\!] \mid (x\colon \text{T}) \in \mathcal{E}\}$. Similarly, if $\mathcal{C}'$ is a type constraint system for $\mathcal{SOOL}$, let $\mathcal{T}_C[\![\mathcal{C}']\!] = \{v <: \mathcal{T}_C[\![\text{T}]\!] \mid (v <: \text{T}) \in \mathcal{C}'\}$.*

The translation of type constraints drops constraints of the form t = T because they have already been taken into consideration in computing $\mathcal{T}_C[\![\text{U}]\!]$ for type U. Of course, $\Lambda^P_{<:}$ does not even include this sort of type constraint, so if we are going to use $\mathcal{T}_C[\![\mathcal{C}']\!]$ in typing expressions of $\Lambda^P_{<:}$ it is also necessary to have eliminated these type definitions.

The following lemma shows that adding a new bounded type identifier to $\mathcal{C}$ makes no difference in the translation of type expressions.

Lemma 13.1.2 *Suppose $\mathcal{C}$ and $\mathcal{C}' = \mathcal{C} \cup \{\text{t} <: \text{T}\}$ are both type constraint systems. Then for all type expressions, S, $\mathcal{T}_{\mathcal{C}'}[\![\text{S}]\!] = \mathcal{T}_C[\![\text{S}]\!]$.*

Proof. The proof is by a trivial induction on the complexity of type expressions using the fact that $\mathcal{T}_{\mathcal{C}'}[\![\text{t}]\!] = \mathcal{T}_C[\![\text{t}]\!]$ by the remark after Definition 12.1.1. ∎

The result of adding a new equational type constraint to $\mathcal{C}$ in translating expressions is described in the following lemmas.

Lemma 13.1.3 *Let $\mathcal{C}$ and $\mathcal{C}'$ be type constraint systems such that $\mathcal{C}' = \mathcal{C} \cup \mathcal{C}''$. Let S be a type expression that contains no type identifiers introduced in $\mathcal{C}''$. Then $\mathcal{T}_C[\![\text{S}]\!] = \mathcal{T}_{\mathcal{C}'}[\![\text{S}]\!]$.*

The Lemma above follows immediately from the following result.

Lemma 13.1.4 *Let $\mathcal{C}_0$ be a type constraint system containing only bounded constraints (i.e., no equations). For all $1 \leq i \leq n$, let $\mathcal{C}_i = \mathcal{C}_{i-1} \cup \{\text{t}_i = \text{T}_i\} \cup \mathcal{C}'_i$ be a type constraint system, where $\mathcal{C}'_i$ contains only bounded constraints. If S is a type* *expression that contains no type variables* t_j, *for* $j > i$, *then for all* $k \geq i$, $\mathcal{T}_{C_k}[\![S]\!] = \mathcal{T}_{C_i}[\![S]\!]$.

Proof.   By induction on i. If $i = 0$, then S contains no type variables involved in a type definition in any of the C_j. In this case it is easy to use Lemma 13.1.2 to prove by induction on the complexity of S that $\mathcal{T}_{C_0}[\![S]\!] = \mathcal{T}_{C_k}[\![S]\!]$ for all k.

Suppose the lemma is true for all $m < i$. We show it for i. The proof is by induction on the complexity of S, where S contains no type variables t_j for $j > i$.

Most cases are trivial. The only interesting case is for type variables. If S is a type variable, then it must be t_m for some $m \leq i$.

If $S = t_m$ for $m < i$, then by induction, $\mathcal{T}_{C_i}[\![t_m]\!] = \mathcal{T}_{C_m}[\![t_m]\!] = \mathcal{T}_{C_k}[\![t_m]\!]$ for all $k \geq i$, because $\mathcal{T}_{C_m}[\![t_m]\!]$ contains no t_j with $j \geq m$.

If $S = t_i$, then $\mathcal{T}_{C_i}[\![t_i]\!] = \mathcal{T}_{C_i}[\![T_i]\!]$. But T_i does not contain t_j for $j > i - 1$. It follows by induction that $\mathcal{T}_{C_i}[\![t_i]\!] = \mathcal{T}_{C_i}[\![T_i]\!] = \mathcal{T}_{C_{i-1}}[\![T_i]\!] = \mathcal{T}_{C_k}[\![T_i]\!] = \mathcal{T}_{C_k}[\![t_i]\!]$ for all $k \geq i$.

Finally if $S = u$ for some type variable different from all t_i, then $\mathcal{T}_{C_i}[\![u]\!] = u = \mathcal{T}_{C_k}[\![u]\!]$ for all k.   ∎

Using the above lemma we show the impact of adding a new type definition to a type constraint used in a translation only adds a simple substitution to the previous translation.

Lemma 13.1.5 *Let* $\mathcal{C}$ *be a type constraint system. Let* t *be a type variable not occurring in* $\mathcal{C}$ *such that* $\mathcal{C}' = \mathcal{C} \cup \{t = T\}$ *is a type constraint system. Then*

1. *For all type expressions,* S, $\mathcal{T}_{C'}[\![S]\!] = [\mathcal{T}_C[\![T]\!]/t]\mathcal{T}_C[\![S]\!]$.

2. *For all expressions,* E, $\mathcal{T}_{C'}[\![E]\!] = [\mathcal{T}_C[\![T]\!]/t]\mathcal{T}_C[\![E]\!]$.

Proof.   The proof of the first part is a simple proof by induction on the construction of type expressions. The only non-trivial part is the case for type identifiers. If $t' \neq t$, then $\mathcal{T}_{C'}[\![t']\!] = \mathcal{T}_C[\![t']\!]$, while $\mathcal{T}_{C'}[\![t]\!] = \mathcal{T}_{C'}[\![T]\!]$. However, T contains no occurrences of t. Thus by Lemma 13.1.3, $\mathcal{T}_{C'}[\![T]\!] = \mathcal{T}_C[\![T]\!]$. Also, $\mathcal{T}_C[\![t]\!] = t$ because t does not occur in $\mathcal{C}$. Thus $\mathcal{T}_{C'}[\![t]\!] = \mathcal{T}_C[\![T]\!] = [\mathcal{T}_C[\![T]\!]/t]\mathcal{T}_C[\![t]\!]$. The other parts of the proof follow easily.

The proof of the second part is a simple induction on the construction of expressions.   ∎

Now we show that iterating this process gives similar results.

Lemma 13.1.6 *Let* $\mathcal{C}_0 = \mathcal{C}$ *and for all* $1 \leq k \leq n$, *let* $\mathcal{C}_k = \mathcal{C}_{k-1} \cup \{t_k = T_k\}$ *be type constraint systems. Then*

1. *For all type expressions,* S, $\mathcal{T}_{C_k}[\![S]\!] = [\mathcal{T}_C[\![T_1]\!]/t_1] \ldots [\mathcal{T}_C[\![T_k]\!]/t_k]\mathcal{T}_C[\![S]\!].$

2. *For all regular expressions,* E, $\mathcal{T}_{C_k}[\![E]\!] = [\mathcal{T}_C[\![T_1]\!]/t_1] \ldots [\mathcal{T}_C[\![T_k]\!]/t_k]\mathcal{T}_C[\![E]\!].$

Proof. The proof is by induction on k for $0 \leq k \leq n$. Both parts of the lemma are clearly true for $k = 0$ as no substitutions are made. Suppose both are true for k, for some $k \geq 0$. We show both are true for $k+1$.

We begin with type expressions, S. By Lemma 13.1.5,

$$\mathcal{T}_{C_{k+1}}[\![S]\!] = [\mathcal{T}_{C_k}[\![T_{k+1}]\!]/t_{k+1}]\mathcal{T}_{C_k}[\![S]\!].$$

But by induction,

$$\mathcal{T}_{C_k}[\![T_{k+1}]\!] = [\mathcal{T}_C[\![T_1]\!]/t_1] \ldots [\mathcal{T}_C[\![T_k]\!]/t_k]\mathcal{T}_C[\![T_{k+1}]\!],$$

and

$$\mathcal{T}_{C_k}[\![S]\!] = [\mathcal{T}_C[\![T_1]\!]/t_1] \ldots [\mathcal{T}_C[\![T_k]\!]/t_k]\mathcal{T}_C[\![S]\!].$$

Thus,

$$
\begin{aligned}
\mathcal{T}_{C_{k+1}}[\![S]\!] &= [[\mathcal{T}_C[\![T_1]\!]/t_1] \ldots [\mathcal{T}_C[\![T_k]\!]/t_k]\mathcal{T}_C[\![T_{k+1}]\!]/t_{k+1}] \\
&\quad ([\mathcal{T}_C[\![T_1]\!]/t_1] \ldots [\mathcal{T}_C[\![T_k]\!]/t_k]\mathcal{T}_C[\![S]\!]) \\
&= [\mathcal{T}_C[\![T_1]\!]/t_1] \ldots [\mathcal{T}_C[\![T_k]\!]/t_k][\mathcal{T}_C[\![T_{k+1}]\!]/t_{k+1}]\mathcal{T}_C[\![S]\!].
\end{aligned}
$$

The proof of the induction case is similar for the second part of the lemma. ∎

When we process declarations of $\mathcal{SOOL}$, the type constraint system is augmented with new type definitions. We show that addition of these definitions has no impact on the translation of static type environments and type constraints.

Lemma 13.1.7 *Let C be a type constraint system and $\mathcal{E}$ be a static type environment. Let* t *be a type variable not occurring in C or $\mathcal{E}$ such that $C' = C \cup \{t = T\}$ is a type constraint system. Then $\mathcal{T}_{C'}[\![C']\!] = \mathcal{T}_C[\![C]\!]$ and $\mathcal{T}_{C'}[\![\mathcal{E}]\!] = \mathcal{T}_C[\![\mathcal{E}]\!].$*

Proof. $\mathcal{T}_{C'}[\![C']\!] = \mathcal{T}_{C'}[\![C]\!]$ because equations are erased in the translation of C'. The fact that $\mathcal{T}_{C'}[\![C]\!] = \mathcal{T}_C[\![C]\!]$ follows easily from Lemma 13.1.5 because t does not occur in C. It again follows from the Lemma and the fact that t does not occur in $\mathcal{E}$ that $\mathcal{T}_{C'}[\![\mathcal{E}]\!] = \mathcal{T}_C[\![\mathcal{E}]\!].$ ∎

Finally we show that substitutions make no difference in translating types.

Lemma 13.1.8 *Let C be a constraint system and* S *a type expression. Then $\mathcal{T}_C[\![S]\!] = \mathcal{T}_C[\![C(S)]\!].$*

Proof. This follows easily from the fact that $\mathcal{T_C}[\![t]\!] = \mathcal{T_C}[\![\mathcal{C}(t)]\!]$ for t a type variable. The other cases follow easily by induction. ∎

Now that we have finished these technical preliminaries, we are ready to begin showing our translation is sound. We begin by showing that subtyping is preserved in the translation from $\mathcal{SOOL}$ to $\Lambda^P_{<:}$. This refinement of Theorem 11.2.1 is necessary because revisions of the type-checking rules changed the definition of $\mathcal{C}$ to include type constraints.

Theorem 13.1.9 *Let S and T be types of $\mathcal{SOOL}$ such that $\mathcal{C} \vdash S <: T$. Then*

$$\mathcal{T_C}[\![\mathcal{C}]\!] \vdash \mathcal{T_C}[\![S]\!] <: \mathcal{T_C}[\![T]\!].$$

Proof. We give a proof by induction on the number of steps in the proof that $\mathcal{C} \vdash S <: T$. That is, we assume that for all proofs of length less than n, if $\mathcal{C} \vdash S <: T$, then $\mathcal{T_C}[\![\mathcal{C}]\!] \vdash \mathcal{T_C}[\![S]\!] <: \mathcal{T_C}[\![T]\!]$. We now must show that the theorem holds for all subtype relations provable in exactly n steps.

Suppose the last step in the proof is *TypeDef* $_{<:}$. Then the last step shows that $\mathcal{C} \vdash S <: T$ based on a shorter proof that $\mathcal{C} \vdash \mathcal{C}(S) <: \mathcal{C}(T)$. By the induction hypothesis, $\mathcal{T_C}[\![\mathcal{C}]\!] \vdash \mathcal{T_C}[\![\mathcal{C}(S)]\!] <: \mathcal{T_C}[\![\mathcal{C}(T)]\!]$. However, by Lemma 13.1.8, $\mathcal{T_C}[\![S]\!] = \mathcal{T_C}[\![\mathcal{C}(S)]\!]$ and similarly for T. Hence $\mathcal{T_C}[\![\mathcal{C}]\!] \vdash \mathcal{T_C}[\![S]\!] <: \mathcal{T_C}[\![T]\!]$.

If the last step in the proof is reflexivity for $\mathcal{SOOL}$, then $S = T$, and hence by the reflexivity rule for $\Lambda^P_{<:}$, $\mathcal{T_C}[\![\mathcal{C}]\!] \vdash \mathcal{T_C}[\![S]\!] <: \mathcal{T_C}[\![S]\!]$.

Transitivity is straightforward, while the other structural rules are all similar. We do the rule *Object* $_{<:}$ as an example.

Suppose that $\mathcal{C} \vdash \texttt{ObjectType M}' <: \texttt{ObjectType M}$ follows from $\mathcal{C} \vdash M' <: M$. By induction, $\mathcal{T_C}[\![\mathcal{C}]\!] \vdash \mathcal{T_C}[\![M']\!] <: \mathcal{T_C}[\![M]\!]$. Let Y be a type variable not occurring in $\mathcal{T_C}[\![\mathcal{C}]\!]$. By the function and product type subtyping rules of $\Lambda^P_{<:}$, it follows that

$$\mathcal{T_C}[\![\mathcal{C}]\!] \vdash Y \times (Y \to \mathcal{T_C}[\![M']\!]) <: Y \times (Y \to \mathcal{T_C}[\![M]\!]).$$

Finally, by rule *Exist* $_{<:}$,

$$\mathcal{T_C}[\![\mathcal{C}]\!] \vdash \exists Y.\, Y \times (Y \to \mathcal{T_C}[\![M']\!]) <: \exists Y.\, Y \times (Y \to \mathcal{T_C}[\![M]\!]).$$

But this simply shows that

$$\mathcal{T_C}[\![\mathcal{C}]\!] \vdash \mathcal{T_C}[\![\texttt{ObjectType M}']\!] <: \mathcal{T_C}[\![\texttt{ObjectType M}]\!].$$

∎

Now we wish to show that if a type can be assigned to an expression of $\mathcal{SOOL}$, then the translation of that type can be assigned to the translated expression.

Theorem 13.1.10 *Let* E *be an expression of* $\mathcal{SOOL}$ *that does not involve* nil, *and suppose* $\mathcal{C}, \mathcal{E} \vdash$ E: S. *Then*

$$\mathcal{T}_\mathcal{C}[\![\mathcal{C}]\!], \mathcal{T}_\mathcal{C}[\![\mathcal{E}]\!] \vdash \mathcal{T}_\mathcal{C}[\![\mathcal{C}, \mathcal{E} \vdash E: S]\!]: \mathcal{T}_\mathcal{C}[\![S]\!].$$

Proof. Following the definition of the translation of expressions, the proof of the theorem is given by induction on the length of the deduction of the typing (*not* the structure of the expression!). We may assume without loss of generality that the typing of E does not include any application of rule Type Abbrev since $\mathcal{T}_\mathcal{C}[\![S]\!] = \mathcal{T}_\mathcal{C}[\![\mathcal{C}(S)]\!]$.

Because the proof is relatively long and notationally dense already, we omit the typing information inside of the translation function. That is, we write $\mathcal{T}_\mathcal{C}[\![E]\!]$ rather than $\mathcal{T}_\mathcal{C}[\![\mathcal{C}, \mathcal{E} \vdash E: S]\!]$ for the translation of expressions in most of the proof. The only exception will be the subsumption case because the added notation clarifies the explanation of the proof. Simplified notation should not result in any ambiguity in the other cases as we will always be discussing the translation in combination with the typing derivation for the expression.

The cases where the last step uses either of the type-checking rules *Constant* or *Void* are trivial. The cases for rules *Value*, *Application*, *Record*, and *Reference* follow easily by induction. The case for the *Function* rule follows from the derived rule for n-ary functions in Section 8.2. The cases for statements are similarly straightforward.

Subsumption Suppose the typing deduction ends with an application of the subsumption rule. In particular, suppose that $\mathcal{C}, \mathcal{E} \vdash$ E: T follows by subsumption from $\mathcal{C}, \mathcal{E} \vdash$ E: S because $\mathcal{C} \vdash$ S <: T. By induction,

$$\mathcal{T}_\mathcal{C}[\![\mathcal{C}]\!], \mathcal{T}_\mathcal{C}[\![\mathcal{E}]\!] \vdash \mathcal{T}_\mathcal{C}[\![\mathcal{C}, \mathcal{E} \vdash E: S]\!]: \mathcal{T}_\mathcal{C}[\![S]\!].$$

But by Theorem 13.1.9, $\mathcal{T}_\mathcal{C}[\![\mathcal{C}]\!] \vdash \mathcal{T}_\mathcal{C}[\![S']\!] <: \mathcal{T}_\mathcal{C}[\![S]\!]$, and hence by subsumption in $\Lambda^P_{<:}$,

$$\mathcal{T}_\mathcal{C}[\![\mathcal{C}]\!], \mathcal{T}_\mathcal{C}[\![\mathcal{E}]\!] \vdash \mathcal{T}_\mathcal{C}[\![\mathcal{C}, \mathcal{E} \vdash E: S]\!]: \mathcal{T}_\mathcal{C}[\![T]\!].$$

But $\mathcal{T}_\mathcal{C}[\![\mathcal{C}, \mathcal{E} \vdash E: T]\!] = \mathcal{T}_\mathcal{C}[\![\mathcal{C}, \mathcal{E} \vdash E: S]\!]$ by the definition of the translation, so

$$\mathcal{T}_\mathcal{C}[\![\mathcal{C}]\!], \mathcal{T}_\mathcal{C}[\![\mathcal{E}]\!] \vdash \mathcal{T}_\mathcal{C}[\![\mathcal{C}, \mathcal{E} \vdash E: T]\!]: \mathcal{T}_\mathcal{C}[\![T]\!].$$

Identifier The case for identifiers is also straightforward. Suppose $\mathcal{C}, \mathcal{E} \vdash$ id: T because (id: T) $\in \mathcal{E}$. Then by definition, (id: $\mathcal{T}_\mathcal{C}[\![T]\!]) \in \mathcal{T}_\mathcal{C}[\![\mathcal{E}]\!]$, and hence $\mathcal{T}_\mathcal{C}[\![\mathcal{C}]\!], \mathcal{T}_\mathcal{C}[\![\mathcal{E}]\!] \vdash$ id: $\mathcal{T}_\mathcal{C}[\![T]\!]$.

Block   Suppose `Block` is

$$\text{type } t_1 = T_1; \ldots; t_n = T_n;$$
$$\text{const } id_1 : U_1 := E_1; \ldots; id_k : U_k := E_k;$$
$$\{ \text{ S return E; } \}$$

Let `TDefs` abbreviate the type declarations, and let `CDefs` abbreviate the constant declarations in `Block`.

For $1 \leq i \leq n$, let

$$\mathcal{C}_i = \mathcal{C} \cup \{t_1 = T_1, \ldots, t_i = T_i\},$$

and for $1 \leq j \leq k$, let

$$\mathcal{E}_j = \mathcal{E} \cup \{id_1 : U_1, \ldots, id_j : U_j\}$$

Let $\mathcal{C}_0 = \mathcal{C}$, $\mathcal{C}' = \mathcal{C}_n$, $\mathcal{E}_0 = \mathcal{E}$, and $\mathcal{E}' = \mathcal{E}_k$.

Suppose $\mathcal{C}, \mathcal{E} \vdash$ `Block`: T where T does not contain any of $t_1, \ldots, t_n$, because

$$\mathcal{C}, \mathcal{E} \vdash \text{TDefs} \diamond \mathcal{C}', \mathcal{E}, \qquad \mathcal{C}', \mathcal{E} \vdash \text{CDefs} \diamond \mathcal{C}', \mathcal{E}', \qquad \mathcal{C}', \mathcal{E}' \vdash \text{S: Command}$$

and

$$\mathcal{C}', \mathcal{E}' \vdash \text{E: T}.$$

By induction,

$$\mathcal{T}_{\mathcal{C}'}[\![\mathcal{C}']\!], \mathcal{T}_{\mathcal{C}'}[\![\mathcal{E}']\!] \vdash \mathcal{T}_{\mathcal{C}'}[\![\text{S}]\!]: Command,$$

and

$$\mathcal{T}_{\mathcal{C}'}[\![\mathcal{C}']\!], \mathcal{T}_{\mathcal{C}'}[\![\mathcal{E}']\!] \vdash \mathcal{T}_{\mathcal{C}'}[\![\text{E}]\!]: \mathcal{T}_{\mathcal{C}'}[\![\text{T}]\!].$$

Hence by the *Sequencing* rule for $\Lambda^P_{\leq :}$,

$$\mathcal{T}_{\mathcal{C}'}[\![\mathcal{C}']\!], \mathcal{T}_{\mathcal{C}'}[\![\mathcal{E}']\!] \vdash \mathcal{T}_{\mathcal{C}'}[\![\text{S}]\!]; \mathcal{T}_{\mathcal{C}'}[\![\text{E}]\!]: \mathcal{T}_{\mathcal{C}'}[\![\text{T}]\!].$$

Suppose, moreover, that $\mathcal{C}', \mathcal{E} \vdash$ `CDefs` $\diamond \mathcal{C}', \mathcal{E}'$ holds because for all $1 \leq j \leq k$, $\mathcal{C}', \mathcal{E}_{j-1} \vdash E_j : U_j$. It follows by induction that, for all $1 \leq j \leq k$,

$$\mathcal{T}_{\mathcal{C}'}[\![\mathcal{C}']\!], \mathcal{T}_{\mathcal{C}'}[\![\mathcal{E}_{j-1}]\!] \vdash \mathcal{T}_{\mathcal{C}'}[\![E_j]\!]: \mathcal{T}_{\mathcal{C}'}[\![U_j]\!].$$

From the last two displayed formulas and the (derived) type rule *Let* presented in Section 8.2 it follows that

$$\mathcal{T}_{\mathcal{C}'}[\![\mathcal{C}']\!], \mathcal{T}_{\mathcal{C}'}[\![\mathcal{E}]\!] \vdash \textit{let } id_1 : \mathcal{T}_{\mathcal{C}'}[\![U_1]\!] := \mathcal{T}_{\mathcal{C}'}[\![E_1]\!] \textit{ in } \ldots$$
$$\textit{let } id_k : \mathcal{T}_{\mathcal{C}'}[\![U_k]\!] := \mathcal{T}_{\mathcal{C}'}[\![E_k]\!] \textit{ in } \mathcal{T}_{\mathcal{C}'}[\![S]\!]; \mathcal{T}_{\mathcal{C}'}[\![E]\!] \textit{ end } \ldots \textit{ end}: \mathcal{T}_{\mathcal{C}'}[\![T]\!]$$

Let Block$_c$ be

$$\text{const } id_1 \colon U_1 := E_1; \ldots; id_k \colon U_k := E_k;$$
$$\{ \text{ S return E; } \}$$

Then the translation of Block$_c$ is the let expression above, and hence

$$\mathcal{T}_{c'}[\![\mathcal{C}']\!], \mathcal{T}_{c'}[\![\mathcal{E}]\!] \vdash \mathcal{T}_{c'}[\![\text{Block}_c]\!] \colon \mathcal{T}_{c'}[\![\text{T}]\!]$$

By repeatedly applying Lemma 13.1.7, $\mathcal{T}_{c'}[\![\mathcal{C}']\!] = \mathcal{T}_c[\![\mathcal{C}]\!]$ and $\mathcal{T}_{c'}[\![\mathcal{E}]\!] = \mathcal{T}_c[\![\mathcal{E}]\!]$. But by Lemma 13.1.6,

$$\mathcal{T}_{c'}[\![\text{Block}_c]\!] = [\mathcal{T}_c[\![\text{T}_1]\!]/t_1] \ldots [\mathcal{T}_c[\![\text{T}_k]\!]/t_k]\mathcal{T}_c[\![\text{Block}_c]\!]$$

and

$$\mathcal{T}_{c'}[\![\text{T}]\!] = [\mathcal{T}_c[\![\text{T}_1]\!]/t_1] \ldots [\mathcal{T}_c[\![\text{T}_k]\!]/t_k]\mathcal{T}_c[\![\text{T}]\!]$$

But $[\mathcal{T}_c[\![\text{T}_1]\!]/t_1] \ldots [\mathcal{T}_c[\![\text{T}_k]\!]/t_k]\mathcal{T}_c[\![\text{T}]\!] = \mathcal{T}_c[\![\text{T}]\!]$ because T does not contain any of the t_i.

Thus,

$$\mathcal{T}_c[\![\mathcal{C}]\!], \mathcal{T}_c[\![\mathcal{E}]\!] \vdash [\mathcal{T}_c[\![\text{T}_1]\!]/t_1] \ldots [\mathcal{T}_c[\![\text{T}_k]\!]/t_k]\mathcal{T}_c[\![\text{Block}_c]\!] \colon \mathcal{T}_c[\![\text{T}]\!].$$

By the definition of the translation,

$$\mathcal{T}_c[\![\text{Block}]\!] = \text{let } t_1 = \mathcal{T}_c[\![\text{T}_1]\!] \text{ in let } t_2 = \mathcal{T}_c[\![\text{T}_2]\!] \text{ in } \ldots \text{ let } t_n = \mathcal{T}_c[\![\text{T}_n]\!] \text{ in}$$
$$\mathcal{T}_c[\![\text{Block}_c]\!] \text{ end } \ldots \text{ end}$$

But it then follows from the previous typing judgement and the derived *TypeLet* rule for type let expressions in Section 9.1 that

$$\mathcal{T}_c[\![\mathcal{C}]\!], \mathcal{T}_c[\![\mathcal{E}]\!] \vdash \mathcal{T}_c[\![\text{Block}]\!] \colon \mathcal{T}_c[\![\text{T}]\!],$$

as desired.

Class   Suppose that

$$\mathcal{C}, \mathcal{E} \vdash \text{class (inst, meth)} \colon \text{ClassType (IV, M)}$$

because

$$\mathcal{C}, \mathcal{E} \vdash \text{inst} \colon \text{IV and } \mathcal{C}', \mathcal{E}' \vdash \text{meth} \colon \text{M}$$

for

- $\mathcal{C}' = \mathcal{C} \cup \{\, \mathtt{M}' <: \mathtt{M},\ \mathtt{IVR}' <: \mathtt{IV}^{ref},$
$$\mathtt{SelfType} = \mathtt{VisObjectType}\,(\mathtt{IVR}', \mathtt{M}')\},$$

- $\mathcal{E}' = \mathcal{E} \cup \{\, \mathtt{self}\colon \mathtt{SelfType},\ \mathtt{close}\colon \mathtt{SelfType} \to \mathtt{ObjectType}\ \mathtt{M}'\}$, and

- $\mathtt{SelfType}$ does not occur in $\mathtt{IV}$ or $\mathtt{M}$.

Now

$\mathcal{T_C}[\![\mathcal{C}, \mathcal{E} \vdash \mathtt{class}(\mathtt{inst}, \mathtt{meth})\colon \mathtt{ClassType}\,(\mathtt{IV}, \mathtt{M})]\!] \triangleq$
$\qquad \Lambda(M' <: \mathcal{T_C}[\![\mathtt{M}]\!]).\,\Lambda(IVR' <: \mathcal{T_C}[\![\mathtt{IV}^{ref}]\!]).\langle \mathcal{T_C}[\![\mathcal{C}, \mathcal{E} \vdash \mathtt{inst}\colon \mathtt{IV}]\!], methfun\rangle,$

where

$$\begin{aligned}
methfun \triangleq{} &\lambda(self\colon VisObj\,(IVR', M')).\\
&\quad let\ close\colon VisObj\,(IVR', M') \to (\exists Y.\ VisObj\,(Y, M'))\\
&\qquad \triangleq closeobj\,[IVR']\,[M']\\
&\quad in\ \mathcal{T}_{C'}[\![\mathcal{C}', \mathcal{E}' \vdash \mathtt{meth}\colon \mathtt{M}]\!]
\end{aligned}$$

and

$$\begin{aligned}
\mathcal{T_C}[\![\mathtt{ClassType}\,(\mathtt{IV}, \mathtt{M})]\!] = {}&\forall(M' <: \mathcal{T_C}[\![\mathtt{M}]\!]).\,\forall(IVR' <: \mathcal{T_C}[\![\mathtt{IV}^{ref}]\!]).\\
&\mathcal{T_C}[\![\mathtt{IV}]\!] \times (VisObj\,(IVR', M') \to \mathcal{T_C}[\![\mathtt{M}]\!])
\end{aligned}$$

By induction,

$$\mathcal{T_C}[\![\mathcal{C}]\!], \mathcal{T_C}[\![\mathcal{E}]\!] \vdash \mathcal{T_C}[\![\mathtt{inst}]\!]\colon \mathcal{T_C}[\![\mathtt{IV}]\!]$$

and

$$\mathcal{T}_{C'}[\![\mathcal{C}']\!], \mathcal{T}_{C'}[\![\mathcal{E}']\!] \vdash \mathcal{T}_{C'}[\![\mathtt{meth}]\!]\colon \mathcal{T}_{C'}[\![\mathtt{M}]\!].$$

It follows from Lemma 13.1.5, our translation rules, and the definition of $VisObj\,(IVR', M')$, that

$$\mathcal{T}_{C'}[\![\mathtt{SelfType}]\!] = \mathcal{T_C}[\![\mathtt{VisObjectType}\,(\mathtt{IVR}', \mathtt{M}')]\!] = VisObj\,(IVR', M').$$

Let

$$\begin{aligned}
meth \triangleq{} &let\ close\colon VisObj\,(IVR', M') \to (\exists Y.\ VisObj\,(Y, M'))\\
&\quad = closeobj\,[IVR']\,[M']\\
&in\ \mathcal{T}_{C'}[\![\mathcal{C}', \mathcal{E}' \vdash \mathtt{meth}\colon \mathtt{M}]\!].
\end{aligned}$$

and hence $methfun = \lambda(self\colon VisObj\,(IVR', M')).meth$.

Let $\mathcal{E}'' \triangleq \mathcal{E} \cup \{\mathtt{self}\colon \mathtt{SelfType}\}$. Then by the derived *Let* rule for $\Lambda^P_{\leq:}$,

$$\mathcal{T}_{C'}[\![\mathcal{C}']\!], \mathcal{T}_{C'}[\![\mathcal{E}'']\!] \vdash meth\colon \mathcal{T}_{C'}[\![\mathtt{M}]\!].$$

By Lemmas 13.1.2 and 13.1.5, $\mathcal{T}_{C'}[\![\mathtt{Z}]\!] = [VisObj\,(IVR',M')\,/\,SelfType]\,\mathcal{T}_C[\![\mathtt{Z}]\!]$ for all $\mathtt{Z}$. Therefore,

$$\mathcal{T}_{C'}[\![\mathcal{C}']\!], \mathcal{T}_{C'}[\![\mathcal{E}'']\!] \vdash meth\colon [VisObj\,(IVR',M')\,/\,SelfType]\,\mathcal{T}_C[\![\mathtt{M}]\!].$$

But $\mathtt{M}$ does not contain $\mathtt{SelfType}$. Thus,

$$\mathcal{T}_{C'}[\![\mathcal{C}']\!], \mathcal{T}_{C'}[\![\mathcal{E}'']\!] \vdash meth\colon \mathcal{T}_C[\![\mathtt{M}]\!].$$

By the fact that $\mathcal{T}_{C'}[\![\mathcal{E}'']\!] = \mathcal{T}_{C'}[\![\mathcal{E}]\!] \cup \{self\colon VisObj\,(IVR',M')\}$ and the *Function* rule for $\Lambda^P_{<:}$,

$$\mathcal{T}_{C'}[\![\mathcal{C}']\!], \mathcal{T}_{C'}[\![\mathcal{E}]\!] \vdash methfun\colon VisObj\,(IVR',M') \to \mathcal{T}_C[\![\mathtt{M}]\!].$$

It follows from this and the type-checking rules *Function* and *Pair* of $\Lambda^P_{<:}$ that

$$\mathcal{T}_{C'}[\![\mathcal{C}']\!], \mathcal{T}_{C'}[\![\mathcal{E}]\!] \vdash \langle \mathcal{T}_C[\![\mathtt{inst}]\!], methfun\rangle\colon \mathcal{T}_C[\![\mathtt{IV}]\!] \times (VisObj\,(IVR',M') \to \mathcal{T}_C[\![\mathtt{M}]\!])$$

Now

$$\begin{aligned} \mathcal{T}_{C'}[\![\mathcal{C}']\!] &= \mathcal{T}_{C'}[\![\mathcal{C}]\!] \cup \{M' <: \mathcal{T}_{C'}[\![\mathtt{M}]\!], IVR' <: \mathcal{T}_{C'}[\![\mathtt{IV}^{ref}]\!]\} = \\ &\quad \mathcal{T}_C[\![\mathcal{C}]\!] \cup \{M' <: \mathcal{T}_C[\![\mathtt{M}]\!], IVR' <: \mathcal{T}_C[\![\mathtt{IV}^{ref}]\!]\} \end{aligned}$$

because none of $\mathcal{C}$, $\mathtt{M}$, or $\mathtt{IV}^{ref}$ contain $\mathtt{SelfType}$. Similarly $\mathcal{T}_{C'}[\![\mathcal{E}]\!] = \mathcal{T}_C[\![\mathcal{E}]\!]$ because $\mathcal{E}$ does not contain $\mathtt{SelfType}$.

Finally, by the expansion of $\mathcal{T}_{C'}[\![\mathcal{C}']\!]$ above and the type-checking rule *Bd-PolyFunc* in Figure 9.9,

$$\begin{aligned} \mathcal{T}_C[\![\mathcal{C}]\!], \mathcal{T}_C[\![\mathcal{E}]\!] \vdash\ & \Lambda(M' <: \mathcal{T}_C[\![\mathtt{M}]\!]).\,\Lambda(IVR' <: \mathcal{T}_C[\![\mathtt{IV}^{ref}]\!]). \\ & \langle \mathcal{T}_C[\![\mathtt{inst}]\!], methfun\rangle\colon \\ & \qquad \forall(M' <: \mathcal{T}_C[\![\mathtt{M}]\!]).\,\forall(IVR' <: \mathcal{T}_C[\![\mathtt{IV}^{ref}]\!]). \\ & \qquad \mathcal{T}_C[\![\mathtt{IV}]\!] \times (VisObj\,(IVR',M') \to \mathcal{T}_C[\![\mathtt{M}]\!]) \end{aligned}$$

Thus

$$\mathcal{T}_C[\![\mathcal{C}]\!], \mathcal{T}_C[\![\mathcal{E}]\!] \vdash \mathcal{T}_C[\![\mathtt{class\,(inst,meth)}]\!]\colon \mathcal{T}_C[\![\mathtt{ClassType\,(IV,M)}]\!].$$

Subclass   The case for subclasses is not much more difficult than that for classes, and we take advantage of some of the work done in that proof.

Suppose that

$$\begin{aligned} \mathcal{C}, \mathcal{E} \vdash\ & \mathtt{class\ inherits\ C\ modifies}\ \mathtt{l}_{i_1}, \ldots, \mathtt{l}_{i_m}\ \mathtt{(inst,meth)}\colon \\ & \qquad\qquad\qquad\qquad \mathtt{ClassType\,(IV,M)} \end{aligned}$$

because

$$\mathcal{C}, \mathcal{E} \vdash \texttt{C: ClassType}\,(\texttt{IV}_{sup}, \texttt{M}_{sup}),$$
$$\mathcal{C}, \mathcal{E} \vdash \texttt{inst: IV}_{sub}, \qquad \mathcal{C}', \mathcal{E}' \vdash \texttt{meth: M}_{sub}, \text{ and}$$
$$\mathcal{C} \vdash \texttt{T}'_{i_j} <: \texttt{T}_{i_j} \text{ for } 1 \leq j \leq m$$

where

- $\texttt{IV} = \texttt{IV}_{sup} \oplus \texttt{IV}_{sub}$ (and hence, $\texttt{IV}^{ref} <: \texttt{IV}_{sup}{}^{ref}$),

- $\texttt{M} = \texttt{M}_{sup} \oplus \texttt{M}_{sub}$ (and hence, $\texttt{M} <: \texttt{M}_{sup}$),

- there is no overlap in the labels occurring in $\texttt{IV}_{sup}$ and $\texttt{IV}_{sub}$, and

- the overlapping labels in $\texttt{M}_{sup}$ and $\texttt{M}_{sub}$ are exactly $\texttt{l}_{i_1}, \ldots, \texttt{l}_{i_m}$.

- The type of $\texttt{l}_{i_j}$ in $\texttt{M}_{sub}$ is $\texttt{T}'_{i_j}$, while the corresponding type in $\texttt{M}_{sup}$ is $\texttt{T}_{i_j}$.

- $\mathcal{C}' = \mathcal{C} \cup \{\, \texttt{M}' <: \texttt{M}, \texttt{IVR}' <: \texttt{IV}^{ref},$
  $\qquad \texttt{SelfType} = \texttt{VisObjectType}\,(\texttt{IVR}', \texttt{M}')\},$

- $\mathcal{E}' = \mathcal{E} \cup \{\, \texttt{self: SelfType, close: SelfType} \rightarrow \texttt{ObjectType M}'\},$ and

- $\texttt{SelfType}$ does not occur in $\texttt{IV}$ or $\texttt{M}$.

By induction,

$$\mathcal{T}_C[\![\mathcal{C}]\!], \mathcal{T}_C[\![\mathcal{E}]\!] \vdash \mathcal{T}_C[\![\texttt{C}]\!] : \mathcal{T}_C[\![\texttt{ClassType}\,(\texttt{IV}_{sup}, \texttt{M}_{sup})]\!],$$

$$\mathcal{T}_C[\![\mathcal{C}]\!], \mathcal{T}_C[\![\mathcal{E}]\!] \vdash \mathcal{T}_C[\![\texttt{inst}]\!] : \mathcal{T}_C[\![\texttt{IV}_{sub}]\!],$$
$$\mathcal{T}_{C'}[\![\mathcal{C}']\!], \mathcal{T}_{C'}[\![\mathcal{E}']\!] \vdash \mathcal{T}_{C'}[\![\texttt{meth}]\!] : \mathcal{T}_{C'}[\![\texttt{M}_{sub}]\!],$$

and

$$\mathcal{T}_C[\![\mathcal{C}]\!] \vdash \mathcal{T}_C[\![\texttt{T}'_{i_j}]\!] <: \mathcal{T}_C[\![\texttt{T}_{i_j}]\!] \text{ for } 1 \leq j \leq m.$$

It is easy to see that

$$\mathcal{T}_C[\![\texttt{IV}]\!] = \mathcal{T}_C[\![\texttt{IV}_{sup}]\!] \oplus \mathcal{T}_C[\![\texttt{IV}_{sub}]\!],$$

and

$$\mathcal{T}_C[\![\texttt{M}]\!] = \mathcal{T}_C[\![\texttt{M}_{sup}]\!] \oplus \mathcal{T}_C[\![\texttt{M}_{sub}]\!].$$

By definition,

$$\mathcal{T}_C[\![\, \mathcal{C}, \mathcal{E} \vdash \texttt{class inherits C modifies } \texttt{l}_{i_1}, \ldots, \texttt{l}_{i_m}\, (\texttt{inst}, \texttt{meth}) :$$
$$\texttt{ClassType}\,(\texttt{IV}, \texttt{M}) \stackrel{\triangle}{=}$$
$$\Lambda(M' <: \mathcal{T}_C[\![\texttt{M}]\!]).\, \Lambda(IVR' <: \mathcal{T}_C[\![\texttt{IV}^{ref}]\!]).\langle inst_{all}, methfun_{all} \rangle,$$

where

$$c = \mathcal{T_C}[\![\mathcal{C}, \mathcal{E} \vdash \mathtt{C: ClassType}(\mathtt{IV}_{sup}, \mathtt{M}_{sup})]\!][M'][IVR']$$
$$inst_{sup} = proj_1(c)$$
$$methfun_{sup} = proj_2(c)$$
$$inst_{all} = inst_{sup} \oplus \mathcal{T_C}[\![\mathcal{C}, \mathcal{E} \vdash \mathtt{inst: IV}_{sub}]\!]$$
$$methfun_{all} = \lambda(self: VisObj(IVR', M')).$$
$$\quad let\ close: VisObj(IVR', M') \to (\exists Y.\ VisObj(Y, M'))$$
$$\quad\quad = closeobj[IVR'][M']$$
$$\quad in\ methfun_{sup}(self) \oplus \mathcal{T}_{\mathcal{C}'}[\![\mathcal{C}', \mathcal{E}' \vdash \mathtt{meth: M}_{sub}]\!].$$

Also,

$$\mathcal{T_C}[\![\mathtt{ClassType}(\mathtt{IV}_{sup}, \mathtt{M}_{sup})]\!] = \forall(M' <: \mathcal{T_C}[\![\mathtt{M}_{sup}]\!]).\ \forall(IVR' <: \mathcal{T_C}[\![\mathtt{IV}_{sup}^{ref}]\!]).$$
$$\mathcal{T_C}[\![\mathtt{IV}_{sup}]\!] \times (VisObj(IVR', M') \to \mathcal{T_C}[\![\mathtt{M}_{sup}]\!])$$

By Theorem 13.1.9,

$$\mathcal{T_C}[\![\mathcal{C}]\!] \vdash \mathcal{T_C}[\![\mathtt{IV}^{ref}]\!] <: \mathcal{T_C}[\![\mathtt{IV}_{sup}^{ref}]\!] \text{ and } \mathcal{T_C}[\![\mathcal{C}]\!] \vdash \mathcal{T_C}[\![\mathtt{M}]\!] <: \mathcal{T_C}[\![\mathtt{M}_{sup}]\!].$$

By the definition of $inst_{sup}$ and $inst_{all}$, the induction hypothesis, and the *Projection* rule for $\Lambda^P_{<:}$,

$$\mathcal{T_C}[\![\mathcal{C}]\!], \mathcal{T_C}[\![\mathcal{E}]\!] \vdash inst_{sub}: \mathcal{T_C}[\![\mathtt{IV}_{sub}]\!],$$

$$\mathcal{T_C}[\![\mathcal{C}]\!], \mathcal{T_C}[\![\mathcal{E}]\!] \vdash inst_{all}: \mathcal{T_C}[\![\mathtt{IV}]\!].$$

By the same reasoning as for classes,

$$\mathcal{T}_{\mathcal{C}'}[\![\mathcal{C}']\!], \mathcal{T}_{\mathcal{C}'}[\![\mathcal{E}]\!] \vdash methfun_{all}: VisObj(IVR', M') \to \mathcal{T_C}[\![\mathtt{M}_{sup}]\!].$$

Thus

$$\mathcal{T}_{\mathcal{C}'}[\![\mathcal{C}']\!], \mathcal{T_C}[\![\mathcal{E}']\!] \vdash methfun_{sup}(self) \oplus \mathcal{T}_{\mathcal{C}'}[\![\mathtt{meth}]\!]: \mathcal{T_C}[\![\mathtt{M}]\!]$$

By the *Function* and *Pair* type-checking rules, it follows that

$$\mathcal{T}_{\mathcal{C}'}[\![\mathcal{C}']\!], \mathcal{T}_{\mathcal{C}'}[\![\mathcal{E}]\!] \vdash \langle inst_{all}, methfun_{all}\rangle: \mathcal{T_C}[\![IV]\!] \times VisObj(IVR', M') \to \mathcal{T_C}[\![\mathtt{M}]\!].$$

As in the case for classes,

$$\mathcal{T}_{\mathcal{C}'}[\![\mathcal{C}']\!] = \mathcal{T_C}[\![\mathcal{C}]\!] \cup \{M' <: \mathcal{T_C}[\![\mathtt{M}]\!], IVR' <: \mathcal{T_C}[\![\mathtt{IV}^{ref}]\!]\}$$

and $\mathcal{T}_{\mathcal{C}'}[\![\mathcal{E}]\!] = \mathcal{T}_{\mathcal{C}}[\![\mathcal{E}]\!]$. Thus by the *BdPolyFunc* rule,

$$\mathcal{T}_{\mathcal{C}}[\![\mathcal{C}]\!], \mathcal{T}_{\mathcal{C}}[\![\mathcal{E}]\!] \vdash \Lambda(M' <: \mathcal{T}_{\mathcal{C}}[\![\mathsf{M}]\!]).\Lambda(IVR' <: \mathcal{T}_{\mathcal{C}}[\![\mathsf{IV}^{ref}]\!]).\langle inst_{all}, methfun_{all}\rangle :$$
$$\forall(M' <: \mathcal{T}_{\mathcal{C}}[\![\mathsf{M}]\!]).\forall(IVR' <: \mathcal{T}_{\mathcal{C}}[\![\mathsf{IV}^{ref}]\!]).$$
$$\mathcal{T}_{\mathcal{C}}[\![\mathsf{IV}]\!] \times (VisObj\,(IVR',M') \to \mathcal{T}_{\mathcal{C}}[\![\mathsf{M}]\!])$$

and hence,

$$\mathcal{T}_{\mathcal{C}}[\![\mathcal{C}]\!], \mathcal{T}_{\mathcal{C}}[\![\mathcal{E}]\!] \vdash$$
$$\mathcal{T}_{\mathcal{C}}[\![\texttt{class inherits C modifies } \mathtt{l}_{i_1}, \dots, \mathtt{l}_{i_m} \,(\texttt{inst}, \texttt{meth})]\!] :$$
$$\mathcal{T}_{\mathcal{C}}[\![\texttt{ClassType}(\texttt{IV}, \texttt{M})]\!]$$

New   Suppose that

$$\mathcal{C}, \mathcal{E} \vdash \texttt{new C}: \texttt{ObjectType M}$$

because

$$\mathcal{C}, \mathcal{E} \vdash \texttt{C}: \texttt{ClassType}(\texttt{IV}, \texttt{M})$$

By induction,

$$\mathcal{T}_{\mathcal{C}}[\![\mathcal{C}]\!], \mathcal{T}_{\mathcal{C}}[\![\mathcal{E}]\!] \vdash \mathcal{T}_{\mathcal{C}}[\![\texttt{C}]\!] : \mathcal{T}_{\mathcal{C}}[\![\texttt{ClassType}(\texttt{IV}, \texttt{M})]\!]$$

The revised translation of new C is

$$\mathcal{T}_{\mathcal{C}}[\![\mathcal{C}, \mathcal{E} \vdash \texttt{new C}: \texttt{ObjectType M}]\!] \triangleq closeobj\,[IVR]\,[M]\langle inst^{ref}, methfun'\rangle$$
where
$$c \triangleq \mathcal{T}_{\mathcal{C}}[\![\mathcal{C}, \mathcal{E} \vdash \texttt{C}: \texttt{ClassType}(\texttt{IV}, \texttt{M})]\!]\,[M]\,[IVR]$$
$$IVR = \mathcal{T}_{\mathcal{C}}[\![\mathsf{IV}^{ref}]\!]$$
$$M = \mathcal{T}_{\mathcal{C}}[\![\mathsf{M}]\!]$$
$$inst = proj_1(c),$$
$$methfun = proj_2(c),$$
$inst^{ref}$ is formed by adding refs to all fields of *inst*, and
$$methfun' = \underline{fix}\,[IVR \to M]\lambda(fm: IVR \to M).$$
$$\lambda(inst': IVR).methfun(\langle inst', fm\rangle).$$

Because

$$\mathcal{T}_{\mathcal{C}}[\![\texttt{ClassType}(\texttt{IV}, \texttt{M})]\!] =$$
$$\forall M' <: \mathcal{T}_{\mathcal{C}}[\![\mathsf{M}]\!].\forall IVR' <: \mathcal{T}_{\mathcal{C}}[\![\mathsf{IV}^{ref}]\!].\mathcal{T}_{\mathcal{C}}[\![\mathsf{IV}]\!] \times (VisObj\,(IVR',M') \to \mathcal{T}_{\mathcal{C}}[\![\mathsf{M}]\!]),$$

it follows that

$$\mathcal{T}_C[\![\mathcal{C}]\!], \mathcal{T}_C[\![\mathcal{E}]\!] \vdash c\colon \mathcal{T}_C[\![\text{IV}]\!] \times \textit{VisObj}\,(\mathcal{T}_C[\![\text{IV}^{\textit{ref}}]\!], \mathcal{T}_C[\![\text{M}]\!]) \to \mathcal{T}_C[\![\text{M}]\!]$$

$$\mathcal{T}_C[\![\mathcal{C}]\!], \mathcal{T}_C[\![\mathcal{E}]\!] \vdash \textit{inst}\colon \mathcal{T}_C[\![\text{IV}]\!]$$

$$\mathcal{T}_C[\![\mathcal{C}]\!], \mathcal{T}_C[\![\mathcal{E}]\!] \vdash \textit{methfun}\colon \textit{VisObj}\,(\mathcal{T}_C[\![\text{IV}^{\textit{ref}}]\!], \mathcal{T}_C[\![\text{M}]\!]) \to \mathcal{T}_C[\![\text{M}]\!]$$

$$\mathcal{T}_C[\![\mathcal{C}]\!], \mathcal{T}_C[\![\mathcal{E}]\!] \vdash \textit{inst}^{\textit{ref}}\colon \mathcal{T}_C[\![\text{IV}^{\textit{ref}}]\!], \text{ and}$$

$$\mathcal{T}_C[\![\mathcal{C}]\!], \mathcal{T}_C[\![\mathcal{E}]\!] \vdash \textit{methfun}'\colon \mathcal{T}_C[\![\text{IV}^{\textit{ref}}]\!] \to \mathcal{T}_C[\![\text{M}]\!].$$

Hence

$$\mathcal{T}_C[\![\mathcal{C}]\!], \mathcal{T}_C[\![\mathcal{E}]\!] \vdash \langle \textit{inst}^{\textit{ref}}, \textit{methfun}'\rangle\colon \mathcal{T}_C[\![\text{IV}^{\textit{ref}}]\!] \times (\mathcal{T}_C[\![\text{IV}^{\textit{ref}}]\!] \to \mathcal{T}_C[\![\text{M}]\!]).$$

Recall that

$$\emptyset, \emptyset \vdash \textit{closeobj}\colon \forall IR.\,\forall M.\,(IR \times (IR \to M)) \to (\exists Y.\,Y \times (Y \to M)).$$

As a result

$$\mathcal{T}_C[\![\mathcal{C}]\!], \mathcal{T}_C[\![\mathcal{E}]\!] \vdash \textit{closeobj}\,[\mathcal{T}_C[\![\text{IV}^{\textit{ref}}]\!]]\,[\mathcal{T}_C[\![\text{M}]\!]]\langle \textit{inst}^{\textit{ref}}, \textit{methfun}'\rangle\colon$$
$$(\exists Y.\,Y \times (Y \to \mathcal{T}_C[\![\text{M}]\!])).$$

Because $\mathcal{T}_C[\![\text{ObjectType M}]\!] = \exists Y.\,Y \times (Y \to \mathcal{T}_C[\![\text{M}]\!])$, it follows that

$$\mathcal{T}_C[\![\mathcal{C}]\!], \mathcal{T}_C[\![\mathcal{E}]\!] \vdash \mathcal{T}_C[\![\text{new C}]\!]\colon \mathcal{T}_C[\![\text{ObjectType } M]\!],$$

as desired.

Message   Suppose
$$\mathcal{C}, \mathcal{E} \vdash \text{E} \Leftarrow \text{m}\colon \text{T}$$
because $\mathcal{C}, \mathcal{E} \vdash \text{E}\colon \text{M}$ and $\mathcal{C} \vdash \text{M} <: \text{ObjectType } \{\!\!| \text{ m}\colon \text{T} \,|\!\!\}$.
  By induction,

$$\mathcal{T}_C[\![\mathcal{C}]\!], \mathcal{T}_C[\![\mathcal{E}]\!] \vdash \mathcal{T}_C[\![\mathcal{C}, \mathcal{E} \vdash \text{E}\colon \text{M}]\!]\colon \mathcal{T}_C[\![\text{M}]\!]$$

and

$$\mathcal{T}_C[\![\mathcal{C}]\!] \vdash \mathcal{T}_C[\![\text{M}]\!] <: \mathcal{T}_C[\![\text{ObjectType } \{\!\!| \text{ m}\colon \text{T} \,|\!\!\}]\!]$$

By subsumption in $\Lambda_{<:}^P$,

(13.1) $$\mathcal{T}_C[\![\mathcal{C}]\!], \mathcal{T}_C[\![\mathcal{E}]\!] \vdash \mathcal{T}_C[\![\text{E}]\!]\colon \mathcal{T}_C[\![\text{ObjectType } \{\!\!| \text{ m}\colon \text{T} \,|\!\!\}]\!].$$

By definition,

$$\mathcal{T}_C[\![\text{ObjectType}\ \{\!|\ \text{m: T}\ |\!\}]\!] = \exists Y.\, Y \times (Y \rightarrow \{\!|\ \text{m:}\ \mathcal{T}_C[\![\text{T}]\!]\ |\!\})$$

and

$$\mathcal{T}_C[\![\text{E}\ \Leftarrow\! \text{m}]\!] = open\ \mathcal{T}_C[\![\text{E}]\!]\ as\ \langle IVR, vo \rangle\ in\ (proj_2(vo)(proj_1(vo))).m$$

It follows from the projection typing rules and the *Selection* rule of $\Lambda^P_{<:}$ that

$$\mathcal{T}_C[\![\mathcal{C}]\!], \mathcal{T}_C[\![\mathcal{E}]\!] \cup \{vo\colon IVR \times (IVR \rightarrow \mathcal{T}_C[\![\text{M}]\!])\} \vdash (proj_2(vo)(proj_1(vo))).m\colon \mathcal{T}_C[\![\text{T}]\!]$$

It follows from 13.1 and the *Unpack* rule that

$$\mathcal{T}_C[\![\mathcal{C}]\!], \mathcal{T}_C[\![\mathcal{E}]\!] \vdash open\ \mathcal{T}_C[\![\text{E}]\!]\ as\ \langle IVR, vo \rangle\ in\ (proj_2(vo)(proj_1(vo))).m\colon \mathcal{T}_C[\![\text{T}]\!]$$

Hence

$$\mathcal{T}_C[\![\mathcal{C}]\!], \mathcal{T}_C[\![\mathcal{E}]\!] \vdash \mathcal{T}_C[\![\text{E} \Leftarrow \text{m}]\!]\colon \mathcal{T}_C[\![\text{T}]\!]$$

Inst Vble   Suppose

$$\mathcal{C}, \mathcal{E} \vdash \text{E.1}\colon \text{T}$$

because $\mathcal{C}, \mathcal{E} \vdash \text{E}\colon \text{VisObjectType}(\text{IVR}, \text{M})$ and $\mathcal{C} \vdash \text{IVR} <: \{\!|\ \text{1:\,T}\ |\!\}$.
By induction,

$$\mathcal{T}_C[\![\mathcal{C}]\!], \mathcal{T}_C[\![\mathcal{E}]\!] \vdash \mathcal{T}_C[\![\text{E}]\!]\colon \mathcal{T}_C[\![\text{VisObjectType}(\text{IVR}, \text{M})]\!]$$

and

$$\mathcal{T}_C[\![\mathcal{C}]\!] \vdash \mathcal{T}_C[\![\text{IVR}]\!] <: \{\!|\ \text{1:}\ \mathcal{T}_C[\![\text{T}]\!]\ |\!\}.$$

By definition,

$$\mathcal{T}_C[\![\text{VisObjectType}(\text{IVR}, \text{M})]\!] = \mathcal{T}_C[\![\text{IVR}]\!] \times (\mathcal{T}_C[\![\text{IVR}]\!] \rightarrow \mathcal{T}_C[\![\text{M}]\!])$$

and

$$\mathcal{T}_C[\![\text{E.1}]\!] = proj_1(\mathcal{T}_C[\![\text{E}]\!]).l$$

By the *Proj* type-checking rule,

$$\mathcal{T}_C[\![\mathcal{C}]\!], \mathcal{T}_C[\![\mathcal{E}]\!] \vdash proj_1(\mathcal{T}_C[\![\text{E}]\!])\colon \mathcal{T}_C[\![\text{IVR}]\!]$$

and by subsumption in $\Lambda^P_{<:}$,

$$\mathcal{T}_C[\![\mathcal{C}]\!], \mathcal{T}_C[\![\mathcal{E}]\!] \vdash proj_1(\mathcal{T}_C[\![\text{E}]\!])\colon \{\!|\ \text{1:}\ \mathcal{T}_C[\![\text{T}]\!]\ |\!\}.$$

By the *Selection* rule,

$$\mathcal{T}_C[\![\mathcal{C}]\!], \mathcal{T}_C[\![\mathcal{E}]\!] \vdash proj_1(\mathcal{T}_C[\![\text{E}]\!]).l\colon \mathcal{T}_C[\![\text{T}]\!].$$

Hence,

$$\mathcal{T}_C[\![\mathcal{C}]\!], \mathcal{T}_C[\![\mathcal{E}]\!] \vdash \mathcal{T}_C[\![\text{E.1}]\!]\colon \mathcal{T}_C[\![\text{T}]\!].$$

Self Message This case is similar to that for sending messages to regular objects except that it is not necessary to unpack the existential. However, because there is no subtyping between visible object types we will need to do things in a slightly different order.

Suppose

$$\mathcal{C}, \mathcal{E} \vdash \text{E} \Leftarrow \text{m: T}$$

because $\mathcal{C}, \mathcal{E} \vdash \text{E: VisObjectType(IVR, M)}$ and $\mathcal{C} \vdash \text{M} <: \{\!| \text{m: T} |\!\}$.

By induction,

$$\mathcal{T}_C[\![\mathcal{C}]\!], \mathcal{T}_C[\![\mathcal{E}]\!] \vdash \mathcal{T}_C[\![\mathcal{C}, \mathcal{E} \vdash \text{E: VisObjectType(IVR, M)}]\!] :$$
$$\mathcal{T}_C[\![\text{VisObjectType(IVR, M)}]\!]$$

and

$$\mathcal{T}_C[\![\mathcal{C}]\!] \vdash \mathcal{T}_C[\![\text{M}]\!] <: \{\!| \text{ m: } \mathcal{T}_C[\![\text{T}]\!] |\!\}$$

By definition,

$$\mathcal{T}_C[\![\text{VisObjectType(IVR, M)}]\!] = IVR \times (IVR \to \mathcal{T}_C[\![\text{M}]\!])$$

and

$$\mathcal{T}_C[\![\text{E} \Leftarrow \text{m}]\!] = (proj_2(\mathcal{T}_C[\![\text{E}]\!])(proj_1(\mathcal{T}_C[\![\text{E}]\!]))).m.$$

Thus,

$$\mathcal{T}_C[\![\mathcal{C}]\!], \mathcal{T}_C[\![\mathcal{E}]\!] \vdash \mathcal{T}_C[\![\text{E}]\!]: IVR \times (IVR \to \mathcal{T}_C[\![\text{M}]\!])$$

It follows from the projection typing rules and the *FuncApp* rule of $\Lambda_{<:}^P$ that

$$\mathcal{T}_C[\![\mathcal{C}]\!], \mathcal{T}_C[\![\mathcal{E}]\!] \vdash proj_2(\mathcal{T}_C[\![\text{E}]\!])(proj_1(\mathcal{T}_C[\![\text{E}]\!])): \mathcal{T}_C[\![\text{M}]\!]$$

By subsumption in $\Lambda_{<:}^P$,

$$\mathcal{T}_C[\![\mathcal{C}]\!], \mathcal{T}_C[\![\mathcal{E}]\!] \vdash proj_2(\mathcal{T}_C[\![\text{E}]\!])(proj_1(\mathcal{T}_C[\![\text{E}]\!])): \{\!| \text{ m: } \mathcal{T}_C[\![\text{T}]\!] |\!\}$$

and hence by the *Selection* rule,

$$\mathcal{T}_C[\![\mathcal{C}]\!], \mathcal{T}_C[\![\mathcal{E}]\!] \vdash (proj_2(\mathcal{T}_C[\![\text{E}]\!])(proj_1(\mathcal{T}_C[\![\text{E}]\!]))).m: \mathcal{T}_C[\![\text{T}]\!] |\!\}$$

Hence

$$\mathcal{T}_C[\![\mathcal{C}]\!], \mathcal{T}_C[\![\mathcal{E}]\!] \vdash \mathcal{T}_C[\![\text{E} \Leftarrow \text{m}]\!]: \mathcal{T}_C[\![\text{T}]\!]$$

■

13.2   The translation is well defined

The proof of Theorem 13.1.10 in the previous section essentially showed how to translate the derivation of $\mathcal{C}, \mathcal{E} \vdash \texttt{E: T}$ in $\mathcal{SOOL}$ to a corresponding derivation of $\mathcal{T}_C[\![\mathcal{C}]\!], \mathcal{T}_C[\![\mathcal{E}]\!] \vdash \mathcal{T}_C[\![\mathcal{C}, \mathcal{E} \vdash \texttt{E: T}]\!]: \mathcal{T}_C[\![\texttt{T}]\!]$ in $\Lambda^P_{<:}$. However, that is not enough to ensure that the definition of $\mathcal{T}_C[\![\mathcal{C}, \mathcal{E} \vdash \texttt{E: T}]\!]$ is well-defined.

The problem arises because of the possibility of two distinct derivations of $\mathcal{C}, \mathcal{E} \vdash \texttt{E: T}$. Because the definition of $\mathcal{T}_C[\![\mathcal{C}, \mathcal{E} \vdash \texttt{E: T}]\!]$ is given by induction on the derivation of the typing, two distinct derivations might give rise to distinct expressions of $\Lambda^P_{<:}$, even though both would end up having the same type.

The `CellExample` program in Figure 13.1 illustrates the problem. The figure contains two different class type definitions, `CellClassType1` and `CellClassType2`. The class `Cell` in the figure will type-check correctly no matter which of these types is assigned to `Cell`. However, the two different typings result in two different translations of `Cell`. If translated with type `CellClassType1` the method suite has both methods, while if translated with `CellClassType2`, the method suite has only the `increase` method, even though the actual code for `CellClass` includes both. As a result, the translation of `new Cell` will have either two or one methods depending on the type given `Cell`. Both of these can be assigned to `cell`, which has type `CellType2`, though the version in which `Cell` has type `CellClassType1` needs the use of subsumption in typing the assignment statement.

This example shows that if one of the subexpressions of a $\mathcal{SOOL}$ program segment is given different types, the translations may not be the same.

In this particular example we were forced to declare a type for `Cell` when we wrote the program, but what if we substituted the definition of `Cell` into the `new Cell` expression in place of the identifier `Cell`? Now we have a context in which we could easily choose either typing derivation for the typing of `new Cell`, and hence get two different translations of the expression.

The two different translations of `new Cell` are not such a big problem as the types of the translations are subtypes and it is not hard to convince oneself that any context using `cell` and returning an element of a base type will get the same results no matter which translation is chosen. In particular, the `bump` method is not accessible from `cell` because it has type `CellType2`.

On the other hand, the two different translations of `Cell` are more of a problem. Not only do they have different class types, but those class types are not subtypes – a class type can only be a subtype of itself.

We can solve this problem by requiring that all classes be declared in the

```
Program CellExample;
type
   CellType1 = ObjectType {|
      increase: Integer → Command;
      bump: Void → Command
   |};
   CellType2 = ObjectType {|
      increase: Integer → Command
   |};
   CellClassType1 = ClassType ({|
      x: Integer
   |}, {|
      increase: Integer → Command;
      bump: Void → Command
   |});
   CellClassType2 = ClassType ({|
      x: Integer
   |}, {|
      increase: Integer → Command;
   |});
const
   Cell: CellClassType? = class ({|
      x: Integer = 0
   |}, {|
      increase: Integer → Command =
         function(dx: Integer): Command is {
           self.x := (val self.x) + dx;
           return nop };
      bump: Void → Command =
         function(): Command is {
           self.x := (val self.x) + 1;
           return nop }
   |});
   cell: Ref CellType2 = ref nil;
{
   cell := new Cell;
}
```

Figure 13.1   CellExample program.

constant section of the program rather than allowing them to be used in a more complex context. Because they are declared along with their types, there is no problem in figuring out with which type they should be translated. This does have the negative consequence that the type of a class expression must now be partially determined from the context of its definition, rather than based on its own internal structure.

A similar though perhaps superior solution in practice for the version of the language with abbreviations (in which programmers normally do not specify class types for class definitions) is to always type classes with the full collection of instance variables and methods in their definitions. The types of class features are always determined by their declarations, either directly for instance variables, or indirectly from the function declarations for methods. The type obtained in this way is essentially the most expressive type for the class and is the one that would naturally be expected by programmers. If the source language that programmers write in allowed identifiers to represent records then we might have added difficulties, but records are not directly supported in $\mathcal{SOOL}$, they are only a convenience for type-checking. As a result, the feature declarations are always directly visible in class declarations.

What about the problems arising with the possibility of two different type derivations for the same expression and type? Aside from classes and subclasses, only the translation of object types depends on the type of the expression being translated. However, the translation of new C depends only on the type of C. Thus if C has a unique type (as it will with the conventions above), then the translation of new C will depend only on that unique type. In other words, with this new restriction on the admissible expressions of class type, the translation no longer depends on type derivations. Instead it can be given inductively on the structure of the expressions. Of course the proof of soundness will still be given by induction on the length of the derivation of types as it is essentially a transformation from type derivations of $\mathcal{SOOL}$ to type derivations in $\Lambda^{P}_{\leq}$.

Alternatively one could continue to use the definition of translation that depends on typing derivations. In this case, one could first show that every typing derivation can be converted to a canonical derivations (for example, by pushing uses of subsumption to uses on as small expressions as possible). (See Section 10.4 of [Mit96], for a similar example.) One could then define the translation as being based on canonical transformations or show that the steps in converting to a canonical derivation all preserve the translation (after all, recall that uses of subtyping have no effect on the translation).

Because the simple modification of $\mathcal{SOOL}$ resulting in unique types for classes is sufficient to ensure that the translation is well-defined, we do not include further discussion of this issue here.

13.3 $SOOL$ is type safe

We would like the type system In an object-oriented language to guarantee that if a message is sent to an object, then that object has a method that can handle the message. The object-oriented programming language Smalltalk [GR83] is not statically typed. As a result, at run time it is possible to get an error message stating "message not understood". This indicates that the receiving object does not have a method with matching name and signature to that of the message.

In Section 13.1, we showed that the translation of $SOOL$ into $\Lambda^P_{\leq}$ is type-preserving. In this section we would like to go further and claim that $SOOL$ is statically type safe. That is, well-typed $SOOL$ programs are guaranteed not to have certain kinds of errors, called type errors, at run time. We begin by providing some background on the notion of safety in programming languages.

TRAPPED AND
UNTRAPPED ERRORS

Cardelli [Car97] distinguishes between what he calls *trapped* and *untrapped errors*. Trapped errors cause a computation to stop immediately, while untrapped errors may allow the computation to continue (at least for a while). An example of an untrapped error might be accessing data beyond the end of an array in a language like C. Cardelli argues that a *safe language* is one that does not allow any untrapped errors to occur at run time.

SAFE LANGUAGE

FORBIDDEN ERRORS

In a given language, a subset of the errors may be designated as *forbidden errors*. The forbidden errors should include all untrapped errors as well as a subset of trapped errors. A language where none of the legal programs can generate forbidden errors is said to be *strongly checked*.

STRONGLY CHECKED

TYPE ERROR

For $SOOL$, as with most typed programming languages, the forbidden errors will include all run-time type errors. A *type error* is an error that can be characterized as being an error based just on the knowledge of the types of the components. For example, if f is a function of type *Integer* $\rightarrow$ *Integer* and *arg* has type *Boolean*, then *f(arg)* results in a type error.

Similarly it is erroneous to attempt to apply an object (as though it were a function) to an integer. The type error we are most concerned with in object-oriented programming languages is to send a message to an object that does not have a method corresponding to the message. This is a type error, because the type of the object specifies the list of messages that it supports.

A *type-safe language* is one in which all type errors are trapped errors. A *static type-safe language* is one in which all type errors are caught statically, *e.g.*, at compile time if a compiler is used.

Smalltalk, LISP, and Scheme are examples of type-safe languages that are not statically type safe. Java, ML, and Haskell are statically type safe.

Examples of non-type errors include dividing an integer by zero (since both operands are integers, the division makes sense based on the types). Similarly sending a message to a `nil` object need not be a type error as long as the static type of the `nil` object includes the message name. Accessing data beyond the end of an array is also not a type error (though it hopefully is a forbidden error in the language). Finally, a non-terminating program is generally not the result of a type error.

Statically type-safe languages ensure that programs that pass the type-checker will not generate type errors at run time (though other forbidden errors may be detected and handled at run time). Programs that do not pass the type-checker are not considered legal programs. Semantics are generally only provided for legal programs of the language.

In the last chapter we provided a translation from $\mathcal{SOOL}$ into $\Lambda^P_{<:}$. We proved in Section 13.1 that well-typed expressions of $\mathcal{SOOL}$ were translated into well-typed expressions of $\Lambda^P_{<:}$. The semantics of $\Lambda^P_{<:}$ are well understood in that there exist both denotational and operational semantics. The translation from $\mathcal{SOOL}$ into $\Lambda^P_{<:}$ provides a semantics for well-typed expressions of $\mathcal{SOOL}$ by first translating to the corresponding $\Lambda^P_{<:}$ program and then determining the semantics of that program.

As defined above, static type safety is a property defined in terms of the run-time behavior of a language. Thus it is most naturally seen as a property of an operational semantics. It is possible to write down a straightforward operational semantics for $\Lambda^P_{<:}$ (recall we only gave fragments of such a semantics) and show that $\Lambda^P_{<:}$ is statically type safe.[1] Using this we can show that $\mathcal{SOOL}$ is statically type safe.

Theorem 13.3.1 $\mathcal{SOOL}$ *is statically type safe.*

Proof.   Let P be a program of $\mathcal{SOOL}$ that is well-typed (i.e., it typable according to the type-checking rules of $\mathcal{SOOL}$). Recall that P is executed by

---

1. There appears to be no published proof that the entire language $\Lambda^P_{<:}$ is type safe. Instead separate proofs of the type safety of the different parts can be found in [Pie02] and other sources. We expect that, aside from the expressions corresponding to the universal and existential types, the language is simple enough that the reader is willing to trust in the type safety of $\Lambda^P_{<:}$.

first using the translation function to obtain a program P' of $\Lambda^P_{<:}$ and then executing P'. By Theorem 13.1.10, P' is also well-typed. However, by the fact that $\Lambda^P_{<:}$ is statically type safe, the execution of P' cannot result in a type error. Thus the execution of P cannot result in a type error. ∎

It is possible to provide a direct operational semantics for $SOOL$ and to show that $SOOL$ is statically type safe with respect to that semantics. (See [BSvG95, BFSvG01] for such a proof for a similar language.) However, that would take us too far afield, so we will be content with this more indirect proof of the static type safety of $SOOL$.

13.4   Errors

We have seen that a static type system like that used for $SOOL$ can guarantee that there are no run-time type errors. In particular, if a message is sent to an object, then that object has a method that can handle the message. Ideally, a static type system could provide an iron-clad guarantee that no run-time errors would occur at all, but this is too much to hope for. For example, no type system could guarantee that program logic is correct. However, without severely restricting the expressiveness of the language, it is even impossible to guarantee that errors like dividing by zero will not occur at run time.

The difficulty is that certain run-time errors are not associated with type systems. For example, if m and n are expressions of type Integer, the expression m/n is well-typed, but if the value of n at run time is 0, an error will occur. Because both zero and non-zero integers are in the same type, there is no way of detecting this problem with a type system.

Of course, one could refine the type system to include a type of non-zero integers. The type system could then require n to have type non-zero integer in order for m/n to be well-typed. This is fine in theory, but in practice this does not work out well at all. Using results in the theory of computation (*e.g.*, see Lewis and Papadimitriou[LP98]), it can be shown that the problem of determining whether an integer-valued expression ever takes the value of zero is undecidable. Thus no algorithm can reliably determine whether or not such an expression can ever evaluate to zero. Because we desire a decidable static type system, no static type system can determine, for an arbitrary integer-valued expression, whether that expression will always result in a non-zero value.

In practice, this means that the programmer will have to insert run-time checks in order to convert the results of an arbitrary arithmetic expression into a type consisting only of non-zero integers. At this point it is not at all clear how much benefit this type system separating non-zero integers from integers is providing, as it will likely be more straight-forward just to insert run-time checks (perhaps using exceptions and their handlers) to ensure that divisions by zero do not occur.

A similar problem occurs in languages with references in dealing with *null* references. Evaluating *val null* results in a run-time error. This is an issue with the polymorphic lambda calculus, which includes a keyword, *null*, which is an element of all reference types. However, $\mathcal{SOOL}$ does not support explicit references, so it is not an issue. A more relevant problem for object-oriented languages is sending messages to `nil`.

The expression `nil` is a member of all object types. We could create object types that also exclude `nil` (like our non-zero integer type above) but we would run into similar difficulties as many classes, such as nodes for linked lists, have instance variables (*e.g.*, next) that need to hold object values that may include `nil`. Certainly it is possible to program around these difficulties, but we adopt the attitude of most popular languages, that expressions of object types may hold the value of `nil`.

We have specifically postponed dealing with the translation of `nil`, partially because of the complications that arise in introducing run-time tests before message sending. We will introduce several alternatives for dealing with this problem in Section 14.2 of the next chapter.

How do we deal with these errors that can generally not be detected statically? They should be detected at run time and result in either aborting a computation or they should raise exceptions that can be caught and handled by the program. We will not discuss such exception handling here. Instead we will require that errors not detected when the program is type checked should result in an error expression of the appropriate type.

Because we have not detailed many of the basic operations of $\mathcal{SOOL}$, we have not included integer division or arrays. However, we will include a check for non-`nil` recipient in the revised definition of message send in Figure 14.5 of Section 14.2 of the next chapter. If the message is sent to a value representing `nil`, then an error expression of the appropriate type is returned. To complete the treatment of such run-time errors we would need to ensure that computation rules are *strict* in error expressions. This means that an operation which involves an expression whose value is an error should evaluate to an error expression of the appropriate type.

We did not provide a direct operational semantics of $\mathcal{SOOL}$ here. Instead we provided a translational semantics into $\Lambda^P_{<:}$, and we have assumed a safe operational semantics of $\Lambda^P_{<:}$ exists. In order to handle errors we would have to ensure that there is an error expression for all types of $\Lambda^P_{<:}$, and that computations involving errors should result in error values.[2] For simplicity in writing our semantics, we ignore the problem of propagating errors in this text.

13.5   Summary

In this chapter we showed that the translation of $\mathcal{SOOL}$ into $\Lambda^P_{<:}$ preserves both subtyping and types of expressions. Given that the type-checking rules of $\Lambda^P_{<:}$ are well-understood, the translation into $\Lambda^P_{<:}$ provides an explanation of $\mathcal{SOOL}$'s type-checking rules as well as providing an actual proof of type safety. This is quite an achievement – we have actually proved (modulo our assumption of the type safety of $\Lambda^P_{<:}$) that no run-time type errors (*e.g.*, "message not understood" errors) can arise with $\mathcal{SOOL}$ programs. Few existing programming languages have such proofs, partially because most languages do not have formal specifications of type-checking rules and semantics (aside from the implicit specifications encoded in compilers for the languages), and partially because real languages are quite complex. Nevertheless, having accomplished this proof we can be confident that the core of object-oriented languages with similar type systems are type safe.

However, in order to simplify our presentation to this point, we have ignored some important constructs in object-oriented languages. In the next chapter we will deal with some of these complicating factors.

---

2. The one exception is that we should ensure that if-then-else statements are evaluated lazily so that if, for example, evaluating the else branch would result in an error, but the boolean condition results in true, then the else branch is ignored. A proper semantics of $\Lambda^P_{<:}$ would ensure that this happens, regardless of whether the ignored branch evaluates to an error or not, so this is usually not a concern.

14

Completing $\mathcal{SOOL}$: super, nil, Information Hiding, and Multiple Inheritance

In this chapter we complete the translation of $\mathcal{SOOL}$ by handling some details that were ignored up to this point in order to simplify the presentation. In particular we discuss the handling of calls to methods in the superclass, the handling of nil, and a problem that arises with returning self from a method. The latter problem will suggest extensions to the language to be discussed in detail in Chapter 16.

In the last few sections of this chapter we describe the semantics of information hiding and multiple inheritance. We include a brief discussion of whether these features are valuable or necessary in an object-oriented language.

14.1 Using methods from superclasses

A common practice in object-oriented languages is to call the version of a method from the superclass when redefining that method. So far we have not explained how to do this, but only a simple extension of our language and translation is needed to handle calls to superclass methods. While it is more common to write a reference to the superclass method as super $\Leftarrow$ m, we will find it technically easier to treat super as a record of methods for the purposes of type-checking.

A revised version of the subclass type-checking rule extended to handle super is contained in Figure 14.1. The only change from the previous version in Figure 12.1 is that $\mathcal{E}'$ now contains a declaration of the keyword super as a record with the type of the record of methods of the superclass.

Figure 14.2 contains the translation of subclasses with super. The only

$$\mathcal{C}, \mathcal{E} \vdash \texttt{C: ClassType}(\texttt{IV}_{sup}, \texttt{M}_{sup}),$$
$$\mathcal{C}, \mathcal{E} \vdash \texttt{inst: IV}_{sub}, \qquad \mathcal{C}', \mathcal{E}' \vdash \texttt{meth: M}_{sub},$$
$$\mathcal{C}' \vdash \texttt{T}'_{i_j} <: \texttt{T}_{i_j} \text{ for } 1 \leq j \leq m$$

Subclass

$$\rule{6cm}{0.4pt}$$

$$\mathcal{C}, \mathcal{E} \vdash \texttt{class inherits C modifies } \texttt{l}_{i_1}, \ldots, \texttt{l}_{i_m}$$
$$(\texttt{inst}, \texttt{meth}): \texttt{ClassType}(\texttt{IV}, \texttt{M})$$

where

- $\texttt{IV} = \texttt{IV}_{sup} \oplus \texttt{IV}_{sub}$,

- $\texttt{M} = \texttt{M}_{sup} \oplus \texttt{M}_{sub}$,

- there is no overlap in the labels occurring in $\texttt{IV}_{sup}$ and $\texttt{IV}_{sub}$, and

- the overlapping labels in $\texttt{M}_{sup}$ and $\texttt{M}_{sub}$ are exactly $\texttt{l}_{i_1}, \ldots, \texttt{l}_{i_m}$.

- The type of $\texttt{l}_{i_j}$ in $\texttt{M}_{sub}$ is $\texttt{T}'_{i_j}$, while the corresponding type in $\texttt{M}_{sup}$ is $\texttt{T}_{i_j}$.

- $\mathcal{C}' = \mathcal{C} \cup \{ \texttt{M}' <: \texttt{M}, \texttt{IVR}' <: \texttt{IV}^{ref},$
  $\quad \texttt{SelfType} = \texttt{VisObjectType}(\texttt{IVR}', \texttt{M}')\}$, and

- $\mathcal{E}' = \mathcal{E} \cup \{ \texttt{self: SelfType}, \texttt{close: SelfType} \rightarrow \texttt{ObjectType M}',$
  $\quad \texttt{super: M}_{sup}\}$

- $\texttt{SelfType}$ does not occur in $\texttt{IV}$ or $\texttt{M}$.

Figure 14.1   Type-checking rules for subclasses with super.

difference from the previous translation is that we interpret the keyword super as *methfun*$_{sup}$(*self*). That is, super is interpreted as the record of methods from the superclass in which self is interpreted in the same way as the subclass.

We illustrate this in Figure 14.3 with an example. Suppose clrCell is an object generated from ClrCellClass, and we wish to evaluate clrCell $\Leftarrow$ bump().

Evaluation of bump() in ClrCellClass involves a call to the method in the superclass, CellClass, because the method was not overridden in ClrCellClass. The evaluation of bump in the superclass results in sending the message set to self.

An important issue is whether the set code for the superclass CellClass

$$\mathcal{T}_C[\![\mathcal{C}, \mathcal{E} \vdash \texttt{class inherits C modifies } \mathtt{l}_{i_1}, \ldots, \mathtt{l}_{i_m} \,(\texttt{inst}, \texttt{meth}):$$
$$\texttt{ClassType}(\texttt{IV}, \texttt{M})]\!] \triangleq$$
$$\Lambda(M' <: \mathcal{T}_C[\![\texttt{M}]\!]).\, \Lambda(IVR' <: \mathcal{T}_C[\![\texttt{IV}^{\mathit{ref}}]\!]).\langle \mathit{inst}_{\mathit{all}}, \mathit{methfun}_{\mathit{all}}\rangle,$$

where
$$c = \mathcal{T}_C[\![\mathcal{C}, \mathcal{E} \vdash \texttt{C}: \texttt{ClassType}(\texttt{IV}_{\mathit{sup}}, \texttt{M}_{\mathit{sup}})]\!][M'][IVR']$$
$$\mathit{inst}_{\mathit{sup}} = \mathit{proj}_1(c)$$
$$\mathit{methfun}_{\mathit{sup}} = \mathit{proj}_2(c)$$
$$\mathit{inst}_{\mathit{all}} = \mathit{inst}_{\mathit{sup}} \oplus \mathcal{T}_C[\![\mathcal{C}, \mathcal{E} \vdash \texttt{inst}: \texttt{IV}_{\mathit{sub}}]\!]$$
$$\mathit{methfun}_{\mathit{all}} = \lambda(\mathit{self}: \mathit{VisObj}(IVR', M')).$$
$$\text{let } \mathit{close}: \mathit{VisObj}(IVR', M') \to (\exists Y.\, \mathit{VisObj}(Y, M'))$$
$$= \mathit{closeobj}[IVR'][M'],$$
$$\mathit{super}: \mathcal{T}_C[\![\texttt{M}_{\mathit{sup}}]\!] = \mathit{methfun}_{\mathit{sup}}(\mathit{self})$$
$$\text{in } \mathit{methfun}_{\mathit{sup}}(\mathit{self}) \oplus \mathcal{T}_{C'}[\![\mathcal{C}', \mathcal{E}' \vdash \texttt{meth}: \texttt{M}_{\mathit{sub}}]\!]$$

Figure 14.2   Translation of subclass with super from $\mathcal{SOOL}$ to $\Lambda_{<:}^P$.

will be executed or the set code for `ClrCellClass`. In object-oriented languages, `self` represents `clrCell`, the receiver of the message, so the selection of appropriate method body should be based on the class of `clrCell`, `ClrCellClass`. Thus the evaluation of `bump()` in `ClrCellClass` should result in increasing the value of x by 1 and changing the color to `red` (the result of executing the code for `set` in the subclass).

The encoding of `super` supports that choice because it is interpreted by $\mathit{methfun}_{\mathit{sup}}(\mathit{self})$. That is, the interpretation of `self` inside the methods of `super` is the same as it is in the methods of the subclass.

Exercise 14.1.1 *To make the translation more concrete, write out carefully the encoding of*

$$(\texttt{new ClrCellClass}) \Leftarrow \texttt{bump()}$$

in order to see that the result ends up increasing the value of x by 1 and setting `color` *to* `red`.

Exercise 14.1.2 *What would be the translation of* `super` $\Leftarrow$ `m` *rather than* `super.m`*? Is there a way of changing the translation of* `super` *so that the first statement gives the desired results?*

```
class CellClass {
  x: Integer = 0;

  function get(): Integer is
  { return x }

  function set(nuVal: Integer): Void is
  { self.x := nuVal }

  function bump(): Void is
  { self ⇐ set(get()+1) }
}

class ClrCellClass inherits CellClass modifies set {

  color: ColorType = blue;

  function getColor(): ColorType is
  { return self.color }

  function set(nuVal: int): Void is
  { super.set(nuVal);
    self.color := red }
}
```

Figure 14.3   Illustration of the use of super in a subclass.

It is straightforward to extend the proof of soundness to include the language with super. Only the subclass case needs to be modified. It is sufficient (and easy) to make sure that the type of $\mathcal{T}_C[\![\text{super}]\!]$ is $\mathcal{T}_C[\![M_{sup}]\!]$.

14.2   Translating nil

So far we have avoided considering how to interpret the expression nil of SOOL. As discussed in Chapter 10, nil's type will depend on its context. This leads us to consider whether we should

- interpret all nil's as the same value, a value which is included in all object types, *or*

- interpret nil differently depending on its type, while ensuring that the values at different types are related.

Even once we have made a choice between these two alternatives, there are several ways of encoding nil. These include

1. Interpret all objects as references and interpret nil as a nil reference.

2. Interpret nil as the only element in a type Bottom which is a subtype of all object types.

3. Interpret all object types as sum types where one summand is a single element type (*e.g.*, Void) and the other summand is our previous definition of object types.

4. Omit nil from $\mathcal{SOOL}$.

The first two of these interpret all nil's as the same value, the third interprets them all differently, and the last attempts to avoid the issue altogether.

For the first suggested solution above, reinterpret $\mathcal{T_C}[\![\text{ObjectType } M]\!]$ as

$$Ref\ \exists Y.\ Y \times (Y \to \mathcal{T_C}[\![M]\!]).$$

This translation is the closest to the implementation of objects in existing object-oriented languages. It has the advantage of providing a mechanism for explaining how subtyping works in a memory model like that in existing computers.

For example, suppose class PointClass has instance variables x and y which hold integers, and class ColorPointClass inherits from PointClass by adding a new instance variable holding a color as well as adding new methods.

The representation of an object in existing languages typically includes a record which contains both the current values of instance variables and information sufficient to locate the code for all methods of the class (often a pointer to a method table for the class). Thus the representation of an object generated from ColorPointClass takes more space than an object generated from PointClass because it needs extra space for a color instance variable. How then can a variable of type PointType hold both points and color points? The solution generally is that objects are held as references to a record or table containing the desired information. While the tables take up different amounts of space, the references can fit in the same amount of memory. In this case it is trivial to represent `nil` as the null pointer.

A detailed translation based on this alternative is presented in Figure 14.4. Unfortunately this alternative has a fatal flaw: it does not preserve subtypes! As noted earlier, reference types do not have subtypes. Thus *Ref T* <: *Ref U* only if *T* = *U*. As a result, if we wish our translation to preserve subtyping, the interpretations of object types can never be references. Thus we must (reluctantly) rule out this solution.

The difficulty arises here because of the possibility of assigning to a reference. No translation of a $\mathcal{SOOL}$ expression will result in making an assignment to such a reference, as objects are represented as *implicit* references as in Java. This problem does arise in C++, where one can update such a reference – hence the failure of subtyping in C++ when directly manipulating an object rather than its reference.

We could work around this problem by creating a form of reference that may not be assigned to, but we prefer a cleaner solution for our translational semantics. Another alternative [BTCGS89] is to translate to a language without subtyping, but instead insert explicit coercion functions to take care of subsumption.

In the second solution we create a new artificial type `Bottom`, which is a subtype of all object types and contains only the single element `nil`. By subtyping, `nil` is an element of all other object types. An advantage of this approach is that we would not have to change the translations of any of the existing types and expressions. However, the existence of a `Bottom` type that is a subtype of all other object types (and only object types) is not very natural. The interpretation of `Bottom` in $\Lambda^P_{<:}$ would have to be a subtype of the interpretations of all object types. Do the interpretations of all existential types in $\Lambda^P_{<:}$ have the interpretation of `Bottom` as a subtype or only some? Why only existential types? This solution seems to raise serious problems with a translational semantics to $\Lambda^P_{<:}$.

In the third solution, presented in Figure 14.5, all object types are interpreted as sum types. For example, we could define $\mathcal{T}_C[\![\texttt{ObjectType M}]\!]$ to be *Void* $+ \exists Y. Y \times (Y \to \mathcal{T}_C[\![\texttt{M}]\!])$. The interpretation of `nil` is the element *null* obtained by injecting $\langle\rangle$ into the first summand. To access an object we would first have to check to see if it is *null*. If not, it could be extracted from the second summand and used as before.

This is a more abstract representation than that represented by the first solution, giving the language implementor more choices in how to represent

$$\mathcal{T}_C[\![\texttt{ObjectType M}]\!] \triangleq Ref\, \exists Y.\, Y \times (Y \to \mathcal{T}_C[\![\texttt{M}]\!]).$$

$$\mathcal{T}_C[\![\mathcal{C},\mathcal{E} \vdash \texttt{E} \Leftarrow \texttt{m: U}]\!] \triangleq open\, val\, \mathcal{T}_C[\![\texttt{E}]\!]\, as\, \langle IR, vo \rangle\, in\, (proj_2(vo)(proj_1(vo))).m$$
if $\mathcal{C},\mathcal{E} \vdash \texttt{E}: \{\!|\ldots,\texttt{m: U},\ldots|\!\}$.

$$\mathcal{T}_C[\![\mathcal{C},\mathcal{E} \vdash \texttt{new C: ObjectType M}]\!] \triangleq ref\, closeobj\,[IVR]\,[M]\langle inst^{ref}, methfun' \rangle$$
where

$c \triangleq \mathcal{T}_C[\![\mathcal{C},\mathcal{E} \vdash \texttt{C: ClassType(IV,M)}]\!]\,[M]\,[IVR]$

$IVR = \mathcal{T}_C[\![\texttt{IV}^{ref}]\!]$

$M = \mathcal{T}_C[\![\texttt{M}]\!]$

$inst = proj_1(c),$

$methfun = proj_2(c),$

$inst^{ref}$ is formed by adding refs to all fields of $inst$, and

$methfun' = \underline{fix}\,[IVR \to M]\lambda(fm: IVR \to M).$

$$\lambda(inst': IVR).methfun(\langle inst', fm \rangle).$$

$$\mathcal{T}_C[\![\mathcal{C},\mathcal{E} \vdash \texttt{nil: ObjectType M}]\!] \triangleq null.$$

Figure 14.4 Alternative 1 for supporting nil: Object types as references.

objects in the computer. Moreover, it makes it clearer that when sending a message to an element of object type, it is necessary to check to see that the element is non-null before attempting to access the methods or instance variables. The problem remains, however, of deciding what to do when a message is sent to an object that is the interpretation of *null*. In the figure, we interpret this by returning an *error* value. We refer the reader back to the discussion in Section 13.4 on the necessity of introducing error expressions in every type and ensuring that errors are propagated during the evaluation of expressions.

The fourth alternative is tempting. If ObjectType M is an object type for which we would like to have an object like nil, we can define a class implementing ObjectType M which has that behavior. For example, suppose we have an object type representing a node with a link to another node, and suppose the method getNext returns the adjacent node. We can create a class NilNode in which the getNext method of an object always returns itself. We could attempt to test for the end of a list by checking to see if

$$\mathcal{T_C}[\![\texttt{ObjectType M}]\!] \triangleq Void + \exists Y. Y \times (Y \to \mathcal{T_C}[\![\texttt{M}]\!]).$$

$$\mathcal{T_C}[\![\mathcal{C}, \mathcal{E} \vdash \texttt{E} \Leftarrow \texttt{m: U}]\!] \triangleq case \ \mathcal{T_C}[\![\mathcal{C}, \mathcal{E} \vdash \texttt{E}: \{\!|\ldots, \texttt{m: U}\ldots|\!\}]\!] \ of$$

$$x_1: \ Void \ then \ error_U \ \|$$

$$x_2: \ \exists Y. Y \times (Y \to \mathcal{T_C}[\![\{\!|\ldots, \texttt{m: U}, \ldots|\!\}]\!]) \ then \ open \ x_2 \ as \ \langle IR, vo \rangle \ in$$

$$(proj_2(vo)(proj_1(vo))).m$$

$$where$$

$$U = \mathcal{T_C}[\![\texttt{U}]\!].$$

$$\mathcal{T_C}[\![\mathcal{C}, \mathcal{E} \vdash \texttt{new C: ObjectType M}]\!] \triangleq$$

$$in_2^{Void, U}(closeobj \ [\mathcal{T_C}[\![\texttt{IV}^{ref}]\!]] \ [\mathcal{T_C}[\![\texttt{M}]\!]] \langle inst^{ref}, methfun' \rangle)$$

$$where$$

$$U = \mathcal{T_C}[\![\texttt{ObjectType M}]\!]$$

$$obj = \mathcal{T_C}[\![\mathcal{C}, \mathcal{E} \vdash \texttt{C: ClassType (IV,M)}]\!] \ [\mathcal{T_C}[\![\texttt{M}]\!]] \ [\mathcal{T_C}[\![\texttt{IV}^{ref}]\!]]$$

$$inst = proj_1(obj),$$

$$methfun = proj_2(obj),$$

$$inst^{ref} \text{ is formed by adding refs to all values of fields of } inst, \text{ and}$$

$$methfun' = \underline{fix} \ [\mathcal{T_C}[\![\texttt{IV}^{ref}]\!] \to \mathcal{T_C}[\![\texttt{M}]\!]] \ \lambda(fm: \mathcal{T_C}[\![\texttt{IV}^{ref}]\!] \to \mathcal{T_C}[\![\texttt{M}]\!]).$$

$$\lambda(inst': \mathcal{T_C}[\![\texttt{IV}^{ref}]\!]). \ methfun(\langle inst', fm \rangle).$$

$$\mathcal{T_C}[\![\mathcal{C}, \mathcal{E} \vdash \texttt{nil}_U: \texttt{ObjectType M}]\!] \triangleq in_1^{Void, U}(\langle\rangle)$$

$$where \ \texttt{U} = \texttt{ObjectType M} \ and \ U = \mathcal{T_C}[\![\texttt{U}]\!].$$

Figure 14.5   Alternative 3 for supporting nil: Object types as sums.

node.getNext() = node, but a real node might need to be allowed to point to itself in some applications, *e.g.*, circular lists. It makes more sense to add a method called isNil to all node classes that returns true only if the object is generated by NilNode. Other methods can be defined to always return an error value or raise an exception when invoked. Many other variations of this technique are also possible, but they all tend to be awkward in practice.

If we wish to present a translational semantics into $\Lambda_{\leq:}^P$, we find ourselves having to choose between the third (sum semantics) and fourth alternatives (eliminate nil altogether). While the last alternative is tempting in that it allows us to ignore nil, existing object-oriented languages do provide for nil. As a result we find the representation of object types as sums as the most attractive.

In order not to clutter our presentation, we will continue to work with the original representation of object types as existentials, ignoring the interpretation of `nil`.

14.3 A complication with `self`

There is one complication with `self` that we have only dealt with indirectly. Suppose a class has a method that returns `self`. In type-checking methods of a class with type `ClassType(IV, M)`, we assumed that the type of `self` was `SelfType = VisObjectType(IVR', M')`, where `IVR'` $<:$ `IV`^{ref} and `M'` $<:$ `M`. Thus if a method returns `self`, then it returns an element of type `SelfType`. We introduced the `close` function, with type `SelfType` $\rightarrow$ `ObjectType M'`, in order to solve that problem. We said earlier that rather than returning `self`, we will instead return `close(self)`, which has type `ObjectType M'`.

However, it makes no sense to write `ObjectType M'` as the return type of the method, as this will mean nothing to the user. In particular, the class type `ClassType(IV, M)` may not mention `M'` because it is only introduced as a type variable in $\mathcal{C}$ in order to write down the type-checking rules. It never appears in the source language!

Luckily, this can be taken care of by using the fact that if `M'` $<:$ `M`, then `ObjectType M'` $<:$ `ObjectType M` by the subtyping rules of $\mathcal{SOOL}$. Thus the type of `close(self)` can be promoted by the *Subsumption* rule to type `ObjectType M`. Hence the return type of a method returning `self` in a class with type `ClassType(IV, M)` can be given as `ObjectType M` (first by replacing `self` by `close(self)` and then by promoting the type using subsumption). Similarly, `close(self)` can be used as an actual parameter whenever the corresponding formal parameter has type `ObjectType M`.

This solves our problem, though at the cost of losing type information. Here is an example. Let `C` be a class with type `ClassType(IV, M)` that has a method `m` that returns `self`. As noted above, the return type of `m` will be `ObjectType M`, the type of objects generated by `C`. Now suppose that `C'` is a subclass of `C` with type `ClassType(IV`$_{all}$`, M`$_{all}$`)` where `IV`$_{all}^{ref}$ $<:$ `IV`^{ref} and `M`$_{all}$ $<:$ `M`. Assume also that `C` does not override method `m`. Then the type checker will assume the return type of the inherited method `m` will also be `ObjectType M`, even though if it were overridden with exactly the same method body, it would type check as having return type `ObjectType M`$_{all}$.

In actuality, of course, this inherited method would return an object with run-time type `ObjectType` M_{all}, but the $SOOL$ type system is not expressive enough to recognize this.

This loss of information is suggestive of that found in Java's type system, where method `clone` is declared in `Object` with return type `Object`. As a result, in all subclasses, `clone` also must return `Object`. In our encoding, as in C++, we can actually do a bit better. If the user is willing to override `clone` in a class, we can change its return type to be the object type corresponding to the class. However, inherited methods never have their types automatically modified. We will return later to this problem and see how we can retain more exact type information by using a `MyType` construct.

14.4   Finer control over information hiding

The typing rules for $SOOL$ provide only very simple support for information hiding. Instance variables are always hidden from outside the object, but are available to subclasses (similarly to "`protected`" in Java and C++), while methods are always available outside of the object as well as to all subclasses (corresponding to "`public`" in Java and C++).

It is easy to make selected instance variables public. Simply provide default "setter" and "getter" methods for the instance variable (*e.g.*, `setX` and `getX`, if `x` is an instance variable), treat an access to an instance variable as syntactic sugar for the corresponding getter method, and treat updates to an instance variable as syntactic sugar for the corresponding setter method. Of course these can be optimized in the translation to provide direct access to the appropriate instance variables, but logically providing these methods is equivalent to making the variables themselves public.

Providing more restricted access to instance variables and methods takes more work (and more complicated rules – at least notationally), but is relatively straightforward. We sketch the changes required below. Rather than use the names `public`, `protected`, and `private` from Java and C++, we adopt the new names `visible`, `hidden`, and `secret` to have similar, although slightly different, meanings.

VISIBLE METHODS   Methods that are declared as `visible` methods have the same visibility as methods treated previously in this text. They are visible from other methods in the class, from methods in any subclasses, and are visible from the outside of objects generated from the class. They are equivalent to the "`public`" methods of Java and C++.

HIDDEN METHODS   Methods that are declared as `hidden` methods are visible from other meth-

$$
Class \quad \frac{\begin{array}{c} \mathcal{C}, \mathcal{E} \vdash \texttt{inst: IV,} \\ \mathcal{C}', \mathcal{E}' \vdash \texttt{smeth: SM,} \qquad \mathcal{C}', \mathcal{E}' \vdash \texttt{hmeth: HM,} \qquad \mathcal{C}', \mathcal{E}' \vdash \texttt{vmeth: VM} \end{array}}{\mathcal{C}, \mathcal{E} \vdash \texttt{class}(\texttt{inst, smeth, hmeth, vmeth}) \texttt{: ClassType}(\texttt{IV, HM, VM})}
$$

where

- $\mathcal{C}' = \mathcal{C} \cup \{\, \texttt{HM}' <: \texttt{HM}, \texttt{VM}' <: \texttt{VM}, \texttt{IVR}' <: \texttt{IV}^{ref},$
  $\qquad \texttt{SelfType} = \texttt{VisObjectType}(\texttt{IVR}', \texttt{M}')\},$

- $\mathcal{E}' = \mathcal{E} \cup \{\texttt{self: SelfType, close: SelfType} \rightarrow \texttt{ObjectType VM}'\}$

$$
New \quad \frac{\mathcal{C}, \mathcal{E} \vdash \texttt{E: ClassType}(\texttt{IV, HM, VM})}{\mathcal{C}, \mathcal{E} \vdash \texttt{new E: ObjectType VM}}
$$

Figure 14.6 Type-checking for classes and objects with hidden and visible methods.

ods in the class and from methods in any subclasses. However they are not visible from the outside of objects generated from the class. That is, if m is a hidden method of class C, and o is an object generated from C, then one may not send the message m to o. (Though one can send the message m to self from methods in C or any of its subclasses.)

This is similar to the use of protected methods in Java and C++.[1] It differs most strikingly from the notion of protected in Java and C++ in the following situation. Let m(C other) be a protected method of C that takes a parameter from the same class. In Java and C++, the method body of m has access to both protected and private methods and instance variables of other. In the model we are describing, classes may not be used as the types of parameters. Thus it is impossible to get access to hidden methods of parameters, even if their type is the same as the type of objects generated by the class. (This should make sense as, even though the parameter has the same type, it may have been generated by a different class.)

SECRET METHODS   Finally, methods that are declared as secret methods are only visible from other methods in the same class. They are not visible in subclasses nor from the outside of objects generated from the class. This is similar to the *private* declaration in C++ and Java. (We do not discuss secret instance variables, but they can be handled similarly to secret methods.)

---

1. For simplicity, we ignore package visibility in Java. Instead we presume that each class is in a separate package so that package scope is not an issue.

We write `class(inst, smeth, hmeth, vmeth )` to represent a class with (hidden) instance variables `inst`, secret methods `smeth`, hidden methods `hmeth`, and `visible` methods `vmeth`. All of the methods are type checked under the same assumptions. (See Figure 14.6.) The class type includes the type of the record of hidden methods, HM, and the type of the record of visible methods, VM, though not that of the secret methods. The function `close` takes `SelfType` to `ObjectType` VM, reflecting the fact that the hidden methods are no longer visible in the type of objects generated from the class.

While we don't bother to write the type-checking rule for subclasses, the modifications necessary from our earlier rule should be obvious from the changes made to the type-checking rule for classes.

The type-checking rule for new expressions given in Figure 14.6 makes it clear that when an object is created from a class, the resulting object's type no longer includes the types of hidden methods. Because the type-checking rules for message sending stay the same, only messages corresponding to the visible methods can be sent to an object.

The semantics of classes change only in relatively insignificant ways to reflect hidden methods, while more work is involved in creating new objects from classes. The new translations are given in Figure 14.7. These translations use the following abbreviations:

$$VisObj\,(IVR,\, SM,\, HM,\, VM) \triangleq IVR \times (IVR \rightarrow SM \times HM \times VM)$$

$$Obj\,(VM) \triangleq \exists HM.\, \exists SM.\, \exists Y.\, VisObj\,(Y,SM,HM,VM))$$

$$closeobj \triangleq \Lambda IVR.\, \Lambda SM.\, \Lambda HM.\, \Lambda VM.\, \lambda(vo: IVR \times (IVR \rightarrow SM \times HM \times VM)).$$
$$pack\,\langle HM, ho \rangle\ as\ Obj\,(VM)$$

where

$$ho \triangleq pack\,\langle SM, so \rangle\ as\ \exists SM.\, \exists Y.\, VisObj\,(Y,SM,HM,VM))$$
$$so \triangleq pack\,\langle IVR, vo \rangle\ as\ \exists Y.\, VisObj\,(Y,SM,HM,VM))$$

The translation of visible objects is a straightforward generalization of the earlier definition. The method portion is represented by a function that takes the instance variables as a parameter and returns a triple consisting of the secret, hidden, and visible methods. The translation of objects differs from the earlier translations by hiding the types of secret and hidden methods with existential quantifiers. Thus we can see that an object type has hidden instance variables and secret and hidden methods, but we do not know anything about their names or types because of the use of existential quantifiers to hide them.

The actual translations of class and new expressions shown in Figure 14.7 are straightforward generalizations of the earlier translations. The function *closeobj* takes care of the work of hiding the instance variables and hidden methods in the construction of new objects.

14.5 Multiple inheritance

MULTIPLE
INHERITANCE

A language supports *multiple inheritance* if a class may directly inherit from two or more superclasses. A common example is defining a class for teaching assistant as being a subclass of both a student class and a teacher class.

The opportunity to inherit from two or more superclasses is often seen as reflecting the fact that objects may be looked at as members of two or more categories, as in the example above of teaching assistant. From the point of view of types, this specification can be understood in a very straightforward way by defining a type TAType which is a subtype of both StudentType and TeacherType. The classification of TA's as both student and teacher indicates that they can respond to messages sent to either students or teachers. This classification need not have anything to do with inherited instance variables or methods, though it may be convenient to implement in this way.

Perhaps surprisingly, it is not difficult to model multiple inheritance of classes in the translational semantics presented here, once one decides what is intended. Moreover, the type rules are relatively straightforward. The only difficulty lies in determining what the intended semantics are when there are conflicts that arise in inheriting from two or more classes.

A classic problem is illustrated with the class hierarchy drawn in Figure 14.8. Let C be a class with a method m. Let subclasses D_1 and D_2 be subclasses of C, each of which overrides method m. Now let E be a subclass of both D_1 and D_2. Which method m should E inherit? Similar and perhaps even more difficult issues arise when instance variables with the same name are inherited through multiple superclasses.

REPLICATED
INHERITANCE
SHARED INHERITANCE

Different languages resolve this difficulty in different ways. The two main strategies are *replicated inheritance* and *shared inheritance*. With replicated inheritance, a subclass inherits all copies of instance variables and methods. Suppose that in the above example both D_1 and D_2 include an instance variable x. With replicated inheritance, subclass E would contain both instance variables, whether or not they had the same type. Methods inherited from D_1

$\mathcal{T}_C[\![\texttt{VisObjectType(IVR, SM, HM, VM)}]\!] \triangleq$
$\qquad VisObj\,(\mathcal{T}_C[\![\texttt{IVR}]\!],\, \mathcal{T}_C[\![\texttt{SM}]\!],\, \mathcal{T}_C[\![\texttt{HM}]\!],\, \mathcal{T}_C[\![\texttt{VM}]\!])$

$\mathcal{T}_C[\![\texttt{ObjectType VM}]\!] \triangleq Obj\,(\mathcal{T}_C[\![\texttt{VM}]\!])$

$\mathcal{T}_C[\![\texttt{ClassType(IV, HM, VM)}]\!] \triangleq$
$\qquad \forall(VM' <: \mathcal{T}_C[\![\texttt{VM}]\!]).\,\forall(HM' <: \mathcal{T}_C[\![\texttt{HM}]\!]).\,\forall(IVR' <: \mathcal{T}_C[\![\texttt{IV}^{ref}]\!]).\,\exists SM.$
$\qquad\qquad \mathcal{T}_C[\![\texttt{IV}]\!] \times (VisObj\,(IVR', SM, HM', VM') \to SM \times \mathcal{T}_C[\![\texttt{HM}]\!] \times \mathcal{T}_C[\![\texttt{VM}]\!])$

$\mathcal{T}_C[\![\mathcal{C}, \mathcal{E} \vdash \texttt{class(inst, smeth, hmeth, vmeth): ClassType(IV, HM, VM)}]\!]$
$\qquad \triangleq \Lambda(VM' <: \mathcal{T}_C[\![\texttt{VM}]\!]).\,\Lambda(HM' <: \mathcal{T}_C[\![\texttt{HM}]\!]).\,\Lambda(IVR' <: \mathcal{T}_C[\![\texttt{IV}^{ref}]\!]).$
$\qquad\qquad pack\,\langle SM, \langle \mathcal{T}_C[\![\mathcal{C}, \mathcal{E} \vdash \texttt{inst: IV}]\!], methfun\rangle\rangle\ as$
$\qquad\qquad\qquad\qquad \exists SM.\,\mathcal{T}_C[\![\texttt{IV}]\!] \times (VO \to SM \times \mathcal{T}_C[\![\texttt{HM}]\!] \times \mathcal{T}_C[\![\texttt{VM}]\!])$
$\quad$ where
$\qquad \mathcal{C}' = \ \mathcal{C} \cup \{\texttt{HM}' <: \texttt{HM}, \texttt{VM}' <: \texttt{VM}, \texttt{IVR}' <: \texttt{IV}^{ref},$
$\qquad\qquad\qquad \texttt{SelfType} = \texttt{VisObjectType(IVR', SM, HM', VM')}\},$
$\qquad SM = \mathcal{T}_C[\![\texttt{SM}]\!],$
$\qquad VO = VisObj\,(IVR', SM, HM', VM'),$ and
$\qquad methfun = \lambda(self: VO).let$
$\qquad\qquad\qquad close: VO \to Obj\,(VM') = closeobj\,[IVR']\,[SM]\,[HM']\,[VM']$
$\qquad\qquad\quad in\,\langle \mathcal{T}_{C'}[\![\mathcal{C}', \mathcal{E}', \vdash \texttt{smeth: SM}]\!], \mathcal{T}_{C'}[\![\mathcal{C}', \mathcal{E}', \vdash \texttt{hmeth: HM}]\!],$
$\qquad\qquad\qquad \mathcal{T}_{C'}[\![\mathcal{C}', \mathcal{E}', \vdash \texttt{vmeth: VM}]\!]\rangle,$

$\mathcal{T}_C[\![\mathcal{C}, \mathcal{E} \vdash \texttt{new E: ObjectType VM}]\!] \triangleq let$
$\qquad protoobj =$
$\qquad\quad \mathcal{T}_C[\![\mathcal{C}, \mathcal{E} \vdash \texttt{C: ClassType(IV, HM, VM)}]\!]\,[\mathcal{T}_C[\![\texttt{VM}]\!]]\,[\mathcal{T}_C[\![\texttt{HM}]\!]]\,[\mathcal{T}_C[\![\texttt{IV}^{ref}]\!]]$
$\qquad open\ protoobj\ as\ \langle SM, visobj\rangle\ in\ let$
$\qquad\quad inst = proj_1\,(visobj),$
$\qquad\quad methfun = proj_2\,(visobj),$
$\qquad\quad inst^{ref}$ is formed by adding refs to all values of fields of $inst$, and
$\qquad\quad methfun' = \underline{fix}\,[\mathcal{T}_C[\![\texttt{IV}^{ref}]\!] \to SM \times \mathcal{T}_C[\![\texttt{HM}]\!] \times \mathcal{T}_C[\![\texttt{VM}]\!]]$
$\qquad\qquad\quad \lambda(fm: \mathcal{T}_C[\![\texttt{IV}^{ref}]\!] \to SM \times \mathcal{T}_C[\![\texttt{HM}]\!] \times \mathcal{T}_C[\![\texttt{VM}]\!]).$
$\qquad\qquad\qquad\qquad\qquad \lambda(inst': \mathcal{T}_C[\![\texttt{IV}^{ref}]\!]).\,methfun(\langle inst', fm\rangle).$
$\qquad in\ obj = closeobj\,[\mathcal{T}_C[\![\texttt{IV}^{ref}]\!]]\,[SM]\,[\mathcal{T}_C[\![\texttt{HM}]\!]]\,[\mathcal{T}_C[\![\texttt{VM}]\!]]\langle inst^{ref}, methfun'\rangle$
$\quad in\ obj$

Figure 14.7 Translation semantics for classes and objects and their types with hidden and visible methods.

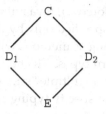

Figure 14.8   A difficult case for multiple inheritance.

that reference x would reference the copy inherited from D_1, while those inherited from D_2 would reference the second copy. Changes to one would not affect the value of the other. Of course some mechanism must be provided to indicate which instance variable is intended when writing new code in E that accesses one of these.

With shared inheritance, only one copy of a method or instance variable is inherited into the subclass. If x has the same type in D_1 and D_2, only one copy is inherited in E. Thus methods inherited from D_1 and D_2 that reference their respective instance variables named x would end up referring to the same instance variable in E. (If the types of the instance variables from the superclasses are distinct then two copies would be inherited if the language supported overloading of instance variable names, and would generate a type error and be disallowed otherwise.)

The default in Eiffel is shared inheritance for circumstances like those in our example above, while replicated inheritance is the default in C++. In circumstances where all copies of the multiply inherited method did not arise from the same class, Eiffel requires the programmer to select which m to inherit. Both Eiffel and C++ provide notational mechanisms for achieving the non-default mechanism. Other languages provide complex mechanisms for determining which version of a method is called when a method or instance variable inherited from multiple superclasses is used.

There seems to be a growing consensus that the complications of multiple inheritance are not worth the dangers of ambiguity. For example, it has been observed that most uses of multiple inheritance in C++ arise in contexts in which one of the superclasses is an abstract class. As a result, the designers of Java decided not to support multiple inheritance of classes, but instead allow classes to implement multiple interfaces. (Java interfaces can be used in ways similar to C++'s abstract classes.)

Moreover, Java interfaces can extend multiple interfaces. Because methods are specified only by their signatures in interfaces, this causes no difficulties as long as methods with the same name and parameter types share the same return types. The effect of this is similar to our uses of object types that can match multiple "super" object types.

We specify typing rules and semantics for multiple inheritance. For simplicity, we assume in the rules that there is no overlap in instance variable or method names in the superclasses. If overlap is to be allowed, the rules can be revised in order to reflect the priorities (e.g., first method declaration prevails, both method types must be the same, etc.).

A type-checking rule for subclasses with multiple inheritance is given in Figure 14.9. We write it here only for the case with exactly two superclasses. It is written so as to be a possible replacement for the corresponding rule of *SOOL*.

The rule is a very straightforward generalization from our earlier subclass rule. We simply make sure both superclasses are type correct, concatenate corresponding records of instance variables and of method types to form the final type for the subclass, and type check the new instance variables and methods under appropriate assumptions on the type of objects generated from the subclass.

The semantics of multiple inheritance can be given as a minor variant of the rules for single inheritance. Figure 14.10 provides a semantic rule appropriate for extending *SOOL* with multiple inheritance.

Because there is no overlap, the translations of the instance variables and methods (and their types) from superclasses can be concatenated with those of the subclass, with priority given to subclass methods over inherited ones from the superclasses. In this way, it is a rather straightforward extension of the earlier translations of subclasses.

We leave it as an exercise for the reader to modify these rules to correspond to the type-checking rules and semantics of any existing language's rules for multiple inheritance.

The author's opinion is that the rules necessary for resolving conflicts are more complex than the construct is worth. The default for the languages described in this book is not to support multiple inheritance, but to allow objects from classes to implement any number of types. This allows objects to take on different roles in different contexts, but avoids the complications of resolving ambiguities arising from having multiple features with the same name coming from different superclasses.

$$C, \mathcal{E} \vdash \mathtt{E}^1 \colon \mathtt{ClassType}\,(\mathtt{IV}^1_{sup},\ \mathtt{M}^1_{sup}),$$
$$C, \mathcal{E} \vdash \mathtt{E}^2 \colon \mathtt{ClassType}\,(\mathtt{IV}^2_{sup},\ \mathtt{M}^2_{sup}),$$
$$C, \mathcal{E} \vdash \mathtt{inst} \colon \mathtt{IV}_{sub}, \qquad C', \mathcal{E}' \vdash \mathtt{meth} \colon \mathtt{M}_{sub},$$

Subclass
$$\frac{C' \vdash \mathtt{T}''_{i_j} <: \mathtt{T}_{i_j} \text{ for } 1 \leq j \leq m}{C, \mathcal{E} \vdash \mathtt{class\ inherits\ E}^1,\ \mathtt{E}^2 \mathtt{\ modifies\ } \mathtt{l}_{i_1}, \ldots, \mathtt{l}_{i_m}}$$
$$(\mathtt{inst}, \mathtt{meth}) \colon \mathtt{ClassType}\,(\mathtt{IV}, \mathtt{M})$$

where

- $\mathtt{IV} = \mathtt{IV}^1_{sup} \oplus \mathtt{IV}^2_{sup} \oplus \mathtt{IV}_{sub}$,

- $\mathtt{M} = \mathtt{M}^1_{sup} \oplus \mathtt{M}^2_{sup} \oplus \mathtt{M}_{sub}$,

- There is no overlap in the labels occurring in $\mathtt{IV}^1_{sup}$, $\mathtt{IV}^2_{sup}$, and $\mathtt{IV}_{sub}$.

- There are no overlapping labels occurring in $\mathtt{M}^1_{sup}$ and $\mathtt{M}^2_{sup}$. The overlapping labels in $\mathtt{M}^1_{sup}$, $\mathtt{M}^2_{sup}$, and $\mathtt{M}_{sub}$ are exactly $\mathtt{l}_{i_1}, \ldots, \mathtt{l}_{i_m}$.

- The type of $\mathtt{l}_{i_j}$ in $\mathtt{M}_{sub}$ is $\mathtt{T}''_{i_j}$, while the corresponding type in $\mathtt{M}^1_{sup}$ or $\mathtt{M}^2_{sup}$ is $\mathtt{T}_{i_j}$.

- $C' = C \cup \{\, \mathtt{M}' <: \mathtt{M},\ \mathtt{IVR}' <: \mathtt{IV}^{ref},$
  $\qquad\qquad \mathtt{SelfType} = \mathtt{VisObjectType}\,(\mathtt{IVR}', \mathtt{M}')\}$, and

- $\mathcal{E}' = \mathcal{E} \cup \{\mathtt{self} \colon \mathtt{SelfType},\ \mathtt{close} \colon \mathtt{SelfType} \to \mathtt{ObjectType\ M}'\}$

Figure 14.9 Type-checking rules for subclasses with multiple inheritance.

14.6 Summary

In this chapter we went back to address details of $\mathcal{SOOL}$ and its translation that we had skipped in order not to complicate the discussion of the semantics of classes and objects. We also addressed the translation of more refined rules for information hiding and of multiple inheritance.

The type checking and translation of calls to methods of a superclass were handled in a relatively straight-forward fashion. The translation of nil was a different matter. We presented four options, selecting the option that interpreted objects as elements of a sum type whose alternatives represent the nil element or the translation of objects discussed in earlier chapters.

In the next section we discussed a problem with typing self (or more

$\mathcal{T_C} [\![\, \mathcal{C}, \mathcal{E} \vdash$
$\quad$ class inherits $\mathtt{E}^1$, $\mathtt{E}^2$ modifies $\mathtt{l}_{i_1}, \ldots, \mathtt{l}_{i_m}$ (inst, meth):
$$\mathtt{ClassType}\,(\mathtt{IV}, \mathtt{M})]\!] \overset{\triangle}{=}$$
$\quad\quad \Lambda(M' <: \mathcal{T_C} [\![\mathtt{M}]\!]).\, \Lambda(IVR' <: \mathcal{T_C} [\![\mathtt{IV}^{ref}]\!]).\, \langle inst_{all}, methfun_{all} \rangle$
$\quad$ where
$\quad\quad c^1 = \mathcal{T_C} [\![\mathcal{C}, \mathcal{E} \vdash \mathtt{E}^1 \colon \mathtt{ClassType}\,(\mathtt{IV}^1_{sup}, \mathtt{M}^1_{sup})]\!]\, [M']\, [IVR']$
$\quad\quad c^2 = \mathcal{T_C} [\![\mathcal{C}, \mathcal{E} \vdash \mathtt{E}^2 \colon \mathtt{ClassType}\,(\mathtt{IV}^1_{sup}, \mathtt{M}^1_{sup})]\!]\, [M']\, [IVR']$
$\quad\quad inst^1_{sup} = proj_1(c^1),$
$\quad\quad inst^2_{sup} = proj_1(c^2),$
$\quad\quad methfun^1_{sup} = proj_2(c^1),$
$\quad\quad methfun^2_{sup} = proj_2(c^2),$
$\quad\quad inst_{all} = inst^1_{sup} \oplus inst^2_{sup} \oplus \mathcal{T_C} [\![\mathcal{C}, \mathcal{E} \vdash \mathtt{inst} \colon \mathtt{IV}_{sub}]\!],$
$\quad\quad methfun_{all} = \lambda(self \colon VisObj\,(IVR', M')).$
$\quad\quad\quad\quad let\ close \colon VisObj\,(IVR', M') \rightarrow (\exists Y.\ VisObj\,(Y, M'))$
$$= closeobj\,[IVR']\,[M']$$
$\quad\quad\quad\quad in\ methfun^1_{sup}(self) \oplus methfun^2_{sup}(self) \oplus \mathcal{T_{C'}} [\![\mathcal{C'}, \mathcal{E'} \vdash \mathtt{meth} \colon \mathtt{M}_{sub}]\!]$
$\quad\quad \mathcal{C'} = \mathcal{C} \cup \{M' <: \mathtt{M}, IVR' <: \mathtt{IV}^{ref},$
$\quad\quad\quad\quad\quad \mathtt{SelfType} = \mathtt{VisObjectType}\,(IVR', M')\},$

Figure 14.10   Semantics of multiple inheritance in $\mathcal{SOOL}$.

accurately close(self). The difficulty is that the type of close(self) obtained by using the type-checking rules is a type that is an artifact of the type-checking rules, rather than something that would be recognizable to the programmer. As a result, subsumption had to be used to obtain a type that makes sense. Unfortunately, this resulted in a loss of information. We will see later that we can obtain more accurate type information using the MyType construct.

We also discussed more refined information hiding strategies that are similar to those of languages like C++ and Java. While there is no difficulty in extending the encoding in this way, we note that from a language design point of view, there may be more advantages to supporting a module system in object-oriented languages to provide the information hiding. Many systems consist of groups of collections of classes in which those classes within a group may need privileged access to features of other classes in the group, while classes outside of the group should not have such access.

Java's packages provide some hints on a possible direction for such modules, but only represent a first step. Module systems need also to provide differential access to types (interfaces) as well as class features. Moreover such modules may need to provide different views to different clients. In particular, they may need to provide more access to classes in the module for clients that wish to create subclasses than for clients who wish simply to use objects from the classes provided.

Finally we addressed typing rules and semantics for multiple inheritance. While multiple inheritance seems to be losing its attraction in object-oriented languages, we showed that there are no serious difficulties in presenting type-checking rules or a translational semantics for this construct. Rather, the difficulty is trying to figure out how to disambiguate the situation when multiple features with the same name are being inherited from different superclasses.

The language designs presented to this point have supported only single inheritance, but allow classes to generate objects whose types match those of many object types. In practice this seems to cover most of the desired uses of multiple inheritance. The designers of Java made a similar decision in allowing classes to only directly inherit from one superclass, but to allow them to implement many interfaces.

This completes our discussion of $\mathcal{SOOL}$. In the next section of the book we examine several extensions to the type system of $\mathcal{SOOL}$. Extensions include parametric polymorphism and support for a `MyType` construct similar to Eiffel's `like Current`. Rather than including all of the subtleties discussed in this chapter, we will build from the core $\mathcal{SOOL}$ language presented earlier. However, each of these features can easily be added to the languages to be presented later using the same ideas discussed here.

Historical Notes and References for Section III

Inspired by the work by Cardelli [Car88], several authors in the late 1980's designed semantics of inheritance for untyped languages. These were presented in papers by Kamin [Kam88], Reddy [Red88], and Cook and Palsberg [Coo89a, CP94] (originally presented in 1989). The Reddy and Cook-Palsberg definitions are based on a denotation semantics in which the meaning of self is determined by a fixed point, while the Kamin definition was more operational and based on self-application. The paper, "Two semantic models of object-oriented languages" [KR94], by Kamin and Reddy compares these models and shows their equivalence.

In 1990 the Abel group [CHC90] and Mitchell [Mit90] independently presented semantics for typed object-oriented languages. The Abel group's semantics relied on fixed points, while Mitchell's model was operational and based on self-application. The Abel group's semantics of classes was defined using bounded polymorphism similar to the definition presented here. (They actually used F-bounded polymorphism to handle a MyType construct like that which will be introduced in Chapter 16.) Interestingly the Abel group provided a semantics, but no actual programming language.

The semantics proposed by Mitchell were for a language that supports delegation rather than inheritance using classes. This definition employed higher-order bounded polymorphism, though with negative information – it specified which method names must *not* occur in a type. Unfortunately the translation of Mitchell's language into a calculus with records and recursive type definitions did not preserve the subtype relation because each method took self as a parameter. Thus the parameter types of methods changed covariantly when overridden in subclasses, breaking subtyping. Bruce [Bru92] showed the rough equivalence of these two approaches to the semantics of inheritance.

Many of these and other early papers are collected by Gunter and Mitchell in *Theoretical Aspects of Object-Oriented Languages* [GM94]. That collection includes many of the most important papers on the foundations of object-oriented languages.

Neither of these semantics for typed object-oriented languages handled instance variables. In 1993, Pierce and Turner [PT94] and Bruce [Bru94] separately provided semantics for typed object-oriented languages with instance variables, though technically each was for a functional language whose instance variables were updated by making a new copy of the object.

Pierce and Turner presented their semantics as a translation from a source language to a higher-order polymorphic lambda calculus. Their semantics used existential types for object definitions, essentially as given in this section. The only (inessential) difference is that in their semantics each individual method takes the record of instance variables as a parameter rather than having it be a parameter to the entire record of methods. Because the type of this parameter was hidden with an existential, subtypes were preserved in the semantics.

Because they wished to avoid the use of recursive types, Pierce and Turner considered the record of instance variables (called `state`) and record of methods (called `self`) separately, rather than considering `self` as a whole. Because there is no `close` function in the source language, it is not easy to define a method that returns an object of the same type as the receiver. Instead, the method returns the record of instance variables of the object, and the code sending the message is responsible for packaging this result into an object using the appropriate method suite. (Hofmann and Pierce [HP95] provided a more abstract approach to modeling these languages.)

Bruce presented his semantics as a denotational semantics of the language TOOPLE in a model of the F-bounded polymorphic lambda calculus. This semantics can be understood as a generalization of the Abel group's semantics to include the encoding of instance variables using existential types. The semantics of objects involved both existential types and fixed points. As with the Abel group's semantics, fixed points were required to handle a `MyType` construct as described in Chapter 16. Similarly, F-bounded polymorphism was required to interpret classes in order to handle `MyType`.

The semantics of classes and objects provided in this section can be seen to be a hybrid of the Pierce-Turner and Bruce semantics. The translational semantics using only existentials (no fixed points) is clearly quite similar to

Pierce-Turner. The semantics can also be seen as a variant of the semantics of Bruce, modified to be a translational semantics and simplified by the omission of `MyType`. In particular, the `close` construct provided the opportunity to write methods that returned an object of the same type as the receiver rather than just its representation. The concerns expressed in Section 14.3 with the typing of `self` will lead to the extension to `MyType` in Chapter 16.

Abadi and Cardelli designed an object calculus because of difficulties in finding a translational semantics for their object-based languages in which the translation preserved subtyping. Such a semantics is more difficult because of the possibility of method override in objects (rather than classes). Later, however, in work with Viswanathan [ACV96], they were able to find a translational semantics that preserved subtyping. This semantics is more complex than either the Pierce-Turner or Bruce semantics, with the meaning of object types expressed in terms of both fixed points and bounded existentials.

The paper "Comparing object encodings" [BCP99] by Bruce, Cardelli, and Pierce provides a careful description of these three encodings along with a simple recursive record translation. (Bruce's semantics is first transformed to be a translation to the polymorphic lambda calculus in this paper.) It also catalogs the advantages and disadvantages of each of the encodings.

Eifrig *et al.* [ESTZ94b, ESTZ94a] provided one of the first semantics for imperative object-oriented languages, as well as making progress on the difficult issue of type inference [EST95b, EST95a] for object-oriented languages. The languages TOIL [vG93] and PolyTOIL [BSvG95, BFSvG01] are examples of imperative languages provided with semantics like that given here.

Abadi and Cardelli also designed imperative object calculi [AC95a] as a foundation for object-based languages. While their text [AC96] focuses primarily on object-based languages, they also show how to model classes in their object calculus, providing the semantics for quite rich class-based object-oriented languages. There has also been a great deal of work by others on extending their object calculi. We omit it here because our focus is on class-based languages.

Other interesting semantics of typed object-oriented languages were provided by Abadi [Aba94] and Palsberg and Schwartzbach [PS94]. Fisher and Mitchell [FM96] provide an interesting survey of research on type systems for object-oriented languages through the mid-90's.

The modeling of information hiding given in Section 14.4 does not correspond exactly to the hiding provided by C++ and Java because we do not allow classes to be used as types. In C++ and Java if a method m of class C takes a parameter c′ of class C, then in the body of m it is possible to access private and protected variables of c′. Fisher and Mitchell [FM98] designed a two phase modeling of classes that provides exactly that access. Their solution involves the use of nested existential types so that subclasses can obtain access to the instance variables of superclasses. The definition involves two kinds of types. Those for the protected interface are modeled by types that support method extension and override, while those for public interfaces only support method invocation. Like Mitchell's earlier work, method invocation is modeled by self-application.

C++ includes support for "friend functions", which allow certain classes to have privileged access to methods and instance variables that are normally hidden. Papers by Pierce and Turner [PT93] and Katiyar *et al.* [KLM94] propose the use of bounded existential types to model privileged access by keeping the privileged classes behind an abstraction barrier, and only providing general access to methods listed in the bound of the existential.

Modula-3 [CDG$^+$88, CDJ$^+$89] uses a module in order to group items which are intended to be "friends". Partial revelations [Fre95] restrict access to full type information from outside of the module. The partial revelations indicate that a type identifier is an extension of a fixed type, but do not reveal what other information values of that type may contain that is not described by the bound. Bruce and Petersen's paper, "Modules in $\mathcal{LOOM}$: Classes are not enough" [BPV98, BFP97], presents an extension of their language $\mathcal{LOOM}$ with a module structure that supports a generalization of partial revelations along with separate access privileges for subclasses of classes in the module.

Fisher and Reppy's language Moby [FR99] supports both classes and modules, and is provided with a firm theoretical foundation. Their later paper, "Extending Moby with inheritance-based subtyping" points out flaws with modeling friends with partial abstraction and suggests that "inheritance-based subtyping" provides better support for friends, binary methods, and object cloning. The underlying semantics is based on an object calculus similar to that used in [FM98].

In Section 13.2, we noted the difficulties with the coherence of a translation based on derivations of typing judgements. The problem is that two different typing derivations of the same judgement may result in different translations. Curien and Ghelli, in their paper "Coherence of subsumption, minimum typing and type-checking in $F_\leq$" [CG92] provided a careful analysis of coherence issues in a version of the bounded polymorphic lambda calculus. They provided a rewriting system for typing derivations that provide the basis of a proof that a semantics is well-defined. Mitchell's text

[Mit96] provides a compact discussion of the issues and techniques to show coherence.

A style of writing semantics for object-oriented languages that we have not discussed here is the use of row variables. Row variables were introduced by Wand [Wan87, Wan89] in connection with a type inference scheme for simple objects, and were used in Mitchell's semantics of typed object-oriented languages [Mit90]. They can be used in specifying partial information about the method suite of an object, but allow further extension. (The version used by Mitchell also allows the specification of negative information.) Row types are especially useful with type inference.

The language Objective ML is the theoretical basis of the language Objective CAML, an extension of ML with classes and objects. The semantics of Objective ML is expressed in terms of row variables. The language supports type inference, but requires explicit coercions to treat an object as having the type of one of its superclasses. The paper, "Objective ML: An effective object-oriented extension to ML" [RV98], describes the language and its semantics, as well as providing a host of references on row variables and type inference in object-oriented languages. Another fairly minimal extension to ML supporting features of object-oriented languages is "Simple Objects for Standard ML" [RR96], by Reppy and Riecke.

There has been a great deal of interest in the semantics of Java and the safety of its type system. Representative papers are by Drossopoulou *et al.* [DE98, DEK99] and Börger and Schulte [BS98]. The design of Featherweight Java by Igarashi *et al.* [IPW99] is an important development for language theoreticians wanting to test their language ideas with a simplified version of Java that is amenable to theoretical analysis. The full Java language is extremely complicated, and many of these complications get in the way of careful study of particular language features. Because Featherweight Java has a simple semantics, it is easy to extend it to encompass new features and yet still prove type soundness.

Part IV

Extending Simple Object-Oriented Languages

15 *Adding Bounded Polymorphism to $\mathcal{SOOL}$*

Adding F-bounded parametric polymorphism of the sort discussed in Section 4.1 to $\mathcal{SOOL}$ is relatively straightforward, as it is not that different from the addition of parametric polymorphism to the lambda calculus. In this chapter we provide the details of an extension, $\mathcal{PSOOL}$, of $\mathcal{SOOL}$. The reader is invited to go back and review Section 4.1 for the motivation to add F-bounded polymorphism.

$\mathcal{PSOOL}$

15.1 Introducing $\mathcal{PSOOL}$

We begin by introducing the syntax of type and value expressions in $\mathcal{PSOOL}$ and then providing type-checking rules. We follow this with a few simple examples of the use of F-bounded polymorphism.

We first add a kind system like that for the polymorphic lambda calculus in Chapter 9. However, for simplicity we restrict the kinds to those that take types as arguments rather than elements of higher kinds. We represent the kind of all types by $*$.

$$\kappa \in \text{Kind} ::= * \mid * \Rightarrow \kappa$$

Type constructors are either types or functions that take a type as a parameter and return a constructor. We write $\mathtt{U} :: \kappa$ to indicate that $\mathtt{U}$ is a type constructor with kind κ. Let $\mathcal{TC}$ be a set of type constants containing the type constant $\mathtt{TopObject}$. Let $\mathcal{L}$ be a set of record labels, and $\mathcal{TI}$ a set of type identifiers. Constructor expressions of $\mathcal{PSOOL}$, $\mathcal{CONSR}_{\mathcal{PSOOL}}(\mathcal{TC}, \mathcal{L}, \mathcal{TI})$, (with their associated kinds) are defined as follows:

1. If $\mathtt{c} \in \mathcal{TC}$, then $\mathtt{c} :: *$.

2. If $\mathtt{t} \in \mathcal{TI}$, then $\mathtt{t} :: *$.

3. If T:: * and U:: κ, then TpFunc(t).U:: * $\Rightarrow \kappa$.

4. If T:: * and F:: * $\Rightarrow \kappa$, then F(T):: κ.

5. If T:: * and U:: *, then ForAll(t <: T).U:: *.

6. ...

The elided elements in the last case consist of all of the type definitions from $\mathcal{SOOL}$, all given with kind *. We omit them here because they would overwhelm the new constructor expressions.

If T has kind *, then we say that T is a type expression of $\mathcal{PSOOL}$ (written $T \in \mathcal{TYPE}_{\mathcal{PSOOL}}(\mathcal{TC}, \mathcal{L}, \mathcal{TI})$). Notice that the constructor identifiers and constants are only of kind * (and hence will be referred to as type identifiers and constants).

Constructor expressions of the form TpFunc(t).U represent functions taking a type T to type [T/t]U. The expression F(T) represents the application of type function F to argument T.

If T and U are types, then ForAll(t <: T).U is the type of polymorphic functions taking subtypes of T to values of type U.

While constructors may only take types as arguments, it is possible to obtain type functions taking several type parameters by writing them in a curried fashion, that is, defining a type function that returns another type function. An example is TpFunc(t).TpFunc(u).t $\rightarrow$ u.

As in $\Lambda^P_{<:}$, we include in Figure 15.1 a congruence rule, *FuncAppCong*, for simplifying constructor applications. In combination with the corresponding subtyping and type-checking rules, *Cong* $_{<:}$ and *Congruence*, this will allow us to simplify constructor applications appearing in expressions to be type-checked. (While we don't bother to write the corresponding rules, the congruence relation is reflexive, symmetric, and transitive.)

It is important not to confuse polymorphic types – those types with the form ForAll(t <: T).U, and functions from types to types – those functions with kind * $\Rightarrow$ *and typically written in the form TpFunc(t).U. Functions from types to types can be applied to a type and return a type, while a polymorphic type is just a type – the type of an expression that takes a type as a parameter and returns an element of the return type.

We now introduce the expressions of $\mathcal{PSOOL}$. New expressions include bounded polymorphic functions and their applications.

Definition 15.1.1 *The set of pre-expressions,* $\mathcal{PEXP}_{\mathcal{PSOOL}}(\mathcal{EC}, \mathcal{L}, \mathcal{EI}, \mathcal{TI})$ *of* $\mathcal{PSOOL}$ *over a set* $\mathcal{EC}$ *of expression constants, a set* $\mathcal{L}$ *of labels, a set* $\mathcal{EI}$ *of expres-*

$$FuncAppCong \qquad \frac{\text{T::}\ *}{\mathcal{C} \vdash (\text{TpFunc(t).U})(\text{T}') \cong [\text{T}'/\text{t}]\text{U}}$$

$$Congruence \qquad \frac{\mathcal{C}, \mathcal{E} \vdash \text{M: T} \qquad \mathcal{C} \vdash \text{T} \cong \text{T}'}{\mathcal{C}, \mathcal{E} \vdash \text{M: T}'}$$

$$Cong_{<:} \qquad \frac{\text{S} \cong \text{S}', \qquad \text{T}' \cong \text{T}, \qquad \mathcal{C} \vdash \text{S} <: \text{T}}{\mathcal{C} \vdash \text{S}' <: \text{T}'}$$

Figure 15.1 Congruence rules for $\mathcal{PSOOL}$.

sion identifiers, and a set $\mathcal{TI}$ of type identifiers, is given by the following context-free grammar (where we assume $\text{t} \in \mathcal{TI}$ *and* $\text{T, U} \in \mathcal{TYPE}_{\mathcal{PSOOL}}(\mathcal{TC}, \mathcal{L}, \mathcal{TI})$ *):*

```
E ∈ Exp   ::=   ... | polyFunc(t <: T): U is Block | E[T]
```

As above, the elided expressions represent the usual expressions of $\mathcal{SOOL}$, which are omitted here.

An expression of the form `polyFunc(t <: T): U is Block` represents a polymorphic function that takes a type parameter and returns the element of type U determined by evaluating `Block`. The second new expression represents the application of a polymorphic function to a type parameter. Notice that `F(T)` represents the application of a type function to a type, while `E[T]` represents the application of a polymorphic function to a type.

We present a detailed example of these constructs later in this chapter. However simple examples of a type function and a polymorphic function follow.

```
PFcn = TpFunc(t).t → Integer;

polyx = polyFunc(t <: Point): t → Integer is
            function(p:t): Integer is p ⇐ getx();
```

PFcn is a type function that send a type T to the type `T → Integer`. On the other hand, `polyx` is a polymorphic function that takes a subtype, T, of `Point`, and a value p of type T, and returns the integer obtained by sending a `getx` message to p. The type of `polyx` is `ForAll(t <: Point).PFcn(t)`.

The subtyping rules are the same as those for $\mathcal{SOOL}$ except for the addition of rules for constructor functions, constructor applications, and bounded

$$Constructor_{<:} \qquad \frac{\mathcal{C} \vdash \mathtt{U'} <: \mathtt{U}}{\mathcal{C} \vdash \mathtt{TpFunc(t).U'} <: \mathtt{TpFunc(t).U}}$$

$$ConstructorApp_{<:} \qquad \frac{\mathcal{C} \vdash \mathtt{F::} * \Rightarrow \kappa, \qquad \mathtt{T::} *, \qquad \mathcal{C} \vdash \mathtt{F'} <: \mathtt{F}}{\mathcal{C} \vdash \mathtt{F'(T)} <: \mathtt{F(T)}}$$

$$BdPoly_{<:} \qquad \frac{\mathcal{C} \cup \{\mathtt{t} <: \mathtt{T}\} \vdash \mathtt{U'} <: \mathtt{U}}{\mathcal{C} \vdash \mathtt{ForAll(t} <: \mathtt{T).U'} <: \mathtt{ForAll(t} <: \mathtt{T).U}}$$

Figure 15.2   New subtyping rules for $\mathcal{PSOOL}$.

$$PolyFcn \qquad \frac{\mathcal{C} \cup \{\mathtt{t} <: \mathtt{T}\}, \mathcal{E} \vdash \mathtt{Block:} \mathtt{U}}{\mathcal{C}, \mathcal{E} \vdash \mathtt{polyFunc(t} <: \mathtt{T):U\ is\ Block:\ ForAll(t} <: \mathtt{T).U}}$$

where T may involve t.

$$PolyFcnApp \qquad \frac{\mathcal{C}, \mathcal{E} \vdash \mathtt{E:\ ForAll(t} <: \mathtt{T).U} \qquad \mathcal{C}, \mathcal{E} \vdash \mathtt{T'} <: \mathtt{[T'/t]T}}{\mathcal{C}, \mathcal{E} \vdash \mathtt{E[T']:\ [T'/t]U}}$$

Figure 15.3   Typing rules for new expressions of $\mathcal{PSOOL}$.

polymorphic types. The rules, which are similar to the corresponding rules for $\Lambda_{<:}^P$, are given in Figure 15.2.

The definition of static type environments, $\mathcal{E}$, does not need to be modified from Definition 10.2.3, nor does the definition of type constraint system, $\mathcal{C}$, from Definition 12.1.1, which already included bounded types.

Type-checking rules for the new expressions are given in Figure 15.3. Because the definition of type constraints allows the constraint T on a type identifier t to involve that identifier, we may type check instances of F-bounded polymorphism.

Recall the following example of GJ code from Section 4.1.

```
interface OrderableF<T> {
    public boolean equal(T other);
    public boolean greaterThan(T other);
    public boolean lessThan(T other);
}
```

In $\mathcal{PSOOL}$ we model `OrderableF` as a function from types to types:

```
OrderableF = TpFunc(t).ObjectType {
    equal: t → Boolean;
    greaterThan: t → Boolean;
    lessThan: t → Boolean
}
```

Thus `OrderableF` takes an object type parameter, `T <: TopObject`, and returns an object type with `equal`, `greaterThan`, and `lessThan` methods that take parameters of type `T`.

`OrderableF` can then be used in a class definition as follows:

```
BPOrderedList: ForAll(Elt <: OrderableF(Elt)).
                                    BPClassTp(Elt) =
    polyFunc(Elt <: OrderableF(Elt)):BPClassTp(Elt) is {
        return class ({| ... |}, {| ... |})
    }
```

if `class ({| ... |}, {| ... |})` has type `BPClassTp(Elt)`.

As with $\mathcal{SOOL}$, we write programs in a language supporting convenient abbreviations. Parametric functions returning classes will be written as parameterized classes. Thus the above examples can be written in the following more readable style:

```
OrderableF(t <: TopObject) = ObjectType {
    equal: t → Boolean;
    greaterThan: t → Boolean;
    lessThan: t → Boolean
}
```

```
class BPOrderedList(Elt <: OrderableF(Elt)) {
    return class { ... };
```

If we also have

```
SomeOrdType = ObjectType {
    equal: SomeOrdType → Boolean;
    greaterThan: SomeOrdType → Boolean;
    lessThan: SomeOrdType → Boolean;
    ...
}
```

then new `BPOrderedList(SomeOrdType)` will create a new ordered list with elements of type `SomeOrdType` if we can show that `SomeOrdType` `<: BPOrderedList(SomeOrdType)`.

Interestingly, we have no way of showing directly that

$$\mathcal{C} \vdash \texttt{SomeOrdType} <: \texttt{OrderableF(SomeOrdType)}.$$

However, `OrderableF(SomeOrdType)` is congruent to

```
SmallOrdType = ObjectType {
    equal: SomeOrdType → Boolean;
    greaterThan: SomeOrdType → Boolean;
    lessThan: SomeOrdType → Boolean
}
```

and $\emptyset \vdash \texttt{SomeOrdType} <: \texttt{SmallOrdType}$. Thus by *Cong*$_{<:}$ it is type safe to apply `BPOrderedList` to `SomeOrdType`.

15.2   Translational semantics of $\mathcal{PSOOL}$

The translation of $\mathcal{PSOOL}$ to $\Lambda^P_{<:}$ is straightforward, as $\Lambda^P_{<:}$ has constructs corresponding to all new constructs added in $\mathcal{PSOOL}$. In order to simplify the notation we assume that restrictions have been made as suggested in Section 13.2 to ensure that class types have unique types. Thus we can define the translation by induction on the expressions rather than on their typings. As a result we will write the translation in the more notationally compact form of $\mathcal{T}_C[\![\mathrm{E}]\!]$ rather than $\mathcal{T}_C[\![\mathcal{C}, \mathcal{E} \vdash \mathrm{E}: \mathrm{T}]\!]$.

The translation of types and type functions is given in Figure 15.4, while the translation of expressions is given in Figure 15.5. We do not bother to repeat the translation of expressions of $\mathcal{SOOL}$ as they are unchanged.

We interpret `TopObject` as an object type with no methods, but it could easily be changed to include methods of the sort contained in Java's Object class, though all other object type definitions would have to implicitly contain those method names.

The proof of type safety is a straightforward extension of that for $\mathcal{SOOL}$, and is left as an exercise for the reader. The proof consists of adding cases for bounded polymorphic functions and polymorphic function application. Type expressions involving function applications may be reduced using the congruence rules.

$$\mathcal{T}_C[\![\texttt{TpFunc(t).U}]\!] \;\triangleq\; \lambda(t <: \mathcal{T}_C[\![\texttt{T}]\!]).\, \mathcal{T}_C[\![\texttt{U}]\!]$$

$$\mathcal{T}_C[\![\texttt{F(T)}]\!] \;\triangleq\; \mathcal{T}_C[\![\texttt{F}]\!](\mathcal{T}_C[\![\texttt{T}]\!])$$

$$\mathcal{T}_C[\![\texttt{TopObject}]\!] \;\triangleq\; \mathcal{T}_C[\![\texttt{ObjectType} \ \{| \ |\}]\!]$$

$$\mathcal{T}_C[\![\texttt{t}]\!] \;\triangleq\; t$$

$$\mathcal{T}_C[\![\texttt{ForAll(t <: T).U}]\!] \;\triangleq\; \forall(t <: \mathcal{T}_C[\![\texttt{T}]\!]).\, \mathcal{T}_C[\![\texttt{U}]\!]$$

Figure 15.4 Translation of type constructors and the new types of $\mathcal{PSOOL}$ to corresponding type constructors and types in $\Lambda^P_{<:}$.

$$\mathcal{T}_C[\![\mathcal{C}, \mathcal{E} \vdash \texttt{E[T']}: \texttt{[T'/t]U}]\!] \triangleq \mathcal{T}^X_C[\![\mathcal{C}, \mathcal{E} \vdash \texttt{E: ForAll(t <: T).U}]\!]\,[\mathcal{T}^X_C[\![\texttt{T'}]\!]]$$

$$\mathcal{T}_C[\![\mathcal{C}, \mathcal{E} \vdash \texttt{polyFunc(t <: T): U is Block: ForAll(t <: T).U}]\!] \triangleq$$
$$\Lambda(t <: \mathcal{T}_C[\![\texttt{T}]\!]).\, \mathcal{T}_C[\![\mathcal{C'}, \mathcal{E} \vdash \texttt{Block: U}]\!]$$

Figure 15.5 Translation of selected expressions of $\mathcal{PSOOL}$ to expressions in $\Lambda^P_{<:}$.

15.3 Summary

In this chapter we showed that the addition of F-bounded polymorphism to $\mathcal{SOOL}$ to form $\mathcal{PSOOL}$ is straightforward and raises no new issues in the translational semantics. This allows us to model object-oriented languages like GJ.

Next chapter we push the boundaries of statically typed object-oriented languages to begin investigating adding extra expressiveness similar to that found in languages like Eiffel and Beta. However, we will accomplish this while retaining a statically type-safe language.

16 Adding *MyType* to *Object-Oriented Programming Languages*

In the last chapter, we added F-bounded parametric polymorphism to $\mathcal{SOOL}$ to obtain the language $\mathcal{PSOOL}$. In this chapter we see how to add, in a statically type-safe way, some of the expressiveness of Eiffel's `like Current` construct, which was discussed in Section 4.2. We also compare the use of F-bounded polymorphism to this new construct.

In Chapter 3, we looked at the limits of the expressiveness of statically typed object-oriented languages with invariant typing disciplines. These are languages in which the types of instance variables and methods of a class are not allowed to vary in going from a class to a subclass. We also found that allowing covariant changes to the return types of methods (like C++ does) provided only a small amount of help in overcoming these limitations, as the other restrictions in the language kept us from defining the instance variables and methods in the subclass as directly as we desired.

In particular, limitations on the definition of subclasses still restricted us from expressing the cloning, node, and circle examples in Chapter 3, even after allowing for covariant changes in the return types of methods. It appeared that covariant changes to the types of instance variables and parameters of methods were required to allow the desired expressiveness of the language. Eiffel allows such changes, but we saw in Section 4.2 that allowing such covariant changes could lead to type errors.

The language $\mathcal{PSOOL}$, which was introduced in the last chapter, added F-bounded polymorphism to $\mathcal{SOOL}$. This added greatly to the expressiveness of the language, but it does not easily help overcome some of the limitations that we described in Chapter 3.[1] In this chapter we show that providing

---

1. Adding a type variable for each instance variable or parameter we wish to have change co-

more accurate information on the type of self will turn out to be the key to overcoming many of these difficulties.

16.1   Typing `self` with `MyType`

In Section 14.3 we discussed some of the difficulties involved in assigning a type to self. In this section we revisit this question in light of some of the typing problems discussed in Chapter 3.

16.1.1   Weaknesses of type-checking rules for classes

Let us review how the two successive type-checking rules introduced for classes in $\mathcal{SOOL}$ (and hence $\mathcal{PSOOL}$) handle the type of self. The original rule for type-checking classes in Figure 10.8 of Section 10.2.3 is similar to that of languages with simple type systems like C++, Java, Object Pascal, and Modula-3. It is based on the assumption that self has essentially the same type as the objects generated from the class being defined. In particular, the type of self was taken to be SelfType = VisObjectType(IV^{ref}, M), and type-checking rules were provided for accessing instance variables and sending methods to objects of this type. We also provided a close operation, that, when applied to an object of type VisObjectType(IV^{ref}, M), returned an object of type ObjectType M. This can be applied to self in order to aid in type checking methods that return self or take self as a parameter.

This rule turned out not to work smoothly with our translation of $\mathcal{SOOL}$ into $\Lambda_{<:}^P$. As a result, in Figure 12.1 in Section 12.1 we introduced a second version of the type-checking rule for classes in $\mathcal{SOOL}$. With this rule, occurrences of self in the definition of a class with type ClassType (IV,M) are assigned the type VisObjectType (IVR',M'), where all that is known about IVR' and M' is that IVR' <: IV^{ref} and M' <: M. This rule provided a better match with our translational semantics since we could ensure that the methods would be type correct in all possible subclasses.

The rules introduced for sending messages to objects of type VisObject-Type (IVR',M') were sufficient to type check message sends to self because the signature of a particular method of M' was guaranteed to be a subtype of the signature of the corresponding method of M. Thus a message send of the form self $\Leftarrow$ m(...) could be treated as having the same signature

---

variantly can help overcome some of these limitations, but only at the cost of nearly incomprehensible code.

as given in M. If methods returned self or took self as a parameter, extra work was required because M' was only defined in the premise of the type-checking rule; it had no meaning in the conclusion of the rule. Thus ObjectType M' could not be used as the return type of a method (or as the parameter type of a publicly available method). The solution, discussed in Section 14.3, was to first apply close to self, resulting in an expression of type ObjectType M', and then to use subtyping to promote the type of close(self) to ObjectType M.

Unfortunately, none of these rules solve all of the expressiveness problems we discussed earlier. For example, suppose C is a class generating objects of type CType. Then in both of the versions of the type-checking rules for classes, a method that takes no parameters and simply returns self would be provided with signature Void → CType (or some supertype of it).

Here is a simple example:

```
class C {
    x: Integer = 0;

    function returnMe(): CType is
    { return close(self) }
}
```

(Normally we will omit the application of close to self in example code, as it will typically be inserted by the type checker. We include it here because we are making a point about typing with self.) Assigning close(self) the type CType requires the use of subtyping, as discussed above.

Now look at what happens when we define a subclass SC of C.

```
class SC inherits C {
    function m'(...): ... is {...}
}
```

Suppose the type of object generated from SC is SCType. One would hope that the return type of the inherited method in SC would be SCType, but even in a language that allows covariant changes to return types, the type of returnMe does not change, because it is inherited without change.

The following code illustrates the problem:

```
sc: SCType;
sc := new SC;
... (sc ⇐ returnMe()) ⇐ m'(...) ... // type error
```

The last line of code will generate a static type error, even though it would be perfectly safe at run time. The problem is that the type checker will determine the type of the expression sc ⇐ returnMe() to be CType, even though we know (by looking at the body of returnMe) that it will really return an object of the same type as the receiver – SCType in this case.

The programmer could add a type cast or typecase statement to test and use the dynamic type of the expression, but this simply highlights the failure of the static type system to determine the best type for the expression.

A workaround exists in a language supporting covariant changes to the return type of methods in subclasses. One would simply override returnMe in SC and copy the code for returnMe from the superclass to the subclass (inheritance by cut and paste!):

```
class SC inherits C modifies returnMe {
    function returnMe(): SCType is
    { return close(self) }

    function m'(...): ... is {...}
}
```

In this case, the fix involves just copying the single line of code that returns self, and would cause no difficulty. However in more complex situations it might result in having to copy over large amounts of code, creating a maintenance nightmare. A call to super.returnMe() could not be used, because it would also return the wrong type (though again, type casts or a typecase statement could be used to overcome the failure of the static type system to capture the correct dynamic type).

```
class SC inherits C modifies returnMe {
    function returnMe(): SCType is
    {
        return super.returnMe() // type error
    }

    function m'(...): ... is {...}
}
```

One would have to insert a downcast (or typecase statement) in order to coerce the results of super.returnMe() to be of type SCType. In summary, one might code around the problem, but it would be far from ideal.

Exercise 16.1.1 *Show how to write the code for* C *and* SC *using F-bounded polymorphism. Include examples generating new objects from classes* C *and* SC.

16.1.2 The changing meaning of self and its type, MyType

The root of the problem arising in the use of inheritance with method returnMe above is that the meaning of self changes in the subclass to denote an element of type SCType rather than CType. Type checking the body of returnMe under the assumption that the type of self is a visible version of CType (as we did in the first version of the type checking rules for classes) is weaker than assuming its type is some visible object type that corresponds to a subtype of CType, as we did in the second version.

That is, from the assumption close(self) has type CType' for some (not yet determined) subtype of CType, we can infer by subsumption that close(self) also has type CType. Thus the second version of our type-checking rule actually allows us to type check methods with a stronger assumption on the type of self. The problem is that the type systems of our languages do not allow us to take advantage of this extra information. What we need is extra expressiveness in the *type expressions* of our language so that we can capture the fact that the type of self changes when methods are inherited in subclasses.

MYTYPE   To get this expressiveness we introduce the new type expression MyType to represent the type of self. The meaning of MyType will be similar to the Eiffel expression like Current.[2] MyType can be used in typing methods and instance variables of classes, where it will always stand for the type of the object executing the code, self.

Suppose o is an object of type CType that was generated by class C. If the keyword self occurs in method m of C, then when $o \Leftarrow m(\ldots)$ is executed, all occurrences of self in the method body will be interpreted as o. Similarly, all occurrences of MyType encountered in evaluating $o \Leftarrow m(\ldots)$ will be interpreted as CType. Thus the semantic interpretations of self and MyType in a message send are just the interpretations of the receiver and its type. When we restrict our attention just to simple classes and objects, it is not at all clear why we need to use MyType, as its meaning is just CType. The advantages really show up, however, in the use of subclasses, as we see next.

---

2. Aside from Eiffel, Trellis/Owl [SCB+86] and Emerald [BHJ+87] also provide constructs giving the type of self an explicit name. MyType is also sometimes written as SelfType in the literature.

In Section 3.2.1 we discussed a more detailed example involving a deep cloning method. The code for it can be found in Figure 3.1. We now show how the use of MyType solves the typing problem discussed there. In that example we presumed that all objects have a pre-defined method clone (inherited from a "Top" class) and wished to define a deepClone method that also cloned instance variables.

In rewriting this example in our more expressive language, we assume that the pre-defined method clone has type Void $\rightarrow$ MyType. We will write deepClone to have the same type. The code in Figure 16.1 contains a definition of class C with method deepClone. It also contains a definition of a subclass SC that adds a new field, nVar, a new method, setNVar, and redefines deepClone. The body of deepClone in SC calls the old version of deepClone in C (via the call to super), and then sets the value of the instance variable nVar in the new, cloned object to be a clone of the value in self.

Figure 16.2 provides an example of the use of these classes. We will provide formal type-checking rules soon, but, following the argument above on the meanings of self and MyType, we see that if c has type CType, then the type of c $\Leftarrow$ deepClone() should also be CType, while if sc has type SCType, then the type of sc $\Leftarrow$ deepClone() should be SCType. Thus the assignments on lines **2** and **3** are safe. This example shows how useful the MyType construct can be in defining subclasses. Because the meaning of MyType changes in going from a class to a subclass, the types of inherited methods can automatically change in subclasses.[3]

The typing of the method body of deepClone in class SC of Figure 16.1 is also quite interesting. The keyword super provides a mechanism to access the methods of the superclass in a subclass. As discussed in Section 14.1, super has the same type as the record of methods of the superclass. Thus super.deepClone() has type MyType. As a result, the assignment **1** to nClone is well-typed, and hence the message send of setNVar to nClone is type-safe. While it is not needed in this example, an expression self $\Leftarrow$ deepClone() would also be given type MyType.

The use of MyType also can solve the typing problem, discussed in Section 3.2.2, of defining a doubly linked node class as a subclass of a singly linked node class. We have rewritten the Node example from Figure 3.2 in Figure

---

3. Because of these automatic changes in the meaning of types in going from a class to a subclass, we will have to be careful in type checking method bodies to ensure that they remain type-safe in subclasses. More on this later.

```
Program DeepCloner;

    CType = ObjectType {
        deepClone: Void → MyType;
    }

    class C {
        ...
        function deepClone(): MyType is
        { super.clone();
            ...
        }
    }

    SCType = ObjectType {
        deepClone: Void → MyType;
        setNVar: nObjType → Void
    }

    class SC inherits C modifies deepClone {
        nVar: nObjType := nil;

        function setNVar(nVarVal: nObjType): Void is
        { nVar := nVarVal }

        function deepClone(): MyType is
            nClone: MyType;
        {                           // no type problems now!
            nClone := super.deepClone();  // **1**
            nClone ⇐ setNVar(nVar ⇐ clone());
            return nClone
        }

        function nMeth(): Void is  { ... }
    }
```

Figure 16.1   Typing `deepClone` methods with `MyType`.

```
    c, c':CType
    sc, sc':SCType


{
  c := new C;
  c' := c ⇐ deepClone();        // **2**
  sc := new SC;
  sc' := sc ⇐ deepClone();      // **3**
    // Assignment safe - type of right side is SCType.
}
```

Figure 16.2   Typing deepClone methods with MyType, *continued*.

16.3, replacing all occurrences of NodeType by MyType. We have also used MyType to specify the type of the instance variable next.

We now define DoubleNode as a subclass of Node in Figure 16.4. The use of MyType in the types of instance variables and methods ensures that all occurrences in inherited methods will change uniformly in the subclass.

In particular, examine the body of setNext in DoubleNode. In the first line, the setNext method of the superclass is invoked. In the superclass setNext took a parameter of type MyType, and that is indeed the type of the parameter, newNext. In the next line, the message setPrevious is sent to newNext, which has type MyType. The method setPrevious takes a parameter of type MyType, which is indeed the type of the receiver. The actual parameter is close(self), which by assumption has type MyType. Thus the body of setNext is well-typed.

16.1.3   Loss of subtyping – gain of matching

The types of objects generated by Node and DoubleNode are given in Figure 16.5. As the reader might suspect from the discussion in Section 4.2 on the failure of static type safety in Eiffel, the types NodeType and DoubleNode-Type cannot be subtypes because of the implicit change in the type of the parameter of setNext between the two types.

As a result we will have to be more careful in type checking methods involving expressions with type MyType. It will no longer be the case that

```
class Node {
    value: Integer := 0;
    next: MyType := nil;

    function getValue(): Integer is
    { return self.value }

    function setValue(newValue: Integer): Void is
    { self.value := newValue }

    function getNext(): MyType is
    { return self.next }

    function setNext(newNext: MyType): Void is
    { self.next := newNext }
}
```

Figure 16.3 Node class with MyType.

```
class DoubleNode inherits Node modifies setNext {
    previous: nil := MyType;

    function getPrevious(): MyType is
    { return self.previous }

    function setPrevious(newPrev: MyType): Void is
    { self.previous := newPrev }

    function setNext(newNext: MyType): Void is
    {                                    // no error!
      super.setNext(newNext);
      newNext ⇐ setPrevious(close(self)) }
}
```

Figure 16.4 Doubly linked node class with MyType.

```
NodeType = ObjectType {
    getValue: Void → Integer;
    setValue: Integer → Void;
    getNext: Void → MyType;
    setNext: MyType → Void
}

DoubleNodeType = ObjectType {
    getValue: Void → Integer;
    setValue: Integer → Void;
    getNext: Void → MyType;
    setNext: MyType → Void;
    getPrevious: Void → MyType;
    setPrevious: MyType → Void
}
```

Figure 16.5   Types of objects generated from node classes with MyType.

subclasses automatically give rise to subtypes.[4] In particular, an element of type DoubleNodeType may not be used in a context expecting an element of type NodeType. This failure of subtyping might be considered to be a great loss, but in practice the failure of subtyping in this case will hardly be missed.

First of all, in a language without MyType, one could not even write DoubleNode as a direct subclass of Node. Separate class definitions would be required, and the types of the corresponding object types would certainly not be in the subtype relation. Thus the use of MyType allows us to write subclasses that could not be written previously. Thus we have the gain of being able to write DoubleNode as a subclass rather than losing an existing subtype.

Second, if a class does not contain occurrences of MyType in its method definitions, then the types of the corresponding object types will still be in the subtype relation. More generally, if MyType only occurs in the return types of methods, the corresponding object types will be in the subtype relation. Thus in the definitions in Figure 16.1 using MyType, SCType <: CType because MyType only occurs as the return type of method deepClone.

---

4. We provide the exact rules for subtyping in the presence of MyType in the next section.

MATCHING   Finally, there is another relation between object types, called *matching*, that
is satisfied by these types.

Definition 16.1.2 *Object type* T *matches object type* U *(written* T <# U*) iff every
method in* U *also occurs in* T, *and the types of corresponding methods in* T *and* U *are
in the subtype relation.*

Of course, type T can also have more methods than U if T <# U. The matching relation is the same as subtyping in the absence of the MyType construct,
but differs in the presence of MyType because MyType implicitly has different meanings in different types. In determining matching, occurrences of
MyType in both types are treated as being the same. Thus DoubleNodeType
matches NodeType, even though they are not subtypes.

While the matching relation does not allow values of one object type to
masquerade as values of the other, as is the case with subtyping, it does
provide information on the availability and types of methods that is often
sufficient in situations where subtyping might seem to be needed.

The most important point to keep in mind with matching is that it provides information about the methods available and their types. Thus knowing that type N matches NodeType provides the information that N has at
least the methods getValue, setValue, getNext, and setNext, and that
their signatures conform to those given in NodeType.

Most of the time, this sort of information is all that is needed in object-
oriented programming. The extra information that one type can masquerade
as another in all possible circumstances is not needed. In the next chapter we
will see that we can replace many occurrences of F-bounded polymorphism
by the use of simple match-bounded polymorphism, providing another benefit of matching.

16.2   *MOOL*: Adding MyType to *SOOL*

MOOL   In this section we provide the formal definition of the language *MOOL*,
which is obtained by adding MyType to *SOOL*. In the next chapter we
will extend *MOOL* with match-bounded polymorphism in order to obtain
PMOOL.

While the source language *MOOL* does not yet actually contain polymorphic functions, it will be notationally convenient to be able to write certain type expressions as the application of a type function to a type and to
write certain value expressions as the application of a polymorphic function

to a type expression. We will do this in order to be able to parameterize
methods and instance variables by MyType. For example, the type of class
Node in Figure 16.3 can be written as ClassType(NodeIV(MyType), No-
deM(MyType)) using the parameterized types NodeIV and NodeM defined
by:

```
NodeIV(MT) = {val: Integer; next: MT}
NodeM(MT) = {getValue:...; setValue:...;
                getNext: Void → MT; setNext: MT → Void}
```

that are formed by replacing MyType by a type variable MT in the types of the
class features. While allowing these type variables will have little impact on
the language, it will make it more convenient to define the translation into
$\Lambda^P_{\leq:}$. Moreover, we will soon extend the language by the addition of type
functions and polymorphic functions. Using this notation now will make it
simpler later to make the transition to the polymorphic language.

The kinds and types are the same as those in $\mathcal{PSOOL}$, except that for now
we omit the types of polymorphic functions. As in $\mathcal{SOOL}$, the type identifier
SelfType will refer to the type of self within the body of a method and
will allow access to instance variables as well as methods. MyType will refer
to the type of self as seen from the outside when only methods are visible.
The new type keyword MyType is allowed to appear in $\mathcal{MOOL}$ programs in
the types of instance variables and methods. However, as before, signatures
of instance variables and methods may not reference SelfType; it is only
used in type checking method bodies.

When writing object and class type expressions, we will write the types of
the records of instance variables and methods as functions applied to My-
Type. In a sense this use of higher-order constructors is merely a notational
convenience. Yet it makes it much easier to write down the type-checking
rules and translation of $\mathcal{MOOL}$ type and value expressions because classes
get translated as polymorphic functions. Thus we will write the expressions
as

```
ObjectType M(MyType),
VisObjectType(IVR(MyType),M(MyType)),
```

and

```
ClassType(IV(MyType),M(MyType)).
```

Each of these type expressions bind all free occurrences of MyType. Thus
MyType, like self, is used as a keyword of $\mathcal{MOOL}$.

We generalize the notion of a type constraint system, C, from that given in $PSOOL$, so that C may contain subtype constraints between elements of higher kinds.

Definition 16.2.1 *Relations of the form* $\mathbf{x}^\kappa = \mathrm{G}$ *and* $\mathbf{x}^\kappa <: \mathrm{G}$, *where* $\mathbf{x}^\kappa$ *is a type constructor variable and* G *is a type constructor expression of the same kind are said*

TYPE CONSTRUCTOR
CONSTRAINTS
TYPE CONSTRUCTOR
CONSTRAINT SYSTEM *to be* **type constructor constraints**. *A* **type constructor constraint system** *is defined as follows:*

1. *The empty set,* $\emptyset$, *is a type constructor constraint system.*

2. *If* C *is a type constructor constraint system,* $\mathbf{x}^\kappa$ *is a constructor identifier that does not appear in* C *or* G, *and* G *is a constructor expression of the same kind, then* $C \cup \{\mathbf{x}^\kappa = \mathrm{G}\}$ *is a type constructor constraint system.*

3. *If* C *is a type constructor constraint system,* $\mathbf{x}^\kappa$ *is a constructor identifier that does not appear in* C, *and* G *is a constructor expression of the same kind, then* $C \cup \{\mathbf{x}^\kappa <: \mathrm{G}\}$ *is a type constructor constraint system.*

We extend the definition of subtyping to handle constructors of higher kinds, and we redefine subtyping for object types to take the presence of MyType into consideration. All other subtyping rules remain the same. The new rules are presented in Figure 16.6. The rule for subtyping type functions could be further generalized by allowing contravariant changes to the bounds on the arguments, but we will only need this simpler version.

The condition relating MT′ and MT on the left side of the hypothesis of the *Object* $_{<:}$ rule ensures that the hypothesis of the rule fails (and hence the conclusion) if M contains any negative occurrences of MyType. (*See example below.*) If M(MyType) and M′(MyType) result in type expressions that do not contain MyType then the rule reduces to our earlier subtyping rule for object types. The hypothesis of this rule should remind the reader of the hypothesis for subtyping of recursive types in $\Lambda^P_{<:}$. In fact, object types will translate to recursive types so the subtyping rule for recursive types will be needed to verify that the translation from $MOOL$ to $\Lambda^P_{<:}$ preserves subtypes.

The other subtyping rules for types are as for $SOOL$.

The matching relation ($<\#$) is only defined on type expressions that represent object types. The matching rules are given in Figure 16.7.

All object types match TopObject, by rule *TopObject* $_\#$. Rule *Cong* $_\#$ states that matching is preserved by congruence.

The *Object* $_{<:}$ rule for subtyping is much more restrictive than the *Object* $_\#$ rule for matching, in that the subtyping rule for object types has a hypothe-

$$TypeFcn_{<:} \quad \frac{\mathcal{C} \vdash \text{U}' <: \text{U}}{\mathcal{C} \vdash \text{TpFunc(t).U}' <: \text{TpFunc(t).U}}$$

where t does not occur in $\mathcal{C}$.

$$TypeFcn\ App_{<:} \quad \frac{\mathcal{C} \vdash \text{F}' <: \text{F}}{\mathcal{C} \vdash \text{F}'\text{(T)} <: \text{F(T)}}$$

$$Object_{<:} \quad \frac{\mathcal{C} \cup \{\text{MT}' <: \text{MT}\} \vdash \text{M}'(\text{MT}') <: \text{M(MT)}}{\mathcal{C} \vdash \text{ObjectType M}'\text{(MyType)} <: \text{ObjectType M(MyType)}}$$

where MT and MT' are new type identifiers not appearing in $\mathcal{C}$, M, or M'.

Figure 16.6 Subtyping rules for higher kinds and replacement subtyping rule for object types.

$$TopObject_{\#} \quad \mathcal{C} \vdash \text{ObjectType M(MyType)} <\!\!\# \text{ TopObject}$$

$$Reflex_{\#} \quad \mathcal{C} \vdash \text{ObjectType M(MyType)} <\!\!\# \text{ ObjectType M(MyType)}$$

$$Transitive_{\#} \quad \frac{\mathcal{C} \vdash \text{S} <\!\!\# \text{T}, \quad \mathcal{C} \vdash \text{T} <\!\!\# \text{U}}{\mathcal{C} \vdash \text{S} <\!\!\# \text{U}}$$

$$Object_{\#} \quad \frac{\mathcal{C} \vdash \text{M}' <: \text{M}}{\mathcal{C} \vdash \text{ObjectType M}'\text{(MyType)} <\!\!\# \text{ ObjectType M(MyType)}}$$

where M' and M have kind $* \Rightarrow *$.

$$Type\ Abbrev_{\#} \quad \frac{\mathcal{C} \vdash \mathcal{C}(\text{T}') <\!\!\# \mathcal{C}(\text{T})}{\mathcal{C} \vdash \text{T}' <\!\!\# \text{T}}$$

$$Cong_{\#} \quad \frac{\text{S} \cong \text{S}', \quad \text{T}' \cong \text{T}, \quad \mathcal{C} \vdash \text{S} <\!\!\# \text{T}}{\mathcal{C} \vdash \text{S}' <\!\!\# \text{T}'}$$

Figure 16.7 Matching rules for object types.

sis that is harder to establish. That is, for proving matching, we can assume the types representing MyType are the same. With subtyping we are only allowed the weaker assumption that the MyType' in the first is a subtype of the MyType of the second. As a result it is harder to show that

$$\mathcal{C} \cup \{\text{MT}' <: \text{MT}\} \vdash \text{M}'(\text{MT}') <: \text{M}(\text{MT})$$

than

$$\mathcal{C} \vdash \text{M}' <: \text{M}.$$

However, we can easily show that if the first assertion is derivable then the second must also be derivable. (Use the same proof, but replace all occurrences of MT' with MT. Then apply rule *TypeFcn* $_{<:}$. Thus if

$$\mathcal{C} \vdash \text{ObjectType M}'(\text{MyType}) <: \text{ObjectType M}(\text{MyType})$$

then

$$\mathcal{C} \vdash \text{ObjectType M}'(\text{MyType}) <\# \text{ObjectType M}(\text{MyType}).$$

The types DoubleNodeType and NodeType, presented in Figure 16.5, are in the matching relation, but they are not subtypes. The difficulty in subtyping results from trying to show that the types of the setNext methods are in the subtype relation. This involves trying to show

$$\mathcal{C} \cup \{\text{MyType}' <: \text{MyType}\} \vdash \text{MyType}' \rightarrow \text{Void} <: \text{MyType} \rightarrow \text{Void}$$

We cannot show this because of the contravariance in the domain of function types. To prove it would require an assumption that MyType <: MyType', the opposite of what is given.

Because the rules for matching are so simple, and match-bound constraints do not occur in $\mathcal{C}$, the following result should be obvious.

Lemma 16.2.2 *Suppose* $\mathcal{C} \vdash \text{T}' <\# \text{T}$ *where* T *is not* TopObject. *Then* $\mathcal{C}(\text{T}')$ = ObjectType M'(MyType) *and* $\mathcal{C}(\text{T})$ = ObjectType M(MyType) *for some type functions* M' *and* M *such that* $\mathcal{C} \vdash \text{M}' <: \text{M}$.

Figure 16.8 provides the rules for a variant, $<\#_{vis}$, of the matching relation for visible object types. This relation also is reflexive and transitive, though we have omitted those rules. The types of the records of instance variables and the types of the records of methods must be subtypes if the visible object types are to be in the $<\#_{vis}$ relation. This relation will be useful in formulating typing rules.

As above, we obtain the following straightforward lemma:

$$VisObj \, \#_{vis} \quad \frac{\mathcal{C} \vdash \texttt{M'} <: \texttt{M} \qquad \mathcal{C} \vdash \texttt{IVR'} <: \texttt{IVR}}{\mathcal{C} \vdash \texttt{VisObjectType(IVR'(MyType), M'(MyType))} \, \#_{vis}}$$
$$\texttt{VisObjectType(IVR(MyType), M(MyType))}$$

where $\texttt{IVR'}$, $\texttt{IVR}$, $\texttt{M'}$, and $\texttt{M}$ have kind $* \Rightarrow *$,

$$Type\ Abbrev \, \#_{vis} \quad \frac{\mathcal{C} \vdash \mathcal{C}(\texttt{T'}) \, \#_{vis} \, \mathcal{C}(\texttt{T})}{\mathcal{C} \vdash \texttt{T'} \, \#_{vis} \, \texttt{T}}$$

$$Cong \, \#_{vis} \quad \frac{\texttt{S} \cong \texttt{S'}, \qquad \texttt{T'} \cong \texttt{T}, \qquad \mathcal{C} \vdash \texttt{S} \, \#_{vis} \, \texttt{T}}{\mathcal{C} \vdash \texttt{S'} \, \#_{vis} \, \texttt{T'}}$$

Figure 16.8 Rules for $\#_{vis}$.

Lemma 16.2.3 *Suppose* $\mathcal{C} \vdash \texttt{T'} \, \#_{vis} \, \texttt{T}$. *Then*

$$\mathcal{C}(\texttt{T'}) = \texttt{VisObjectType(IVR'(MyType), M'(MyType))},$$

and

$$\mathcal{C}(\texttt{T}) = \texttt{VisObjectType(IVR(MyType), M(MyType))},$$

for some type functions $\texttt{IVR'}$, $\texttt{IVR}$, $\texttt{M'}$, *and* $\texttt{M}$ *such that* $\mathcal{C} \vdash \texttt{IVR'} <: \texttt{IVR}$ *and* $\mathcal{C} \vdash \texttt{M'} <: \texttt{M}$.

The expressions of $\mathcal{MOOL}$ are the same as those of $\mathcal{SOOL}$ (modulo the addition of MyType as a type keyword). The difference in expressiveness comes entirely through the use of MyType in the types of methods and instance variables.

The type-checking rules of $\mathcal{MOOL}$ are similar to those for $\mathcal{SOOL}$, except for those for classes, subclasses, and message sends, which now involve My-Type and matching. Figures 16.9 and 16.10 contain the new type checking rules for these expressions. As mentioned earlier, for notational convenience, we write the record of methods and values of instance variables as if they were polymorphic functions that take type parameters.

There are several differences between these rules and the type-checking rules for classes and subclasses for $\mathcal{SOOL}$ given in Figure 12.1. As before, new subtype constraints are added to $\mathcal{C}$ for the purpose of type checking. However, this time the variables, $\texttt{M'}$ and $\texttt{IVR'}$, and their constraints, $\texttt{M}$ and $\texttt{IV}^{ref}$, are functions from types to types. We also add to $\mathcal{C}$ a definition for $\texttt{MT}$,

$$\text{Class} \quad \frac{\begin{array}{c} \mathcal{C}', \mathcal{E} \vdash \texttt{inst}\,[\texttt{MT}]\colon \texttt{IV}\,(\texttt{MT})\,, \\ \mathcal{C}', \mathcal{E}' \vdash \texttt{meth}\,[\texttt{MT}]\,[\texttt{SelfType}]\colon \texttt{M}\,(\texttt{MT}) \end{array}}{\begin{array}{c} \mathcal{C}, \mathcal{E} \vdash \texttt{class}\,(\texttt{inst}\,[\texttt{MyType}], \texttt{meth}\,[\texttt{MyType}]\,[\texttt{SelfType}])\colon \\ \texttt{ClassType}\,(\texttt{IV}(\texttt{MyType}), \texttt{M}(\texttt{MyType})) \end{array}}$$

where

- $\mathcal{C}' = \mathcal{C} \cup \{ \texttt{M}' <: \texttt{M}, \texttt{IVR}' <: \texttt{IV}^{\mathit{ref}}, \texttt{MT} = \texttt{ObjectType}\,\texttt{M}'\,(\texttt{MyType}),$
  $\texttt{SelfType} = \texttt{VisObjectType}(\texttt{IVR}'(\texttt{MyType}), \texttt{M}'(\texttt{MyType}))\,\},$

- $\mathcal{E}' = \mathcal{E} \cup \{\,\texttt{self}\colon \texttt{SelfType}, \texttt{close}\colon \texttt{SelfType} \to \texttt{MT}\,\}.$

- None of $\texttt{M}'$, $\texttt{IVR}'$, $\texttt{MT}$, or $\texttt{SelfType}$ occurs free in $\texttt{inst}$, $\texttt{meth}$, $\texttt{IV}$, $\texttt{M}$, $\mathcal{C}$, or $\mathcal{E}$.

$$\text{Subclass} \quad \frac{\begin{array}{c} \mathcal{C}, \mathcal{E} \vdash \texttt{E}\colon \texttt{ClassType}\,(\texttt{IV}_{\mathit{sup}}(\texttt{MyType}), \texttt{M}_{\mathit{sup}}(\texttt{MyType}))\,, \\ \mathcal{C}', \mathcal{E} \vdash \texttt{inst}\,[\texttt{MT}]\colon \texttt{IV}_{\mathit{sub}}(\texttt{MyType})\,, \\ \mathcal{C}', \mathcal{E}' \vdash \texttt{meth}\,[\texttt{MT}]\,[\texttt{SelfType}]\colon \texttt{M}_{\mathit{sub}}(\texttt{MyType})\,, \\ \mathcal{C}' \vdash \texttt{T}'_{i_j} <: \texttt{T}_{i_j}, \text{ for } 1 \le j \le m \end{array}}{\begin{array}{c} \mathcal{C}, \mathcal{E} \vdash \texttt{class inherits E modifies } \texttt{l}_{i_1}, \ldots, \texttt{l}_{i_m} \\ (\texttt{inst}\,[\texttt{MyType}], \texttt{meth}\,[\texttt{MyType}]\,[\texttt{SelfType}])\colon \\ \texttt{ClassType}\,(\texttt{IV}(\texttt{MyType}), \texttt{M}(\texttt{MyType})) \end{array}}$$

where

- $\texttt{IV} = \texttt{IV}_{\mathit{sup}} \oplus \texttt{IV}_{\mathit{sub}}$ and $\texttt{M} = \texttt{M}_{\mathit{sup}} \oplus \texttt{M}_{\mathit{sub}}$,

- There is no overlap in the labels occurring in $\texttt{IV}_{\mathit{sup}}$ and $\texttt{IV}_{\mathit{sub}}$, and

- The overlapping labels in $\texttt{M}_{\mathit{sup}}$ and $\texttt{M}_{\mathit{sub}}$ are exactly $\texttt{l}_{i_1}, \ldots, \texttt{l}_{i_m}$,

- The type of $\texttt{l}_{i_j}$ in $\texttt{M}_{\mathit{sub}}\,(\texttt{MT})$ is $\texttt{T}'_{i_j}$, while the corresponding type in $\texttt{M}_{\mathit{sup}}\,(\texttt{MT})$ is $\texttt{T}_{i_j}$.

- $\mathcal{C}' = \mathcal{C} \cup \{ \texttt{M}' <: \texttt{M}, \texttt{IVR}' <: \texttt{IV}^{\mathit{ref}}, \texttt{MT} = \texttt{ObjectType}\,\texttt{M}'\,(\texttt{MyType}),$
  $\texttt{SelfType} = \texttt{VisObjectType}(\texttt{IVR}'(\texttt{MyType}), \texttt{M}'(\texttt{MyType}))\,\},$

- $\mathcal{E}' = \mathcal{E} \cup \{\,\texttt{self}\colon \texttt{SelfType}, \texttt{close}\colon \texttt{SelfType} \to \texttt{MT}\,\}.$

- None of $\texttt{M}'$, $\texttt{IVR}'$, $\texttt{MT}$, or $\texttt{SelfType}$ occurs free in $\texttt{inst}$, $\texttt{meth}$, $\texttt{IV}$, $\texttt{M}$, $\mathcal{C}$, or $\mathcal{E}$.

Figure 16.9 Typing rules for classes and subclasses in *MOOL*.

an identifer that will eventually be interpreted as MyType, the type of self from outside the object.

As before, in type checking method bodies, $\mathcal{E}$ is extended to include a type for self, and the function close is also added with type SelfType $\rightarrow$ MT. As mentioned earlier, in the source language, the type checker would generally be smart enough to be able to insert close automatically wherever it is needed so that the user would not even have to be aware of it. See the example in the next section.

Even though M' and IVR' are introduced in new constraints, they may not appear in the methods or instance variables. Rather the identifier MT, whose definition in $\mathcal{C}'$ involves M', replaces MyType in instance variables and method bodies when they are type checked. Notice that

$$\mathcal{C}' \vdash \text{MT} <\!\!\# \text{ObjectType M(MyType)}$$

because $\mathcal{C}' \vdash \text{M}' <: \text{M}$ and $\mathcal{C}'(\text{MT}) = \text{ObjectType M'(MyType)}$. Similarly

$$\mathcal{C}' \vdash \text{SelfType} <\!\!\#_{vis} \text{VisObjectType}(\text{IV}^{ref}(\text{MyType}), \text{M(MyType)})$$

because of the definition of SelfType, $\mathcal{C}' \vdash \text{IVR}' <: \text{IV}^{ref}$, and $\mathcal{C}' \vdash \text{M}' <: \text{M}$.

When the user is checking to see whether the instance variables and methods type check, it will generally be by using these matching relations rather than the higher-order subtyping. Anything provable from these matching relations will also be provable from $\mathcal{C}'$. When presenting this system to a programmer, only these relations (rather than the higher-order subtyping) will normally be presented in explaining how programs are type checked. The stronger rule presented here is needed only for the proof of soundness of the type system.

Later we will show how to translate class expressions to the extended lambda calculus, and that our translation is sound. For now we simply remark that, as in $\mathcal{SOOL}$, the constraints on the type functions used in defining SelfType and MyType ensure that methods that type check correctly in a class will remain type safe in all possible subclasses.

The type-checking rule for subclasses is obtained from the previous rule for type checking subclasses in a way similar to the changes made for classes. As before, we have not included the use of super in type checking subclasses. It can be added similarly to the way indicated in Section 14.1.

The new rules for message sending and instance variable access are given in Figure 16.10. One change in the new message-sending rule is that the type of an expression representing sending a message to an object is the type of

Message
$$\frac{\mathcal{C}, \mathcal{E} \vdash \texttt{E: U}, \quad \mathcal{C} \vdash \texttt{U} <\!\!\# \texttt{ObjectType } \{\!|\, \texttt{m: T(MyType)}\,|\!\}}{\mathcal{C}, \mathcal{E} \vdash \texttt{E} \Leftarrow \texttt{m: T(U)}}$$

Inst Vble
$$\frac{\mathcal{C}, \mathcal{E} \vdash \texttt{E: U}, \quad \mathcal{C} \vdash \texttt{U} <\!\!\#_{vis} \texttt{VisObjectType}(\{\!|\, \texttt{l: T(MyType)}\,|\!\}, \{\!|\,\,|\!\})}{\mathcal{C}, \mathcal{E} \vdash \texttt{E.l: T(V)}}$$

where $\mathcal{C}(\texttt{U}) = \texttt{VisObjectType}(\texttt{IVR(MyType)}, \texttt{M(MyType)})$, for some type
constructors $\texttt{IVR}$ and $\texttt{M}$, and $\texttt{V}$ is a type such that $\mathcal{C}(\texttt{V}) = \texttt{ObjectType}$
$\texttt{M(MyType)}$.

VisObj Message
$$\frac{\mathcal{C}, \mathcal{E} \vdash \texttt{E: U}, \quad \mathcal{C} \vdash \texttt{U} <\!\!\#_{vis} \texttt{VisObjectType}(\{\!|\,\,|\!\}, \{\!|\, \texttt{m: T(MyType)}\,|\!\})}{\mathcal{C}, \mathcal{E} \vdash \texttt{E} \Leftarrow \texttt{m: T(V)}}$$

where $\mathcal{C}(\texttt{U}) = \texttt{VisObjectType}(\texttt{IVR(MyType)}, \texttt{M(MyType)})$, for some type
constructors $\texttt{IVR}$ and $\texttt{M}$, and $\texttt{V}$ is a type such that $\mathcal{C}(\texttt{V}) = \texttt{ObjectType}$
$\texttt{M(MyType)}$.

Figure 16.10 Typing rules for message sending and instance variables in $\mathcal{MOOL}$.

the method, updated so that all occurrences of MyType are replaced by the
type of the receiver. For example, if n: NodeType and the type of method
getNext in NodeType is Void → MyType, then the type of n ⇐ getNext
is Void → NodeType. Similarly, n ⇐ setNext has type NodeType → Void
because setNext has type MyType → Void. In each case, all occurrences
of MyType in the method signature are replaced by the type of the receiver,
NodeType.

As before, we have generalized the hypothesis for the type-checking rule
for message sends to handle the case in which the only information known
about the type of the methods in the receiver is via an upper bound with
respect to the matching ordering. This generalized form is used when we
send a message to an object with type MyType.

For example, in the body of method setNext of DoubleNodeClass, the
method setPrevious is sent to instance variable newNext of type MyType.
When type checking the class, the type constraints include the information
that MyType <# DoubleNodeType, where DoubleNodeType includes the
method setPrevious with type MyType → Void. As a result, the type

of newNext $\Leftarrow$ setPrevious is MyType $\rightarrow$ Void,[5] and hence the type of newNext $\Leftarrow$ setPrevious(close(self)) is Void.

This new rule for type checking message passing formalizes the earlier discussion of MyType and message sending, and should make intuitive sense in that MyType is supposed to stand for the type of the receiver of a message. Thus when we actually know the receiver and its type, we can replace MyType by the actual type. Because the keyword MyType is a bound variable inside the object type, it would be a serious mistake to allow it as a free variable in the type of the message send expression. Thus we must replace it when the type of the method is extracted from the object type.

The rules for extracting instance variables and sending messages to expressions whose types are visible object types are similar. Note that while the expression itself has a visible object type, U, we must replace occurrences of MyType in the method body or instance variable by the object type, V, which corresponds to the visible object type, U. A consequence of this correspondence is that a value of object type V is obtained by applying close to an expression of type U.

In practice, each of these rules will typically only be applied in type checking the body of methods when the receiver, E, is actually the expression self with type SelfType. In this case, SelfType corresponds to U, and MT will be the corresponding V to be substituted for MyType in the conclusion of the rule. (After all, MT = ObjectType M'(MyType), and SelfType = VisObjectType(IVR'(MyType),M'(MyType)) in $\mathcal{C}'$.)

Rather than writing a rule that applies only to self: SelfType, we have included a more general rule. However, the simplified rules for when we have an expression of type SelfType are given below.

$$\textit{Inst Vble} \quad \frac{\mathcal{C}, \mathcal{E} \vdash \text{E: SelfType,} \quad \mathcal{C} \vdash \text{SelfType} <\#_{vis} \text{VisObjectType}(\{\!| \text{ l: T(MyType)}|\!\}, \{\!| \; |\!\})}{\mathcal{C}, \mathcal{E} \vdash \text{E.l: T(MT)}}$$

where close: SelfType $\rightarrow$ MT $\in \mathcal{E}$, MT = ObjectType M'(MyType) $\in \mathcal{C}$,

---

5. We have replaced all occurrences of MyType by the type of the receiver, MyType, so it looks like we haven't made any changes. However, we followed the type-checking rule and made the required replacement of all occurrences of MyType in the type of the method by the type of the receiver, also MyType, which doesn't actually change anything!

and SelfType $=$ VisObjectType(IVR'(MyType), M'(MyType)) $\in \mathcal{C}$ for some type constructor identifiers, IVR' and M'.

$$
\textit{VisObj Message} \quad \frac{\begin{array}{c} \mathcal{C}, \mathcal{E} \vdash \text{E: SelfType,} \\ \mathcal{C} \vdash \text{SelfType} <\#_{vis} \\ \text{VisObjectType}(\{\!| \;|\!\}, \{\!| \text{ m: } \text{T(MyType)} |\!\}) \end{array}}{\mathcal{C}, \mathcal{E} \vdash \text{E} \Leftarrow \text{ m: T(MT)}}
$$

where close: SelfType $\rightarrow$ MT $\in \mathcal{E}$, MT $=$ ObjectType M'(MyType) $\in \mathcal{C}$, and SelfType $=$ VisObjectType(IVR'(MyType), M'(MyType)) $\in \mathcal{C}$ for some type constructor identifiers, IVR' and M'.

16.3 Translational semantics of $\mathcal{MOOL}$

The translation of $\mathcal{MOOL}$ into $\Lambda^{P}_{<:}$ is only a bit more complex than before. One of the main differences is that the types of methods and instance variables are parameterized by MyType. Thus in the translation of classes and their types we will use subtyping on functions from types to types rather than just on simple types. We must also take a fixed point in order to obtain the meaning of MyType.

The translations of type expressions and type constructor constraint systems are mutually recursive. We will begin with the translation of type constructor constraint systems. Our definition will follow the cases in the definition of type constructor constraint systems. Let $\mathcal{C}'$ be a type constructor constraint system. Then,

1. $\mathcal{T}_{\mathcal{C}'}[\![\emptyset]\!] \triangleq \emptyset$.

2. If $\mathcal{C} \cup \{x^{\kappa} = \text{G}\}$ is a type constructor constraint system, then
$\mathcal{T}_{\mathcal{C}'}[\![\mathcal{C} \cup \{x^{\kappa} = \text{G}\}]\!] \triangleq \mathcal{T}_{\mathcal{C}'}[\![\mathcal{C}]\!]$.

3. If $\mathcal{C} \cup \{x^{\kappa} <: \text{G}\}$ is a type constructor constraint system, then
$\mathcal{T}_{\mathcal{C}'}[\![\mathcal{C} \cup \{x^{\kappa} <: \text{G}\}]\!] \triangleq \mathcal{T}_{\mathcal{C}'}[\![\mathcal{C}]\!] \cup \{x^{\kappa} <: \mathcal{T}_{\mathcal{C}'}[\![\text{G}]\!]\}$.

As before, type definitions are defined away, and subtype constraints are translated in a straightforward way.

The translation of $\mathcal{E}$ is simply done pointwise. That is, $(x : T) \in \mathcal{E}$ iff $(x : \mathcal{T}_{\mathcal{C}}[\![T]\!]) \in \mathcal{T}_{\mathcal{C}}[\![\mathcal{E}]\!]$.

$$\mathcal{T}_C [\![\texttt{TpFunc(t).U}]\!] \triangleq \lambda(t).\,\mathcal{T}_C [\![\texttt{U}]\!],$$

$$\mathcal{T}_C [\![\texttt{F (U)}]\!] \triangleq \mathcal{T}_C [\![\texttt{F}]\!] (\mathcal{T}_C [\![\texttt{U}]\!])$$

$$\mathcal{T}_C [\![\texttt{ObjectType M(MyType)}]\!] \triangleq Obj\,(\mathcal{T}_C [\![\texttt{M}]\!])$$

$$\mathcal{T}_C [\![\texttt{VisObjectType(IVR(MyType),M(MyType))}]\!] \triangleq$$
$$VisObj\,(\mathcal{T}_C [\![\texttt{IVR}]\!] (Obj\,(\mathcal{T}_C [\![\texttt{M}]\!])),\,\mathcal{T}_C [\![\texttt{M}]\!] (Obj\,(\mathcal{T}_C [\![\texttt{M}]\!])))$$

$$\mathcal{T}_C [\![\texttt{ClassType(IV(MyType),M(MyType))}]\!] \triangleq$$
$$\forall (M' <:\, \mathcal{T}_C [\![\texttt{M}]\!]).\, \forall (IVR' <:\, \mathcal{T}_C [\![\texttt{IV}^{ref}]\!]).$$
$$\mathcal{T}_C [\![\texttt{IV}]\!] (Obj\,(M')) \times$$
$$(VisObj\,(IVR'(Obj\,(M')),M'(Obj\,(M'))) \to \mathcal{T}_C [\![\texttt{M}]\!] (Obj\,(M')))$$

where

$$Obj\,(M) \triangleq Fix(\lambda MT.\,\exists Y.\,Y \times (Y \to M(MT)))$$
$$= \exists Y.\,Y \times (Y \to M(Obj\,(M))).$$

$$VisObj\,(IVR,M) \triangleq IVR \times (IVR \to M).$$

Figure 16.11   Translation of new types and constructors.

Figure 16.11 contains the translations of the new types and type constructors of $\mathcal{MOOL}$, as well as those that changed because of the addition of My-Type. Most of the basic non-object types are interpreted as before, and hence are not included in the figure.

The translation of type functions is straightforward as they are simply translated pointwise. Type function applications are also translated as the application of the translation of the function applied to the translation of the argument.

In the following paragraphs, let IV, M:: $* \Rightarrow *$ represent type functions that, when provided with the meaning of MyType, return the types of the records of instance variables and methods of an object. (See the examples of NodeIV and NodeM in Section 16.2.)

Before the introduction of MyType, visible object types were translated as pairs of the type of instance variables and method suite (parameterized by the instance variables). Object types were defined similarly except that the type of the record of instance variables was abstracted away using an existential type. The only thing different here is that we must interpret MyType. Because MyType is supposed to represent the type of the object, we can define it using a recursive type. Thus the translation of object types in the figure begins with a fixed point on a type variable, MT, representing MyType:

$$\mathcal{T}_C[\![\texttt{ObjectType M(MyType)}]\!] \triangleq Fix(\lambda MT. \exists Y. Y \times (Y \rightarrow \mathcal{T}_C[\![\texttt{M}]\!](MT)))$$

The definition in the figure has been simplified by using the updated abbreviation for $Obj(M)$ contained in the figure.

Because of the strong hypotheses in the Fix rule in Figure 9.6 for proving subtyping of recursive types, knowing that M' $<:$ M (as functions from types to types) is *not* sufficient to guarantee that

$$\mathcal{T}_C[\![\texttt{ObjectType M'(MyType)}]\!] <: \mathcal{T}_C[\![\texttt{ObjectType M(MyType)}]\!],$$

unless the type argument of M (representing MyType) occurs only positively, *i.e.*, as a return type, in M.

In the interpretation of "visible object types", MyType will again be interpreted as $Obj(\mathcal{T}_C[\![\texttt{M}]\!])$, but now the types of the instance variables will also be visible.

$$\mathcal{T}_C[\![\texttt{VisObjectType(IVR(MyType), M(MyType))}]\!] \triangleq$$
$$\mathcal{T}_C[\![\texttt{IVR}]\!](Obj(\mathcal{T}_C[\![\texttt{M}]\!])) \times (\mathcal{T}_C[\![\texttt{IVR}]\!](Obj(\mathcal{T}_C[\![\texttt{M}]\!])) \rightarrow \mathcal{T}_C[\![\texttt{M}]\!](Obj(\mathcal{T}_C[\![\texttt{M}]\!]))).$$

(Recall that we use IVR to suggest that this is the type of the record of instance *variables* rather than just their values.) The definition in the figure utilizes the (old) abbreviation $VisObj(IVR,M)$ to simplify notation.

As before, the meaning of classes is parameterized by the types of all possible subclasses. Again, because both $\mathcal{T}_C[\![\texttt{IV}]\!]$ and $\mathcal{T}_C[\![\texttt{M}]\!]$ are functions from types to types, they will need to be applied to the meaning of MyType in the subclass, $Obj(M')$. Moreover, the bounded quantification in the translation of class types is based on subtyping of functions from types to types.

As with the earlier translation of classes, the translation is parameterized over all extensions of the types of the instance *variables* (not just the types of their *values*) and methods, and returns a pair composed of the record of initial *values* and the methods, where the methods are parameterized by the meaning of self (which has type $VisObj(IVR'(Obj(M')),M'(Obj(M')))$).

Comparing this definition with the one given in Section 12.1, the main differences are that IV and M are now functions from types to types, and thus $\mathcal{T}_C[\![\,\text{IV}\,]\!]$ and $\mathcal{T}_C[\![\text{M}]\!]$ must be applied to $Obj(M')$ in order to provide the interpretation of MyType.

We now provide the new translations of expressions for $\mathcal{MOOL}$. The translation of most expressions is the same as for $\mathcal{SOOL}$. The only ones that have changed are for classes, subclasses, new expressions, message sending, and access to instance variables.

$$\mathcal{C}, \mathcal{E} \vdash closeobj : \forall IVR. \forall M. VisObj(IVR(Obj(M)), M(Obj(M)))) \to Obj(M)$$

Thus the interpretation of close is a function with type $\mathcal{T}_C[\![\text{SelfType}]\!] \to \mathcal{T}_C[\![\text{MyType}]\!]$.

The new translation of classes, subclasses, and new expressions is given in Figure 16.12. In the translation for both classes and subclasses, the type parameters M' and IVR' now represent functions from types to types. Notice also that the interpretation of MyType in both instance variables and methods is $Obj(M')$. Thus MyType is interpreted as the type of objects generated when the type function determining the type of the method suite is M'. Similarly, SelfType is interpreted as $VisObj(IVR'(Obj(M')), M'(Obj(M')))$, the visible object type that results when the type function determining the type of the instance variables is IVR', and the type function M' determines the type of the methods. Notice that we follow our earlier convention and translate classes and subclasses as having the most expressive type, *i.e.*, the one that includes all instance variables and methods.

The expression close, which may occur in method definitions, is interpreted as an instantiation of the function *closeobj*, which was defined in Section 11.2, and takes visible object types to object types.

16.4   Soundness of translation for $\mathcal{MOOL}$

In this section we show that the translational semantics for $\mathcal{MOOL}$ is sound. We will not bother to repeat the portions of the proof that are nearly identical to those for $\mathcal{SOOL}$, but instead focus on the new encoding of classes and objects. We begin by showing the preservation of subtyping.

Theorem 16.4.1 *Let* S *and* T *be type constructor expressions of* $\mathcal{MOOL}$ *such that* $\mathcal{C} \vdash \text{S} <: \text{T}$. *Then* $\mathcal{T}_C[\![\mathcal{C}]\!] \vdash \mathcal{T}_C[\![\text{S}]\!] <: \mathcal{T}_C[\![\text{T}]\!]$.

Proof. We only provide the proof for object types. The other cases are easy.

$$\mathcal{T}_C[\![\,\mathcal{C}, \mathcal{E} \vdash \texttt{class}\,(\texttt{inst}\,[\texttt{MyType}], \texttt{meth}\,[\texttt{MyType}]\,[\texttt{SelfType}]):$$
$$\texttt{ClassType}\,(\texttt{IV}(\texttt{MyType}), \texttt{M}(\texttt{MyType}))]\!] \triangleq$$
$$\Lambda(M' <: \mathcal{T}_C[\![\texttt{M}]\!]).\Lambda(IVR' <: \mathcal{T}_C[\![\texttt{IV}^{ref}]\!]).$$
$$\langle \mathcal{T}_{C'}[\![\mathcal{C}', \mathcal{E} \vdash \texttt{inst}\,[\texttt{MyType}]: \texttt{IV}(\texttt{MyType})]\!], methfun \rangle$$

where $MyType = Obj\,(M')$, $SelfType = VisObj\,(IVR'(MyType), M'(MyType))$,
$methfun = \lambda(self: SelfType).$
$$\text{let } close: SelfType \to \exists Y.\, VisObj\,(Y, M'(MyType))$$
$$= closeobj\,[IVR'(MyType)]\,[M'(MyType)]$$
$$\text{in } \mathcal{T}_{C'}[\![\mathcal{C}', \mathcal{E}' \vdash \texttt{meth}\,[\texttt{MyType}]\,[\texttt{SelfType}]: \texttt{M}(\texttt{MyType})]\!].$$
$\mathcal{C}' = \mathcal{C} \cup \{M' <: M, IVR' <: IV^{ref}, MT = \texttt{ObjectType M}'(\texttt{MyType}),$
$\texttt{SelfType} = \texttt{VisObjectType}\,(IVR'(\texttt{MyType}), M'(\texttt{MyType}))\}$

$$\mathcal{T}_C[\![\mathcal{C}, \mathcal{E} \vdash \texttt{class inherits E modifies } \texttt{l}_{i_1},\ldots,\texttt{l}_{i_m}$$
$$(\texttt{inst}\,[\texttt{MyType}], \texttt{meth}\,[\texttt{MyType}]\,[\texttt{SelfType}]):$$
$$\texttt{ClassType}\,(\texttt{IV}(\texttt{MyType}), \texttt{M}(\texttt{MyType}))]\!] \triangleq$$
$$\Lambda(M' <: \mathcal{T}_C[\![\texttt{M}]\!]).\Lambda(IVR' <: \mathcal{T}_C[\![\texttt{IV}^{ref}]\!]).\langle inst_{all}, methfun_{all} \rangle$$

where $MyType = Obj\,(M')$, $SelfType = VisObj\,(IVR'(MyType), M'(MyType))$,
$inst_{sup} = proj_1($
$$\mathcal{T}_C[\![\mathcal{C}, \mathcal{E} \vdash \texttt{E: ClassType}\,(\texttt{IV}_{sup}(\texttt{MyType}), \texttt{M}_{sup}(\texttt{MyType}))]\!]$$
$$[M']\,[IVR']),$$
$inst_{all} = inst_{sup} \oplus \mathcal{T}_{C'}[\![\mathcal{C}', \mathcal{E} \vdash \texttt{inst}\,[\texttt{MyType}]: \texttt{IV}_{sub}(\texttt{MyType})]\!]$,
$methfun_{sup} = proj_2(\,\mathcal{T}_C[\![\texttt{E}]\!]\,[M']\,[IVR'])$,
$methfun_{all} = \lambda(self: SelfType).$
$$\text{let } close: SelfType \to \exists Y.\, VisObj\,(Y, M'(MyType))$$
$$= closeobj\,[IVR'(MyType)]\,[M'(MyType)]$$
$$\text{in } methfun_{sup}\,(self) \oplus$$
$$\mathcal{T}_{C'}[\![\mathcal{C}', \mathcal{E}' \vdash \texttt{meth}\,[\texttt{MyType}]\,[\texttt{SelfType}]: \texttt{M}_{sub}(\texttt{MyType})]\!].$$

$$\mathcal{T}_C[\![\mathcal{C}, \mathcal{E} \vdash \texttt{new C: ObjectType M}(\texttt{MyType})]\!] \triangleq$$
$$closeobj\,[IVR]\,[M](\langle inst^{ref}, methfun' \rangle).$$

where $MyType = Obj\,(\mathcal{T}_C[\![\texttt{M}]\!])$, $IVR = \mathcal{T}_C[\![\texttt{IV}^{ref}]\!](MyType)$, $M = \mathcal{T}_C[\![\texttt{M}]\!](MyType)$,
$c = \mathcal{T}_C[\![\mathcal{C}, \mathcal{E} \vdash \texttt{C: ClassType}\,(\texttt{IV}(\texttt{MyType}), \texttt{M}(\texttt{MyType}))]\!]$
$$[\mathcal{T}_C[\![\texttt{M}]\!]]\,[\mathcal{T}_C[\![\texttt{IV}^{ref}]\!]],$$
$inst = proj_1(c)$, $methfun = proj_2(c)$,
$inst^{ref}$ is formed by adding ref's to all fields of $inst$,
$methfun' = \underline{fix}\,[IVR \to M]\,\lambda(fm: IVR \to M).\lambda(inst': IVR).$
$$methfun(\langle inst', fm \rangle).$$

Figure 16.12   Translation of classes and subclasses of $\mathcal{MOOL}$ to $\Lambda^P_{<:}$.

Suppose $\mathcal{C} \vdash$ `ObjectType M'(MyType)` $<:$ `ObjectType M(MyType)`. By the subtyping rules for $\mathcal{MOOL}$, this can only occur if $\mathcal{C}' \vdash$ `M'(MT')` $<:$ `M(MT)` where $\mathcal{C}' = \mathcal{C} \cup \{$`MT'` $<:$ `MT`$\}$.

By induction, $\mathcal{T}_{\mathcal{C}'}[\![\mathcal{C}']\!] \vdash \mathcal{T}_{\mathcal{C}'}[\![$`M'(MT')`$]\!] <: \mathcal{T}_{\mathcal{C}'}[\![$`M(MT)`$]\!]$. By Lemma 13.1.2, it follows that $\mathcal{T}_{\mathcal{C}'}[\![$`F`$]\!] = \mathcal{T}_{\mathcal{C}}[\![$`F`$]\!]$, for all constructors `F`. By this, the function and product type subtyping rules of $\Lambda^P_{<:}$, it follows that

$$\mathcal{T}_{\mathcal{C}}[\![\mathcal{C}']\!] \vdash Y \times (Y \to \mathcal{T}_{\mathcal{C}}[\![$`M'(MT')`$]\!]) <: Y \times (Y \to \mathcal{T}_{\mathcal{C}}[\![$`M(MT)`$]\!]).$$

Because $\mathcal{T}_{\mathcal{C}}[\![\mathcal{C}']\!] = \mathcal{T}_{\mathcal{C}'}[\![\mathcal{C}]\!] \cup \{MT' <: MT\}$, $\mathcal{T}_{\mathcal{C}}[\![$`M'(MT')`$]\!] = \mathcal{T}_{\mathcal{C}}[\![$`M'`$]\!](MyType')$, and $\mathcal{T}_{\mathcal{C}}[\![$`M(MT)`$]\!] = \mathcal{T}_{\mathcal{C}}[\![$`M`$]\!](MyType)$

$$\mathcal{T}_{\mathcal{C}}[\![\mathcal{C}]\!] \cup \{MT' <: MT\} \vdash Y \times (Y \to \mathcal{T}_{\mathcal{C}}[\![$`M'`$]\!](MyType')) <:$$
$$Y \times (Y \to \mathcal{T}_{\mathcal{C}}[\![$`M`$]\!](MyType)).$$

Then, by rule *Exist* $_{<:}$,

$$\mathcal{T}_{\mathcal{C}}[\![\mathcal{C}]\!] \cup \{MT' <: MT\} \vdash \exists Y. Y \times (Y \to \mathcal{T}_{\mathcal{C}}[\![$`M'`$]\!](MT')) <:$$
$$\exists Y. Y \times (Y \to \mathcal{T}_{\mathcal{C}}[\![$`M`$]\!](MT)).$$

Finally by the subtyping rule for recursive types, *Fix* $_{<:}$,

$$\mathcal{T}_{\mathcal{C}}[\![\mathcal{C}]\!] \vdash Fix(\lambda MyType. \exists Y. Y \times (Y \to \mathcal{T}_{\mathcal{C}}[\![$`M'`$]\!](MyType))) <:$$
$$Fix(\lambda MyType. \exists Y. Y \times (Y \to \mathcal{T}_{\mathcal{C}}[\![$`M`$]\!](MyType))).$$

But this simply shows that

$$\mathcal{T}_{\mathcal{C}}[\![\mathcal{C}]\!] \vdash \mathcal{T}_{\mathcal{C}}[\![$`ObjectType M'(MyType)`$]\!] <: \mathcal{T}_{\mathcal{C}}[\![$`ObjectType M(MyType)`$]\!].$$

■

Now that we know that the translation preserves subtypes, we continue to show that the translation preserves the types of expressions.

Theorem 16.4.2 *Suppose* $\mathcal{C}, \mathcal{E} \vdash$ `E`: `S`. *Then* $\mathcal{T}_{\mathcal{C}}[\![\mathcal{C}]\!], \mathcal{T}_{\mathcal{C}}[\![\mathcal{E}]\!] \vdash \mathcal{T}_{\mathcal{C}}[\![$`E`$]\!]$: $\mathcal{T}_{\mathcal{C}}[\![$`S`$]\!]$.

Proof. As before, the proof will be by induction on the proof of the typing of expressions. Most of the proof proceeds just like Theorem 13.1.10. We will only include here those parts of the proof that have changed.

Class   Suppose that

$$\mathcal{C}, \mathcal{E} \vdash \texttt{class (inst[MyType], meth[MyType][SelfType])}:$$
$$\texttt{ClassType(IV(MyType), M(MyType))}$$

because

$$\mathcal{C}', \mathcal{E} \vdash \texttt{inst}\,[\texttt{MT}]\colon \texttt{IV}\,(\texttt{MT})$$

and

$$\mathcal{C}', \mathcal{E}' \vdash \texttt{meth}\,[\texttt{MT}]\,[\texttt{SelfType}]\colon \texttt{M}\,(\texttt{MT})$$

where

- $\mathcal{C}' \triangleq \mathcal{C} \cup \{\texttt{M}' <: \texttt{M}, \texttt{IVR}' <: \texttt{IV}^{ref}, \texttt{MT} = \texttt{ObjectType}\,\texttt{M}'\,(\texttt{MyType}),$
  $\texttt{SelfType} = \texttt{VisObjectType}\,(\texttt{IVR}'\,(\texttt{MyType}), \texttt{M}'\,(\texttt{MyType}))\,\}$,

- $\mathcal{E}' \triangleq \mathcal{E} \cup \{\texttt{self}\colon \texttt{SelfType}, \texttt{close}\colon \texttt{SelfType} \to \texttt{MT}\,\}$, and

- none of $\texttt{M}'$, $\texttt{IVR}'$, $\texttt{MT}$, or $\texttt{SelfType}$ occurs free in $\texttt{inst}$, $\texttt{meth}$, $\texttt{IV}$, $\texttt{M}$, $\mathcal{C}$, or $\mathcal{E}$.

Now

$$\mathcal{T}_{\mathcal{C}}[\![\texttt{class}\,(\texttt{inst}\,[\texttt{MyType}], \texttt{meth}\,[\texttt{MyType}]\,[\texttt{SelfType}])]\!] \triangleq$$
$$\Lambda(M' <: \mathcal{T}_{\mathcal{C}}[\![\texttt{M}]\!]).\Lambda(IVR' <: \mathcal{T}_{\mathcal{C}}[\![\texttt{IV}^{ref}]\!]).$$
$$\langle \mathcal{T}_{\mathcal{C}'}[\![\texttt{inst}]\!]\,[MyType], methfun \rangle$$

where $MyType = Obj\,(M')$,

$SelfType = VisObj\,(IVR'\,(MyType), M'\,(MyType))$,

$methfun = \lambda(self\colon SelfType).$
$\quad\quad\quad\quad let\ close\colon SelfType \to \exists Y.\,VisObj\,(Y, M'\,(MyType))$
$\quad\quad\quad\quad\quad = closeobj\,[IVR'\,(MyType)]\,[M'\,(MyType)]$
$\quad\quad\quad\quad in\ \mathcal{T}_{\mathcal{C}'}[\![\texttt{meth}]\!]\,[MyType]\,[SelfType].$

Also

$$\mathcal{T}_{\mathcal{C}}[\![\texttt{ClassType}\,(\texttt{IV}(\texttt{MyType}), \texttt{M}(\texttt{MyType}))]\!] \triangleq$$
$$\forall(M' <: \mathcal{T}_{\mathcal{C}}[\![\texttt{M}]\!]).\,\forall(IVR' <: \mathcal{T}_{\mathcal{C}}[\![\texttt{IV}^{ref}]\!]).$$
$$\mathcal{T}_{\mathcal{C}}[\![\texttt{IV}]\!]\,(Obj\,(M')) \times$$
$$(VisObj\,(IVR'\,(Obj\,(M')), M'\,(Obj\,(M'))) \to \mathcal{T}_{\mathcal{C}}[\![\texttt{M}]\!]\,(Obj\,(M')))$$

For simplicity, we will use the abbreviations for *MyType*, *SelfType*, and *meth* for the rest of this part of the proof. For example, we can rewrite the above equation as:

$$\mathcal{T}_{\mathcal{C}}[\![\texttt{ClassType}\,(\texttt{IV}(\texttt{MyType}), \texttt{M}(\texttt{MyType}))]\!] \triangleq$$
$$\forall(M' <: \mathcal{T}_{\mathcal{C}}[\![\texttt{M}]\!]).\,\forall(IVR' <: \mathcal{T}_{\mathcal{C}}[\![\texttt{IV}^{ref}]\!]).$$
$$\mathcal{T}_{\mathcal{C}}[\![\texttt{IV}]\!]\,(MyType) \times (SelfType \to \mathcal{T}_{\mathcal{C}}[\![\texttt{M}]\!]\,(MyType)).$$

By induction,

$$\mathcal{T}_{\mathcal{C}'}[\![\mathcal{C}']\!], \mathcal{T}_{\mathcal{C}'}[\![\mathcal{E}]\!] \vdash \mathcal{T}_{\mathcal{C}'}[\![\texttt{inst}\,[\texttt{MT}]]\!] \colon \mathcal{T}_{\mathcal{C}'}[\![\texttt{IV}(\texttt{MT})]\!]$$

and

$$\mathcal{T}_{\mathcal{C}'}[\![\mathcal{C}']\!], \mathcal{T}_{\mathcal{C}'}[\![\mathcal{E}']\!] \vdash \mathcal{T}_{\mathcal{C}'}[\![\texttt{meth}\,[\texttt{MT}]\,[\texttt{SelfType}]]\!] \colon \mathcal{T}_{\mathcal{C}'}[\![\texttt{M}(\texttt{MT})]\!],$$

By the definition of the translation of type variables,

$$\mathcal{T}_{\mathcal{C}'}[\![\texttt{IV}(\texttt{MT})]\!] = \mathcal{T}_{\mathcal{C}'}[\![\texttt{IV}]\!](Obj\,(M')) = \mathcal{T}_{\mathcal{C}'}[\![\texttt{IV}]\!](MyType)$$

and

$$\mathcal{T}_{\mathcal{C}'}[\![\texttt{M}(\texttt{MT})]\!] = \mathcal{T}_{\mathcal{C}'}[\![\texttt{M}]\!](Obj\,(M')) = \mathcal{T}_{\mathcal{C}'}[\![\texttt{M}]\!](MyType).$$

Also,

$$\mathcal{T}_{\mathcal{C}'}[\![\texttt{inst}\,[\texttt{MT}]]\!] = \mathcal{T}_{\mathcal{C}}[\![\texttt{inst}]\!][Obj\,(M')] = \mathcal{T}_{\mathcal{C}}[\![\texttt{inst}]\!][MyType],$$

and

$$\begin{aligned}
\mathcal{T}_{\mathcal{C}'}&[\![\texttt{meth}\,[\texttt{MT}]\,[\texttt{SelfType}]]\!] \\
&= \mathcal{T}_{\mathcal{C}}[\![\texttt{meth}]\!][Obj\,(M')][VisObj\,(IVR'\,(Obj\,(M')), M'(Obj\,(M')))] \\
&= \mathcal{T}_{\mathcal{C}}[\![\texttt{meth}]\!][MyType][SelfType].
\end{aligned}$$

Thus,

$$\mathcal{T}_{\mathcal{C}'}[\![\mathcal{C}']\!], \mathcal{T}_{\mathcal{C}'}[\![\mathcal{E}]\!] \vdash \mathcal{T}_{\mathcal{C}}[\![\texttt{inst}]\!][MyType] \colon \mathcal{T}_{\mathcal{C}'}[\![\texttt{IV}]\!](MyType)$$

and

$$\mathcal{T}_{\mathcal{C}'}[\![\mathcal{C}']\!], \mathcal{T}_{\mathcal{C}'}[\![\mathcal{E}']\!] \vdash \mathcal{T}_{\mathcal{C}'}[\![\texttt{meth}]\!][MyType][SelfType] \colon \mathcal{T}_{\mathcal{C}'}[\![\texttt{M}]\!](MyType).$$

Now

$$\begin{aligned}
\mathcal{T}_{\mathcal{C}'}[\![\mathcal{C}']\!] &= \mathcal{T}_{\mathcal{C}'}[\![\mathcal{C} \cup \{\texttt{M}' <: \texttt{M},\, \texttt{IVR}' <: \texttt{IV}^{ref}, \\
&\qquad \texttt{MT} = \texttt{ObjectType}\,\texttt{M}'\,(\texttt{MyType}), \\
&\qquad \texttt{SelfType} = \texttt{VisObjectType}(\texttt{IVR}'(\texttt{MyType}), \texttt{M}'(\texttt{MyType}))\}]\!] \\
&= \mathcal{T}_{\mathcal{C}'}[\![\mathcal{C}]\!] \cup \{M' <: \mathcal{T}_{\mathcal{C}'}[\![\texttt{M}]\!], IVR' <: \mathcal{T}_{\mathcal{C}'}[\![\texttt{IV}^{ref}]\!]\} \\
&= \mathcal{T}_{\mathcal{C}}[\![\mathcal{C}]\!] \cup \{M' <: \mathcal{T}_{\mathcal{C}}[\![\texttt{M}]\!], IVR' <: \mathcal{T}_{\mathcal{C}}[\![\texttt{IV}^{ref}]\!]\}
\end{aligned}$$

and

$$\begin{aligned}
\mathcal{T}_{\mathcal{C}'}[\![\mathcal{E}']\!] &= \mathcal{T}_{\mathcal{C}'}[\![\mathcal{E} \cup \{\texttt{self}\colon \texttt{SelfType}, \texttt{close}\colon \texttt{SelfType} \to \texttt{MT}\}]\!] \\
&= \mathcal{T}_{\mathcal{C}}[\![\mathcal{E}]\!] \cup \{self\colon SelfType, close\colon SelfType \to MyType\}.
\end{aligned}$$

In each of the above derivations, we can replace expressions of the form $\mathcal{T}_{\mathcal{C}'}[\![\ldots]\!]$ by $\mathcal{T}_{\mathcal{C}}[\![\ldots]\!]$ in the last line because the argument of $\mathcal{T}_{\mathcal{C}}[\![\ldots]\!]$ involves only type variables already in $\mathcal{C}$.

Recall that

$$methfun \triangleq \lambda(self\colon SelfType).$$
$$\text{let } close\colon SelfType \rightarrow \exists Y. VisObj\,(Y, M'(MyType))$$
$$= closeobj\,[IVR'(MyType)]\,[M'(MyType)]$$
$$\text{in } \mathcal{T}_{\mathcal{C}}[\![\texttt{meth}]\!]\,[MyType]\,[SelfType].$$

By the *Let* and *Function* typing rules,

$$\mathcal{T}_{\mathcal{C}'}[\![\mathcal{C}']\!], \mathcal{T}_{\mathcal{C}}[\![\mathcal{E}]\!] \vdash methfun\colon SelfType \rightarrow \mathcal{T}_{\mathcal{C}}[\![\texttt{M}]\!](MyType).$$

It follows from the above and the type-checking rules *Function* and *Pair* of $\Lambda_{<:}^{P}$ that

$$\mathcal{T}_{\mathcal{C}'}[\![\mathcal{C}']\!], \mathcal{T}_{\mathcal{C}}[\![\mathcal{E}]\!] \vdash \langle \mathcal{T}_{\mathcal{C}}[\![\texttt{inst}]\!], methfun \rangle\colon$$
$$\mathcal{T}_{\mathcal{C}}[\![\texttt{IV}]\!](MyType) \times (SelfType \rightarrow \mathcal{T}_{\mathcal{C}}[\![\texttt{M}]\!](MyType))$$

Finally, by the type-checking rule *BdPolyFunc* in Figure 9.9,

$$\mathcal{T}_{\mathcal{C}}[\![\mathcal{C}]\!], \mathcal{T}_{\mathcal{C}}[\![\mathcal{E}]\!] \vdash \Lambda(M' <: \mathcal{T}_{\mathcal{C}}[\![\texttt{M}]\!]).\, \Lambda(IVR' <: \mathcal{T}_{\mathcal{C}}[\![\texttt{IV}^{ref}]\!]).$$
$$\langle \mathcal{T}_{\mathcal{C}}[\![\texttt{inst}]\!]\,[MyType], methfun \rangle\colon$$
$$\forall(M' <: \mathcal{T}_{\mathcal{C}}[\![\texttt{M}]\!]).\, \forall(IVR' <: \mathcal{T}_{\mathcal{C}}[\![\texttt{IV}^{ref}]\!]).$$
$$\mathcal{T}_{\mathcal{C}}[\![\texttt{IV}]\!](MyType) \times (SelfType \rightarrow \mathcal{T}_{\mathcal{C}}[\![\texttt{M}]\!](MyType))$$

Thus

$$\mathcal{T}_{\mathcal{C}}[\![\mathcal{C}]\!], \mathcal{T}_{\mathcal{C}}[\![\mathcal{E}]\!] \vdash \mathcal{T}_{\mathcal{C}}[\![\texttt{class}(\texttt{inst}, \texttt{meth})]\!]\colon \mathcal{T}_{\mathcal{C}}[\![\texttt{ClassType}(\texttt{IV}, \texttt{M})]\!].$$

Subclass Omitted here. Similar to class.

Message Suppose

$$\mathcal{C}, \mathcal{E} \vdash \texttt{E} \Leftarrow \texttt{m}\colon \texttt{T}(\texttt{U})$$

because

$$\mathcal{C}, \mathcal{E} \vdash \texttt{E}\colon \texttt{U}$$

and

$$\mathcal{C} \vdash \texttt{U} <\!\!\# \texttt{ObjectType}\,\{\!|\, \texttt{m}\colon \texttt{T}(\texttt{MyType})\,|\!\}$$

By Lemma 16.2.2, $\mathcal{C}(\mathtt{U}) = \mathtt{ObjectType}\ \mathtt{M}(\mathtt{MyType})$ for some $\mathtt{M}$ such that

$$\mathcal{C} \vdash \mathtt{M} <: \mathtt{TpFunc}(\mathtt{MT}) . \{| \ \mathtt{m} \colon \mathtt{T}(\mathtt{MT}) \ |\}.$$

By Theorem 16.4.1,

$$\mathcal{T}_C[\![\mathcal{C}]\!] \vdash \mathcal{T}_C[\![\mathtt{M}]\!] <: \mathcal{T}_C[\![\mathtt{TpFunc}(\mathtt{MT}). \{| \mathtt{m} \colon \mathtt{T}(\mathtt{MT}) |\}]\!],$$

where $\mathcal{T}_C[\![\mathtt{TpFunc}(\mathtt{MT}). \{| \mathtt{m} \colon \mathtt{T}(\mathtt{MT}) |\}]\!] = \lambda(MT). \{| \ m \colon \mathcal{T}_C[\![\mathtt{T}]\!](MT) |\}$.
Hence for all type identifiers, IVR', MT',

$$(16.1) \qquad \begin{aligned} \mathcal{T}_C[\![\mathcal{C}]\!] \vdash IVR' &\times (IVR' \to \mathcal{T}_C[\![\mathtt{M}]\!](MT')) <: \\ IVR' &\times (IVR' \to \{| m \colon \mathcal{T}_C[\![\mathtt{T}]\!](MT') |\}). \end{aligned}$$

By induction,

$$\mathcal{T}_C[\![\mathcal{C}]\!], \mathcal{T}_C[\![\mathcal{E}]\!] \vdash \mathcal{T}_C[\![\mathtt{E}]\!] \colon \mathcal{T}_C[\![\mathtt{U}]\!].$$

Let

$$\begin{aligned} MT = \mathcal{T}_C[\![\mathtt{U}]\!] &= \mathcal{T}_C[\![\mathtt{ObjectType}\ \mathtt{M}(\mathtt{MyType})]\!] = Obj\,(\mathcal{T}_C[\![\mathtt{M}]\!]) \\ &= \exists Y. Y \times (Y \to \mathcal{T}_C[\![\mathtt{M}]\!](MT)). \end{aligned}$$

By definition,

$$\mathcal{T}_C[\![\mathtt{E} \Leftarrow \mathtt{m}]\!] = open\ \mathcal{T}_C[\![\mathtt{E}]\!]\ as\ \langle IVR, vo \rangle\ in\ (proj_2(vo)(proj_1(vo))).m$$

By equation 16.1 and subsumption,

$$\begin{aligned} \mathcal{T}_C[\![\mathcal{C}]\!], \mathcal{T}_C[\![\mathcal{E}]\!] \cup \{vo \colon IVR \times (IVR \to \mathcal{T}_C[\![\mathtt{M}]\!](MT))\} &\vdash \\ vo \colon IVR \times (IVR \to \{| m \colon \mathcal{T}_C[\![\mathtt{T}]\!](MT) |\}) \end{aligned}$$

By the projection typing rules and the *Selection* rule of $\Lambda^P_{<:}$,

$$\begin{aligned} \mathcal{T}_C[\![\mathcal{C}]\!], \mathcal{T}_C[\![\mathcal{E}]\!] \cup \{vo \colon IVR \times (IVR \to \mathcal{T}_C[\![\mathtt{M}]\!](MT))\} &\vdash \\ (proj_2(vo)(proj_1(vo))).m \colon \mathcal{T}_C[\![\mathtt{T}]\!](MT). \end{aligned}$$

It follows from the *Unpack* rule that

$$\mathcal{T}_C[\![\mathcal{C}]\!], \mathcal{T}_C[\![\mathcal{E}]\!] \vdash open\ \mathcal{T}_C[\![\mathtt{E}]\!]\ as\ \langle IVR, vo \rangle\ in\ (proj_2(vo)(proj_1(vo))).m \colon \mathcal{T}_C[\![\mathtt{T}]\!](MT)$$

Hence

$$\mathcal{T}_C[\![\mathcal{C}]\!], \mathcal{T}_C[\![\mathcal{E}]\!] \vdash \mathcal{T}_C[\![\mathtt{E} \Leftarrow \mathtt{m}]\!] \colon \mathcal{T}_C[\![\mathtt{T}(\mathtt{U})]\!]$$

The reader should be sure to understand why the match, rather than subtype, bound on $\mathtt{U}$ was sufficient for proving the soundness of this rule.

Inst Vble   Suppose

$$\mathcal{C}, \mathcal{E} \vdash \texttt{E.l} : \texttt{T(V)}$$

because

$$\mathcal{C}, \mathcal{E} \vdash \texttt{E} : \texttt{U}$$

and

$$\mathcal{C} \vdash \texttt{U} <\#_{vis} \texttt{VisObjectType}(\{\mskip-5mu| \ \texttt{l}: \texttt{T(MyType)}|\mskip-5mu\}, \{\mskip-5mu| \ |\mskip-5mu\})$$

where $\mathcal{C}(\texttt{U}) = \texttt{VisObjectType(IVR(MyType), M(MyType))}$ and $\mathcal{C}(\texttt{V}) = \texttt{ObjectType M(MyType)}$.

By Lemma 16.2.3,

$$\mathcal{C} \vdash \texttt{IVR} <: \texttt{TpFunc(MT)}. \{\mskip-5mu| \ \texttt{l}: \texttt{T(MT)}|\mskip-5mu\},$$

and hence by Theorem 16.4.1,

$$\mathcal{T_C}[\![\mathcal{C}]\!] \vdash \mathcal{T_C}[\![\texttt{IVR}]\!] <: \mathcal{T_C}[\![\texttt{TpFunc(MT)}. \{\mskip-5mu| \ \texttt{l}: \texttt{T(MT)}|\mskip-5mu\}]\!].$$

By induction,

$$\mathcal{T_C}[\![\mathcal{C}]\!], \mathcal{T_C}[\![\mathcal{E}]\!] \vdash \mathcal{T_C}[\![\texttt{E}]\!] : \mathcal{T_C}[\![\texttt{VisObjectType(IVR(MyType), M(MyType))}]\!],$$

while, by definition,

$$\begin{aligned} &\mathcal{T_C}[\![\texttt{VisObjectType(IVR(MyType), M(MyType))}]\!] \\ &= \textit{VisObj} \, (\mathcal{T_C}[\![\texttt{IVR}]\!](MT), \mathcal{T_C}[\![\texttt{M}]\!](MT)) \\ &= \mathcal{T_C}[\![\texttt{IVR}]\!](MT) \times (\mathcal{T_C}[\![\texttt{IVR}]\!](MT) \to \mathcal{T_C}[\![\texttt{M}]\!](MT)), \end{aligned}$$

where $MT = \mathcal{T_C}[\![\texttt{V}]\!] = \mathcal{T_C}[\![\texttt{ObjectType M(MyType)}]\!] = \textit{Obj} \, (\mathcal{T_C}[\![\texttt{M}]\!])$.

By rule *Proj*,

$$\mathcal{T_C}[\![\mathcal{C}]\!], \mathcal{T_C}[\![\mathcal{E}]\!] \vdash \textit{proj}_1(\mathcal{T_C}[\![\texttt{E}]\!]) : \mathcal{T_C}[\![\texttt{IVR}]\!](MT)$$

and thus by subsumption in $\Lambda^P_{<:,}$

$$\mathcal{T_C}[\![\mathcal{C}]\!], \mathcal{T_C}[\![\mathcal{E}]\!] \vdash \textit{proj}_1(\mathcal{T_C}[\![\texttt{E}]\!]) : \{\mskip-5mu| \ \texttt{l}: \mathcal{T_C}[\![\texttt{T}]\!](MT)|\mskip-5mu\}$$

By definition,

$$\mathcal{T_C}[\![\texttt{E.l}]\!] = \textit{proj}_1(\mathcal{T_C}[\![\texttt{E}]\!]).l$$

Therefore, by the *Selection* type-checking rule of $\Lambda^P_{<:,}$

$$\mathcal{T_C}[\![\mathcal{C}]\!], \mathcal{T_C}[\![\mathcal{E}]\!] \vdash \mathcal{T_C}[\![\texttt{E.l}]\!] : \mathcal{T_C}[\![\texttt{T}]\!](MT)$$

and thus

$$\mathcal{T_C}[\![\mathcal{C}]\!], \mathcal{T_C}[\![\mathcal{E}]\!] \vdash \mathcal{T_C}[\![\texttt{E.l}]\!] : \mathcal{T_C}[\![\texttt{T(V)}]\!]$$

Self Message   This case is similar to sending messages to regular objects except that it is not necessary to unpack the existential.

■

16.5   Summary

In this chapter we designed the language $\mathcal{MOOL}$ by adding a MyType construct to $\mathcal{SOOL}$. The type expression MyType represents the type of self inside of a class definition. As the meaning of self changes automatically when moving from a class to a subclass, so does the meaning of MyType.

Just as this automatic change of the meaning of self is extremely helpful when inheriting methods from a superclass, so is the automatic change in the meaning of MyType. In particular, it provides a way to support covariant changes to types in classes, whether they are the types of instance variables, method parameters, or method return types.

While subclasses of classes whose methods have parameters with type MyType do not generate object types that are in the subtype relation, they do generate object types that match. While the loss of subtyping might be seen to be a disadvantage, we saw that matching is often all that is needed. In particular, if type T $<\#$ S then any method of S will also be in T, and the type of that method in T will be a subtype of that in S.

In the next chapter we will extend $\mathcal{MOOL}$ with match-bounded polymorphism and show the expressiveness of the combination of MyType and matching.

17 *Match-Bounded Polymorphism*

In this chapter we add bounded polymorphism to $\mathcal{MOOL}$. Of course we have already done this in extending $\mathcal{SOOL}$ to $\mathcal{PSOOL}$. The difference is that this time we will be more interested in introducing match-bounded polymorphism rather than polymorphism in which the bounds are expressed in terms of the subtyping relation.

We have already seen that in languages with MyType, subclasses generate types that are in the matching relation, and thus seems a more natural relation than subtyping. We will also see that we can simplify many occurrences of F-bounded polymorphism to simple match-bounded polymorphism. Match-bounded polymorphism also has the added benefit of fitting more smoothly with subclasses than does F-bounded polymorphism.

17.1 Benefits of match-bounded polymorphism

While the matching relation does not allow values of one object type to masquerade as values of the other, as is the case with subtyping, we have seen it provides useful information on the availability and types of methods. Interestingly, it is also very useful as a constraint on type variables for polymorphism. In fact, the use of MyType and matching will allow the possibility of dispensing with most of the uses of F-bounded polymorphism.

Recall from the last chapter the following example of F-bounded polymorphism.

```
OrderableF(t <: TopObject) = ObjectType {
    equal: t → Boolean;
    greaterThan: t → Boolean;
    lessThan: t → Boolean
}
```

```
class BPOrderedList(Elt <: OrderableF(Elt)) { ...};
```

The use of F-bounded polymorphism was needed in parameterized class `BPOrderedList` because the constraint on `Elt` was that it have `equal`, `greaterThan`, and `lessThan` methods that took parameters of type `Elt`. Thus when one of these methods is sent to an element of type `Elt`, it should have the same type as the receiver. Of course this should suggest to us the use of `MyType`.

Define

```
OrderableMT = ObjectType {
    equal: MyType → Boolean;
    greaterThan: MyType → Boolean;
    lessThan: MyType → Boolean
}
```

Unlike `OrderableF`, the type `OrderableMT` need not be parameterized. The class `BPOrderedListMT` is still defined with bounded polymorphism, but the bound is now expressed with the *matching* relation, and *no* F-bounded polymorphism is required.

```
class BPOrderedListMT(Elt <# OrderableMT) { ... };
```

MATCH-BOUNDED
POLYMORPHISM

Thus the uses of F-bounded polymorphism occurring in our earlier examples can be replaced with simple *match-bounded polymorphism* (bounded polymorphism in which the bound is expressed with matching) with the introduction of `MyType`.

The most important point to keep in mind with matching is that it provides information about the methods available and their types. Thus knowing that type `Elt` matches `OrderableMT` provides the information that `Elt` has at least the methods `equal`, `greaterThan`, and `lessThan`, and that their signatures conform to those given in `OrderableMT`. Most of the time, this sort of information is all that is needed in object-oriented programming. The extra information that one type can masquerade as another in all possible circumstances is not needed. We will present a more careful comparison of F-bounded polymorphism and match-bounded polymorphism after we discuss the type-checking rules and translation of this extended language.

17.2   Introducing $\mathcal{PMOOL}$

In Section 17.1 we discussed the benefits of using match-bounded polymorphism rather than using subtyping to restrict type variables. Adding match-
bounded polymorphism to $\mathcal{MOOL}$ to form $\mathcal{PMOOL}$ is straightforward,
though the translational semantics will be a bit tricky.

$\mathcal{PMOOL}$

We begin by generalizing type constructor constraint systems to allow
matching relations.

Definition 17.2.1 *Relations of the form* $\mathtt{x}^\kappa = \mathtt{G}$, $\mathtt{t} <\!\!\#\ \mathtt{T}$, *and* $\mathtt{x}^\kappa <: \mathtt{G}$, *where* $\mathtt{x}^\kappa$
is a type constructor variable, $\mathtt{G}$ *is a type constructor expression of the same kind,* $\mathtt{t}$
is a type variable, and $\mathtt{T}$ *is a type expression are said to be . Because matching is only*
defined for types, rather than constructors of higher kind, constraints of the form $\mathtt{t}$
$<\!\!\#\ \mathtt{T}$ *will be restricted to those in which* $\mathtt{t}$ *and* $\mathtt{T}$ *are both types, and* $\mathtt{T}$ *represents*
an object type. A is defined as follows:

1. *The empty set,* $\emptyset$, *is a generalized type constructor constraint system.*

2. *If* $\mathcal{C}$ *is a generalized type constructor constraint system,* $\mathtt{x}^\kappa$ *is an identifier that*
   does not appear in $\mathcal{C}$ *or* $\mathtt{G}$, *and* $\mathtt{G}$ *is a constructor expression of the same kind, then*
   $\mathcal{C} \cup \{\mathtt{x}^\kappa = \mathtt{G}\}$ *is a generalized type constructor constraint system.*

3. *Let* $\mathcal{C}$ *be a generalized type constructor constraint system, let* $\mathtt{t}$ *be a type identifier*
   that does not appear in $\mathcal{C}$, *and let* $\mathtt{T}$ *either be of the form* $\mathtt{ObjectType}\ \mathtt{M}$, *for*
   some $\mathtt{M}$, *or be a type identifier representing an object type with respect to* $\mathcal{C}$. *Then*
   $\mathcal{C} \cup \{\mathtt{t} <\!\!\#\ \mathtt{T}\}$ *is a generalized type constructor constraint system.*

4. *If* $\mathcal{C}$ *is a generalized type constructor constraint system,* $\mathtt{x}^\kappa$ *is a type constructor*
   identifier that does not appear in $\mathcal{C}$, *and* $\mathtt{G}$ *is a constructor expression of the same*
   kind, then $\mathcal{C} \cup \{\mathtt{x}^\kappa <: \mathtt{G}\}$ *is a generalized type constructor constraint system.*

The definition above allowed type identifiers to serve as upper bounds
of matching relationships only if the upper bounds themselves represented
object types. The formal definition follows:

Definition 17.2.2 *A type identifier* $\mathtt{t}$ represents an object type *with respect to* $\mathcal{C}$
if $(\mathtt{t} = \mathtt{T}) \in \mathcal{C}$, $(\mathtt{t} <: \mathtt{T}) \in \mathcal{C}$, *or* $(\mathtt{t} <\!\!\#\ \mathtt{T}) \in \mathcal{C}$, *where* $\mathtt{T}$ *is* $\mathtt{TopObject}$, *is of the*
form $\mathtt{ObjectType}\ \mathtt{M}$ *for some* $\mathtt{M}$, *or is a type identifier representing an object type*
with respect to $\mathcal{C}$ *with the constraint on* $\mathtt{t}$ *removed.*

That is, $\mathtt{t}$ represents an object type if it is explicitly bounded above or equal
to an object type or it is bounded above or equal to another type identifier
that represents an object type.

$$MPolyFcn \quad \frac{\mathcal{C} \cup \{t \lessdot\!\!\# \; T\}, \mathcal{E} \vdash \texttt{Block: U}}{\mathcal{C}, \mathcal{E} \vdash \texttt{polyFunc(t} \lessdot\!\!\# \; \texttt{T): U is Block: ForAll(t} \lessdot\!\!\# \; \texttt{T).U}}$$

where T may involve t.

$$MPolyFcnApp \quad \frac{\begin{array}{c} \mathcal{C}, \mathcal{E} \vdash \texttt{E: ForAll(t} \lessdot\!\!\# \; \texttt{T).U} \\ \mathcal{C} \vdash \texttt{T}' \; \lessdot\!\!\# \; [\texttt{T}'/\texttt{t}]\,\texttt{T} \end{array}}{\mathcal{C}, \mathcal{E} \vdash \texttt{E[T']}: [\texttt{T}'/\texttt{t}]\,\texttt{U}}$$

$$MPolyFcn_{<:} \quad \frac{\mathcal{C} \cup \{t \lessdot\!\!\# \; T\} \vdash \texttt{U}' <: \texttt{U}}{\mathcal{C} \vdash \texttt{ForAll(t} \lessdot\!\!\# \; \texttt{T).U}' <: \texttt{ForAll(t} \lessdot\!\!\# \; \texttt{T).U}}$$

Figure 17.1   Typing and subtyping rules for new expressions of $\mathcal{PMOOL}$.

We could loosen the definition to allow bounds, T, where T only reduces to an object type, but that would greatly complicate our translation function later. In fact, such expressions would normally be reduced during type-checking anyway.

Now that our type constraints include matching relations, we add match-bounded polymorphic expressions and their typing rules in Figure 17.1. While these rules allow F-bounded matching, the use of matching removes the necessity for most uses requiring the bounded type variable to appear in the bound.

17.3   Examples and comparison with F-bounded polymorphism

A complete example of a $\mathcal{PMOOL}$ program manipulating ordered lists is given in Figures 17.2, 17.3, and 17.4. It uses match-bounded polymorphism to create ordered lists that hold elements of any (fixed) type that matches `OrderableMT`. (The MT in `OrderableMT` stands for `MyType`.)

The `NodeType` type constructor takes type T as a parameter to form a type for objects providing methods to set and get values of type T and providing methods to access and change a `next` field of the same type. Class `Node` is polymorphic, taking a type parameter T that is restricted to be an object type, and a value of type T, generating objects of type `NodeType(T)`.[1]

---

1. We implicitly extend our abbreviations available for $\mathcal{PMOOL}$ programs in order to write these examples more simply.

The type constructor `BPOrdListMTType` takes a type parameter, `T`, and returns an object type with `find` and `add` methods for a list with elements of type `T`. The polymorphic class `BPOrdListMT` takes a type parameter `T` that is restricted to be an object type with `equal`, `greaterThan`, and `lessThan` methods that can be used to compare objects of the same type. The definitions of methods `add` and `find` use the comparison relations on `T`.

The main part of the program depends on the assumption that `StringMT` $<\#$ `OrderableMT`. It creates a new ordered list, adds a string, and then checks to see if a different string is contained in it.

In Section 4.1.4 we remarked that F-bounded polymorphism did not interact well with the subtype or subclass hierarchies in object-oriented languages. We recast the example in that section in terms of $\mathcal{PSOOL}$.

Recall the examples in Section 15.1. We had parameterized type `OrderableF`, and parameterized class `BPOrdList` that takes a type parameter `Elt` $<:$ `OrderableF(Elt)`. We also had object type `String` such that `String` $<:$ `OrderableF(String)`.

Suppose `CaseString` is a subtype of `String` that also includes a method `setUpper:Void` $\to$ `Void` that is to convert the string to all caps. This could easily be obtained as a subclass of a class generating objects of type `String`. While `CaseString` is a subtype of `String`, the type `CaseString` does not satisfy the F-bounded constraint on `BPOrdList` because `CaseString` is a subtype of `OrderableF(String)` rather than being a subtype of `OrderableF(CaseString)`.

An important feature of match-bounded polymorphism is that this problem goes away. If `StringMT` matches `OrderableMT`, *i.e.*, its methods all have type `MyType` $\to$ `Boolean`, then adding new methods like `setUpper` result in types matching `StringMT`, and hence `OrderableMT`. Thus we could apply parameterized class `BPOrdListMT` to these extensions. This consistency with extensions of both classes and object types is an important advantage of match-bounded polymorphism over F-bounded polymorphism.

17.4   Translational semantics of $\mathcal{PMOOL}$

The only new cases we must deal with in the translation of $\mathcal{PMOOL}$ into $\Lambda^P_{<:}$ are those corresponding to match-bounded polymorphism. However, because we modified the definition of constraint systems, we will need to modify their translations as well.

```
program linkedlist;

    OrderableMT = ObjectType {
        equal: MyType → Boolean;
        greaterThan: MyType → Boolean;
        lessThan: MyType → Boolean } ;

    // Type of singly linked node objects
    NodeType(T) = ObjectType {
        getValue: Void → T;
        setValue: T → Void;
        getNext: Void → MyType;
        setNext: MyType → Void } ;

    // Type of ordered linked lists of T
    BPOrdListMTType(T) = ObjectType {
        find: T → Boolean;
        add: Void → T } ;

    // class for singly linked nodes w/values of type T
    class Node(T <# TopObject; a: T) {
        value: T := a;
        next: MyType := nil;

        function getValue(): T is
        { return self.value };

        function setValue(newValue: T): Void is
        { self.value := newValue };

        function getNext(): MyType is
        { return self.next };

        function setNext(newNext: MyType): Void is
        { self.next := newNext }
    };
```

Figure 17.2   Linked list example in $\mathcal{PMOOL}$. Part 1.

```
class BPOrdListMT(T <# OrderableMT) {
   head: NodeType(T) := nil;
   function find(match: T): Boolean is
   {  done: Boolean := false;
      current: NodeType(T) := head;
      while not(done) & not(current = nil) do
      {  done := current ⇐ getVal() ⇐ eq(match);
         if not(done) then
            {  current := current ⇐ getNext(); } }
      return (done);
   };

   function add(a: T): Void is
   {  prev: NodeType(T); current: NodeType(T);
      newNode: NodeType(T) = new Node(T,a);
      if head = nil then
      {  head := newNode;
         newNode ⇐ setNext(nil); }
      else if head⇐ getVal()⇐ ge(
                   newNode⇐ getVal()) then
      {  newNode ⇐ setNext(head);
         head := newNode; }
      else
      {  prev := head;
         current := head ⇐ getNext();
         while not(current = nil) &
            current ⇐ getVal() ⇐ ge(
                   newNode ⇐ getVal()) do
            {  prev := current;
               current := current ⇐ getNext(); }
         if current = nil then
            {  prev ⇐ setNext(newNode);
               newNode ⇐ setNext(nil); }
         else
            {  newNode ⇐ setNext(current);
               prev ⇐ setNext(newNode); }  }  }
   };
```

Figure 17.3 Linked list example in $\mathcal{PMOOL}$. Part 2.

```
// Assume StringType <# OrderableMT
aString: StringMT := ``First Node'';
lnode: NodeType (StringMT);
   // singly linked list
slist: BPOrdListMTType (StringMT);

{
    slist := new (BPOrdListMT[StringMT]);
    slist ⇐ add(``1st Node'');
    printBool (slist ⇐ find (aString));
}
```

Figure 17.4   Linked list example in $\mathcal{PMOOL}$. Part 3.

17.4.1   Translational semantics of types

The difficulty here is that $\Lambda^P_{<:}$ does not include syntax for the matching relation. As a result, we must encode it using higher-order subtyping. We encode
matching as higher-order subtyping using the following correspondence:

$$\mathcal{C} \vdash \text{ObjectType M' (MyType)} <\# \text{ObjectType M (MyType)}$$
$$iff \qquad \mathcal{C} \vdash \text{M'} <: \text{M}.$$

Of course we have already been using this encoding implicitly when writing
down type-checking rules and the translations for classes and subclasses.

This encoding works fine as long as the type expressions on both sides of
$<\#$ are object type expressions, but what do we do in the case where one
or both are type variables? To solve this problem we will interpret a type
identifier t as a type constructor identifier $t^{\star \Rightarrow \star}$ of $\Lambda^P_{<:}$ with kind $\star \Rightarrow \star$. (We
will use the same letter for the translated type identifier, even though the
original has kind $\star$ while the translation has kind $\star \Rightarrow \star$.) Then when we are
ready to actually use the variable in a context requiring an object type, we
will convert it into an object type by using $Obj(t)$.

This brings up the unfortunate complication that we must have two ways
of interpreting object types and type variables. We need one translation
where both are translated as functions from types to types so that they may
be used in match-bounded polymorphism. The second translation is used
where we actually need these to be object types and used as types of expressions.

When we translate ForAll(t $<$: U). V, the type variable t and its bound U will be translated as functions from types to types, while V should be translated as a regular type. Thus we will need context sensitive translations of types in order to translate the extension of the language with match-bounded polymorphism.

Moreover we will need to distinguish between identifiers introduced in match-bounded polymorphic types and those occurring as formal parameters of type constructors. That is, we will translate the identifier t introduced in match-bounded polymorphism of the form ForAll(t $<\#$ U). V differently from other type identifiers.

We distinguish between these two translations by introducing the notation $\mathcal{T}_{\mathcal{C}}^{\mathcal{M},X}[\![\text{U}]\!]$ for the translation of type variables in X and object types to be $\Lambda_{<:}^{P}$ functions from types to types. It is undefined on other types. (Think of the superscript $\mathcal{M}$ as referring to "match-bounded".)

The notation $\mathcal{T}_{\mathcal{C}}^{X}[\![\text{U}]\!]$ will represent the translation of types of $\mathcal{PMOOL}$ to types of $\Lambda_{<:}^{P}$. It is very similar to the translation function $\mathcal{T}_{\mathcal{C}}[\![\text{U}]\!]$ that we used in our earlier translations.

The translation of polymorphic types and type variables is given in Figure 17.5. Translation of types not included are as before, except with $\mathcal{T}_{\mathcal{C}}[\![\ldots]\!]$ replaced by $\mathcal{T}_{\mathcal{C}}^{X}[\![\ldots]\!]$.

At the top level, we begin translating types using $\mathcal{T}_{\mathcal{C}}^{X}[\![\text{U}]\!]$. The reader will note that the alternative translation function, $\mathcal{T}_{\mathcal{C}}^{\mathcal{M},X}[\![\text{U}]\!]$, is introduced only in the translation of polymorphic types where the new type variable is match-bound by another type. In that cases both the type variable and its bound is translated using $\mathcal{T}_{\mathcal{C}}^{\mathcal{M},X}[\![\ldots]\!]$.

We illustrate the new functions by translating the three types introduced in the program linkedlist in Figure 17.2. We begin by translating the type NodeType defined by:

```
NodeType = TpFunc(T). ObjectType {|
    getValue: Void → T;
    setValue: T → Void;
    getNext: Void → MyType;
    setNext: MyType → Void |}
```

(We have given the definition in the form without abbreviations here.) We will omit the translation of methods setValue and setNext because they are similar to the two corresponding "get..." methods. By the definition

$\mathcal{T}_{\mathcal{C}}^{\mathcal{M},X}[\![\mathtt{t}]\!] \triangleq t, \qquad$ *for* $\mathtt{t} \in X$ *a type identifier and where* $\mathtt{t}$ *has kind* $* \Rightarrow *$.

$\mathcal{T}_{\mathcal{C}}^{\mathcal{M},X}[\![\mathtt{TopObject}]\!] \triangleq \lambda mt.\{\!|\ |\!\}$

$\mathcal{T}_{\mathcal{C}}^{\mathcal{M},X}[\![\mathtt{ObjectType\ M(MyType)}]\!] \triangleq \mathcal{T}_{\mathcal{C}}^{X}[\![\mathtt{M}]\!]$

$\mathcal{T}_{\mathcal{C}}^{\mathcal{M},X}[\![\mathtt{T}]\!]$ *is undefined if* $\mathtt{T}$ *is not a type variable of* X *or an object type.*

$\mathcal{T}_{\mathcal{C}}^{X}[\![\mathtt{TpFunc(t).U}]\!] \triangleq \lambda t.\,\mathcal{T}_{\mathcal{C}}^{X}[\![\mathtt{U}]\!],$
  where t *is a type variable and does not occur in* $\mathcal{C}$.

$\mathcal{T}_{\mathcal{C}}^{X}[\![\mathtt{F(U)}]\!] \triangleq \mathcal{T}_{\mathcal{C}}^{X}[\![\mathtt{F}]\!](\mathcal{T}_{\mathcal{C}}^{X}[\![\mathtt{U}]\!])$

$\mathcal{T}_{\mathcal{C}}^{X}[\![\mathtt{t}]\!] \triangleq \begin{cases} Obj(t), & \text{if } \mathtt{t} \in X \\ t, & \text{otherwise} \end{cases}$

$\mathcal{T}_{\mathcal{C}}^{X}[\![\mathtt{ForAll(t\ \texttt{<\#}\ T).U}]\!] \triangleq \forall(t <: \mathcal{T}_{\mathcal{C}}^{\mathcal{M},X \cup \{t\}}[\![\mathtt{T}]\!]).\,\mathcal{T}_{\mathcal{C}}^{X \cup \{t\}}[\![\mathtt{U}]\!]$
  where t *has kind* $* \Rightarrow *$ *and does not occur in* $\mathcal{C}$.

$\mathcal{T}_{\mathcal{C}}^{X}[\![\mathtt{ObjectType\ M(MyType)}]\!] \triangleq Obj(\mathcal{T}_{\mathcal{C}}^{X}[\![\mathtt{M}]\!])$

$\mathcal{T}_{\mathcal{C}}^{X}[\![\mathtt{VisObjectType(IVR(MyType),M(MyType))}]\!] \triangleq$
$\qquad\qquad VisObj(\mathcal{T}_{\mathcal{C}}^{X}[\![\mathtt{IVR}]\!]\,(Obj(\mathcal{T}_{\mathcal{C}}^{X}[\![\mathtt{M}]\!])), \mathcal{T}_{\mathcal{C}}^{X}[\![\mathtt{M}]\!](Obj(\mathcal{T}_{\mathcal{C}}^{X}[\![\mathtt{M}]\!])))$

$\mathcal{T}_{\mathcal{C}}^{X}[\![\mathtt{ClassType(IV(MyType),M(MyType))}]\!] \triangleq$
$\qquad \forall(M' <: \mathcal{T}_{\mathcal{C}}^{X}[\![\mathtt{M}]\!]).\,\forall(IVR' <: \mathcal{T}_{\mathcal{C}}^{X}[\![\mathtt{IV}^{ref}]\!]).$
$\qquad\quad \mathcal{T}_{\mathcal{C}}^{X}[\![\mathtt{IV}]\!](Obj(M')) \times$
$\qquad\quad (VisObj(IVR'(Obj(M')),M'(Obj(M'))) \to \mathcal{T}_{\mathcal{C}}^{X}[\![\mathtt{M}]\!](Obj(M')))$

where

$Obj(M) \triangleq Fix(\lambda MT.\exists Y.\,Y \times (Y \to M(MT)))$
$\qquad\quad = \exists Y.\,Y \times (Y \to M(Obj(M))).$

$VisObj(IVR,M) \triangleq IVR \times (IVR \to M).$

Figure 17.5   Translations of selected types and constructors of $\mathcal{PMOOL}$.

of $\mathcal{T}_{\mathcal{C}}^{X}[\![\mathtt{U}]\!]$ in Figure 17.5:

$\mathcal{T}_{\mathcal{C}}^{\emptyset}[\![\mathtt{NodeType}]\!] = \lambda T.\,\mathcal{T}_{\mathcal{C}}^{\{\emptyset\}}[\![\mathtt{ObjectType\ \{|\,getValue:\ Void \to T;}$
$\qquad\qquad\qquad\qquad\qquad\qquad\qquad \mathtt{getNext:\ Void \to MyType|\}}]\!]$
$\qquad\qquad\quad = \lambda T.\,Obj(\mathcal{T}_{\mathcal{C}}^{\{\emptyset\}}[\![\lambda mt.\{\!|\ldots|\!\}]\!])$
$\qquad\qquad\quad = \lambda T.\,Obj(\lambda mt.\{\!| getValue:\ Void \to \mathcal{T}_{\mathcal{C}}^{\{\emptyset\}}[\![\mathtt{T}]\!];$
$\qquad\qquad\qquad\qquad\qquad\quad getNext:\ Void \to \mathcal{T}_{\mathcal{C}}^{\{\emptyset\}}[\![mt]\!] |\!\})$
$\qquad\qquad\quad = \lambda T.\,Obj(\lambda mt.\{\!| getValue:\ Void \to T;$
$\qquad\qquad\qquad\qquad\qquad\quad getNext:\ Void \to mt |\!\})$

The type `OrderableMT`, which is defined by

```
OrderableMT = ObjectType {|
    equal: MyType → Boolean;
    greaterThan: MyType → Boolean;
    lessThan: MyType → Boolean |}
```

appears as a type bound in the definition of `BPOrdListMT`. As a result, we will need to compute the alternate translation, $\mathcal{T}_c^{\mathcal{M},\{T\}}[\![BPOrdListMTType]\!]$. Because the three methods of `OrderableMT` all have the same signature, we will only include the `equal` method in our translation.

$$
\begin{aligned}
OrderMT &= \mathcal{T}_c^{\mathcal{M},\{T\}}[\![OrderableMT]\!] \\
&= \mathcal{T}_c^{\mathcal{M},\{T\}}[\![ObjectType\ \{|equal: MyType \to Boolean|\}]\!] \\
&= \mathcal{T}_c^{\{T\}}[\![\lambda mt. \{|equal:\ mt \to Boolean|\}]\!] \\
&= \lambda mt.\ \mathcal{T}_c^{\{T\}}[\![\{|equal:\ mt \to Boolean|\}]\!] \\
&= \lambda mt.\ \{|equal:\ mt \to Boolean\ |\}
\end{aligned}
$$

whereas

$$
\mathcal{T}_c^{\{T\}}[\![OrderableMT]\!] = Obj\,(\lambda mt.\ \{|equal:\ mt \to Boolean\ |\}).
$$

With this, we can now translate `BPOrdListMTType`:

```
BPOrdListMTType = TpFunc(T). ObjectType {|
    find: T → Boolean;
    add: Void → T |}
```

as

$$
\begin{aligned}
\mathcal{T}_c^{\emptyset}&[\![BPOrdListMTType]\!] \\
&= \lambda T.\ \mathcal{T}_c^{\{\emptyset\}}[\![ObjectType\ \{|\ find:\ T \to Boolean; \\
&\hspace{6.5em} add:\ Void \to T|\}]\!] \\
&= \lambda T.\ Obj\,(\mathcal{T}_c^{\{\emptyset\}}[\![ObjectType\ \{|\ldots|\}]\!]) \\
&= \lambda T.\ Obj\,(\mathcal{T}_c^{\{\emptyset\}}[\![\lambda mt.\ \{|\ldots|\}]\!]) \\
&= \lambda T.\ Obj\,(\lambda mt.\ \{|\ find:\ \mathcal{T}_c^{\{\emptyset\}}[\![T]\!] \to Boolean; \\
&\hspace{6.5em} add:\ Void \to \mathcal{T}_c^{\{\emptyset\}}[\![T]\!]|\}) \\
&= \lambda T.\ Obj\,(\lambda mt.\ \{|\ find:\ T \to Boolean; \\
&\hspace{6.5em} add:\ Void \to T|\})
\end{aligned}
$$

17.4.2   Translational semantics of value expressions

Not surprisingly, the extra complications of translating types will result in similar complications for translating expressions, especially those reflecting match-bounded polymorphism and applications of polymorphic functions to types. The translation for selected expressions is given in Figure 17.6. We only include those expressions where types play a visible role. Others are translated similarly to before.

Only a single translation function, $\mathcal{T}_{\mathcal{C}}^{X}[\![\ldots]\!]$, is used for value expressions, though $\mathcal{T}_{\mathcal{C}}^{\mathcal{M},X}[\![\ldots]\!]$ is used for translating some of the types.

Notice the difference between the translations of subtype-bounded polymorphic functions and match-bounded polymorphic functions. In the former, the bound type identifier and its bound are both translated as types, while in the latter, both are translated as functions from types to types. Similarly, there is a distinction in the translation of expressions representing the application of polymorphic functions to types. If they represent match-bounded polymorphism then the type arguments are translated as functions from types to types, while with subtype-bounded polymorphism the type arguments are translated as types.

The translation of other expressions is exactly as before except that $\mathcal{T}_{\mathcal{C}}^{X}[\![\ldots]\!]$ is used in place of $\mathcal{T}_{\mathcal{C}}[\![\ldots]\!]$. We will come back to this topic later, but we remark now that in a language with match-bounded polymorphism, there is little need to also support subtype-bounded polymorphism. This provides for a simpler language at little cost in expressiveness.

17.5   Soundness of the translation of $\mathcal{PMOOL}$

In order to prove the translation of $\mathcal{PMOOL}$ is sound we must first determine how to translate type constraints. Our definition is by induction on the definition of generalized type constructor constraint systems. Let $\mathcal{C}'$ be a generalized type constructor constraint system and X a set of variables of $\Lambda_{<:}^{P}$. Then

1. $\mathcal{T}_{\mathcal{C}'}^{X}[\![\emptyset]\!] = \emptyset$.

2. $\mathcal{T}_{\mathcal{C}'}^{X}[\![\mathcal{C} \cup \{\mathtt{t} = \mathtt{T}\}]\!] = \mathcal{T}_{\mathcal{C}'}^{X}[\![\mathcal{C}]\!]$.

3. $\mathcal{T}_{\mathcal{C}'}^{X}[\![\mathcal{C} \cup \{\mathtt{t} <: \mathtt{T}\}]\!] = \mathcal{T}_{\mathcal{C}'}^{X}[\![\mathcal{C}]\!] \cup \{t <: \mathcal{T}_{\mathcal{C}'}^{X}[\![\mathtt{T}]\!]\}$.

4. $\mathcal{T}_{\mathcal{C}'}^{X \cup \{t\}}[\![\mathcal{C} \cup \{\mathtt{t} <\!\!\# \ \mathtt{T}\}]\!] = \mathcal{T}_{\mathcal{C}'}^{X}[\![\mathcal{C}]\!] \cup \{t <: \mathcal{T}_{\mathcal{C}'}^{\mathcal{M},X \cup \{t\}}[\![\mathtt{T}]\!]\}$, where t is a type

$\mathcal{T}_C^X[\![\mathcal{C}, \mathcal{E} \vdash \text{polyFunc(t <: T): U is Block: ForAll(t <: T).U}]\!] \triangleq$
$$\Lambda(t <: \mathcal{T}_C^X[\![\mathrm{T}]\!]).\, \mathcal{T}_{C'}^X[\![\mathcal{C}', \mathcal{E} \vdash \text{Block: U}]\!]$$
where t has kind $*$.

$\mathcal{T}_C^X[\![\mathcal{C}, \mathcal{E} \vdash \text{polyFunc(t <\# T): U is Block: ForAll(t <\# T).U}]\!] \triangleq$
$$\Lambda(t <: \mathcal{T}_C^{M,X \cup \{t\}}[\![\mathrm{T}]\!]).\, \mathcal{T}_{C'}^{X \cup \{t\}}[\![\mathcal{C}', \mathcal{E} \vdash \text{Block: U}]\!]$$
where t has kind $* \Rightarrow *$.

$\mathcal{T}_C^X[\![\mathcal{C}, \mathcal{E} \vdash \text{E[T']: [T'/t]U}]\!] \triangleq$
$$\begin{cases} \mathcal{T}_C^X[\![\mathcal{C}, \mathcal{E} \vdash \text{E: ForAll(t <\# T).U}]\!]\,[\mathcal{T}_C^{M,X}[\![\mathrm{T'}]\!]], & \textit{if } \text{E} \textit{ is match-bounded} \\ \mathcal{T}_C^X[\![\mathcal{C}, \mathcal{E} \vdash \text{E: ForAll(t <: T).U}]\!]\,[\mathcal{T}_C^X[\![\mathrm{T'}]\!]], & \textit{if } \text{E} \textit{ is subtype-bounded} \end{cases}$$

$\mathcal{T}_C^X[\![\mathcal{C}, \mathcal{E} \vdash \text{function}(id_1\colon \mathrm{T}_1, \ldots, id_n\colon \mathrm{T}_n)\colon \mathrm{T} \text{ is Block:}$
$$\mathrm{T}_1 \times \ldots \times \mathrm{T}_n \rightarrow \mathrm{T}]\!] \triangleq$$
$$\lambda(\langle id_1\colon \mathcal{T}_C^X[\![\mathrm{T}_1]\!], \ldots, id_n\colon \mathcal{T}_C^X[\![\mathrm{T}_n]\!]\rangle).\, \mathcal{T}_C^X[\![\mathcal{C}, \mathcal{E}' \vdash \text{Block: T}]\!]$$

$\mathcal{T}_C^X[\![\mathcal{C}, \mathcal{E} \vdash \{\!| l_1\colon \mathrm{T}_1 = \mathrm{E}_1; \ldots; l_n\colon \mathrm{T}_n = \mathrm{E}_n |\!\}\colon \{\!| l_1\colon \mathrm{T}_1; \ldots; l_n\colon \mathrm{T}_n |\!\}]\!] \triangleq$
$$\{\!| l_1\colon \mathcal{T}_C^X[\![\mathrm{T}_1]\!] = \mathcal{T}_C^X[\![\mathcal{C}, \mathcal{E} \vdash \mathrm{E}_1\colon \mathrm{T}_1]\!]; \ldots;$$
$$l_n\colon \mathcal{T}_C^X[\![\mathrm{T}_n]\!] = \mathcal{T}_C^X[\![\mathcal{C}, \mathcal{E} \vdash \mathrm{E}_n\colon \mathrm{T}_n]\!] |\!\}$$

$\mathcal{T}_C^X[\![\mathcal{C}, \mathcal{E} \vdash \text{Block: T}]\!] = \textit{let } t_1 = \mathcal{T}_C^X[\![\mathrm{T}_1]\!] \textit{ in } \ldots \textit{let } t_n = \mathcal{T}_C^X[\![\mathrm{T}_n]\!] \textit{ in}$
$$\textit{let } id_1\colon \mathcal{T}_C^X[\![\mathrm{U}_1]\!] = \mathcal{T}_C^X[\![\mathcal{C}, \mathcal{E} \vdash \mathrm{E}_1\colon \mathrm{U}_1]\!] \textit{ in } \ldots$$
$$\textit{let } id_k\colon \mathcal{T}_C^X[\![\mathrm{U}_k]\!] = \mathcal{T}_C^X[\![\mathcal{C}, \mathcal{E} \vdash \mathrm{E}_k\colon \mathrm{U}_k]\!] \textit{ in}$$
$$\mathcal{T}_C^X[\![\mathcal{C}, \mathcal{E} \vdash \text{S: Command}]\!]; \mathcal{T}_C^X[\![\mathcal{C}, \mathcal{E} \vdash \text{E: T}]\!] \textit{ end } \ldots \textit{ end}$$
where Block is type $t_1 = \mathrm{T}_1; \ldots; t_n = \mathrm{T}_n$
$$\text{const } id_1\colon \mathrm{U}_1 = \mathrm{E}_1; \ldots; id_k\colon \mathrm{U}_k = \mathrm{E}_k$$
$$\{ \text{ S return E } \}$$

Figure 17.6 Translation of $\mathcal{PMOOL}$ expressions involving polymorphism.

identifier of $\mathcal{PMOOL}$, and t is a type constructor variable that has kind $* \Rightarrow *$.

The translation of $\mathcal{E}$ is similar to that given earlier:

$$\mathcal{T}_C^X[\![\mathcal{E}]\!] = \{x\colon \mathcal{T}_C^X[\![\mathrm{T}]\!] \mid (\mathrm{x}\colon \mathrm{T}) \in \mathcal{E}\}$$

Before proving the soundness theorems for this extended system we must first determine the appropriate initial value of X, the set of type constructor identifiers of kind $* \Rightarrow *$ to be treated as types. The rather simple solution is to initialize X to the set of all type identifiers that are declared with a match-bound in the generalized type constructor constraint system used in the corresponding typing, subtyping, or matching rule.

The following theorem corresponds to Theorem 13.1.9 and is proved in the same way.

Theorem 17.5.1 *Let* S *and* T *be types of* $\mathcal{SOOL}$ *such that*

$$\mathcal{C} \vdash \text{S} <: \text{T},$$

and let

$$X = \{ \text{t} \mid \text{there exists a T such that } (\text{t} <\!\!\#\ \text{T}) \in \mathcal{C} \}.$$

Then

$$\mathcal{T}_{\mathcal{C}}^{X}[\![\mathcal{C}]\!] \vdash \mathcal{T}_{\mathcal{C}}^{X}[\![\text{S}]\!] <: \mathcal{T}_{\mathcal{C}}^{X}[\![\text{T}]\!].$$

The translation of matching types results in functions from types to types that are in the subtype relation.

Theorem 17.5.2 *Let* S *and* T *be types of* $\mathcal{SOOL}$ *such that*

$$\mathcal{C} \vdash \text{S} <\!\!\#\ \text{T},$$

and let

$$X = \{ \text{t} \mid \text{there exists a T such that } (\text{t} <\!\!\#\ \text{T}) \in \mathcal{C} \}.$$

Then

$$\mathcal{T}_{\mathcal{C}}^{X}[\![\mathcal{C}]\!] \vdash \mathcal{T}_{\mathcal{C}}^{\mathcal{M},X}[\![\text{S}]\!] <: \mathcal{T}_{\mathcal{C}}^{\mathcal{M},X}[\![\text{T}]\!].$$

Proof.   We give a proof by induction on the number of steps in the proof that $\mathcal{C} \vdash \text{S} <\!\!\#\ \text{T}$. The proofs for *TopObject* $_\#$, *Reflex* $_\#$, *Transitive* $_\#$, and *Type Abbrev* $_\#$ are trivial.

Suppose

$$\mathcal{C} \vdash \texttt{ObjectType M'(MyType)} <\!\!\#\ \texttt{ObjectType M(MyType)}$$

because

$$\mathcal{C} \vdash \text{M}' <: \text{M}.$$

By Theorem 17.5.1,

$$\mathcal{T}_{\mathcal{C}}^{X}[\![\mathcal{C}]\!] \vdash \mathcal{T}_{\mathcal{C}}^{X}[\![\text{M}']\!] <: \mathcal{T}_{\mathcal{C}}^{X}[\![\text{M}]\!].$$

But

$$\mathcal{T}_{\mathcal{C}}^{\mathcal{M},X}[\![\texttt{ObjectType M'(MyType)}]\!] = \mathcal{T}_{\mathcal{C}}^{X}[\![\text{M}']\!],$$

and

$$\mathcal{T}_{\mathcal{C}}^{\mathcal{M},X}[\![\text{ObjectType M(MyType)}]\!] = \mathcal{T}_{\mathcal{C}}^{X}[\![\text{M}]\!],$$

so we are done.   ∎

Now we wish to show that if a type can be assigned to an expression of $\mathcal{SOOL}$, then the translation of that type can be assigned to the translated expression.

Theorem 17.5.3 *Let* E *be an expression of* $\mathcal{SOOL}$ *that does not involve* nil, *let*

$$X = \{t \mid \text{there exists a } T \text{ such that } (t \mathrel{<\!\#} T) \in \mathcal{C}\},$$

and suppose

$$\mathcal{C}, \mathcal{E} \vdash \text{E: S}.$$

Then

$$\mathcal{T}_{\mathcal{C}}^{X}[\![\mathcal{C}]\!], \mathcal{T}_{\mathcal{C}}^{X}[\![\mathcal{E}]\!] \vdash \mathcal{T}_{\mathcal{C}}^{X}[\![\text{E}]\!]: \mathcal{T}_{\mathcal{C}}^{X}[\![\text{S}]\!].$$

Proof.   We only show the cases for expression identifiers and for match-bounded polymorphic expressions.

Identifier   Suppose $\mathcal{C}, \mathcal{E} \vdash$ id: T because (id: T) $\in \mathcal{E}$. Then (*id:* $\mathcal{T}_{\mathcal{C}}^{X}[\![\text{T}]\!]$) $\in \mathcal{T}_{\mathcal{C}}^{X}[\![\mathcal{E}]\!]$, and hence $\mathcal{T}_{\mathcal{C}}^{X}[\![\mathcal{C}]\!], \mathcal{T}_{\mathcal{C}}^{X}[\![\mathcal{E}]\!] \vdash$ *id:* $\mathcal{T}_{\mathcal{C}}^{X}[\![\text{T}]\!]$.

Match-bounded polymorphism   Suppose

$$\mathcal{C}, \mathcal{E} \vdash \text{polyFunc(t} \mathrel{<\!\#} \text{T): U is Block: ForAll(t} \mathrel{<\!\#} \text{T).U}$$

because $\mathcal{C} \cup \{\text{t} \mathrel{<\!\#} \text{T}\}, \mathcal{E} \vdash$ Block: U.
Let $\mathcal{C}' = \mathcal{C} \cup \{\text{t} \mathrel{<\!\#} \text{T}\}$ and $X' = X \cup \{\text{t}\}$. By induction,

$$\mathcal{T}_{\mathcal{C}'}^{X'}[\![\mathcal{C}']\!], \mathcal{T}_{\mathcal{C}'}^{X'}[\![\mathcal{E}]\!] \vdash \mathcal{T}_{\mathcal{C}'}^{X'}[\![\text{Block}]\!]: \mathcal{T}_{\mathcal{C}'}^{X'}[\![\text{U}]\!].$$

By definition $\mathcal{T}_{\mathcal{C}'}^{X'}[\![\mathcal{C}']\!] = \mathcal{T}_{\mathcal{C}}^{X}[\![\mathcal{C}]\!] \cup \{t <: \mathcal{T}_{\mathcal{C}'}^{\mathcal{M},X'}[\![\text{T}]\!]\}$. Thus,

$$\mathcal{T}_{\mathcal{C}}^{X}[\![\mathcal{C}]\!] \cup \{t <: \mathcal{T}_{\mathcal{C}'}^{\mathcal{M},X'}[\![\text{T}]\!]\}, \mathcal{T}_{\mathcal{C}'}^{X'}[\![\mathcal{E}]\!] \vdash \mathcal{T}_{\mathcal{C}'}^{X'}[\![\text{Block}]\!]: \mathcal{T}_{\mathcal{C}'}^{X'}[\![\text{U}]\!],$$

and hence by the *PolyFunc* rule of $\Lambda_{<:}^{P}$,

$$\mathcal{T}_{\mathcal{C}'}^{X}[\![\mathcal{C}]\!], \mathcal{T}_{\mathcal{C}'}^{X'}[\![\mathcal{E}]\!] \vdash \Lambda(t <: \mathcal{T}_{\mathcal{C}'}^{\mathcal{M},X'}[\![\text{T}]\!]). \mathcal{T}_{\mathcal{C}'}^{X'}[\![\text{Block}]\!]: \forall(t <: \mathcal{T}_{\mathcal{C}'}^{\mathcal{M},X'}[\![\text{T}]\!]). \mathcal{T}_{\mathcal{C}'}^{X'}[\![\text{U}]\!],$$

But

$$\mathcal{T}_{\mathcal{C}}^{X}[\![\text{ForAll(t} \mathrel{<\!\#} \text{T). U}]\!] \stackrel{\triangle}{=} \forall(t <: \mathcal{T}_{\mathcal{C}}^{\mathcal{M},X'}[\![\text{T}]\!]). \mathcal{T}_{\mathcal{C}}^{X'}[\![\text{U}]\!],$$

and

$$\mathcal{T}_{\mathcal{C}}^{X}[\![\texttt{polyFunc(t <\!\!\# T): U is Block}]\!] \triangleq \Lambda(t <: \mathcal{T}_{\mathcal{C}}^{\mathcal{M},X'}[\![\texttt{T}]\!]).\, \mathcal{T}_{\mathcal{C}}^{X'}[\![\texttt{Block}]\!].$$

By the equivalent of Lemma 13.1.2, $\mathcal{T}_{\mathcal{C}'}^{X}[\![\texttt{M}]\!] = \mathcal{T}_{\mathcal{C}}^{X}[\![\texttt{M}]\!]$ for all $\texttt{M}$. Putting this all together, we get

$$\mathcal{T}_{\mathcal{C}}^{X}[\![\mathcal{C}]\!],\mathcal{T}_{\mathcal{C}}^{X}[\![\mathcal{E}]\!] \vdash \mathcal{T}_{\mathcal{C}}^{X}[\![\texttt{polyFunc(t <\!\!\# T): U is Block}]\!]:$$
$$\mathcal{T}_{\mathcal{C}}^{X}[\![\texttt{ForAll(t <\!\!\# T).U}]\!],$$

Match-bounded polymorphic application   Suppose

$$\mathcal{C},\mathcal{E} \vdash \texttt{E[T']}: [\texttt{T'}/\texttt{t}]\,\texttt{U},$$

because

$$\mathcal{C},\mathcal{E} \vdash \texttt{E: ForAll(t <\!\!\# T).U},$$

and

$$\mathcal{C} \vdash \texttt{T'} <\!\!\# [\texttt{T'}/\texttt{t}]\texttt{T}.$$

By induction,

$$\mathcal{T}_{\mathcal{C}}^{X}[\![\mathcal{C}]\!],\mathcal{T}_{\mathcal{C}}^{X}[\![\mathcal{E}]\!] \vdash \mathcal{T}_{\mathcal{C}}^{X}[\![\texttt{E}]\!]: \mathcal{T}_{\mathcal{C}}^{X}[\![\texttt{ForAll(t <\!\!\# T).U}]\!]$$

and

$$\mathcal{T}_{\mathcal{C}}^{X}[\![\mathcal{C}]\!] \vdash \mathcal{T}_{\mathcal{C}}^{\mathcal{M},X}[\![\texttt{T'}]\!] <: \mathcal{T}_{\mathcal{C}}^{\mathcal{M},X}[\![[\texttt{T'}/\texttt{t}]\,\texttt{T}]\!].$$

The typing judgement translates to

$$\mathcal{T}_{\mathcal{C}}^{X}[\![\mathcal{C}]\!],\mathcal{T}_{\mathcal{C}}^{X}[\![\mathcal{E}]\!] \vdash \mathcal{T}_{\mathcal{C}}^{X}[\![\texttt{E}]\!]: \forall(t <: \mathcal{T}_{\mathcal{C}}^{\mathcal{M},X'}[\![\texttt{T}]\!]).\,\mathcal{T}_{\mathcal{C}}^{X'}[\![\texttt{U}]\!]$$

where $X' = X \cup \{\texttt{t}\}$.

It is easy to show that $\mathcal{T}_{\mathcal{C}}^{\mathcal{M},X}[\![[\texttt{T'}/\texttt{t}]\,\texttt{T}]\!] = [\mathcal{T}_{\mathcal{C}}^{\mathcal{M},X}[\![\texttt{T'}]\!]/t]\,\mathcal{T}_{\mathcal{C}}^{\mathcal{M},X'}[\![\texttt{T}]\!]$, where t has kind $* \Rightarrow *$.

It follows that

$$\mathcal{T}_{\mathcal{C}}^{X}[\![\mathcal{C}]\!],\mathcal{T}_{\mathcal{C}}^{X}[\![\mathcal{E}]\!] \vdash \mathcal{T}_{\mathcal{C}}^{\mathcal{M},X}[\![\texttt{T'}]\!] <: [\mathcal{T}_{\mathcal{C}}^{\mathcal{M},X}[\![\texttt{T'}]\!]/t]\,\mathcal{T}_{\mathcal{C}}^{\mathcal{M},X'}[\![\texttt{T}]\!],$$

and hence by rule *BdPolyApp* of $\Lambda_{<:}^{P}$ that

$$\mathcal{T}_{\mathcal{C}}^{X}[\![\mathcal{C}]\!],\mathcal{T}_{\mathcal{C}}^{X}[\![\mathcal{E}]\!] \vdash \mathcal{T}_{\mathcal{C}}^{X}[\![\texttt{E}]\!]\,[\mathcal{T}_{\mathcal{C}}^{\mathcal{M},X}[\![\texttt{T'}]\!]]: [\mathcal{T}_{\mathcal{C}}^{\mathcal{M},X}[\![\texttt{T'}]\!]/t]\,\mathcal{T}_{\mathcal{C}}^{\mathcal{M},X}[\![\texttt{U}]\!].$$

As a result,

$$\mathcal{T}_{\mathcal{C}}^{X}[\![\mathcal{C}]\!],\mathcal{T}_{\mathcal{C}}^{X}[\![\mathcal{E}]\!] \vdash \mathcal{T}_{\mathcal{C}}^{X}[\![\texttt{E}]\!]\,[\texttt{T'}]: \mathcal{T}_{\mathcal{C}}^{X}[\![[\texttt{T'}/\texttt{t}]\,\texttt{U}]\!].$$

∎

17.6 Summary

In this chapter we extended $\mathcal{MOOL}$ to a language $\mathcal{PMOOL}$ that supports match-bounded polymorphism, a form of bounded polymorphism in which the bound on type parameters is expressed in terms of the matching relation rather than subtyping. As the examples in Section 17.3 illustrate, this is often exactly what is needed. While F-bounded polymorphism can also express many of the same examples, match-bounded polymorphism is a simpler construct from the point of view of programmers and fits better with subclasses in languages with MyType.

The language $\mathcal{PMOOL}$ is very rich, including MyType, subtyping and matching, and F-bounded polymorphism where the bounds may be given in terms of either subtyping or matching. In the next chapter we step back to investigate the possibility of simplifying the language while retaining similar expressiveness. In particular, we will consider the possibility of dropping subtyping from the language.

18 *Simplifying: Dropping Subtyping for Matching*

"Perfection is finally attained not when there is no longer anything to add, but when there is no longer anything to take away ..."

– Antoine de Saint-Exupéry

In this chapter we provide a brief introduction to a simplified version of the language $\mathcal{PMOOL}$ that arises by dropping the notion of subtype and replacing it with a notion of *hash types*.

While the language $\mathcal{PMOOL}$ is very expressive, it may be too rich a language. The notions of subtyping and matching are very similar, differing on object types only based on whether or not MyType occurs as the type of a parameter in a method. Because both subtype and match-bounded polymorphism are available to programmers, they will have to decide which relation is most appropriate whenever defining polymorphic functions.

Moreover, while subclasses will always give rise to object types which *match* those of the superclass, they will not always be in the subtype relation. However, we have seen that subclasses always result in object types that match those of the superclass. Thus, if we believe the MyType construct to be useful (and we do!), it may be worth exploring whether it might be possible to have matching replace subtyping in an object-oriented language.

18.1 Can we drop subtyping?

Because it is not wise to include extraneous features in programming languages, it is worth considering whether or not one of these relations can be omitted. The language $\mathcal{PSOOL}$ omitted MyType and matching, but did not have the expressiveness of $\mathcal{PMOOL}$. In particular, reusable binary methods are hard to write safely. Once MyType is included in the language, matching seems forced on the programmer. But what about dropping subtyping from the language?

At first that seems to be a rather extreme position – after all subtyping is one of the key features of object-oriented languages! However, in practice it is usually *not* necessary for objects of one type to be able to masquerade as another. Instead what is important is to be able to predict which methods (and signatures) are supported by objects. This is exactly what matching guarantees. If T <# U the objects of type T support all of the same methods as U.

Virtually every use of subtype-bounded polymorphism can be replaced by match-bounded polymorphism. Moreover in section 17.3 we saw that match-bounded polymorphism is more compatible with the subclass relation (subclasses generate matching types) than is the F-bounded polymorphism that was necessary to get similar expressiveness.

What about the ability to replace the types of methods by subtypes in subclasses? It turns out that this ability is actually rarely used by programmers (helping to explain why most statically typed object-oriented languages don't support it). In Chapter 3 we discussed a number of problematic examples that illustrated the lack of expressiveness in object-oriented languages. These included classes with a clone method, and classes with binary methods like equals or the setNext method in the Node class. These examples are handled extremely well with the use of MyType – without needing support for changing method types.

The only example not handled easily by the use of MyType was the example with CircleClass and ColorCircleClass in Section 3.2.3, where it would have been useful to change the type of an instance variable, center. There is no advantage gained by using a language with subtyping, because it would require an illegal covariant change to the type of an instance variable. Instead, this example could be handled by writing it as a class, say PolyCircleClass, that is parameterized by a type parameter that matches PointType (the type of the instance variable center). A programmer would get a usable CircleClass by applying PolyCircleClass to PointType. We could extend PolyCircleClass to a subclass, PolyColorCircleClass, and then apply that to ColorPointType to get a usable ColorCircleClass. Subtype-bounded polymorphism would also work – if PointType does not have any covariant occurrences of MyType – but matching is just as good.

Of course, this is a bit awkward, and is similar to the difficulties in using F-bounded polymorphism. One alternative is to use Beta's virtual classes to change the type of the center instance variable, though this would introduce a dynamic type check at run time. Recall that Eiffel allows this sort of covariant type change in instance variables, though this is the source of Eiffel's type insecurities with existing compilers.

A statically safe alternative is to use a generalization of MyType that allows programmers to change simultaneously a mutually recursive group of types. In the paper [BV99], Bruce and Vanderwaart introduce the concept of a type group and type group extensions to group together several mutually recursive types and allow them all to be extended simultaneously. The type-checking rules for classes implementing these types are similar to those using MyType in that the type checker may only uses matching information about the types in the type group when type checking the methods of the class.

However, there are examples in which subtyping seems to play a crucial role. For example, one might want to have an array of graphical objects of different types, as long as they all include at least a certain collection of methods with given signatures. In a language with subtyping, this array can be declared to hold items of a type Graphical, where all of the objects to be placed in the array have types which are subtypes of Graphical. Because of subtyping, elements of subtypes can be assigned to components of the array expecting elements of type Graphical. This would not be possible if we only had matching.

Similarly we might want to define a method draw that takes a parameter that supports at least the methods of Graphical. This would normally be done by declaring:

draw: Graphical → Void

Then draw can be applied to any object with a type that is a subtype of Graphical.

Without the use of subtyping, this is more difficult. One possibility is to change the signature of the method to:

pdraw: ForAll (G <# Graphical). G → Void

This method requires the user to pass the type of the parameter as well as the parameter itself. This is more painful for the programmer. For example, if s is an object of type Square, where Square <# Graphical, the programmer would need to write pdraw[Square](x), rather than just draw(x), to invoke the function. It is clearly easier to use subtyping rather than requiring the programmer to pass both the type and regular parameter.

We do note that if `Graphical` has a binary method (*i.e.*, a method with a parameter of type `MyType`), then the more verbose signature is actually more flexible, because `Graphical` would have no subtypes, but does have many possible matching types.

The problem is worse for the array described above or variables that are intended to hold different types of values, because in the absence of subtyping there is no way of using type parameters to specify a variable that can hold values of different types. Without subtyping, variables can only contain elements with exactly their declared type.

Thus it appears that we cannot just drop subtyping and replace it with matching. We need a way for programmers to specify that an identifier can have a value corresponding to a range of types rather than just a single type.

$\mathcal{NOOL}$ In the rest of this chapter we provide a brief sketch of a language, $\mathcal{NOOL}$, with the following properties. The language will contain a `MyType` construct and support match-bounded polymorphism. Subtyping will not be a part of the language, but we will introduce a new type constructor for "hash" types. The combination of the weaker relation of matching and hash types will allow us to emulate the flexibility provided by subtyping.

18.2   Introducing hash types

In a traditional object-oriented language, a type declaration, `x: T`, indicates that the value of `x` may be of type `T` or any subtype of `T`. The subsumption type-checking rule provides the formal justification for this behavior.

While it is often convenient to have this flexibility, there are times when it is useful to be guaranteed that an expression has a fixed exact type as opposed to knowing the type up to subtyping. This is especially the case with binary methods, where one often wishes to guarantee that the receiver and parameter of the method are of the exact same type. For example, it takes only a little thought to realize it would be disastrous to try to build a linked list where some of the nodes are singly linked and others are doubly linked. This is one reason why it is important that doubly linked nodes are not allowed to be defined as subclasses of singly linked nodes in languages where subclasses always result in subtypes.

In order to provide the programmer with the capability to decide whether or not a type declaration should restrict an identifier to represent only a single type or a range of types, we introduce the following notations in $\mathcal{NOOL}$. We write

```
x: T
```

to indicate that the value of x must be of type T, but not a subtype of T. We write

```
x: #T
```

to indicate that the value of x must be of some type T' such that T' <# T.

HASH TYPE　　　We call types of the form #T, *hash types*. Because matching is only defined on object types, only object types (including type variables representing object types) can be used in constructing hash types. For example, one may not use hash types with function types.

Here is a simple example of the use of hash types. Suppose we wish to define a node class (similar to that in Figure 16.3) that holds items from any object type matching String. Then we could declare the instance variable:

```
value: #String
```

Because declaring a variable or formal parameter to have a hash type T allows it to hold values of all types matching T, items with hash types are used in a very similar way as regular variables or formal parameters in languages with subtyping.

While hash types add expressiveness to $\mathcal{NOOL}$, there are some restrictions on their use that are necessary to preserve type safety. We illustrate the possible problems with a familiar example.

Recall the definitions of NodeType and DoubleNodeType in Figure 16.5. While DoubleNodeType <# NodeType, they are not subtypes. The classes Node and DoubleNode generate objects of those types.

In anticipation of the discussion below, we repeat method setNext from DoubleNode below:

```
function setNext(newNext: MyType): Void is
{
    super.setNext(newNext);
    newNext ⇐ setPrevious(close(self))
}
```

Recall that method setPrevious was introduced in DoubleNodeType but was not contained in NodeType.

Suppose that n1, n2: #NodeType. Then their values could either be of type NodeType or of type DoubleNodeType (or potentially any other extension of NodeType). Suppose we wished to attach n2 as the "next" element from n1. That is, we would like to write the statement:

```
n1  ⇐  setNext(n2)
```

While this seems quite plausible, there are problems. Suppose that at run time, n1 is actually an object of type DoubleNodeType, while n2 is of type NodeType. If n1 is generated by class DoubleNode, execution of the above code will result in a type error. In particular, execution of the code for set-Next in DoubleNode results in sending the message setPrevious to n2, an object of type NodeType that does not have a method with that name.

This is essentially the same argument we gave back in Section 4.2 to show that extensions of object types with methods having parameters of type My-Type (or in Eiffel's case, like Current), did not result in subtypes. We must prevent this method invocation from being legal if we wish to have a statically type-safe language.

If we think more carefully about what is going on, we can see that the problem is that setNext requires a parameter that has exactly type MyType. However, because we do not know the exact type of n1, we cannot know at type-checking time what MyType is supposed to represent!

It might seem that changing the signature of setNext so that it takes a parameter of type #MyType might help, but changing that and the type of the instance variable next to #MyType do not help, as the same counterexample shows this is not type safe. As before, in order to understand whether a parameter to setNext is legal, we must know the meaning of MyType at the time of type checking. In this example, we definitely do not know the meaning of MyType if all that we know is that the type of n1 is #NodeType.

There is no difficulty in determining what is legal if we know the exact type of the receiver, n1, even in the case where we make the parameter type of setNext and the type of instance variable next be #MyType.[1] Suppose the parameter type is #MyType. If n1:NodeType then actual parameters for n1 ⇐setnext of type #NodeType, NodeType, and DoubleNodeType all work without type problems. If n1 has type (exactly) DoubleNodeType, then actual parameters of setNext with type #DoubleNodeType or Dou-bleNodeType both work without difficulty. Of course, the use of an actual parameter of type NodeType will not be type safe. The use of an actual parameter of type #NodeType also should not type check because it may not be safe.

---

1. Actually, while there are no type problems, we will find the class is not very usable if the type of next and the associated method parameters and return types are declared to have type #MyType. If we get a node as a result of sending getNext to another node, we lose the exact type and hence can't send setNext messages to it.

As a general rule, we will find the use of MyType very handy whenever we have a homogeneous collection of values to be dealt with. However, MyType is rarely appropriate when we have a heterogeneous collection of values. Thus MyType is very handy in the definition of singly or doubly linked nodes, because lists are composed of either homogeneous collections of singly linked nodes or homogeneous collections of doubly linked nodes.[2]

We can define a class for binary search trees as follows:

```
class BinarySearchTree(T <# OrderableMT) {
      function insert(T): Void is ...;
      function find(T): Boolean is ...;
      function remove(T): Boolean is ...
}
```

An object generated from BinarySearchTree(U) will represent a binary search tree in which all elements have exactly type U. Thus an object generated from BinarySearchTree(U) contains a homogeneous collection of elements.

However, suppose we wished to define a parameterized binary search tree, all of whose elements were of any type matching a type U. We would proceed as follows.

First recall type constructor OrderableF from Section 15.1. We modify its methods to take parameters of type #T:

```
OrderableM(T) = ObjectType {|
      equal: #T → Boolean;
      greaterThan: #T → Boolean;
      lessThan: #T → Boolean
|}
```

Objects of type OrderableM(T) are able to compare themselves with objects of any type matching T.

Then we can use F-bounded matching to write:

```
class HeteroBinarySearchTree(T <# OrderableM(T)) {
      function insert(#T): Void is ...;
      function find(#T): Boolean is ...;
      function remove(#T): Boolean is ...
}
```

---

2. Of course the values stored in the list can be specified to be either homogeneous or heterogeneous. It is the nodes that we are concerned with here!

If U <# OrderableM(U), objects generated from class HeteroBinary-SearchTree(U) represent binary search trees containing items of any type matching U. It is important that U <# OrderableM(U) because this way an object with type V matching U can be compared with an object with any other type W that matches T. Notice that it makes no sense to use MyType in any of the types associated with these heterogeneous data structures because we would then be unable to compare elements of type V with elements of type W.

Thus while objects with parameters of type MyType do not work well in heterogeneous collections, MyType is also typically not the correct modeling choice in expressing what must be done. Instead, MyType is most useful in working with homogeneous collections. However, matching continues to be useful in both situations.

18.3   Type-checking rules

We make no changes to the syntax of the language from $\mathcal{PMOOL}$ aside from dropping subtype-bounded polymorphic expressions. We also make no changes to the definition of static type assignments, $\mathcal{E}$. We simplify the definition of type constraints from Definition 17.2.1 by no longer including subtype constraints in $\mathcal{C}$.

Definition 18.3.1 *Relations of the form* $x^\kappa = G$ *and* $t <\# T$, *where* x^κ *is a type constructor variable,* G *is a type constructor expression of the same kind,* t *is a type variable, and* T *is a type expression are said to be* generalized type constructor constraints. *Because matching is only defined for types, rather than constructors of higher kind, constraints of the form* $t <\# T$ *will be restricted to those in which* t *and* T *are both types, and* T *represents an object type. A* generalized type constructor constraint system *for* $\mathcal{NOOL}$ *is defined as follows:*

GENERALIZED TYPE
CONSTRUCTOR
CONSTRAINTS

GENERALIZED TYPE
CONSTRUCTOR
CONSTRAINT SYSTEM

1. *The empty set,* ∅, *is a generalized type constructor constraint system.*

2. *If* $\mathcal{C}$ *is a generalized type constructor constraint system,* x^κ *is an identifier that does not appear in* $\mathcal{C}$ *or* G, *and* G *is a constructor expression of the same kind, then* $\mathcal{C} \cup \{x^\kappa = G\}$ *is a generalized type constructor constraint system.*

3. *Let* $\mathcal{C}$ *be a generalized type constructor constraint system, let* t *be a type identifier that does not appear in* $\mathcal{C}$, *and let* T *either be of the form* ObjectType M, *for some* M, *or be a type identifier representing an object type with respect to* $\mathcal{C}$. *Then* $\mathcal{C} \cup \{t <\# T\}$ *is a generalized type constructor constraint system.*

We also simplify the definition of when a type identifier represents an object type by no longer considering bounds involving subtypes.

REPRESENTS AN OBJECT
TYPE

Definition 18.3.2 *A type identifier* t *represents an object type with respect to* $\mathcal{C}$ *if* (t = T) $\in$ $\mathcal{C}$ *or* (t $<\!\#$ T) $\in$ $\mathcal{C}$, *where* T *is* TopObject, *is of the form* Object-Type M *for some* M, *or is a type identifier representing an object type with respect to* $\mathcal{C}$ *with the constraint on* t *removed.*

Because we will no longer allow the subtyping of method signatures in matching types, we can get along with the much simpler notion of extension.

EXTENDS

Definition 18.3.3 *1. Let* M *and* N *be record types. Then* M *extends* N, *written* M $\prec$ N *if and only if every label* l *of* N *is also included in* M *and the types associated with corresponding labels in* M *and* N *are exactly the same.*

2. Let F *and* G *be type constructors with kind* $* \Rightarrow *$. *Then* F $\prec$ G *iff for all types* t, F(t) *and* G(t) *are record types such that* F(t) $\prec$ G(t).

As usual, the matching relation ($<\!\#$) is only defined on type expressions that represent object types. The matching rules are given in Figure 18.1. The main difference between these rules and the rules for $\mathcal{MOOL}$ given in Figure 16.7 is in the hypothesis for rule *Object* $_{\#}$. Now the types of corresponding methods in matching object types must be identical (up to the implied change of meaning in MyType in different contexts).

Type-checking rules for $\mathcal{NOOL}$ are almost identical to those for $\mathcal{PMOOL}$. However, occurrences of subtyping in the type-checking rules are replaced by extension. We include the revised rules for classes and subclasses in Figure 18.2 as an example.

The rules in Figure 18.3 for message sending are the same as before when the receiver is an exact type, but are restricted for hash types.

Messages corresponding to binary methods may not be sent to expressions with hash types. When (non-binary) messages *are* sent to expressions with hash types, the resulting type is found by replacing all occurrences of My-Type by the hash type. Thus, if the clone method of type T has signature Void $\rightarrow$ MyType and E is an expression of type #T, then the type of E $\Leftarrow$ clone() is #T, as expected.

There are no changes to the type-checking rules for accessing instance variables or sending messages to visible objects because neither involves object types.

Of course the subsumption rule for subtypes goes away, but it is replaced by rules involving hash types. The *#Subsumption* rule allows one to treat an

TopObject $_{<\!\!\#}$ $\mathcal{C} \vdash \texttt{ObjectType M(MyType)} <\!\!\# \texttt{TopObject}$

Reflex $_{<\!\!\#}$ $\mathcal{C} \vdash \texttt{ObjectType M(MyType)} <\!\!\# \texttt{ObjectType M(MyType)}$

Transitive $_{<\!\!\#}$ $$\frac{\mathcal{C} \vdash \texttt{S} <\!\!\# \texttt{T}, \quad \mathcal{C} \vdash \texttt{T} <\!\!\# \texttt{U}}{\mathcal{C} \vdash \texttt{S} <\!\!\# \texttt{U}}$$

Object $_{<\!\!\#}$ $$\frac{\texttt{M}' \prec \texttt{M}}{\mathcal{C} \vdash \texttt{ObjectType M'(MyType)} <\!\!\# \texttt{ObjectType M(MyType)}}$$

where M$'$ and M have kind $* \Rightarrow *$.

Type Abbrev $_{<\!\!\#}$ $$\frac{\mathcal{C} \vdash \mathcal{C}(\texttt{T}') <\!\!\# \mathcal{C}(\texttt{T})}{\mathcal{C} \vdash \texttt{T}' <\!\!\# \texttt{T}}$$

Cong $_{<\!\!\#}$ $$\frac{\texttt{S} \cong \texttt{S}', \quad \texttt{T}' \cong \texttt{T}, \quad \mathcal{C} \vdash \texttt{S} <\!\!\# \texttt{T}}{\mathcal{C} \vdash \texttt{S}' <\!\!\# \texttt{T}'}$$

Figure 18.1   Matching rules for object types in $\mathcal{NOOL}$.

expression of type #T as though it had the type #U if T $<\!\!\#$ U. The weakening rule allows one to treat an expression with an exact type as though it had the corresponding hash type.

The `linkedlist` program from Figures 17.2, 17.3, and 17.4 of the last chapter is an example of a legal $\mathcal{NOOL}$ program. In fact nearly all of the $\mathcal{SOOL}, \mathcal{PSOOL}, \mathcal{MOOL}$, and $\mathcal{PMOOL}$ programs exhibited in this text are legal $\mathcal{NOOL}$ programs – or would be so by simply converting certain object types to hash types. As mentioned earlier, programmers tend not to use the full strength of subtyping as much as might be expected, even when subclasses are being defined. As a result matching and hash types can be used to give similar expressiveness.

In fact, if the type system of a language like $\mathcal{SOOL}$ were to use an invariant type system like Java, then there would be a simple translation from type-safe programs of $\mathcal{SOOL}$ to type-safe programs of $\mathcal{NOOL}$, where the translation simply replaces occurrences of object types with their hashed versions. Thus the use of hash types actually gives a language which properly extends languages with type systems like Java's.

$$C', \mathcal{E} \vdash \texttt{inst}\,[\texttt{MT}]\colon \texttt{IV}\,(\texttt{MT})\,,$$
$$C', \mathcal{E}' \vdash \texttt{meth}\,[\texttt{MT}]\,[\texttt{SelfType}]\colon \texttt{M}\,(\texttt{MT})$$

Class $\dfrac{}{C, \mathcal{E} \vdash \texttt{class}\,(\texttt{inst}\,[\texttt{MyType}], \texttt{meth}\,[\texttt{MyType}]\,[\texttt{SelfType}])\colon}$
$$\texttt{ClassType}\,(\texttt{IV}(\texttt{MyType}), \texttt{M}(\texttt{MyType}))$$

where

- $C' = C \cup \{\texttt{M}' \prec \texttt{M}, \texttt{IVR}' \prec \texttt{IV}^{ref}, \texttt{MT} = \texttt{ObjectType}\,\texttt{M}'(\texttt{MyType}),$
  $\texttt{SelfType} = \texttt{VisObjectType}\,(\texttt{IVR}'(\texttt{MyType}), \texttt{M}'(\texttt{MyType}))\,\}$,

- $\mathcal{E}' = \mathcal{E} \cup \{\texttt{self}\colon \texttt{SelfType}, \texttt{close}\colon \texttt{SelfType} \to \texttt{MT}\,\}$.

- None of $\texttt{M}'$, $\texttt{IVR}'$, $\texttt{MT}$, or $\texttt{SelfType}$ occurs free in $\texttt{inst}$, $\texttt{meth}$, $\texttt{IV}$, $\texttt{M}$, C, or $\mathcal{E}$.

$$C, \mathcal{E} \vdash \texttt{E}\colon \texttt{ClassType}\,(\texttt{IV}_{sup}(\texttt{MyType}), \texttt{M}_{sup}(\texttt{MyType})),$$
$$C', \mathcal{E} \vdash \texttt{inst}\,[\texttt{MT}]\colon \texttt{IV}_{sub}(\texttt{MyType}),$$
$$C', \mathcal{E}' \vdash \texttt{meth}\,[\texttt{MT}]\,[\texttt{SelfType}]\colon \texttt{M}_{sub}(\texttt{MyType}),$$
$$C' \vdash \texttt{T}'_{i_j} \prec \texttt{T}_{i_j}, \text{ for } 1 \le j \le m$$

Subclass $\dfrac{}{C, \mathcal{E} \vdash \texttt{class inherits E modifies } \texttt{l}_{i_1}, \ldots, \texttt{l}_{i_m}}$
$$(\texttt{inst}\,[\texttt{MyType}], \texttt{meth}\,[\texttt{MyType}]\,[\texttt{SelfType}])\colon$$
$$\texttt{ClassType}\,(\texttt{IV}(\texttt{MyType}), \texttt{M}(\texttt{MyType}))$$

where

- $\texttt{IV} = \texttt{IV}_{sup} \oplus \texttt{IV}_{sub}$ and $\texttt{M} = \texttt{M}_{sup} \oplus \texttt{M}_{sub}$,

- There is no overlap in the labels occurring in $\texttt{IV}_{sup}$ and $\texttt{IV}_{sub}$, and

- The overlapping labels in $\texttt{M}_{sup}$ and $\texttt{M}_{sub}$ are exactly $\texttt{l}_{i_1}, \ldots, \texttt{l}_{i_m}$,

- The type of $\texttt{l}_{i_j}$ in $\texttt{M}_{sub}\,(\texttt{MT})$ is $\texttt{T}'_{i_j}$, while the corresponding type in $\texttt{M}_{sup}\,(\texttt{MT})$ is $\texttt{T}_{i_j}$.

- $C' = C \cup \{\texttt{M}' \prec \texttt{M}, \texttt{IVR}' \prec \texttt{IV}^{ref}, \texttt{MT} = \texttt{ObjectType}\,\texttt{M}'(\texttt{MyType}),$
  $\texttt{SelfType} = \texttt{VisObjectType}\,(\texttt{IVR}'(\texttt{MyType}), \texttt{M}'(\texttt{MyType}))\,\}$,

- $\mathcal{E}' = \mathcal{E} \cup \{\texttt{self}\colon \texttt{SelfType}, \texttt{close}\colon \texttt{SelfType} \to \texttt{MT}\}$.

- None of $\texttt{M}'$, $\texttt{IVR}'$, $\texttt{MT}$, or $\texttt{SelfType}$ occurs free in $\texttt{inst}$, $\texttt{meth}$, $\texttt{IV}$, $\texttt{M}$, C, or $\mathcal{E}$.

Figure 18.2   Typing rules for classes and subclasses in $\mathcal{NOOL}$.

Message
$$\frac{\mathcal{C},\mathcal{E} \vdash \text{E: U}, \quad \mathcal{C} \vdash \text{U} <\!\!\# \ \texttt{ObjectType} \ \{\!\!| \text{m: T(MyType)} |\!\!\}}{\mathcal{C},\mathcal{E} \vdash \text{E} \Leftarrow \text{m: T(U)}}$$

#Message
$$\frac{\mathcal{C},\mathcal{E} \vdash \text{E: \#U}, \quad \mathcal{C} \vdash \text{U} <\!\!\# \ \texttt{ObjectType} \ \{\!\!| \text{m: T(MyType)} |\!\!\}}{\mathcal{C},\mathcal{E} \vdash \text{E} \Leftarrow \text{m: T(\#U)}}$$

where `MyType` only occurs positively in `T(MyType)`.

#Subsumption
$$\frac{\mathcal{C} \vdash \text{T} <\!\!\# \ \text{U} \quad \mathcal{C},\mathcal{E} \vdash \text{E: \#T}}{\mathcal{C},\mathcal{E} \vdash \text{E: \#U}}$$

Weakening
$$\frac{\mathcal{C},\mathcal{E} \vdash \text{E: T}}{\mathcal{C},\mathcal{E} \vdash \text{E: \#T}}$$

Figure 18.3   Typing rules for message sending and subsumption in $\mathcal{NOOL}$.

18.4   An informal semantics of hash types

Because $\mathcal{NOOL}$ does not support subtyping, it would make more sense to provide a translation to Λ_{rr}^P than to $\Lambda_{<:}^P$. However, this would require more space than we would like to devote here. (See [BFP97] for an alternative approach to the semantics of a language, $\mathcal{LOOM}$, that is very similar to $\mathcal{NOOL}$.) However, we do wish to explain hash types in terms of existential types.

We can understand the type `#T` as an abbreviation for $\exists(\text{t} <\!\!\# \ \text{T}).\text{t}$. In words, an expression has type `#T` iff it has a type t, where t $<\!\!\#$ T. While we did not include existential types, let alone match-bound existential types, in any of our object-oriented languages, the reader should be able to understand their use in explaining the meaning of hash types.

With this understanding of the translation of hash types, we can explain why the *#Subsumption* and *Weakening* rules are true. If the value of E has type $\exists(\text{t} <\!\!\# \ \text{T}).\text{t}$, then it is easy to unpack the value and repack it with type $\exists(\text{t} <\!\!\# \ \text{U}).\text{t}$ as long as T $<\!\!\#$ U, validating the *#Subsumption* rule. Similarly, if E has type T, then it is easy to pack it to have type $\exists(\text{t} <\!\!\# \ \text{T}).\text{t}$.

The interesting thing about this understanding of these rules is that use of these two rules has a semantic effect on the values of the expressions. However the original value is still available unchanged.

18.5   Summary

In this section we have given a brief description of a language $\mathcal{NOOL}$ which results (roughly) from replacing uses of subtyping in $\mathcal{PMOOL}$ by matching and newly introduced hash types. The purpose of the design of this new language was to provide a simpler language. In particular, we desired to avoid the confusion of supporting two very similar relations on object types, subtyping and matching. More details, including a proof of type safety based on an operational semantics, may be found in the paper [BFP97].

Though we did not have space to include many examples, we assert that the use of $\mathcal{NOOL}$ allows the programmer more expressiveness than working in a language without MyType. At this point, that is only a claim rather than a statement of fact. Further experience with languages like $\mathcal{NOOL}$ will be necessary in order to evaluate this assertion. The language $\mathcal{LOOJ}$ (referred to as Rupiah in [Bur98, Fos01]), is an extension of Java using similar ideas.

Historical Notes and References for Section IV

As we noted earlier, bounded polymorphism was introduced by Cardelli and Wegner. F-bounded polymorphism was introduced when it was realized that regular bounded polymorphism was not adequate to express many of the restrictions on polymorphism required in object-oriented languages, particularly when the bounds on the parameter identifiers involved binary methods. Eiffel appears to be the first commercial language to provide formal support for bounded polymorphism.

The notion of an explicit type identifier, MyType, representing the type of self appears to have first arisen in Trellis/Owl [SCB+86]. As we saw earlier, Eiffel's use of anchored types provides an even more general construct. One of the first theoretical papers to discuss MyType, and the one that most influenced the material presented here, was the paper, "Inheritance is not subtyping" [CHC90], by Cook *et al.*.

Mitchell's object-based calculus, presented in [Mit90], also includes a way of referring to the type of self, though a bound variable rather than a keyword is used. Later work by Fisher *et al.* [FHM94] continued development of this calculus.

The language Emerald [BH91, BHJ+87] also allows references to the type of self in method signatures via a bound local name for the type. Emerald provides constrained parametric polymorphism where the constraint on type variables is given via a "such that" clause similar to the "where" clauses in Ada that allow the programmer to specify the names and signatures of methods that the type variable must support. However, Emerald also allows the use of named types in these clauses with a syntax similar to F-bounded polymorphism.

The languages Theta [DGLM94, DGLM95] and PolyJ [MBL97] use "where" clauses to constrain type variables. Constraints of this sort are essentially equivalent to match-bounded polymorphism. The main differences involve whether one has to write out all of the methods one wishes to require or just has to write out the name of a type containing those methods.

The discussion of `MyType` in Chapters 16 and 17 is based on the development and analysis of the languages TOOPLE [Bru94, BCD+93, BCK94], TOIL [vG93], and PolyTOIL [BSvG95, BFSvG01]. These language were designed by Bruce and his students, extending the ideas of [CHC90]. The language $\mathcal{MOOL}$ in this book is very similar to TOIL, while $\mathcal{PMOOL}$ is similar to PolyTOIL.

Eifrig *et al.* [ESTZ94b, ESTZ94a] also presented a semantics for an imperative object-oriented language containing a `MyType` construct. As noted earlier, the language Strongtalk [BG93], a typed version of Smalltalk, also involves a `MyType` construct (called `Self` there). Its type system is based on the type rules for TOOPLE.

The definition of matching as originally given in [Bru94] was based on F-bounded polymorphism. Abadi and Cardelli, in "On subtyping and matching" [AC95b], argue that higher-order subtyping is more general than F-bounded polymorphism and serves as a better interpretation for the matching relation introduced in Chapter 16. We have followed their lead in our presentation.

The language Objective ML also supports the notion of MyType by allowing the use of a local bound type variable to stand for the type of `self`. The use of row variables in object types provides a mechanism for the expression of a matching relation.

Bono and Bugliesi, in their paper, "Matching for the lambda calculus of objects", discuss replacing polymorphism over row variables in Mitchell's object calculus by matching and implicit match-bound polymorphism, carefully examining the connections between these schemes.

After completing the design of PolyTOIL, Bruce was concerned that it was confusing to have such similar relations as subtyping and matching coexisting in a language. As a result he and his coworkers began looking at the design of a language, $\mathcal{LOOM}$ [BFP97], with matching only. Gawecki and Matthes [GM96] reported an interesting study that showed that when programmers worked with a language supporting both subtype-bounded polymorphism and match-bounded polymorphism, they had difficulty determining which to use. While PolyTOIL only supported match-bound polymorphism at the source program level, these results strengthened the appeal of $\mathcal{LOOM}$.

More recent work on $\mathcal{LOOM}$ has included the addition of a module system [Pet96, BPV98] to the language in order to provide more refined information hiding facilities. Work in another direction has included the design and implementation of an extension to Java, now called $\mathcal{LOOJ}$ [Bur98, Fos01], that adds `MyType` (called `ThisType` in $\mathcal{LOOJ}$), match-bounded polymorphism, and exact types to Java. Finally, Bruce and Vanderwaart [BV99] present the design and translational semantics of a mutually recursive generalization of `MyType` that supports the simultaneous specializations of mutually recursive types, adding expressiveness similar to that of virtual classes.

Bibliography

[Aba94] Martin Abadi. Baby Modula-3 and a theory of objects. *Journal of Functional Programming*, 4:249–283, 1994.

[AC93] Roberto Amadio and Luca Cardelli. Subtyping recursive types. *ACM Transactions on Programming Languages and Systems*, 15(4):575–631, 1993.

[AC95a] Martin Abadi and Luca Cardelli. An imperative object calculus. In P.D. Mosses and M. Nielsen, editors, *TAPSOFT '95: Theory and Practice of Software Development*, pages 471–485. Springer-Verlag, LNCS 915, 1995.

[AC95b] Martin Abadi and Luca Cardelli. On subtyping and matching. In *Proceedings ECOOP '95*, pages 145–167, 1995.

[AC96] Martin Abadi and Luca Cardelli. *A Theory of Objects*. Springer-Verlag, 1996.

[ACV96] Martin Abadi, Luca Cardelli, and Ramesh Viswanathan. An interpretation of objects and object types. In *Proc. ACM Symp. on Principles of Programming Languages*, pages 396–409, 1996.

[AFM97] Ole Ageson, Stephen Freund, and John C. Mitchell. Adding parameterized types to Java. In *ACM Symposium on Object-Oriented Programming: Systems, Languages, and Applications*, pages 49–65, 1997.

[AGH99] Ken Arnold, James Gosling, and David Holmes. *The Java Programming Language*. Addison Wesley, third edition, 1999.

[Ame87] Pierre America. Inheritance and subtyping in a parallel object-oriented language. In Jean Bezivin et al., editor, *ECOOP '87*, pages 234–242. Springer-Verlag, LNCS 276, 1987.

[AvdL90] Pierre America and Frank van der Linden. A parallel object-oriented language with inheritance and subtyping. In *OOPSLA-ECOOP '90 Proceedings*, pages 161–168. ACM SIGPLAN Notices,25(10), October 1990.

[Bac81] J. W. Backus. The history of FORTRAN I, II, and III. In R. L. Wexelblatt, editor, *History of Programming Languages*, pages 25–45. Academic Press, 1981.

[Bar84] Henk P. Barendregt. *The Lambda Calculus: Its Syntax and Semantics*. North Holland, 1984.

[Bar92] Henk P. Barendregt. Lambda calculus with types. In *Handbook of Logic in Computer Science*, volume 2. Oxford University Press, 1992.

[BCC+95] Kim B. Bruce, Luca Cardelli, Giuseppe Castagna, The Hopkins Objects Group, Gary T. Leavens, and Benjamin Pierce. On binary methods. *Theory and Practice of Object Systems*, 1(3):221–242, 1995.

[BCD+93] Kim B. Bruce, J. Crabtree, A. Dimock, R. Muller, T. Murtagh, and R. van Gent. Safe and decidable type checking in an object-oriented language. In *Proc. ACM Symp. on Object-Oriented Programming: Systems, Languages, and Applications*, pages 29–46, 1993.

[BCK94] Kim B. Bruce, J. Crabtree, and G. Kanapathy. An operational semantics for TOOPLE: A statically-typed object-oriented programming language. In S. Brookes, M. Main, A. Melton, M. Mislove, and D. Schmidt, editors, *Mathematical Foundations of Programming Semantics*, pages 603–626. LNCS 802, Springer-Verlag, 1994.

[BCP99] Kim B. Bruce, Luca Cardelli, and Benjamin C. Pierce. Comparing object encodings. *Information and Computation*, 155:108–133, 1999. A preliminary version appeared in Proceedings of TACS '97 (Theoretical Aspects of Computer Science), LNCS 1281, pp. 415-438.

[BDMN73] G.M. Birtwistle, O.-J. Dahl, B. Myhrhaug, and K. Nygaard. *SIMULA Begin*. Aurbach, 1973.

[BFP97] Kim B. Bruce, Adrian Fiech, and Leaf Petersen. Subtyping is not a good "match" for object-oriented languages. In *ECOOP '97*, pages 104–127. LNCS 1241, Springer-Verlag, 1997.

[BFSvG01] Kim B. Bruce, Adrien Fiech, Angela Schuett, and Robert van Gent. PolyTOIL: A type-safe polymorphic object-oriented language. Technical report, Williams College, 2001. submitted for publication.

[BG93] Gilad Bracha and David Griswold. Strongtalk: Typechecking Smalltalk in a production environment. In *Proc. ACM Symp. on Object-Oriented Programming: Systems, Languages, and Applications*, pages 215–230, 1993.

[BH91] A. Black and N. Hutchinson. Typechecking polymorphism in Emerald. Technical Report CRL 91/1 (Revised), DEC Cambridge Research Lab, 1991.

[BHJ+87] A. P. Black, N. Hutchinson, E. Jul, H. M. Levy, and L. Carter. Distribution and abstract types in Emerald. *IEEE Transactions on Software Engineering*, SE-13(1):65–76, 1987.

[BI82] A.H. Borning and D.H. Ingalls. A type declaration and inference system for Smalltalk. In *ACM Symp. Principles of Programming Languages*, pages 133–141, 1982.

[BL90] Kim B. Bruce and G. Longo. A modest model of records, inheritance and bounded quantification. *Information and Computation*, 87(1/2):196–240, 1990. Reprinted in *Theoretical Aspects of Object-Oriented Programming*, ed. Gunter and Mitchell, MIT Press (1994), pp. 151-195.

[BOSW98] Gilad Bracha, Martin Odersky, David Stoutamire, and Philip Wadler. Making the future safe for the past: Adding genericity to the java programming language. In *Object-Oriented Programming: Systems, Languages, Applications (OOPSLA)*, Vancouver, October 1998. ACM.

[BOW98] Kim B. Bruce, Martin Odersky, and Philip Wadler. A statically safe alternative to virtual types. In *ECOOP '98*, pages 523–549. LNCS 1445, Springer-Verlag, 1998.

[BPV98] Kim B. Bruce, Leaf Petersen, and Joseph C. Vanderwaart. Modules in LOOM: Classes are not enough. Technical report, Williams College, 1998.

[Bru92] Kim B. Bruce. The equivalence of two semantic definitions of inheritance in object-oriented languages. In S. Brookes, M. Main, A. Melton, M. Mislove, and D. Schmidt, editors, *Proceedings of the 7th International Conference on Mathematical Foundations of Programming Semantics*, pages 102–124. LNCS 598, Springer-Verlag, 1992.

[Bru94] Kim B. Bruce. A paradigmatic object-oriented programming language: design, static typing and semantics. *Journal of Functional Programming*, 4(2):127–206, 1994. An earlier version of this paper appeared in the 1993 POPL Proceedings.

[Bru97] Kim B. Bruce. Increasing Java's expressiveness with ThisType and match-bounded polymorphism. Technical report, Williams College, 1997.

[BS98] Egon Börger and Wolfram Schulte. A programmer friendly modular definition of the semantics of Java. In Jim Alves-Foss, editor, *Formal Syntax and Semantics of Java*. Springer, 1998.

[BSvG95] Kim B. Bruce, Angela Schuett, and Robert van Gent. PolyTOIL: A type-safe polymorphic object-oriented language, extended abstract. In *ECOOP '95*, pages 27–51. LNCS 952, Springer-Verlag, 1995.

[BTCGS89] V. Breazu-Tannen, T. Coquand, C.A. Gunter, and A. Scedrov. Inheritance and explicit coercion. In *Fourth IEEE Symp. Logic in Computer Science*, pages 112–129, 1989.

[BTCGS91] V. Breazu-Tannen, T. Coquand, C.A. Gunter, and A. Scedrov. Inheritance and implicit coercion. *Information and Computation*, 93(1):172–221, 1991.

[Bur98] Jon Burstein. *Rupiah: An extension to Java supporting match-bounded parametric polymorphism, ThisType, and exact typing*. Williams College Senior Honors Thesis, 1998.

[BV99] Kim B. Bruce and Joseph C. Vanderwaart. Semantics-driven language design: Statically type-safe virtual types in object-oriented languages. In

Electronic Notes in Theoretical Computer Science, volume 20, 1999.   URL:
`http://www.elsevier.nl/locate/entcs/volume20.html`, 26 pages.

[BW90] Kim B. Bruce and Peter Wegner. An algebraic model of subtype and inheritance. In Francois Bancilhon and Peter Buneman, editors, *Advances in Database Programming Language*, pages 75–96. Addison-Wesley, Reading, MA, 1990.

[Car88] L. Cardelli. A semantics of multiple inheritance. *Information and Computation*, 76:138–164, 1988. Special issue devoted to *Symp. on Semantics of Data Types*, Sophia-Antipolis (France), 1984.

[Car97] Luca Cardelli. Type systems. In Allen Tucker, editor, *Handbook of Computer Science and Engineering*, pages 2208–2236. CRC Press, 1997.

[Cas95] Giuseppe Castagna. Covariance and contravariance: Conflict without a cause. *ACM Transactions on Programming Languages and Systems*, 17:431–447, 1995.

[Cas97] Giuseppe Castagna. *Object-Oriented Programming: A unified foundation*. Progress in Theoretical Computer Science. Birkhauser, 1997.

[CCH+89] P. Canning, W. Cook, W. Hill, J. Mitchell, and W. Olthoff. F-bounded quantification for object-oriented programming. In *Functional Prog. and Computer Architecture*, pages 273–280, 1989.

[CDG+88] L. Cardelli, J. Donahue, L. Galssman, M. Jordan, B. Kalsow, and G. Nelson. Modula-3 report. Technical Report SRC-31, DEC systems Research Center, 1988.

[CDJ+89] L. Cardelli, J. Donahue, M. Jordan, B. Kalsow, and G. Nelson. The Modula-3 type system. In *Sixteenth ACM Symp. Principles of Programming Languages*, pages 202–212, 1989.

[CG92] P.L. Curien and G. Ghelli. Coherence of subsumption, minimum typing and type-checking in $F_\le$. *Mathematical Structures in Computer Science*, 2:55–91, 1992.

[Cha95] Craig Chambers. The cecil language: Specification and rationale, version 2.1. Technical report, University of Washington, 1995.

[CHC90] William R. Cook, Walter L. Hill, and Peter S. Canning. Inheritance is not subtyping. In *Proc. 17th ACM Symp. on Principles of Programming Languages*, pages 125–135, January 1990.

[Chu32] Alonzo Church. A set of postulates for the foundations of logic. *Annals of Mathematics*, 33:346–366, 1932. A second paper with the same title appeared in Volume 33, pp. 839-864 of the same journal.

[Chu36] Alonzo Church. An unsolvable problem of elementary number theory. *American Journal of Mathematics*, 58:345–363, 1936.

[Chu40] Alonzo Church. A formulation of the simple theory of types. *Journal of Symbolic Logic*, 5:56–68, 1940.

[Chu41] Alonzo Church. *The Calculi of Lambda Conversion*. Princeton Univ. Press, 1941. Reprinted 1963 by University Microfilms Inc., Ann Arbor, MI.

[CL95] Craig Chambers and Gary T. Leavens. Typechecking and modules for multimethods. *TOPLAS*, 17:805–843, 1995.

[CM99] C. Chambers and Todd Millstein. Modular statically typed multimethods. In *ECOOP*, pages 279–303, 1999.

[Coo89a] W.R. Cook. *A Denotational Semantics of Inheritance*. PhD thesis, Brown University, 1989.

[Coo89b] W.R. Cook. A proposal for making Eiffel type-safe. In *European Conf. on Object-Oriented Programming*, pages 57–72, 1989.

[Coo92] William R. Cook. Interfaces and specifications for the smalltalk-80 collection classes. In *Proc. ACM Conf. on Object-Oriented Programming: Systems, Languages and Applications*, pages 1–15, 1992.

[Cox86] Brad Cox. *Object-oriented programming; an evolutionary appoach*. Addison-Wesley, 1986.

[CP94] William Cook and Jens Palsberg. A denotational semantics of inheritance and its correctness. *Information and Computation*, 114:329–350, 1994. An earlier version of this paper appeared in the 1989 OOPSLA Proceedings.

[CU89] C. Chambers and D. Ungar. Customization: Optimizing compiler technology for Self, a dynamically-typed object-oriented programming language. In *SIGPLAN '89 Conf. on Programming Language Design and Implementation*, pages 146–160, 1989.

[CW85] L. Cardelli and P. Wegner. On understanding types, data abstraction, and polymorphism. *Computing Surveys*, 17(4):471–522, 1985.

[DE98] Sophia Drossopoulou and Susan Eisenbach. Describing the semantics of Java and proving type soundness. In Jim Alves-Foss, editor, *Formal Syntax and Semantics of Java*. Springer, 1998.

[DEK99] Sophia Drossopoulou, Susan Eisenbach, and Sarfraz Khurshid. Is the Java type system sound? *Theory and Practice of Object Systems*, pages 3–24, 1999.

[DG87] L. G. DeMichiel and R. P. Gabriel. Common Lisp Object System overview. In *Proceedings of ECOOP '87*, pages 151–170. Springer-Verlag LNCS 276, 1987.

[DGLM94] Mark Day, Robert Gruber, Barbara Liskov, and Andrew C. Myers. Abstraction mechanisms in Theta. Technical report, MIT Laboratory for Computer Science, 1994.

[DGLM95] Mark Day, Robert Gruber, Barbara Liskov, and Andrew C. Myers. Subtypes vs. where clauses: Constraining parametric polymorphism. In *Proc. ACM Symp. on Object-Oriented Programming: Systems, Languages, and Applications*, pages 156–168, 1995.

[ES90] Margaret A. Ellis and Bjarne Stroustrop. *The annotated C^{++} reference manual*. Addison-Wesley, 1990.

[EST95a] J. Eifrig, S. Smith, and V. Trifonov. Sound polymorphic type inference for objects. In *Proceedings of OOPSLA '95*, pages 169–184, 1995.

[EST95b] Jonathan Eifrig, Scott Smith, and Valery Trifonov. Type inference for recursively constrained types and its application to OOP. In *Mathematical Foundations of Programming Semantics, New Orleans*, volume 1 of *Electronic Notes in Theoretical Computer Science*. Elsevier, 1995. http://www.elsevier.nl:80/mcs/tcs/pc/volume01.htm.

[ESTZ94a] J. Eifrig, S. Smith, V. Trifonov, and A. Zwarico. Application of OOP type theory: State, decidability, integration. In *Proceedings of OOPSLA '94*, pages 16–30, 1994.

[ESTZ94b] J. Eifrig, S. Smith, V. Trifonov, and A. Zwarico. An interpretation of typed OOP in a language with state. *LISP and Symbolic Computation*, 1994. To appear.

[FHM94] K Fisher, F. Honsell, and John C. Mitchell. A lambda calculus of objects and method specialization. *Nordic Jounral of Computing*, 1:3–37, 1994. An earlier version of this paper appeared in Proc. 8th IEEE Symp. on Logic in Computer Science, 1993, pp. 26-38.

[FM96] Kathleen Fisher and John C. Mitchell. The development of type systems for object-oriented languages. *TAPOS*, pages 189–220, 1996.

[FM98] Kathleen Fisher and John C. Mitchell. On the relationship between classes, objects, and data abstraction. *TAPOS*, pages 3–32, 1998.

[Fos01] John N. Foster. *Rupiah: Towards an expressive static type system for Java*. Williams College Senior Honors Thesis, 2001.

[FR99] Kathleen Fisher and John Reppy. The design of a class mechanism for Moby. In *ACM SIGPLAN '99 Symposium on Programming Language Design and Implementation*, pages 37–49. ACM, 1999.

[Fre95] Steve Freeman. Partial revelation and Modula-3. *Dr. Dobb's Journal*, 20(10):36–42,110–112, October 1995.

[Gir71] J.-Y. Girard. Une extension de l'interpretation de Gödel à l'analyse, et son application à l'élimination des coupures dans l'analyse et la théorie des types. In J.E. Fenstad, editor, *2nd Scandinavian Logic Symposium*, pages 63–92. North-Holland, 1971.

[Gir86] J.-Y. Girard. The system F of variable types, fifteen years later. *Theor. Comp. Sci.*, 45(2):159–192, 1986.

[GJSB00] James Gosling, Bill Joy, Guy Steele, and Gilad Bracha. *The Java Language Specification*. Addison Wesley, second edition, 2000.

[GLP00] Vladimir Gapeyev, Michael Levin, and Benjamin Pierce. Recursive subtyping revealed. In *Proceedings of the International Conference on Functional Programming (ICFP)*, pages 221–231, 2000.

[GM94] Carl A. Gunter and John C. Mitchell. *Theoretical Aspects of Object-Oriented Programming*. MIT Press, Cambridge, MA, 1994.

[GM96] Andreas Gawecki and Florian Matthes. Integrating subtyping, matching and type quantification: A practical perspective. In *ECOOP '96*, pages 26–47. LNCS 1098, Springer-Verlag, 1996.

[GR83] A. Goldberg and D. Robson. *Smalltalk–80: The language and its implementation*. Addison Wesley, 1983.

[GTW78] J.A. Goguen, J.W. Thatcher, and E.G. Wagner. An initial algebra approach to the specification, correctness, and implementation of abstract data types. In R.T. Yeh, editor, *Current Trends in Programming Methodology*, volume 4. Prentice-Hall, 1978.

[Gun92] Carl A. Gunter. *Semantics of Programming Languages: Structures and Techniques*. MIT Press, 1992.

[Gut77] J.V. Guttag. Abstract data types and the development of data structures. *Communications of ACM*, 20(6):396–404, 1977.

[Hen50] L. Henkin. Completeness in the theory of types. *Journal of Symbolic Logic*, 15(2):81–91, June 1950.

[Hin97] J.R. Hindley. *Basic Simple Type Theory*, volume 42 of *Cambridge Tracts in Theoretical Computer Science*. Cambridge University Press, 1997.

[HJW92] Paul Hudak, S. Peyton Jones, and Philip Wadler. Report on the programming language Haskell, a non-strict purely functional language (version 1.2). *SIGPLAN Notices*, 27(5), May 1992.

[HMM86] R. Harper, D.B. MacQueen, and R. Milner. Standard ML. Technical Report ECS–LFCS–86–2, Lab. for Foundations of Computer Science, University of Edinburgh, March 1986.

[HP95] Martin Hofmann and Benjamin Pierce. A unifying type-theoretic framework for objects. *Journal of Functional Programming*, 5(4):593–635, October 1995. Previous versions appeared in the Symposium on Theoretical Aspects of Computer Science, 1994, (pages 251–262) and, under the title "An Abstract View of Objects and Subtyping (Preliminary Report)," as University of Edinburgh, LFCS technical report ECS-LFCS-92-226, 1992.

[HS86] J.R. Hindley and J.P. Seldin. *Introduction or Combinators and Lambda Calculus*. London Mathematical Society, 1986.

[IP99] Atsushi Igarashi and Benjamin C. Pierce. Foundations for virtual types. In *ECOOP '99*, 1999. Full version to appear in *Information and Computation*.

[IPW99] Atsushi Igarashi, Benjamin Pierce, and Philip Wadler. Featherweight Java: A minimal core calculus for Java and GJ. In *OOPSLA '99*, pages 132–146, 1999. Full version to appear in ACM Transactions on Programming Languages and Systems, 2001.

[Joy98] Bill Joy. Re: Do parametric types beat virtual types? Message to Java-genericity electronic mail list, October, 1998.

[Kam88] S. Kamin. Inheritance in Smalltalk-80: a denotational definition. In *ACM Symp. Principles of Programming Languages*, pages 80–87, 1988.

[Kle36] Stephen C. Kleene. Lambda definability and recursiveness. *Duke Mathematical Journal*, 2:340–353, 1936.

[KLM94] Dinesh Katiyar, David Luckham, and John Mitchell. A type system for pro-totyping languages. In *21st ACM Symp. Principles of Programming Languages*, pages 138–150, 1994.

[KMMPN87] Bent Bruun Kristensen, Ole Lehrmann Madsen, Birger Moller-Pedersen, and Kristen Nygaard. The Beta programming language. In Bruce Shriver and Peter Wegner, editors, *Research Directions in Object-Oriented Programming*, pages 7–48. M.I.T. Press, Cambridge, MA, 1987.

[KPS93] Dexter Kozen, Jens Palsberg, and Michael I. Schwartzbach. Efficient recur-sive subtyping. In *20th ACM Symp. Principles of Programming Languages*, 1993.

[KR78] B. W. Kernighan and D. M. Ritchie. *The C programming language*. Prentice-Hall, 1978.

[KR94] Samuel N. Kamin and Uday S. Reddy. Two semantic models of object-oriented languages. In Carl A. Gunter and John C. Mitchell, editors, *Theoretical Aspects of Object-Oriented Programming*, pages 463–495. MIT Press, 1994.

[L+81] B. Liskov et al. *CLU Reference Manual*, volume 114 of *Lecture Notes in Computer Science*. Springer-Verlag, 1981.

[Lan65] P.J. Landin. A correspondence between algol 60 and church's lambda nota-tion. *CACM*, 8:89–101; 158–165, 1965.

[Lan66] P.J. Landin. The next 700 programming languages. *CACM*, 9:157–166, 1966.

[Lou93] Kenneth C. Louden. *Programming Languages: Principles and Practice*. PWS, 1993.

[LP98] Harry R. Lewis and Christos H. Papadimitriou. *Elements of the Theory of Com-putation*. Prentice-Hall, 2nd edition, 1998.

[MAE+65] J. McCarthy, P. W. Abrahams, D. J. Edwards, T. P. Hart, and M.I. Levin. *LISP 1.5 Programmer's Manual, 2nd Edition*. MIT Press, 1965.

[MBL97] Andrew C. Myers, Joseph A. Bank, and Barbara Liskov. Parameterized types for Java. In *ACM Symposium on the Principles of Programming Languages*, pages 132–145. ACM, 1997.

[McC79] N. McCracken. *An Investigation of a Programming Language with a Polymorphic Type Structure*. PhD thesis, Syracuse Univ., 1979.

[Mey88] Bertrand Meyer. *Object-Oriented Software Construction*. Prentice-Hall, 1988.

[Mey92] Bertrand Meyer. *Eiffel: the language*. Prentice-Hall, 1992.

[Mey95a] B. Meyer. Static typing and other mysteries of life. Technical report, Interactive Software Engineering, Inc., 1995. Text of invited address to OOPSLA '95.

[Mey95b] Bertrand Meyer. Static typing. *OOPS Messenger*, 6(4):20–29, 1995. Text of an OOPSLA '95 address.

[Mit84] J.C. Mitchell. Coercion and type inference (summary). In *Proc. 11th ACM Symp. on Principles of Programming Languages*, pages 175–185, January 1984.

[Mit90] J.C. Mitchell. Toward a typed foundation for method specialization and inheritance. In *Proc. 17th ACM Symp. on Principles of Programming Languages*, pages 109–124, January 1990.

[Mit96] John C. Mitchell. *Foundations for Programming Languages*. Foundations of Computing Series. MIT Press, 1996.

[MP88] J.C. Mitchell and G.D. Plotkin. Abstract types have existential types. *ACM Trans. on Programming Languages and Systems*, 10(3):470–502, 1988. Preliminary version appeared in *Proc. 12th ACM Symp. on Principles of Programming Languages*, 1985.

[MPS86] D. MacQueen, G Plotkin, and R. Sethi. An ideal model for recursive polymorphic types. *Information and Control*, 71(1/2):95–130, 1986.

[MTH90] Robin Milner, Mads Tofte, and Robert Harper. *The Definition of Standard ML*. MIT Press, 1990.

[Omo91] Stephen M. Omohundro. The Sather language. Technical report, International Computer Science Institute, 1991.

[Omo93] Stephen M. Omohundro. The Sather programming language. *Dr. Dobb's Journal*, 18(11):42–48, October 1993.

[OW97] Martin Odersky and Philip Wadler. Pizza into Java: Translating theory into practice. In *24th ACM Symp. on the Principles of Programming Languages*, pages 146–159. ACM, 1997.

[Pet96] Leaf Petersen. *A module system for LOOM*. Williams College Senior Honors Thesis, 1996.

[Pie94] Benjamin C. Pierce. Bounded quantification is undecidable. *Information and Computation*, 112(1):131–165, July 1994. Reprinted in *Theoretical Aspects of Object-Oriented Programming*, ed. Gunter and Mitchell, MIT Press (1994), pp. 427-459. Summary in POPL '92.

[Pie97] Benjamin C. Pierce. Foundational calculi for programming languages. In Allen Tucker, editor, *Handbook of Computer Science and Engineering*, pages 2190–2207. CRC Press, 1997.

[Pie02] Benjamin C. Pierce. *Types and Programming Languages*. MIT Press, Cambridge, Massachusetts, 2002.

[PS94] J. Palsberg and M. Schwartzbach. *Object-oriented type systems*. Wiley & Sons, 1994.

[PT93] Benjamin C. Pierce and David N. Turner. Statically typed friendly functions via partially abstract types. Technical Report ECS-LFCS-93-256, University of Edinburgh, 1993.

[PT94] Benjamin C. Pierce and David N. Turner. Simple type-theoretic foundations for object-oriented programming. *Journal of Functional Programming*, 4:207–247, 1994. An earlier version appeared in Proc. of POPL '93, pp. 299-312.

[Red88] U.S. Reddy. Objects as closures: Abstract semantics of object-oriented languages. In *Proc. ACM Symp. Lisp and Functional Programming Languages*, pages 289–297, July 1988.

[Rey74] J.C. Reynolds. Towards a theory of type structure. In *Paris Colloq. on Programming*, pages 408–425. Springer-Verlag LNCS 19, 1974.

[Rey75] John C. Reynolds. User-defined types and procedural data structures as complementary approaches to data abstraction. In Stephen A. Schuman, editor, *New Directions in Algorithmic Languages*, pages 157–168. IFIP Working Group 2.1 on Algol, INRIA, 1975. Reprinted in *Theoretical Aspects of Object-Oriented Programming*, ed. Gunter and Mitchell, MIT Press (1994), pp. 13-23.

[Rey80] J.C. Reynolds. Using category theory to design implicit conversions and generic operators. In N.D. Jones, editor, *Semantics-Directed Compiler Generation*, pages 211–2580. Springer-Verlag Lecture Notes in Computer Science, Vol. 94, 1980.

[RR96] John H. Reppy and Jon G. Riecke. Simple objects for standard ML. In *ACM SIGPLAN '96 Conference on Programming Language Design and Implementation*, pages 171–180, 1996.

[RV98] Didier Rémy and Jérôme Vouillon. Objective ML: An effective object-oriented extension to ML. *Theory and Practice of Object-Oriented Systems*, 4:27–50, 1998.

[SCB⁺86] C. Schaffert, T. Cooper, B. Bullis, M. Kilian, and C. Wilpolt. An introduction to Trellis/Owl. In *OOPSLA '86 Proceedings*, pages 9–16. ACM SIGPLAN Notices,21(11), November 1986.

[Sco76] D. Scott. Data types as lattices. *Siam J. Computing*, 5(3):522–587, 1976.

[SS75] G.L. Steele and G.J. Sussman. Scheme: an interpreter for the extended lambda calculus. Technical Report 349, MIT Artificial Intelligence Laboratory, 1975.

[Str67] C. Strachey. Fundamental concepts in programming languages. Lecture Notes, International Summer School in Computer Programming, Copenhagen, August 1967.

[Str86] B. Stroustrup. *The C^{++} Programming Language*. Addison-Wesley, 1986.

[Tes85] L. Tesler. Object Pascal report. Technical Report 1, Apple Computer, 1985.

[Tho97] Kresten Krab Thorup. Genericity in Java with virtual types. In *ECOOP '97*, pages 444–471. LNCS 1241, Springer-Verlag, 1997.

[Tor97] Mads Torgersen. Virtual types *are* statically safe. In *Informal FOOL 5 electronic proceedings*. http://pauillac.inria.fr/~remy/fool/abstracts/5.html, 1997.

[TT97] Kresten Krab Thorup and Mads Torgersen. Unifying genericity – combining the benefits of virtual types and parameterized classes. In *ECOOP '99*, pages 186–204. LNCS 1628, Springer-Verlag, 1997.

[Tur37] Alan Turing. Computability and lambda definability. *Journal of Symbolic Logic*, 2:153–163, 1937.

[Tur86] D. A. Turner. An overview of Miranda. *SIGPLAN Notices*, 21:158–166, 1986.

[US 80] US Dept. of Defense. *Reference Manual for the Ada Programming Language*. GPO 008-000-00354-8, 1980.

[US87] D. Ungar and R.B. Smith. Self: The power of simplicity. In *Proc. ACM Symp. on Object-Oriented Programming: Systems, Languages, and Applications*, pages 227–241, 1987.

[vG93] Robert van Gent.   *TOIL: An imperative type-safe object-oriented language*. Williams College Senior Honors Thesis, 1993.

[Wan87] M. Wand. Complete type inference for simple objects. In *Proc. 2nd IEEE Symp. on Logic in Computer Science*, pages 37–44, 1987. Corrigendum in *Proc. 3rd IEEE Symp. on Logic in Computer Science*, page 132, 1988.

[Wan89] M. Wand. Type inference for record concatenation and simple objects. In *Proc. 4th IEEE Symp. on Logic in Computer Science*, pages 92–97, 1989.

[Weg87] Peter Wegner. Dimensions of object-oriented language design. In *Proceedings of OOPSLA '87*, pages 168–182, 1987.

[Weg90] Peter Wegner. Concepts and paradigms of object-oriented programming. *OOPS Messenger*, 1(1):7–87, August 1990.

[Wir71] Niklaus Wirth. The programming language Pascal. *Acta Informatica*, 1:35–63, 1971.

[Wir85] Niklaus Wirth. *Programming in Modula-2, 3rd edition*. Springer-Verlag, 1985.

[Wir88] N. Wirth. The programming language Oberon. *Software - Practice and Experience*, 18:671–690, 1988.

Index

Printed in the United States
by Baker & Taylor Publisher Services

Printed in the United States
by Baker & Taylor Publisher Services